Matthias

BUDDHIST PSYCHOTHERAPY

A Guideline
for Positive
Changes

Translated by Craig Meulen

LOTUS PRESS

Original title: *Buddhistische Psychotherapie*
Published by Windpferd Verlagsgesellschaft mbH, Oberstdorf, Germany
www.windpferd.de
Original German language edition ©2010 by Windpferd
Translated from German by Craig Meulen

1st English edition 2014
by Lotus Press
published in cooperation with ©Inner Worlds Music
Box 325, Twin Lakes, WI 53181, USA
www.lotuspress.com · lotuspress@lotuspress.com
All rights reserved
Cover design: Kuhn Grafik Communication Design, Amden, Switzerland
by using a photo from iStock · Layout: Marx Grafik & ArtWork
ISBN: 978-0-9406-7622-0
Library of Congress Control Number: 2014936546
Printed in USA

Table of Contents

Introduction   5

1. Recognise and Convey the Essence of Buddhism.   17
2. Buddhist Psychotherapy is Suitable for Everybody.   31
3. Buddhist Psychotherapists Take Care of Others and Themselves   45
4. Buddhist Psychotherapy Unites Theory and Practice   67
5. Recognise and Convey the Significance of the Body   85
6. Recognise and Convey the Significance of Mental States   123
7. Recognise and Convey the Truth About Our Feelings   157
8. Recognise and Convey the Truth of Our Inner Nobility   179
9. Recognise and Convey the Wisdom of the Middle Way   193
10. Use the Insights to Stay in the Here and Now and Help Yourself and Others   205
11. Recognise and Convey the First Noble Truth of Suffering   215
12. Recognise and Convey the Significance of Karma for Our Suffering   229
13. Recognise and Convey the Noble Truth of Our Ignorance   241
14. Recognise and Convey the Noble Truth about Our Attachment   275
15. Recognise and Convey the Noble Truth of Our Resistance   291
16. Recognise and Convey the Noble Truth of the Liberation from Suffering   303
17. Recognise and Convey the Noble Truth of the Right Path   321
18. The Teachings: The Right Measure for Each of Us   345
19. Recognise and Convey Practical Buddhist Techniques   369
20. Our Whole Life is Practice   433
21. Recognise and Convey the Step from the Relative to the Absolute Truth   447
22. Study Buddhist Literature   459

About the Author   464

Introduction

This book is intended for people looking for help and inspiration. I hope it addresses readers interested in Buddhism, psychotherapy, spirituality, science or even general opportunities for further personal development. It could also be of interest to people active in a wide range of different healing professions.

Buddhist Psychotherapy (BPT) is a cross-cultural integration project: Tried and tested methods of healing from Buddhist teachings are linked with successful techniques from Western cultures. BPT is not only designed to treat problems; it is also a well-tested collection of Buddhist-psychotherapeutic theory and practice to promote *healthy* states of mind in *all* people. It does not concentrate solely on removing *negative* conditions but also emphasises supporting and stabilising our *positive* characteristics. This is why BPT does not focus exclusively on illnesses, conflicts and problems. It opens up a much larger framework of reference to allow us to unfold our human potential in a healthy way.

For therapists and others treating help-seekers, this book is designed to be a source of inspiration to encourage them to compare their own treatment methods and concepts with those in Buddhist Psychotherapy and, where appropriate, to combine them. The book also serves as an introduction to the everyday relevance of Buddhism and invites the reader him- or herself to make use of the rich wealth of resources available within Buddhism and Buddhist Psychotherapy. Readers who carry out the exercises and put into practice the ideas within this book stand a good chance of experiencing tangible personal enrichment—but, of course, as the author of this book I cannot guarantee this.

The idea behind Buddhist Psychotherapy is to make this tangible enrichment available to help-seekers and, in particular, to therapists. It can be an additional resource for therapists in every specialist area and is applicable for every help-seeker, regardless of religion, age and education or reason for resorting to therapy (severity of disorder or illness, etc.). Of course, the exercises therapists offer to help-seekers who are psychologically and mentally relatively stable will differ from those they recommend to those who are suffering from severe illnesses. If someone is walking too far to the right, they will be instructed to move to the left; if someone is walking too far to the left, they will be instructed to move to the right. (This *Wisdom of the Middle Way* will be dealt with later in more detail.)

What does the term Buddhist Psychotherapy mean? In general, *psycho*therapy refers to a method of treatment designed to achieve healing or alleviation of symptoms with regard to the *mind, soul* or *psyche*. This compares to *physio*therapy as treatment of the *body*. Buddhist Psychotherapy as a method is designed to be holistic: It includes treatment on both *psycho*logical and *physio*logical levels. In addition it also integrates *social* aspects.

The intention behind this book is to present a modern, skilful and technically well-founded school of therapy and body of exercises that are strongly influenced by Buddhist teachings. In this regard, it is not an exclusively Buddhist book. I hope instead that it will be received as an inspiring and highly relevant integration of helpful Buddhist approaches and insights from Western sciences with a focus on healthy, enduring, practical training for the unity of body, mind and spirit. The book will shed light on some core Buddhist topic sand present a variety of practical Buddhist techniques and exercises. These include various forms of meditation, techniques taken from a range of different modern forms of therapy, and some Buddhist exercises which have remained largely unknown until now but whose quality and usefulness have been proven for hundreds of years. In some cases, the sources only became accessible to us very recently; translations and transmission lines for certain exercises only came to Europe a few years ago, for example. So BPT may well be described as a new form of psychotherapy but its roots are as old as we can imagine—it could be described as a rediscovery.

Prior knowledge of Buddhism is not necessary to read this book. Key terms are always explained in context and presented in an understandable way. It is designed to be a practical book explaining how Buddhist philosophy and methods can easily offer comprehensive and permanent enrichment in the treatment of help-seekers.

The phenomenon of globalisation is leading to some very obvious problems but it also offers us the great potential of a meeting of cultures. The treatment of people seeking help has always been dependent on cultural influences, including the spirit of the times *(zeitgeist)* and the current state of scientific knowledge. Our western healthcare system and—connected to this—our psychotherapy can surely only benefit from innovations based on proven resources, including—or especially—those from other cultures. If we study the extraordinarily large body of literature from the Western traditions of clinical psychology, psychotherapy and psychiatry, it immediately becomes clear that all of them focus almost exclusively on pathology, illness, deficits, disorders etc. This has led to a great deal of research into such issues as violence, stress, aggression and prejudice. However, Western researchers have only just recently begun to research topics such as kindness, compassion, love or happiness. Even elements from humanist and anthroposophical philosophy are rarely encountered in the field of clinical treatment. Concepts of healing are mostly based on the desire to reduce or remove symptoms. This approach treats healing as a process of realignment with "normality". For example, the aim of "normal" psychotherapy could be as far as possible to eliminate a panic disorder. After this the treatment would be regarded as successful and brought to an end. Only a few Western clinical models actively include *positive* human potential.

In contrast, Buddhist Psychotherapy clearly names and focuses on the goals we can achieve as well as what we want to alleviate or eliminate. In addition to alleviating and removing suffering, we also aspire to the active and practical promotion of positive mental states such as happiness, compassion, love and joy. BPT clearly expands the scope of action of Western psychotherapy by not limiting its focus to the treatment of disorders, problems and illnesses. Since their revelation over 2500 years ago, Buddhist teachings (a foundation of BPT) have been serving human growth in general, specifically the cause of liberation from unhealthy mental states and the promotion of healthy ones.

The goals of BPT are open to everyone and *everyone* can benefit from this. In fact, rather than assuming that just a small percentage of the population is ill, Buddhist philosophy sets out to show that the *whole* of humanity repeatedly experiences suffering. Much of this is *unavoidable* but there is also a very large proportion of *avoidable* suffering. We will grow old, occasionally fall ill and surely die—this is *unavoidable* suffering. In the same way it is inevitable that people we love will sometimes leave us or fall ill or die. And there are an infinite number of minor and major everyday problems which are also *unavoidable*. Nonetheless there are forms of suffering which we *could* actually avoid, including our unhealthy reactions to the unavoidable suffering; these include anger, hate, rage, bickering, grumbling, self-doubt, self judgement and self-pity. These are secondary emotional reactions which have damaging effects on ourselves and others; they count as *avoidable* suffering.

Buddhism and Buddhist Psychotherapy communicate specific insights and techniques on how to deal with and eradicate *avoidable* types of suffering and cope better with the *unavoidable* suffering.

This principle will be presented in this book in a way which enables the readers to check its validity for themselves.

Western humanities such as psychology, theology, philosophy and sociology have developed amazing qualities but reveal at the same time a clear bias toward the *theoretical;* they cannot generally be described as based on direct experience. Many people consider this to be a deficit. In fact, one of the aspects that make Buddhism so attractive to so many people today seems to be its more pronounced balance of theory and practice.

Right at the start we need to note that Buddhism is one of the non-theistic world religions: a religion without belief in a divine being. Nonetheless many people from the Western cultures still think of Buddhism as a rather exotic Far Eastern religion. Buddhism is special because it does not define itself exclusively in terms of typical religious aspects although it does include many of these, such as the veneration of saints, religious holidays, rituals, ceremonies, prayer recitations and chanting. Important Buddhist representatives from East and West, such as the Dalai Lama, Yongey Mingyur Rinpoche or Jack Kornfield, have explained that Buddhism is and has always been less of a religion and more of a science of the mind. This science has been tested for centuries and delivers detailed, verifiable explanations and descriptions of human experience and behaviour. It also offers practical exercises and techniques to overcome many human conflicts and worries. So Buddhism bridges the often painful gap between science and religion, between innovation and ancient tradition or heritage. Albert Einstein is reported once to have said that, if there was any religion compatible with the demands of modern science, then it would be Buddhism. The German physicist and philosopher Carl Friedrich von Weizsäcker imagined the human being of the future to be an individual bringing together Christian ethics, scientific thinking and Buddhist strengths.

This book mainly describes the theoretical contents and practical techniques offered by Buddhism and a Buddhist approach to psychotherapy, forming an essential basis for BPT. Nonetheless, BPT is also more than this: It is a project of integration which seeks to use as many resources as are possible and useful, taken from many different sources and traditions. Furthermore, we also need to remember that, although we often refer to *Buddhism* as if there were only one form, in fact there are many different Buddhist traditions. During its 2500-year history, Buddhism spread from its Indian origins across Asia and recently throughout the world. In every country where Buddhists lived, they developed their own characteristics and focus based on their own culture. So today we can see many different forms, including Japanese, Vietnamese, Tibetan, Chinese,

Indian and even American and European "Buddhisms". The Western cultures are, however, still in the early stages of finding their own Buddhist forms.

In this way, over the course of many centuries a body of teachings and practice has developed which is diverse, practical and relevant to everyday life and which exhibits many well-developed features specific to the various traditions. One of Buddhism's particular achievements is the considerable flexibility of the teachings and its masters and disciples. This ability to integrate new insights enabled Buddhism to preserve its coherence and stay true to its fundamentals whilst developing an enormous variety of individual schools coexisting without an overarching institution (such as the Vatican).

Buddhist Psychotherapy uses the common features from within the different schools of Buddhism and brings them together in a constructive synthesis with other cultures and sciences. Although we often contrast *Eastern* and *Western,* this is a simplification which we use purely for the purpose of illustration; please remember that BPT is an integrative project which renders a range of approaches accessible to us and brings together psychological, medical and psychosomatic insights from all kinds of cultures, whether Buddhist or not.

Our modern era is characterised by segregation, specialisation and polarisation in many important areas of life: the world of work versus creativity; formal education versus character building; bureaucratic administration versus a human approach; religion versus worldly needs; consumerism versus actual basic human needs; and more besides. For many people, these polarisations are distressing, and BPT can be considered a model which can help reconcile these differences and reintegrate areas of life that have been split asunder. Depending on the needs of the individual help-seeker, the integrative approach of Buddhist Psychotherapy offers a blend of breadth and depth; the former corresponding to practical, everyday assistance and the latter to support in finding inspiration on quests for spiritual meaning. BPT integrates both individual-personal references and universal ones. In other words, it sees the individuality of every person seeking help but also recognises that each person belongs to larger systems, beginning with the family, various groups, wider society and continuing on to the human being's place in nature and beyond. This expansion of the frame of reference is constructive and advantageous for both therapist and help-seeker. BPT has a clear spiritual dimension, but the focus nonetheless remains on the connection between psycho-spiritual aspects of existence and the practical elements of our everyday life; in this respect BPT does not differ from Buddhism as a whole. Contrary to some popular understandings, Buddhism is not about running away from the world; instead, the teachings convey the art of remaining *fully* in the world, but without getting tangled up in it. The Buddha summarised this with the instruction: Meditate, but tether your elephant. Which means: Pray or meditate, but pay attention to everyday necessities. The Buddha emphasised strongly that individual personal progress be pursued in such a way as to benefit all beings.

If we look back to the roots of Buddhism we should be aware that the historical Buddha was also a human being. Before his enlightenment or awakening his name was Siddhartha Gautama; *Buddha* is a term in Sanskrit and Pali which means "the awakened one". Another epithet we often hear is Buddha Shakyamuni, which refers to the fact that Siddhartha was born into the noble Shakya tribe, in the region that is now on the border between India and Nepal. The roots of Buddhism are not religious: A man at the end of his twenties, Siddhartha did not set off on a quest to find God but rather to find a way to end human suffering for himself and all his fellow people. After he discovered his path when he was 35 years old—his awakening—he developed a large following and was able to establish secure lines of transmission through his disciples by means of his public teachings and the practical techniques which he taught.

His teachings—*sutras*—were first written down centuries after his death; until this point his teachings were passed on by *oral* transmission from teacher to disciple. This is probably one reason why Buddhist teachings tend to relate important facts in numerical lists, since these are easier to remember: Four Noble Truths, Eightfold Path, Four Immeasurables, Seven Factors of Awakening, Three Jewels etc.

This book will also attempt to illustrate how the Buddhist science of the mind is a very detailed and exact consideration and description of how human beings work, even measured against the yardstick of modern scientific standards. Furthermore, we will also show that Buddhism, as one of the roots of modern psychotherapeutic methods, is still as valid as ever in terms of the relevance, applicability and effectiveness of its profound and ancient practice. Buddhism provides a comprehensive and integrative healing understanding of human problems as well as the necessary methods and a variety of practical techniques to reduce and even overcome a very wide range of difficulties. It can be considered as one of the oldest and most intensively proven psychotherapeutic treatment methods. In comparison, Western psychology is still in its infancy, having taken its first faltering steps with William James about 100 years ago. The roots of this young science can clearly be traced back to traditional sources in the humanities. Many psychoanalytic and depth psychology methods, such as personality and character typology, formulating problems in connection with the concept of a human unconscious, and the recognition of the relevance of dreams, have also been a feature of Buddhism for over 2500 years. Buddhist teachings include a refined structural presentation of human awareness, perception and cognitive abilities. Buddhism's understanding of the world is deeply systemic and centred in the present moment. It shares these exact same focal points with modern systemic and behaviour therapists.

Behaviour therapy—one of the main Western therapy forms alongside psychoanalysis and depth psychology—is undergoing constant change. Behaviour therapists speak of "waves" of development: In the first wave, at the beginning of BT's development, the therapy concentrated exclusively on *behaviour*. Training programmes were used to promote new forms of behaviour. Later, a second wave occurred, with cognitions (thoughts) now playing a central role. Now known as cognitive behavioural therapy (CBT), its main interest lay with a person's judgement and expectations. The third generation or wave is still in the process of development: CBT is discovering *mindfulness*, with the effect that one of the cornerstones of Buddhist practice is now establishing itself in the world of Western therapy. The topic of mindfulness will appear frequently in this book.

The way of presenting Buddhist Psychotherapy chosen for this book focuses on two main areas. Firstly, the more theoretical aspects with relevance to psychotherapy are introduced, including the most important Buddhist teachings. Then practical Buddhist-psychotherapeutic techniques are described, with examples to show how they can work. These include exercises which feature a variety of meditations. BPT also integrates some very old, previously almost unknown liberation and healing processes. The book also presents real examples to illustrate all of this.

Anybody seeking therapeutic or counselling support today is confronted by a confusing diversity of very different professions offering relevant treatment, such as doctors, psychologists, psychotherapists (from different schools), mental health and other counsellors, natural health practitioners, coaches, life coaches, neurologists and psychiatrists. The range of therapy forms is even more diverse including such schools as psychoanalysis, deep psychology, systemic therapy, behaviour therapy, Gestalt therapy, counselling, hypnosis and many more. Each of these has a range of different techniques and models to explain how disorders and illnesses arise. There seems to be a lack of competitive alternatives to the classical psychoanalytic models of illness because a large majority of these therapeutic schools still use these models, which tend to focus on childhood in their search for the causes of current conflicts and symptoms. Some research metabolic processes in the brain; others concentrate on problematic systemic interactions; for yet others the most important point might be the individual aspects of a client's social status or their gender. And there are therapists who completely avoid this type of deliberation and assume that we come into this world as an "blank page" and that the whole spectrum of emotions and behaviour can be trained and re-trained.

The concepts and explanations or models of illnesses used by a therapist play a very important role in a course of therapy. However, help-seekers cannot always clearly recognise these extremely relevant aspects, even though all of the therapeutic measures, from the search for causes through to methods of treatment, depend on them.

Many treatment models concentrate only on eradicating symptoms, often ignoring or simply not seeing the positive human potential. We human beings, however, want more than simply 'not to suffer'—we also want to be happy. So we urgently need working models whose aim is to actively and practically promote *positive* mental states such as kindness, satisfaction, compassion and joy.

The definition of the word "health" was broadened as long ago as 1948 with the drafting of the constitution of the World Health Organisation (WHO), which starts with the following principle:

Health is a state of complete physical, mental and social well-being and not merely the absence of disease or infirmity.

More than 60 years after this benchmark statement by the WHO, many methods of therapy still cannot present any concepts beyond the simple removal of symptoms. This does not show sufficient respect for human beings with their needs and potential. Buddhist Psychotherapy does full justice to the principle stated by the WHO because it goes beyond the treatment of illnesses by also actively assisting in the unfolding of the potential for positive growth inherent in everybody. One central feature of Buddhist Psychotherapy is the attention that it pays to explaining the concepts behind its methods. These form a significant component of the treatment and are presented as the "22 Fundamentals of Buddhist Psychotherapy".

In order to give the reader an advance overview of the contents of this book, we will briefly present the structure of the 22 Fundamentals, which also forms the underlying framework of the therapy itself, including its form, procedure, schedule and contents as well as possible aims.

The 1st Fundamental is intended to provide a concise presentation of the essence of Buddhism as a whole and of Buddhist Psychotherapy.

The 2nd to 4th Fundamentals describe details and aspects of the course of treatment and its schedule which are relevant to both the help-seeker and the therapist.

The 5th to 7th Fundamentals convey necessary basic knowledge about our physical, mental and emotional concerns.

The 8th to 18th Fundamentals convey the necessary Buddhist theory and introductions to the practice.

The 19th Fundamental includes practical Buddhist-psychotherapeutic exercises, measures, interventions and techniques. Examples from real practice are described (we refer to "examples" and not to "case studies" because BPT treats real *people* and not cases). Some of the techniques presented are much more than 2500 years old, others have been tested for over 1000 years, but only made accessible to Western help-seekers fairly recently. However, before we turn to the 19th Fundamental we need to study the prior 18 Fundamentals—recognising, understanding and internalising the insights they present. We need to set an approximate course and establish secure foundations before we actually set off and start active training.

The 20th Fundamental of BPT concentrates on the practical implementation of Buddhist measures and our own insights and progress in everyday life.

To conclude, the 21st Fundamental offers a glimpse of further prospects whilst also putting everything into perspective.

The 22nd Fundamental offers a selected bibliography. Studying the books referred to here can be helpful for BPT.

The BPT Fundamentals presented here have proven themselves during many years of application in individual and group work in the institutional surroundings of various psychosomatic clinics and in private therapeutic practice. The sequence in which these principles are presented is derived from the experiences gained here; it is an established sequence, but each therapist is nonetheless encouraged to select their own key issues based on their own experiences or the needs of a particular help-seeker.

If readers find particular sections of this book less inviting, they are free to choose their own priorities. The body of Buddhist theory and practice is thoroughly holistic, which means that the whole spirit is in fact contained within every little fragment. So we can choose an individual topic which we are particularly interested in and study this intensively as our own individual and beneficial way in to the whole. Nonetheless, clear instructions are always needed *before* a particular practical exercise in order to ensure the necessary knowledge of the background and aim of the exercise. If this sequence is not followed we run the risk of losing track of our goal and becoming very confused.

The good news is that Buddha was (and still is) a very valuable pioneer, paving the way with detailed theoretical and practical instructions which give us a chance to follow him. Being able to follow in his tracks and share in his path gives us a lot of hope.

Possibly less welcome is the realisation that following the path— or rather, paths—still requires courage and represents an adventure which, whilst exciting, is also challenging and perhaps strenuous for each of us, even though they are well signposted and relatively clear thanks to all those who have trodden them before us. We are embarking on a journey with its own hidden dangers, pitfalls, temptations and distractions. However, as the reader has probably already guessed, the path is well worth following!

Reading a book is always a decision to take precious time away from other things in our life, so I hope everyone reading this book has an enjoyable time!

Matthias Ennenbach
2010

The 1st
Fundamental of Buddhist Psychotherapy

Recognise and Convey the Essence of Buddhism

> "Strictly speaking, there are no enlightened people: there is only enlightened activity."
>
> SHUNRYU SUZUKI ROSHI

The discussion of the essence of Buddhism and Buddhist Psychotherapy (BPT) presented here is designed to serve as a common guideline for the wide variety of approaches we will later take. Additionally, many readers might find it interesting to read a summary of what Buddhism is—a distilled essence of what is, after all, a very comprehensive set of teachings. We will see that this essence pervades both the theory and the practical exercises. If we sharpen our perception we will recognise that this very same essence is contained within every aspect of the extremely wide-ranging Buddhist teachings.

So what makes up this essence? Do all Buddhists really aspire to attain enlightenment? Does Buddhist Psychotherapy aim to provide training in enlightenment for all of its clients?

Perhaps we should start with more basic questions, such as whether it is even realistic to speak of enlightenment. And what does this term mean anyway? What consequences does enlightenment have for my life? All of these questions are both perfectly reasonable and very important.

Let us begin by considering what Buddhism and Buddhist Psychotherapy are really all about. It is always helpful if we can take complex and complicated topics and express them in a simple way, and this is indeed possible for multifaceted systems such as Buddhism and BPT. In fact, their goals can be expressed in one sentence:

The essence of Buddhism is liberation

All books about Buddhism, the contents of every teaching, every practical exercise and all Buddhist practices pursue the same goal: liberation. In the huge selection of Buddhist texts and their numerous translations, you will find a series of terms used mostly synonymously to refer to the same thing: liberation, great awakening, enlightenment, extinguishment, Nirvana. (The Sanskrit term *Nirvana* can be translated as *"blown out"*—as in a candle.) Whatever term we choose, we are using it to describe a condition or state of liberation in this world and not to refer to some mystical place in the world beyond—such as the Jewish, Christian or Islamic idea of *paradise*.

It is a core intention of BPT to enable its clients to *experience* these fundamental truths. After all, a purely theoretical teaching of knowledge can never replace an experience, no matter how detailed it might be: Wonderful tales of mountain climbing can never replace the experience of actually standing high up on a mountain top for yourself.

Buddhism is often wrongly treated as a negative philosophy concentrating on a revelation of all-encompassing suffering. We will later discover the truth behind this, but here we already need to make clear that identifying and analysing the suffering we experience is the first step. This needs to be followed immediately by the next steps, which are intended to lead to liberation from suffering. This is the Buddha's central message: Yes, there is suffering, and yes, we can free ourselves from it. We can free ourselves from human suffering and thus achieve liberation from the eternal cycle of (distressing) existence, known as *Samsara*.

Identifying and describing a cycle to be interrupted and permanently broken is akin to a negative definition. Turning this on its head then shows a positive definition in the sense of goals to which we can aspire. These goals actually refer to the development and maintenance of wholesome states of mind: kindness, love, compassion, serenity and the improved ability to control oneself, i.e. to really slow down in calm phases and to really have enough energy and determination during active phases in order to pursue our goals.

If we do not do anything to change it, we spend our whole life moving along a continuum between the two poles of happiness and unhappiness (whereby happiness here represents everything positive and unhappiness everything negative). During this lifelong tug-of-war we are sometimes pulled more strongly towards one pole and sometimes more strongly to the other. Once at the happy end we do our best to stay there, and we try our hardest to avoid the unhappy end. However, there are some experiences we can have which show us that the problem is not being unhappy; the problem is living our life between these two extremes. Once we understand this, we then understand that happiness and unhappiness are actually one and the same; it is relatively futile to constantly strive for happiness and no longer surprising to find that unhappiness always follows. Liberation from this cycle means living our life beyond this compulsive oscillation between two opposite poles. Peace and liberation lie beyond happiness and unhappiness.

Indeed, we have all experienced this peace many times, even if it only lasted for an instant. These were the moments when we were able to experience the here and now—moments when we were not thinking about what happened yesterday or what might happen tomorrow and were able to experience the present moment peacefully. Many people experience this after physical exertion or sexual intercourse, in nature, at the top of a mountain, on the beach looking at the ocean, etc. Experiences like this are important and valuable but will always be of short duration and, unless we undertake mind training, dependent on external conditions.

The path of liberation
is connected with concentration on the here and now

Buddhists do indeed all aspire to liberation from painful states of mind and the attachment to positive states which inevitably lead to painful consequences. Later we will describe in more detail why Buddhists do not fundamentally distinguish between positive and negative feelings. Both types of feeling can chain us in their own way, so the aspiration to liberation is affected by both. For example, a feeling that is pleasant at first sight, such as pleasure or desire, can lead to unhealthy states of mind such as greed, longing, envy or jealousy.

Nonetheless, it can generally be seen that healthy states of mind should be cultivated and negative or unhealthy ones eliminated. This book demonstrates a variety of ways to achieve this, each of which leads to a different type of positive effect. Healthy changes in our consciousness (such as a reduction in feelings of isolation and negativity) can be the result of continually reducing our ignorance and delusion, removing attachments and breaking down feelings of aversion. This all serves to help liberate us. The explanations in this book will offer a more detailed look at all of this so that the reader may understand what Buddhists mean when they talk of liberation.

> In this context we need to understand a very clear distinction: We are not seeking to liberate ourselves *from* our feelings; we are seeking to liberate ourselves *in the midst of* our feelings.

This is a very significant distinction because it is this which makes our path human. It is natural for us to want to retain our skills and qualities by continuing to feel all of our emotional, human impulses. So even at an advanced stage of Buddhist practice we are not freeing ourselves *from* troublesome feelings; rather we are freeing ourselves *in the midst of* our troublesome feelings.

The Buddha said that his whole teaching, regardless of which aspects we look at, can be compared to the ocean: Wherever we choose to taste it, it always has one and the same "salty" taste—of liberation. As a consequence, we do not have to work our way through the whole teaching of the Dharma or meditate for years and years in order to have a chance of gaining freedom. We will repeatedly see that we already have everything we need for this. BPT can help us to learn how to channel our resources in order to reach our goal.

Christianity also offers a comparable teaching when it asks the question: Do we have to punish ourselves and do penance in order to be able to discover a distant and remote God? No, he is already with us; we simply have to look and listen carefully.

What does liberation mean?

There are many names for the process of spiritual breakthrough that occurs with liberation, awakening, or enlightenment, but what does this actually mean? Freedom from what? Awakening out of what? Enlightenment from what sort of darkness?

Our life has both minor and major types of inherent and unavoidable suffering: illnesses, deaths, losses, separations, negative changes etc. We strive to achieve security and often realise that we can try as hard as we want, but we will never find absolute security. Even if we accumulate wealth, this does not grant absolute security and definitely does not grant us real peace. Even if at the moment we are not faced with any external causes of unhappiness and stress, we often make life difficult for ourselves with our self-criticism, restlessness, ruminations, fears, worries, irritation and anger. This is the ongoing cycle of life which Buddhists call *Samsara:* the wheel of life and suffering.

Siddhartha Gautama wanted to free himself and all other beings from this cycle. So we can see him as one of the first and most famous (and most successful) "dropouts" in history! However, we will see that he only dropped out of this cycle of suffering and dissatisfaction, not out of life itself. Buddhism is a very worldly philosophy with a high relevance to everyday life, so it is really more suitable for "dropping in". After his awakening, Siddhartha became known as the *Buddha*—the Awakened One. For the rest of his life he lived as a monk and a teacher, passing on his experience of how to achieve this state and the responsibility that goes with it to many other people, forever seeking to show his fellow beings the path to freedom.

Buddhism has ancient roots

The Buddha is not and never was a god. He was an (almost) ordinary person who lived some 2500 years ago in what is now northern India and Nepal. According to the legends, he lived a life of luxury for the first years of his life as Prince Siddhartha Gautama. It was not a search for God which Siddhartha undertook before he became the

Buddha but instead a search for a method to end human suffering for himself and his fellow human beings. His quest lasted many years, during which he followed the ancient Indian tradition of spending time with various gurus and engaging in intensive meditative absorption and extreme ascetic practices (which he later recognised as being unhelpful). Finally, he did indeed reach his goal of discovering a path that can end human suffering and lead to lasting happiness and freedom from unhealthy mental states. He discovered this path with his Awakening (in Sanskrit *Bodhi*) at the age of 35. He also told us that there had been other "Awakened Ones" or Buddhas before him and that there will be others after him. So we are talking about a tradition that is thousands of years old: a traditional science of the mind which generations of students, teachers, learners and practitioners have tried out and tested over and over again, carrying it over into everyday life. And this tradition will continue into the future.

The beginnings and propagation of the teaching

According to legend, the Buddha remained silent for 49 days after his awakening before he began to tell others of his experience and insights. First of all, he sought out the five companions with whom he had previously practised asceticism for a long time. He explained his enlightenment experience thoroughly to them and told them about the insights he had gained, and this first teaching came to be known as the "First Turning of the Wheel of the Dharma". It already contained the central aspects of the Buddhist teachings which would continue to develop afterwards.

The famous teaching of the First Turning of the Wheel of Dharma contains three significant statements:
- Follow the Middle Way (see 9th Fundamental of BPT)
- Use the insights to stay in the here and now and help yourself and others (see 10th Fundamental of BPT)
- Understand the Four Noble Truths (see 11th and 13th to 17th Fundamentals of BPT)

For a long time the teachings were passed on orally from teacher to students and it was only some 500 years after Buddha passed away that his teachings first were written down. Here it is worth noting that Buddha only spoke Magadhi/Ardhamagadhi—a regional Indian dialect—but his teachings were written down in Pali (as suttas) or Sanskrit (as sutras). The Collection of Middle-Length Discourses brings together 152 of these *suttas* (see the Bibliography in 22nd Fundamental of BPT). When we read the Buddha's teachings today there are many features we notice. The language is characterised by deep insights into the human psyche and the social aspects of human coexistence. The texts and phrasing also demonstrate great clarity in their structure. Most of the translations available today retain the original strategies that even then were designed to help the Buddha's students understand, internalise and implement the teaching. For example, the teachings utilise the special feature of listing important facts in numbered collections, such as The Four Noble Truths or the Eightfold Path. The texts also sound like songs, which reminds us that they were originally passed on orally; they all have a similar beginning, a middle section with the important information, and the closing chorus. The suttas all convey a number of factors such as the "sutta of the Seven Factors of Awakening", with seven repetitions of an initial verse, a middle section with one of the seven pieces of information and a closing verse that refers back to the opening verse.

The Buddhist path comprises two fundamental, inseparable aspects:
- The *theory,* or teachings (recognise and internalise)
- The *practice* (convey and implement in everyday life)

We will return again and again to the fact that theory and practice are of equal value and relevance.

Keeping the goal in sight

The Buddha himself said that we should never lose sight of the goal—liberation. We should not get trapped in the details of the theory; the theory should never become an end in itself.

The Buddha compared the teachings with a raft that we use to cross the river and reach the other bank. The other bank of the river is liberation, and as soon as we have reached this, the raft is not important any more. This metaphor warns us against placing too much importance on the nature of the raft and embellishing it, or developing pride because we own a raft. Instead we should practice steering the raft with our mindfulness, keeping our destination in sight (the other bank—liberation). BPT helps us to remember these key points. There are, however, two possible misunderstandings in this metaphor. One is that we could take it to mean that we face a long struggle in a life on the river. The other could be that we assume that our journey is over when we have reached the other bank and we can rest there forever.

This book will also deal with the questions: How do we cross the river? What does the destination look like exactly? What happens when we get there?

By taking a look at both Buddhism and Buddhist Psychotherapy, we will gain detailed insights to help us recognise that suffering is not a mistake that we make (see 11th Fundamental of BPT) nor do we belong to some unfortunate minority of unhappy people. Rather, suffering is something universal which affects all human beings. However, this somewhat negative conclusion is not the final balance drawn by either Buddhism or Buddhist Psychotherapy. They both go on to explain in a detailed way how this suffering arises (see 12th to 15th Fundamentals of BPT), what causes it, how we can permanently eradicate these causes (see 16th and 19th Fundamentals of BPT) and what consequences this has for our everyday life (see 17th and 20th Fundamentals of BPT).

Demystifying liberation

The good news is that everybody is capable of achieving freedom and already has everything they need to fulfil the conditions for this. We will discover that liberation is a thoroughly attainable condition which we can implement in the here and now whenever we want.

Without a doubt there are many different ideas of what the goal of liberation, freedom, enlightenment or whatever term we choose actually looks like. Many Buddhists speak of *absolute* or *ultimate* liberation, referring to a state which can only be reached after extremely intensive practice. If a person experiences this type of breakthrough they can be considered to be absolutely and perfectly enlightened. Other Buddhists refer to this topic with somewhat less high-flying concepts of the goal. Jack Kornfield, for example, a famous American meditation teacher, wrote a book on this called *After the Ecstasy, the Laundry.* In this book, Buddhist and other spiritual masters are asked to describe their awakening and the author conveys the quintessential insight that liberation is not a permanent state which we reach once and remain in forever. Enlightenment or liberation cannot be described as an *either-or* phenomenon but rather as a sort of growth process with various phases of progress and regress.

It also has to be considered that many spiritual masters were living as monks or nuns and therefore were not even confronted with many of the everyday problems most people have to deal with. Nonetheless, it needs to be noted that a monastic life is not considered as the highest goal in Buddhism. We will discover how clearly the Buddha phrased his instructions for living in the world—demonstrably preaching anything but escapism.

Over-estimating enlightened masters would be similar to the veneration of saints; even if enlightened beings can serve as motivating role models for many people, venerating them generally creates an unproductive sense of remoteness between the venerators and venerated. And of course this also applies to the way we treat Buddhist teachers, masters and saints.

The Buddhist understanding of interconnectedness can create a wholesome link between the venerated and the venerator, but careful observation is nonetheless required to watch for a tendency amongst some people for remoteness to increase through the practice of worship. Those who started along a path then desperately need encouragement to continue—we need to recognise that if we place the goals too high people will possibly turn back out of fear, doubt or insecurity ("I will never be able to attain that state, only the Dalai Lama can do that.") The Buddha himself emphasised the closeness of enlightenment by making it clear that every single person can attain it in the here and now.

The essence of Buddhist Psychotherapy

The first fundamental of Buddhist Psychotherapy (Recognise and Convey the Essence of Buddhism) challenges Buddhist Psychotherapists to recognise and internalise the essence of Buddhism and then convey this to their clients.

This broadens the focus, often found in Western psychotherapy, on eradicating the symptoms. So BPT is already meeting the benchmark standard set by the WHO as mentioned in the introduction, which defines health as much more than just the absence of illness. More than 60 years ago the WHO laid down this challenge to health professionals to rethink their understanding of illness and health so that aspects of health promotion conducing to further-reaching health and wellbeing might be put in place. Well-being or health should not be reduced simply to the absence of disorders. We have to make the most of our human potential and incorporate this into considerations of how to promote an idea of health that encompasses all aspects of our being.

How do we get closer to the essence?

We will find out what Buddhist Psychotherapy can mean for clients and what it demands from them when we look at the second fundamental of BPT; what it means for and demands from the therapists will then be shown as part of the third fundamental. Special exercises and techniques will be presented in the 19th fundamental.

Buddhism itself has been delivering very good, tried and tested techniques to relieve human suffering and promote healthy states of mind for many centuries. In fact, all of today's schools of psychotherapy have profited from these, directly or indirectly (and mostly unacknowledged); all that BPT is doing in this regard is making the connection to the roots of psychotherapy in Buddhism more explicit. This school of psychotherapy draws on important sources, bringing together classical knowledge and modern science. In this way we can build a genuinely multipurpose house out of medical, psychological, psychotherapeutic, sociological, educational, theological and spiritual bricks. The basic theory is centred on the individual while also being deeply systemic. Of course, the roots and character of BPT are both completely client-centred, which means that the wishes, ideas and worldview of the individual help-seeker are respectfully accepted, appreciated and acknowledged. Most of the time people come to BPT with a very specific issue, for example with the wish to free themselves from their current sadness, fear or anger. The BPT can then offer reassurance and a secure framework for the therapeutic processes to come; it also delivers further and more comprehensive structures, offers of help and perspectives.

The relative and ultimate levels

Finally it needs to be mentioned that we have been speaking here about important aspects of the *relative* essence. These should serve as guidelines and assistance for us. We are speaking about relative things (such as the essence) in order to make sure we have a common language and understanding at a practical level, so we can convey these elements more easily.

Approaching the *ultimate* (or *absolute*) elements is much more difficult since they cannot be experienced practically and are somewhat inaccessible. Nonetheless, as our practice continues we shouldn't let this stop us trying to open our awareness for the *ultimate* essence, too. For this approach we need a good and deep practice (see 21ˢᵗ Fundamental of BPT, which takes a detailed look at the relative and ultimate aspects). The absolute should not be considered as higher than the relative essence nor is it more important; instead it simply shows a different level. At the relative level we can talk about feelings, objects, principles etc. but at the ultimate level none of these things really exist. For this reason we do not grasp tightly to any sort of dogma, instead remaining open for life's flow.

In this book we have to use words in order to express ideas that often lie beyond words. So it is important to try not to get too fixated on the words themselves, and instead to remain mindful of the spirit that they are intended to convey. We can try our best to describe an apple using words but nothing has the same effect as the direct experience of biting into an apple. Knowing that we are dealing with something that is "round, juicy, a little sweet and a little sour" is not enough: We need guidance to find it and have our own experience of eating it.

Even terms such as "Buddhism" and "Buddhist Psychotherapy" are just labels that are intended to convey something beyond words. We should not spend too much time and effort on the names, instead remaining aware of the (false) expectations that might be associated with them. The terms are simply intended, where possible, to be an aid. We remain open for the message behind them—a message about our own experiences.

Describing an essence does not mean in any way that we are suggesting that all personal striving, thinking and feeling will lead to an identical goal. The common denominator is liberation, but this will look very different for each individual person.

In August 2009 the Dalai Lama took part in *a symposium entitled One World, One Mind, One Heart.* The Dalai Lama commented to the effect of: *"One world? Yes. One mind? I don't know, I think no. One heart? No."* Yes, we share one world, but we will soon be seven billion people and thus seven billion different ideas, wishes, characters etc. On a very fundamental level we are all the same—we are all human beings—but generally we are very different. And even one individual person can be completely different in the morning and in the evening.

So when we are dealing with the essence we need to assign the important insights about our *sameness* to the right level and keep open our awareness for the wonderful *diversity* of all the individuals there are.

Henry B came to BPT in order to learn how to relax in every situation and to meditate, and by doing this to free himself from all of his worries. He said that he had heard that Buddhism offers exercises which can help people to free themselves from all their problems. Above all, his idea of meditation was that it should help him get rid of his burdensome feelings. After studying the Fundamentals of BPT, visiting Dharma lectures and speaking to other participants, he was able to see what a more realistic path for him could be. In particular, Henry experienced a momentary flash of insight when he heard the phrase: "We are not liberating ourselves from our feelings; we are liberating ourselves in the midst of our feelings."

In the meditations he also experienced how little meditation is about "switching off" and how much it is concerned with "switching on".

This Fundamental Should Convey the Following:

The aim of the 1st Fundamental of Buddhist Psychotherapy is to describe the possible path and the destination (= liberation) and also to promote the demystification of the term enlightenment (awakening, liberation etc.), which is of paramount importance.

Conveying this in a believable way can hardly be achieved by a written description, however convincing this may be. It has to be conveyed directly by the Buddhist Psychotherapist and become something the help-seeker can experience in an unmediated way

The **2**nd
Fundamental of Buddhist Psychotherapy

Buddhist Psychotherapy is Suitable for Everybody

> The unhealthy patterns of our personality can be recognised and transformed into a healthy expression of our natural temperament.
>
> JACK KORNFIELD

When we hear about Buddhist Psychotherapy for the first time, we might ask ourselves: Could that be something for me? It sounds interesting, but I know little or nothing about Buddhism. Perhaps this type of therapy is only for Buddhists?

The wording of the second fundamental in the title of this chapter has already given it away: BPT is equally suitable for every person, every age group and people from every cultural or intellectual background. The overall aim of liberation will be the same, yet the individual goals of the individual people seeking help will be very different. Therefore the exercises and other measures chosen within BPT will be different, too. We will discover that a course of Buddhist Psychotherapy always respects and follows the individual goals and wishes of the help-seeker in addition to offering universal goals that go beyond them, such as liberation or enlightenment, for which it also has practical advice. In this way we can integrate both aspects in a way that is highly productive and client-orientated, which guarantees that its effects last significantly longer and also contributes to the growth of the individual, their family, their environment and all other beings (thanks to its comprehensive notion of interconnectedness).

In BPT we want to convey that *every* person is capable of achieving liberation or awakening—at any time. The liberated state, Nirvana, is not reserved for old, wise, Tibetan meditation masters but is rather a universal state or condition, accessible to everyone and attainable in the here and now.

Treatment requires active cooperation

The treatment or course of therapy offered by Buddhist Psychotherapy requires its clients to be much more fundamentally open-minded and adopt a more active approach than some other psychotherapeutic measures. For example, a surgeon simply requires his patients to have a certain amount of trust; otherwise the patient is more or less *passive* during the necessary interventions. However, BPT requires a very high degree of readiness to *actively* cooperate. It also needs a degree of motivation to regularly perform exercises and practice. This attitude is particularly desired in BPT because the weekly 50-minute sessions are not the only type of treatment or activity requiring the help-seeker's attention: The therapy includes daily practice and the performance of various exercises. In return, the person seeking help experiences a tangibly quick and lasting effect.

For these reasons, soon after the therapy starts there will be pressure on the help-seeker to adopt this attitude. However, it might be advisable not to call this "self-discipline" because this term often has negative associations. Instead, the term "patience" is preferable. We all need patience for ourselves and for others as well. Although patience is often the last thing that a suffering person wants to summon up, a targeted approach can usually create the necessary confidence. So every person coming to BPT seeking help is requested to bring a little patience for themselves and for the exercises. They should also clearly understand that this form of therapy is a very active and practical form of treatment. The treatment is almost equally divided into spoken exchanges and practical exercises. Other than this need to be active and motivated, there are no other requirements on the clients, and no further prior knowledge or experience, Buddhist or otherwise, is needed.

The Buddha took anybody into his community

In addition to the regular practice and exercises, basic Buddhist theory also forms a significant component of the BPT. The Buddha passed on his teachings to everyone who was interested, regardless of their personal, material or intellectual background. By making his teachings accessible to simple farmers and cowherds as well as officials or nobles, the Buddha was consciously rebelling against the traditional caste system in ancient Indian society. In particular, by accepting disciples from among the so-called "untouchables"—people who lived below the lowest of the castes—he was making it clear that *anyone* could find acceptance in the Buddhist community—the *Sangha*. The acceptance of women—at least as lay practitioners—was also significant, considering that women were then (and often still are) not granted any equality at all. The Buddha himself grew up in the noble family of the Shakyas, but as he began his quest to find liberation he is said to have exchanged his luxurious clothes with those of a poor person and later wore nothing but a monk's robes.

He also seems to have found it easy to speak with people from *all* classes of society, possessing the ability to adapt his speech and tune in to the individual needs of each person he spoke to. This ability could very well be described as *therapeutic* and is still as relevant as ever. Each of his disciples received personalised guidance for the exercises, and if his instructions sometimes appeared contradictory, the Buddha himself is reported to have responded by saying that someone who has a tendency to "walk too far to the left" will receive the instruction to "walk further to the right" but the opposite instruction would be needed for someone who has the opposite problem.

An important aspect of the art of treatment is to be able to find the right tone and the right words for each individual person who seeks our help. Without doubt, Buddha will have had different ways of expressing himself when talking to ox herders, soldiers or officials and nobles. For our work, this means that we should also appreciate the individual background of each help-seeker and adapt our approach accordingly. Someone who is more comfortable with the intellectual, logical and rational aspects of life needs to be given a more logical explanation of the teachings in order for their meaning to be conveyed. A more practically minded person might find the intellectual aspects less easily accessible and should therefore be given clear, explicable practical instructions. Once these experiences have been conveyed and made more tangible, a second step would then be to make the teachings themselves more accessible.

So Buddhist Psychotherapy has universal and individual aspects. The universal aspect casts light on the principles of human behaviour which have remained unchanged and valid for 2500 years. The eastern science of the mind has gathered very comprehensive, well-founded and well-recorded knowledge of the human mind (see the 6th Fundamental of the BPT).

The individual aspect allows everybody to find their very own way in and to use the Buddhist exercises to deal with their special issues. Whatever form the individual issues take, the BPT's combination of universal and individual aspects allows it to offer every help-seeker the appropriate support, instructions and exercises. This is true whether they have problems of a more psychological nature (such as fears, obsessive brooding, anger, depression) or issues directly connected to particular people (partnership conflicts, bullying, workplace bullying) and substances (addiction or abuse). It also applies if the issues are psychosomatic in nature (sleep disorders, pain, physical discomforts) or if the person is seeking help to find meaning in their life or orientation on a spiritual search. Their level of education, intelligence, prior knowledge of Buddhism, gender, sexual orientation and religious connections are only of concern in BPT insofar as the Buddhist Psychotherapist has to be aware of them and their potential relevance in a non-judgemental way.

What people seeking help from a therapist should be aware of

A client seeking help from BPT will find a Buddhist Psychotherapist who has a high degree of serenity, mindfulness, humour and empathy and gives them a clear feeling of acceptance. The therapist is not a strict teacher dishing out instructions to his or her disciples. Clear language does sometimes need to be used but this will always be done with an underlying attitude of appreciation and respect. The help-seeker will be able to experience a sense of belonging, relating to the principle of interconnection and compassion that is a central aspect of Buddhist teachings and practice.

Many aspects of the cooperation between therapist and client reveal it to be an alliance. In this book we will discover much more about interconnectedness as a fundamentally important aspect with significant consequences, so here it will suffice to remind ourselves of the way in which this interconnectedness makes us what we are today.

The neuroscientist Prof. Gerald Hüther explains that, although we each have genetic predispositions to various skills and abilities, whether we actually develop these depends entirely on the world with which we are connected in such an intense way. For example, every "healthy" person is born with a "language centre" in the left side of their brain (nerve cells that control our ability to speak), but if nobody actually speaks to us then we remain mute and this ability does not develop. And this applies equally to many other essential characteristics and traits. We have an aptitude for love, compassion, serenity, self-discipline and more besides, but if we grow up in an environment where we never or rarely experience these qualities then unfortunately we will not be able to develop them to any more than a very limited extent, if at all. Western scientists speak of aptitudes or genetic predispositions where Buddhists have been speaking for centuries about "seeds" in our "store-house or substrate consciousness" (see 6th Fundamental of the BPT on the topic of the mind). These seeds are said to have a "quality" with either healthy or unhealthy consequences. By means of targeted training, such as that offered within BPT, we can decide which seeds we would like to cultivate and which we do not wish to activate.

Thich Nhat Hanh, a Vietnamese Buddhist teacher also says that the seeds of everything positive and everything negative are already within us. Even if we cannot feel some of these elements or we deny their presence, they are nonetheless there. We have to be very careful which seeds we nourish ourselves or allow others to nourish.

Each help-seeker comes to us in the BPT with their own very different set of resources, problems and strengths. An individual, customised strategy can be developed for everyone (see 19th Fundamental, for example) in order to alleviate or remove their suffering and to stabilise, secure and promote their health. Whether or not the higher goal of liberation is pursued depends on the individual concerned.

Buddhist Psychotherapy can be (almost) everything for us

BPT offers far more than just constructive assistance in times of crisis—it offers long-term support and a refuge in good *and* bad times. In addition to a means of orientation in the form of *Buddha* and his teachings (the *Dharma*), BPT also offers a community (*Sangha*) with weekly group instruction sessions followed by meditation. This is clearly a reference to the Three Jewels to which Buddhists formally take refuge.

The Three Jewels are: the Buddha, the Dharma, and the Sangha.

Following the path of the Buddha, studying the teachings, and practicing within a community are the three pillars of Buddhism. They can simply be used as tools but they can also be seen as a type of key which we can use to open doors and gain access to areas that were previously closed to us or simply did not even seem to exist.

An appeal to people seeking help from BPT

We should take our time and carefully observe whether we feel a healthy connection with our Buddhist Psychotherapist. The "chemistry" between the people involved is of crucial importance for the whole process and success of a course of therapy. A "working alliance" is sufficient for the help-seeker to make many new discoveries, receive instructions and learn how to conduct their exercises, but ideally therapist and client should also have a feeling of equality and connection with each other. Furthermore, people seeking help from a Buddhist Psychotherapist should also make sure that, as well as being authentic and skilled, he or she also has a good sense of humour, serenity and genuine appreciation for all people (including any previous therapists of the client, specialists from other disciplines and followers of other religions).

Enlightened Buddhist Psychotherapists?

Yes, we psychotherapists are also striving for liberation or enlightenment just like the people coming to us for help. In this book we will hear much more about how we can achieve this and how we can maintain this condition of liberation for ever longer periods of time. This will strongly characterise our working alliance with the help-seeker.

As help-seekers, when we discover more about BPT and hear about interconnectedness, working alliances, and in particular, the equality of therapist and help-seeker, we may feel a sense of disappointment: Buddhist healers and psychotherapists are (generally) not enlightened beings far more advanced than ourselves. After all, many of us have a deep-seated longing for an enlightened guru. So we should carefully monitor the underlying expectations and hopes that are motivating us. Perhaps we are secretly hoping to find an Enlightened One who will perform some remarkable feat, allowing us to effortlessly and miraculously experience enlightenment, or perhaps even salvation?

Many of us might want to bypass everything else and receive instructions directly from the Dalai Lama. A very well-known German magazine ran a cover story about him in 2007 with the title "A God Up Close", concisely expressing something which many of us deeply desire. However, the Dalai Lama himself takes this sort of statement very seriously when he says that some people worship him as a god and others fear him as a devil. The Dalai Lama never tires of prefacing his lectures, teachings and discussions with the statement that he is just a simple Buddhist monk or practitioner. We may interpret this as a deliberate expression of his humility; it nonetheless bears witness to his profound underlying insight that, on a fundamental level, we are all equal human beings striving towards similar goals and obstructed by very similar mental afflictions.

So the "bad" news is: There is no Guru who can pass on his enlightenment to us directly, without effort on our part. We have to proceed along the path ourselves. The "good" news is: Buddhists have been treading this path for over 2500 years and it has been well signposted, so we should not have too much trouble following it. Of course we need to note that the path is an inner path and not an outer one—from retreats to meditation session to therapy to prayer etc. Nonetheless, we sometimes need more time for inner journeys than outer ones.

On equality (including that of client and therapist)

We all have both universal and individual characteristics. The Dalai Lama explains that we are fundamentally, i.e. universally, virtually identical as human beings. Building upon this we individualise ourselves more and more; we belong to a particular continent, race, nation, gender, faith, profession, political orientation or sports fan club and take on other roles such as son, daughter, father or mother. So the Dalai Lama emphasises that it is our way of viewing ourselves which determines whether we see ourselves as *same* or *different*. None of these possible affiliations or roles should be granted higher priority than the basic level on which we are all people. Our roles as members of a political group, nation or religious community should never take precedence over our fundamental role as a human being. No grouping should consider itself as higher than humanity; human rights are the most important of all. Buddhism therefore considers the dignity of each individual and the equality of everyone to be inalienable.

Here we could perhaps note that these basic values have unfortunately still not been implemented in many societies (including Buddhist ones such as Myanmar). We should ask ourselves whether we truly implement them in our society and also whether we personally live them out. If this is the case, at least most of the time, then we really have already reached a high degree of realisation. Buddhism supplies us with a range of helpful models here (see 8th Fundamental of BPT) and practical measures (see 19th and 20th Fundamentals of BPT).

So let us resist the temptation to put our Buddhist Psychotherapists or anyone else on a pedestal and instead remain careful to check the source of our desire to idealise others. Interconnection is always present but it may feel significantly different during different phases of therapy; it should, however, never be allowed to develop into a dependency. We should never make ourselves dependent on a master or anyone else. The Buddha himself told us to be our own master. So as a help-seeker we have a responsibility to maintain a good balance between closeness and distance.

In general, BPT helps us to help ourselves. It should not be oriented towards the wishes and progress of the therapist. Instead, we should recognise that we are all pursuing liberation for all beings.

It's always possible to start again

If we are struggling and self-doubt is causing us trouble, if we think we never make any real personal or spiritual progress, or if we are disheartened because we think we will never lead such pure or perfect lives as monks or nuns, then we need to remind ourselves that all of the prerequisites for achieving liberation are within us already. We already contain all the healthy seeds (as well as the unhealthy ones). So it is up to us whether we activate them or not.

Sometimes we can seek motivation by looking toward our main role models—the 14th Dalai Lama, perhaps. However, this can just as easily demotivate us if they appear distant, out of reach and aloof. So it might be useful to seek out some other examples. The Buddhist literature offers a variety of famous liberation stories, even including tales of dangerous criminals (Angulimala, Milarepa) who finally ended up on a healthy path after recognising, understanding and internalising the Buddhist teachings.

Angulimala (Sanskrit *Anguli* = "finger", *Mala* = "garland, necklace") was a murderer who, as his name suggests, collected one finger from each of his victims and wore them as a garland around his neck. This was during Buddha's lifetime and it was Buddha's completely fearless approach when confronted by Angulimala which served to bring him onto a healthy path. The moral of the story is clear: Even someone like Angulimala can find peace and freedom. Another example is Milarepa, who lived from 1040-1123 CE. Struck by twists of fate, he exacted deadly revenge on his relatives but later he was able to turn his life around and find a healthy path to awakening.

Numerous advanced meditation masters undertake programmes of Buddhist activity in prisons and similar detention centres, where they offer meditation instruction and Buddhist teachings. They report very positive experiences even with the most hardened criminals. Perhaps this should not surprise us too much since even they humans like us; at a more profound level they are very similar to us but the unhealthy seeds latent within them were activated much more strongly. Negative life circumstances or other people are often the agents that activate these latent seeds, but sometimes people deliberately activate the unhealthy seeds themselves (for example, in order to survive a threatening experience or achieve a perceived short-term gain). If we label such people "monsters" this is actually a form of self-protection, wanting to see them as different from us and not wanting to see that we, too, carry all sorts of both healthy and unhealthy seeds within us without being able to fully control which of them are activated. At least, this is the case if we do not practice extensive mind training, such as offered by Buddhism and Buddhist Psychotherapy. Without this, we humans have our individual *patterns of behaviour*, but we do not always have a free of how to behave.

Everyone is human

This might appear blatantly obvious but we want to make sure that no-one is raised onto a pedestal. Having taken a quick look at how even people with the most difficult problems who have acted in the most misguided of ways have been able to purify them and achieve liberation, it is now necessary to take a look at the "other end of the spectrum" and remind ourselves that the people there—the people we worship—are also human and exhibit very human behaviour patterns. One example is Mahatma Gandhi, who is known all over the world as the embodiment of peace and non-violence even though he had serious conflicts with his son—breaking off all contact to him—and also had problems in his relationship with his wife—who apparently did not always live up to his high expectations. Just as other people do, Gandhi also had "behavioural roles": his roles as a father, a husband, a politician, a practitioner of a religion, and more. Without targeted mind training, behaviour can be very different in different roles: a level-headed politician is not always a level-headed father, or vice versa.

So we have to exercise caution when we begin to idealise our teachers too much. Idealisation (not to mention idolisation) creates a feeling of remoteness which can in certain circumstances be obstructive to our own growth. We have to understand that although people can be very different, we do in fact exhibit many fundamental similarities. Each one of us carries our "Innate Nobility" within us (see 8th Fundamental of BPT) and everyone already has everything they need to free themselves.

Kathrin K is a single mother who initially came to BPT alone. She complained about severe feelings of stress and excessive demands being placed on her. As therapy progressed and she carried out her regular exercises, she gradually learnt to Pay attention to her own limits and needs. This improved her ability to calm down and relax, but she also became more aware of her concerns about her 14-year-old son. One evening she brought him with her to the meditation session and he quickly and easily discovered his own enthusiasm for the practice. He was proud of his initial success and curious to know more so he attended regularly, treating the meditation evenings a little like a new sport to learn. As his practice continued, his understanding of the wider context also developed.

This Fundamental Should Convey the Following:

Buddhist Psychotherapy is suitable for everyone, regardless of their education, religion, gender, sexual orientation, age, race etc. People seeking help from BPT need to clearly understand that the therapy involves their active cooperation. For successful treatment it is essential to carry out some exercises on a *daily* basis and attend *weekly* individual and group sessions.

The 3rd
Fundamental of Buddhist Psychotherapy

Buddhist Psychotherapists Take Care of Others and Themselves

> Listening itself is an art. When we listen with a still and concentrated mind, it's possible to actually be responsive to what the words are saying.
>
> JOSEPH GOLDSTEIN

> Remain natural while changing your aspiration.
>
> GESHE KELSANG GYATSO

The role of the Buddhist Psychotherapist is both amazing and amazingly difficult. It offers a wonderful chance to engage in daily practice and ongoing personal growth-and to get paid for it! We earn money while we are enjoying the opportunity to practice and pass on the Dharma many hours a day. From a Buddhist point of view- and that of many religions-the helping professions are particularly honourable occupations that contribute to personal and universal growth, benefitting all sentient beings.

So it is all the more remarkable that, although there is almost unanimous agreement with the above viewpoint, this is not reflected in the support provided to these professional groups within the healthcare and social sectors. When it comes to savings and cuts, they are often the first targets.

Occupational hazards

The helping professions all count as high-risk occupations. In other words, people carrying out these occupations (nurses, carers, paramedics, doctors, Samaritans, pastors, counsellors, psychotherapists etc.) are subject to increased levels of risk and therefore need ongoing assistance and support. Their jobs become even more difficult in the prevailing economic situations in the healthcare and social sectors, where more often than not constant rounds of savings and cuts are accompanied by a lack of experience and expertise in the HR departments and at upper management levels, where there is little appreciation of the resources their employees urgently need.

Perhaps it should also be taken more strongly into account that many people in these professions were drawn to their occupation by a strong social desire to help people. Dealing with people in need requires a high level of skill when it comes to managing interpersonal distance and intimacy and distinguishing between one's own needs and those of others. We are talking about a phenomenon often called the "helper syndrome", which more or less *every* person has the potential to experience, since everybody is capable of empathy and the impulse to help that arises from this-this is one ability that characterises us as human beings. In a book published in 2005, the editors Otto F. Kernberg, Birger Dulz and Jochen Eckert gave a range of psychotherapists an opportunity to talk about themselves and their 'impossible' profession (see Bibliography in 22nd Fundamental). Risks faced by the helpers that are mentioned by the authors and the studies they cite include: increased risk of addictions, suicidal tendencies, higher divorce rates, psychological disorders, burn-out. Other less dramatic particularities were also observed; one example was the tendency of people in the helping professions not to take enough care of themselves. Signs of this include the following: they generally are not well organised; as employees they rarely speak out to request support; the design and appearance of the rooms they work in has a low priority for them.

The basic therapeutic attitude

We have already appealed to the help-seekers to take a closer look at their Buddhist Psychotherapists with regard to particular personality traits (see 2nd Fundamental of BPT). Psychotherapists should ideally exhibit a range of desirable characteristics, or at least be doing their utmost to develop them. A helpful Buddhist teaching to guide us here is that of the *Four Immeasurables,* which are also sometimes translated as the *Four Illimitable Mental States.* These serve as excellent cornerstones for a healthy and therapeutically effective basic attitude.

The Four Immeasurables
1) Loving-Kindness
2) Compassion
3) Joy
4) Equanimity

The first immeasurable is also translated as *love,* by which we obviously mean an absolutely non-sexual feeling: an attitude or mental state which unites acceptance, helpfulness, respect and appreciation. This should not be understood as a wishy-washy approach to kindness: Boundaries need to be drawn and clear words spoken. *Loving-kindness* can be understood as a general attitude to life itself and all sentient beings, rather than a form of love targeted at one specific object or person. It is comparable with the Western concept of *agape,* which the theologian Thomas Jay Oord defined as "an intentional response to promote well-being when confronted by that which generates ill-being".

Compassion expresses the therapist's ability to empathise with the help-seeker, clearly feeling the other's suffering whilst not being drawn into the suffering themselves. The latter point is important because in this way they do not lose their resources of creativity, healing energy, motivation and confidence and thus remain able to help. In this Buddhist sense, the compassion of the therapist is supported by an awareness of the inseparable connection between the two of them because of the interconnection of all sentient beings. A person feeling compassion does not feel superior to the person suffering; the therapist does not *pity* the help-seeker in the modern usage of this term.

Buddhism is sometimes accused of being a pessimistic religion whose followers believe that life is suffering. Although this is indeed part of the Buddhist message-that suffering is unavoidable for us all-the second part of the message is equally important and much more upbeat: This suffering can be overcome. So Buddhist Psychotherapists should not cease to convey and exemplify this joyful spirit. The third immeasurable is *joy*. It can also be seen in Buddhist symbolism, with its joyful, optimistic and serene approach clearly visible as millions of Buddha statues smile at us all over the world. As an expression of joy, humour is also essential for even the most serious course of therapy. And there is now scientific evidence offering further proof that laughter is indeed one of the best medicines.

Equanimity and a calm composure are two important basic attitudes which can only fully be attained by means of an intensive daily practice. However, the aim is not equanimity at any cost but rather the quality known as "congruence", referring to a therapist who is authentic and genuine. As a therapist, expressing our feelings and emotions satisfactorily is not at all inconsistent with the desire to be calm; expressing our feelings is not the same as having an attachment to them. We try to see our emotions as a storm cloud which we notice, look at, appreciate for what it is and then let drift by, freeing up the sky so we can continue to work with a clear view and calm composure.

When considering the Four Immeasurables and how to develop them in good measure, we should also keep in mind the Wisdom of the Middle Way (see 9th Fundamental of BPT).

The composure or attitude that Buddhist Psychotherapists adopt and exhibit can serve as an example to the help-seeker, with a healing energy already developing on this level. This basis is essential if the further methods and contents of the teachings are to be communicated. A moody, stressed psychotherapist cannot convey the principles of BPT in a believable way. Loving-kindness, compassion, joy and equanimity serve as tangible expressions of a constructive basic attitude of acceptance and respect. In order to develop and maintain these valuable characteristics as individuals and especially in the role of therapist, all Buddhist therapists have to go through Buddhist Psychotherapy themselves in order to internalise the experiences it leads to. And this should also express itself in the form of committed daily practice.

Humour plays a particularly important role: a serious, or sincere, therapy should not be a "deadly serious" therapy—both parties are allowed and encouraged to laugh. This laughter should not be *about* the client but *with* them.

BPT therapists are not authoritative teachers who looking down on their followers, nor are they zealous missionaries bending over backwards to convert others. If we have made a healthy discovery, such as finding the Buddhist teachings, we might easily be convinced that others have to understand them and adopt them as eagerly as we. However, this impulse to proselytise is nipped in the bud if we remain mindful, of course, this does not mean we need to let go of our intention to help the other person. We might do well to remember the tortoise with his slow and steady approach, feeling no compulsion to match the hare's pace, but nonetheless confident that he would reach his destination—in the end he actually wins the race. As therapists we open ourselves up to the world as seen by the person seeking our help and let go of any inflexible prior notions of what the outcome will be. The aims of the therapy are then worked out together with the help-seeker.

A calm composure is important

Jack Kornfield tells the story of a man who loved his Doberman and began to give it large doses of cod-liver oil. He would hold the head of the protesting dog and forcefully pour the liquid down its throat. The man noticed that the dog didn't like the cod-liver oil but had been told that it was good for dogs and so continued the struggle. One day the dog broke loose and the oil spilled on the floor. To the man's great surprise, the dog returned and lapped up the puddle. So the man discovered that what the dog had been fighting was not the oil but the forced way of administering it.

An attitude of serenity or calmness can mean that we do not *have* to heal anyone directly. We can make suggestions, invite our patients to try things and make offers. But everybody has to walk the healing path themselves.

In the 2nd Fundamental we explained that the BPT is suitable for anyone, so we need to realise that this is not the same as guaranteeing its success for everyone. Each person is on their very own path, which does not always or automatically lead them in the right direction. For many of us it (unfortunately) takes painful experiences to learn some of life's important lessons, so in a wider sense it is almost impossible to clearly assess any one particular experience as positive or negative. Much of what we initially experience as negative later turns out to have been very helpful and instructive. So we cannot and should not prevent anyone from learning these lessons.

There are even cases which make it clear that psychotherapy is not always the most fruitful course of action, so we should always check if the person seeking our help can really benefit from our efforts. Jack Kornfield cites a very pithy Indian saying to illustrate this: "When a pickpocket meets a saint, all he sees are pockets." We can show someone as many healthy paths as possible and even practice the first few steps together, but in the end they have to choose and walk a path themselves.

As Buddhist Psychotherapists we are perhaps in a better position to take care of our own health and composure since we can remind ourselves that we cannot—and must not even try to—heal everyone. Furthermore, the insights of the Middle Way approach (see 9th Fundamental of BPT) serve as a guide to help us maintain a healthy balance between the extremes of serving others and serving ourselves.

Is confrontation a technique?

It is very important to note that confrontation is *not* a therapeutic technique and definitely not a therapeutic attitude. Confrontation remains a therapeutic treatment *skill* which can, in particular circumstances, serve as a powerful instrument to generate or force rapid therapeutic changes. However, it should only be applied within the wider context of a secure, safe and appreciative therapeutic working alliance. Regrettably, this is often forgotten. The impressive effects achieved by skilled therapists lead to the technique being blindly copied by their less skilled colleagues, mostly leading to unnecessary and even destructive conflicts. So it appears better to stay on the safe side, giving a supportive and cooperative approach one more chance before prematurely trying confrontation. As the proverb says: You catch more flies with a teaspoon of honey than with a barrel full of vinegar.

Therapist and client are a team

In comparison with some other schools of therapy and forms of treatment, Buddhist Psychotherapy works with a more open disclosure of its principles. So one cornerstone of the therapy is to convey the relevant contents of Buddhist teachings and the practical exercises that go along with them. In our treatment framework there is no "healthy" person carrying out the treatment and "sick" person receiving it. Rather, we are all trapped within the wheel of life's suffering and we are all (hopefully) on the path to freedom. In our context this means, for example, that the Buddhist treatment methods are not only applied to the help-seeker. Rather, the focus is just as much on the therapists themselves, who are required to put the Buddhist principles into practice and live them out in an exemplary way. Put bluntly, this can be summarised thus: The Buddhist therapist is his or her own first client.

Of course, this should not be understood as indiscriminately claiming that "everyone is the same". It is highly probable that the Buddhist Psychotherapist has well-trained specialist skills and expertise but they should not enjoy any special privileges or a higher status because of this. BPT psychotherapists do not wear white or any other uniform, since this would clearly signal a desire for distance or fixed roles. Although one part of BPT is indeed the conveyance of some important elements from Buddhist teachings, the way this is done is only superficially similar to a traditional teacher-disciple relationship. If we look more closely we will realise that as help-seekers we do not really have to learn anything completely new; everything we will hear actually sounds like an old familiar truth.

As human beings we are all interconnected, we are not truly separate from each other. This applies within BPT, too. The therapists are not "higher", nor are they "separate" from the therapy process; they are part of what happens.

As therapists we need to frequently check how we are defining ourselves. Have we fallen into the trap of identification again? *Are* we Buddhists? *Are* we therapists? *Are* we Europeans? *Are* we women, men, children, mothers, fathers, etc.? The identification with one or more roles is something we want to learn how to avoid.

Buddhist Psychotherapists may well serve a sort of function as role model or even teacher for some people but all the other people we deal with can also serve as *our* teachers. People we are dealing with in one way or another and people we have problems with are our greatest teachers. Every situation, no matter how difficult, can be our teacher. As therapists we are grateful for these opportunities to continually practice and keep learning. In apparently uncomfortable situations, even those where negative emotions arise in us, we can laugh—even if only inwardly—and tell ourselves that we are now experiencing an opportunity to learn a great lesson.

A critical eye

With the basis provided by a constantly appreciative and respectful attitude towards everyone, as therapists we can then look very carefully at the people coming to us for help in order to give them the best possible advice and treatment. With our critical yet respectful eye we should be looking for risk factors that could reduce the chances of a productive therapy or even pose a real danger to the help-seeker. Things that need to be identified include the following: possible influencing factors; the individual functioning level, especially the ego structures and unconscious psychological defence mechanisms; the help-seeker's worldview; and their explanations for and interpretations of their current situation.

1. Risk factors: physical fitness; possible serious illnesses, including those in need of medical treatment; drug use/abuse, including alcohol, medicines, nicotine, hard and soft drugs; addictive behaviour, including gambling, sex, shopping and eating disorders; obesity; lack of exercise; genetic predispositions; etc.

2. Influencing factors: capacity to work; threatened or actual unemployment; family status; relationships; material and financial security; level of education; motivation; prior knowledge and experience; expectations; urgency etc.

3. Ego structures: We come into this world extremely helpless, without any ego structures. These form slowly as we grow older, until the end of puberty. The term refers to a variety of skills and competences such as the following: delayed gratification; frustration tolerance; reality testing; space-time orientation; affect regulation and impulse control; flexibility; ability to form attachments; deferred behaviour; anticipation; empathy; self-reflection or introspection; social behaviour; psychological defence mechanisms; self-protection resources; object representations (see below).

Many of these aspects are very relevant to how psychotherapists handle contact with the help-seeker and conduct the therapy, as well as to the prognosis.

> **Extra tip:** Psychoanalysts, depth psychologists and psychodynamic therapists all work with models where these ego structures form our "innermost scaffolding". Buddhist Psychotherapists as-

> sume that our innermost core is an innate inner nobility (see 8th Fundamental of BPT), with protective layers around it. The "ego structures" can be said to build up in and on these *external* protective layers, serving both as defence and coping mechanisms.

When building the therapeutic working alliance and selecting Buddhist therapy measures, the ego structures known as *object representations* are particularly significant. One of the factors here is the help-seeker's assessment of their fellow human beings. Do they assess and evaluate their attachment figures in a relatively stable way? Or do their feelings waver significantly depending on their mood? If people suffer from "personality disorders", their object representations fluctuate considerably. These "disorders" are defined in terms of very immature (under-developed) or damaged ego structures. One way this might express itself in the therapy context is through an initial idealisation of the therapist followed by a dramatic devaluation as soon as the help-seeker experiences some problems, perhaps leading them to call off the therapy.

The level of the client's psychological defence mechanisms also needs to be carefully observed. This defence generally happens unconsciously by means of techniques such as: sublimation, denial, repression, projection, reversal into the opposite, rationalisation, identification (with the aggressor), or dissociation.

As psychotherapists we have to understand that everybody—even someone who has taken the decision to start therapy—has parts of his character that want to maintain the *status quo,* no matter how uncomfortable this may be. We may rationally desire change but this triggers emotional alarm functions at deeper levels of our psyche which in turn automatically activate self-defence mechanisms. No-one *really* wants to change fundamentally, which is one reason why the most radical changes in our lives often only happen after we have lived through a crisis.

4. Worldview: It might be helpful to pose the following questions in order to shed light on this: How does the help-seeker interpret their situation? What hypotheses do they put forward? Which problems are externalised, i.e. which other people and circumstances are blamed for the situation? Or are the problems interpreted in an excessively self-judgmental way? How grounded is the help-seeker?

Regarding the help-seeker with a critical eye does not in the slightest contradict an appreciative and respectful attitude. As psychotherapists we actually have a responsibility to maintain an all-encompassing view of the situation. This includes critical observation whilst continuing to offer understanding and compassion, as well as loving and kind attention. Only then can the partners in the working alliance really join forces to process the critical areas where it is necessary to do so.

So we pay careful attention to both the help-seeker and our own position in order to make sure that the therapy work we do together always includes "relationship work". This is where we stay in the here and now to try and uncover the typical reaction, emotion and transference patterns of the help-seeker and our own reactions to these.

Namaste instead of idealisation

A moderate level of gentle idealisation at the beginning can actually help to forge the working alliance in certain circumstances. However, the therapist needs to keep this aspect in view at all times, since constant idealisation frequently creates an unproductive sense of separation and remoteness.

Often our unconscious defence mechanisms are also part of this phenomenon. As help-seekers we might think we will never be able to become as calm and serene as the therapist, so we might as well give up and remain the way we are. Or we could bide our time until this ever-so-perfect therapist finally catapults us into enlightenment. And if they cannot, then at least we can remain the way we are and even contribute to their dethroning!

By idealising the therapist, the help-seekers very often make it more difficult for themselves to find their own path, their own liberation and their own Buddha nature. For this reason, as therapists and teachers we will always remain disciples, too. When we receive praise, we should take a careful look at our tendency to identify with it and be mindful of any hidden narcissism. As therapists we regularly need to practice coming down from our imaginary throne.

Buddhist teachers and masters generally sit on a throne or podium when they give teachings and instructions or lead meditation seminars. This should not be confused with the similar symbolism in monarchical or clerical seating arrangements with thrones. In a Buddhist context, the person sitting on a throne is in an absolute sense equal with everyone else; as human beings we all bring with us everything we need for enlightenment. One of the most fundamental Buddhist convictions is the understanding that we are all *interconnected* with all other beings.

Knowing this, we can show respect and worship for Buddhist teachers sitting on podiums, in the conviction we are also worshipping that same potential within ourselves. And the worship of Buddha statues or saintly monks and advanced masters can also be understood as worshipping both these beings and the corresponding sacred aspects of our own nature

This is exactly what is meant when we use the greeting *Namaste*, which literally means: "I greet the light within you." It is a very common way for people to greet each other in south-east Asia, accompanied by the gesture of folded hands held to one's breast and a slight bow: I bow to the inner light, divine spark or Buddha nature we all carry within us.

Respect

Buddhist Psychotherapists are mindful and respectful with regard to all other forms of treatment and other lifestyles in general. The Buddha, 2500 years ago, and the Dalai Lama today both show a great deal of respect for *all* religions. They emphasise that every person should be conscious of their own roots and respect them. This does not exclude the possibility of changing paths later on in life.

Many people coming to seek help from BPT have previous experience of other forms of therapy. At various stages of their life, these other therapies may very well have been the most appropriate, but as therapists we should nonetheless listen carefully for signs of negative experiences during past therapies. It takes a particularly careful approach to deal with help-seekers whose opinion of all their previous therapists is negative.

The BPT is not a form of therapy offering the help-seeker a panacea which they only need to take (passively) in order to be healed. It needs to be made very clear to them from the beginning that their *active* cooperation is required.

It might be appropriate here to mention the parable of the treasure chest: In the middle of a town there is a beggar sitting on a box, asking passers-by to give him some money for food. Years go by and he never receives the right help or enough money, so he grows bitter and begins to despair, asking himself whether the right person will ever turn up and really help him. One day, an old man comes along and says, "I have no money to give you, but what's in that box you're sitting on?" Unwilling at first, the "poor" beggar then pries the lid off the box and discovers that it is full of gold coins.

The same pattern can be discovered time and time again in our consultation rooms. The help-seeker demands the *right* therapist and the *right* method that will *deliver them* health or happiness. From the viewpoint of Buddhist Psychotherapy, the help-seeker is already in possession of their own treasure chest full of everything they need for a satisfying and peaceful life.

Supporting Factors for a Successful Therapy

The therapist's credibility

The therapist and the consultation rooms are both practical factors that contribute to the therapy's success. It has long been known that the therapeutic relationship itself guarantees the success of the therapy more than the particular therapeutic methods applied. So it is clear that the credibility and authenticity of the therapist is of crucial significance.

Jack Kornfield describes an interesting observation: On the way to a particular hospital there was a toll road, where an almost insignificant toll had to be thrown into a collection box at the roadside. A hidden camera was put in place, filming the doctors to see if they paid this fee on their way to work. This experiment yielded a very interesting result: Patients of the doctors who paid the toll showed faster rates of healing than those being treated by doctors who did not.

Of course, simple conclusions should not be drawn from a study such as this without posing more questions, but it does lend support to the claim that the attitude and integrity of those in the healing professions has a valuable influence on the success of the assistance they provide.

Even if they do not state it openly, all help-seekers would like more than just relief from their oppressive emotions such as fear, worry, anger, disappointment or sadness: They also want to become calm, happy and satisfied. Therapists are well advised to mention that these states are possible, but more importantly it should be possible for the client to *feel that* this type of development is within their grasp during their time together with the therapist.

The therapeutic surroundings

Another practical aspect of relevance to re the mindfulness displayed by therapists towards their help-seekers is the consultation room: Is it spacious enough? Does it have enough light, are there windows for daylight or only lamps? Does (creative) chaos prevail or is there a recognisable sense of design and tidiness? Is the room regularly ventilated and cleaned? Are there any noticeable odours? Can candles or incense sticks be lit without setting off the smoke detector or fire alarm?

Particular attention needs to be paid to the setting if it is shared by several different therapists, which is often the case for rooms where the group sessions are held. Unfortunately they are often designed for functionality and resemble a sports hall or waiting room more than a therapeutic setting.

For many of us active in a Buddhist context, it will be a source of inspiration if we have Buddhist images or statues present. The Medicine Buddha can lend us especially suitable support.

The relevance of healing therapeutic surroundings cannot be stressed enough. For example, studies have shown that people in a positive environment have significantly better chances of healing. Other studies showed that people who work next to a mirror maintain a more upright posture while working. Although different, both examples serve to highlight the same point: Let us take a careful look at the room(s) where we work.

Helpful rituals

Starting and finishing our therapy sessions with rituals can be very helpful. Since ancient times, symbols and rituals have served humanity as important and therapeutic supports. Proven methods include breathing exercises or a simple sounding of cymbals or a singing bowl. A closing ritual is especially important for the therapist, who often needs a very clear cleansing, closing and letting-go exercise in order to clear his or her mind between two different clients or sessions. For the therapist it might even be advisable to adopt a special "clocking off" ritual to help them leave the help-seekers' issues and energies behind in the consultation room. Opening the windows and airing the room as part of this is also a good idea. It is not advisable to routinely take work home, even report writing-if we do not have working space there which is clearly separate from our living space.

The Therapist as Personification of the Link Between Psychotherapy and Buddhism

Can Buddhist Psychotherapy only be carried out by Buddhists?

In order to consider this question, we first have to ask ourselves: When does someone become a Buddhist? What characterises a Buddhist?

We can call ourselves a Buddhist if:

we accept the Buddha as a teacher;

we are studying the teachings (Dharma) and investigating how to apply them to our lives; and

we regularly practice in a community (Sangha) of like-minded people (meditation and Dharma discussions), where possible under the direction of a Buddhist teacher.

Furthermore, there are a variety of different precepts offering us guidance for daily life as Buddhists. We will take a closer look at these later, but when considering the basic question posed here regarding being a Buddhist, the Buddha listed five precepts for lay people:

Refrain from deliberately killing or injuring living beings (including animals).

Refrain from taking anything that is not freely given.

Lead an ethical life.

Refrain from lying and harsh speech.

Refrain from blurring consciousness by taking drugs.

Of course it is up to each one of us to decide how we pursue the Buddhist path and how far we take it. For example, after putting the guidelines mentioned above into practice, we might wish to take another step and begin the bodhisattva path. This decision can be reinforced in a formal way by taking the Bodhisattva Vow. A bodhisattva is a human being who dedicates his or her life to working intensively towards the liberation of all beings, not only themselves.

For Buddhist Psychotherapists, caring for themselves goes beyond the usual mental hygiene necessary for everyone working in the healing professions because of the Buddhist view that everything is *interconnected* and other experiences or concepts such as the value of *compassion*, the inherent *emptiness* of objects and the *illusory nature* of an independent self. It is typically Buddhist to place equal emphasis on taking care of oneself (as a therapist) and taking care of others (the help-seekers), although similar concepts are found in other religions, such as the Christian commandment: *"Thou shalt love thy neighbour as thyself."*

Buddhist Psychotherapists do not have to be ordained Buddhists in order to practice BPT but they should definitely have some basic qualities and prior knowledge. So what qualifications do we mean?

The great significance of the therapist's *integrity* has already been emphasised above. Of course, this does not only refer to their credibility but to their qualification, their ability to ensure the best and most well-founded treatment for the people coming to them for help.

A course of therapy that claims to be based on Buddhist principles needs therapists that are very familiar with these principles, so in order to practice BPT a therapist needs good training, skills and confidence in both psychotherapy and Buddhist teachings. Healers offering BPT need to study and internalise the core Buddhist principles and live their lives accordingly. This book is intended to present these core principles.

Training to become a Buddhist Psychotherapist

The BPT does not replace vocational training. Basic professional training as a psychotherapist is necessary in order to offer well-founded Buddhist Psychotherapy. These initial qualifications ensure that help-seekers can find the safest and most professional conditions possible.

For many people who turn to psychotherapy looking for help, the range of different professional qualifications and titles can be very confusing. Is there a difference between *psychotherapy* and *mental health counselling*? What are the differences between *therapists*, *counsellors, psychotherapists, psychoanalysts, psychologists* and *psychiatrists*? Which countries have legal regulation of these professions?

As therapists, we have a duty to make our professional background clear to anyone coming to us for help. For example, we should ensure that we do not use any titles that are regulated or protected unless we are entitled to do so. We could make it clear whether we have a medical education and training. The most important factor is to follow a path available in our country that genuinely qualifies us to offer safe and professional support to the people turning to us for help. And to maintain full transparency regarding our qualifications in order to maximise our credibility and authenticity as a therapist.

Assuming that the therapist has a solid professional training consisting of a relevant combination of, for example, medical and psychological qualifications with particular training in one or more schools of psychotherapy, this is then the perfect foundation for further training in Buddhist Psychotherapy. This includes undertaking the therapy as a help-seeker, a regular and intensive study of the Buddhist teachings, daily Buddhist practice and abiding by the five lay precepts (see above).

If we then decide to go further along the Buddhist path and develop the approach of a Bodhisattva, is this at all realistic? Or are we setting ourselves goals that are too lofty, thereby dooming ourselves to failure?

One of the Dalai Lama's favourite authors is Shantideva, who lived in India around the 8th century CE. In his basic text, the *Bodhicaryavatara,* known in English as *A Guide to the Bodhisattva's Way of Life,* he describes how crazy he considers the swearing of such lofty oaths. He recognises how the idea of working towards a good

---

Translator's note: The English edition of this book is intended for an international audience in many different countries and therefore cannot provide a detailed overview of the regulations covering the above-mentioned professions in the reader's country, as was provided for Germany in the original book.

cause can be very inspiring but how difficult it then is to really put this into practice in our lives.

So making a decision and taking vows are not enough. With Buddhist Psychotherapy we then benefit from a very healthy outer framework—and, with time, an inner one—to help us become more effective in our work for the benefit of ourselves and all other beings. Progress will become tangible, which in turn increases confidence and certainty. Healing takes effect right from the very first steps and not only when the goal is reached.

The teachings and exercise instructions in this book are suitable for *everyone*—for therapists and help-seekers alike. After all, the distinction between "healthy" therapists and "ill" clients is preposterous: We are all help-seekers and therefore equal in this regard.

Is a healer always healthy?

The old question of whether a teacher should always embody their own teachings is an important consideration for Buddhist Psychotherapy too. There are various types of efficacy which make a treatment successful. A mathematics teacher obviously has to understand mathematics, but an unathletic teacher can show others how to play sport. Nietzsche even wrote: "One who is unable to loosen his own chains may yet be a redeemer for his friend."

So we return to the issue of a therapist's qualifications and qualities. As well as those which can be taught and assessed practically, with the awarding of a certificate, there are also the less objectively measurable human characteristics previously mentioned such as authenticity, credibility, human warmth and empathy. Perhaps this is why we often speak of the *art* of healing and why the Latin phrase *lege artis* came to stand for a (medical) practice that is genuine and carried out correctly.

Inner and outer rules for Buddhist Psychotherapists

If we want to further deepen our interest in the Buddhist path to liberation, it can be helpful to take a fresh look at the path every day, as if we were repeatedly taking our first step. Beneficial rituals, such as prayers and vows, can support us in this, especially as we seek to reinforce the *inner* rules which can often be lacking in comparison to the *external* rules, such as instructions and prohibitions. In further chapters of this book we will discover more details regarding prayers, vows, rituals and symbols. And in particular, we will learn how mental activities can have practical, tangible effects on us and our surroundings (see 6th and 19th Fundamentals of BPT).

For many people who have taken a conscious decision to live their life for the liberation of themselves and others, the Bodhisattva Vow offers them a helpful guideline for their way of life, this applies equally to therapeutic work and everyday matters. By taking the vow we are confirming our decision to cultivate qualities within us which are healthy for us and for everybody else. Reciting the vow regularly and thus using it as a prayer (see 20th Fundamental of BPT), is a way of benefitting from its positive effect on us and other people.

We will describe how mental activities such as the daily recitation of a vow can lead to tangible beneficial effects and we will also explore some practical exercises which allow anyone to understand and experience this with their own senses, check it against their experience and feel its validity. After all, our goal is to convey experiences, not beliefs. We can test every aspect to see if it is correct and relevant.

As well as existing vows, during Buddhist Psychotherapy we also develop a personal vow for each help-seeker.

Since the Bodhisattva Vow can have a very helpful and healing effect, especially for therapists, we reproduce it here:

The Bodhisattva Vow

Beings are numberless; I vow to free them all.

Delusions are inexhaustible; I vow to end them fully.

Dharma gates are boundless; I vow to enter them all.

The ways to awakening are unsurpassable; I vow to embody them all.

Frank H is a psychotherapist himself. It took many years of suffering before he looked for help because of the strong feelings of shame which arose when he—a helper—admitted he needed help. He had already been showing symptoms of burn-out for a long time. He said he always looked after his patients very carefully and could never refuse a new patient, even when his schedules were already full. Studying this 3rd Fundamental offered some inspiring and helpful insights. The experience of interconnection within his BPT group and the mindfulness exercises were particularly useful, helping Frank to discover self-confidence in his relationship to himself. He recognised that the need for both appreciation and help are universal and therefore apply equally to him. Frank developed a new way of looking at the world which helped him to understand that we *all* need help and support.

This Fundamental Should Convey the Following:

Buddhist Psychotherapists take care of their help-seeking clients *and* themselves. Thanks to a deep respect for everyone's individuality we recognise and respect our interconnection at the deeper levels of being human.

Buddhist Psychotherapists and their help-seeking clients form a community with beneficial, healing effects for everyone.

The 4th
Fundamental of Buddhist Psychotherapy

Buddhist Psychotherapy Unites Theory and Practice

> Buddhism is an empirical science and a path for transforming the mind.
>
> Matthieu Ricard

> Buddhism is not a religion but rather a science of mind.
>
> Dalai Lama XIV

We will use the 4th Fundamental of Buddhist Psychotherapy to present a few *theoretical* aspects of the therapy. The Buddhist path is ideally suited to everyday life; it is a very practical philosophical, spiritual and therapeutic tradition enriched with centuries of experience, enabling it to become very sophisticated yet remain down-to-earth and modern. The 14th Dalai Lama made it clear that Buddhism has always incorporated new insights with his provocative assertion: "If science proves some belief of Buddhism wrong, then Buddhism will have to change." This clearly means we do not have to blindly believe in any "exotic oriental ideas". Rather, we should follow Buddhist tradition by listening attentively to any new statement and carefully examining it, checking it against our experience and trying it out. If the results are positive, we should take it on board and practice it further. This learning process is also important for Buddhist Psychotherapy since following it is the perfect guide to making the best use of both theory and practice in our lives and passing these insights on to others.

The following three-step process is a rough description of the main points of how the theory/teachings can be conveyed. It is particularly important to note how important and characteristically Buddhist the third step is—putting into practice or implementation in everyday life—following the first and second steps—recognising/understanding and contemplating/internalising, respectively. The basic Buddhist approach shines through again here: We do not only want to make progress for *ourselves,* but also for *all sentient beings.* Studying and analysing the teachings cannot remain a purely intellectual occupation because the process only becomes complete and only has a justification after its practical implementation in everyday life.

Three-Step Process for Buddhist Teachings within BPT

1. *Recognise and Understand:* Acquiring knowledge of Buddhist teachings takes place in individual and group sessions, with both formal teachings and discussions. Plus: Self-study of relevant literature and the Fundamentals of Buddhist Psychotherapy.

2. *Contemplate and Internalise:* As part of the therapy, individual understanding of the teachings will be internalised.

3. *Realise and Implement:* Parallel to this, the theory is *put into practice* in everyday life. Here, the 20th Fundamental (amongst others) provides practical guidance.

So it becomes very clear that we are talking about the unity of theory and practice. One significant aspect of Buddhism is that we should not blindly believe in some kind of dogma. The Buddha used the imagery of the pre-dawn colours or "red sky" (wisdom) as always preceding the sunrise (state of liberation). One implication of this for Buddhist Psychotherapy is that we as therapists have to internalise the important aspects of the Buddhist teachings in order to be able to convey them in an understandable way. Recognition and an initial understanding of the Dharma are necessary before we can go on to practice it.

The Structure of a Course of Buddhist Psychotherapy

The initial phase of BPT has two main components:

1. *Establishing contact* with the client by means of an *anamnesis* (recording the life history and current issues) and initial or *trial sessions* of spoken therapy.

2. *Conveying the first basics* of Buddhism and psychotherapy basics by means of the following questions:
What will the treatment be like? What needs to be considered?
What individual agreements and information could be important?
What specific aim will be pursued?

Establishing contact, trial sessions and anamnesis

Once contact has been established with the patient, BPT envisages 3 to 5 trial sessions of oral therapy. This allows the therapist and the client to "check each other out" and try out the working alliance; it also includes a thorough anamnesis (biography, educational and professional background and situation, social status, medical history with current symptoms, ideas and attributions of the client regarding the illness, psychological diagnosis with determination of psychological stability, assessment of factors such as thought patterns, tendency to complain, possible suicidal tendencies, inner drive, affect stability, previous diagnoses etc.).

During the first sessions—often in the first few minutes—the help-seeker gains that all-important first impression of the therapist. It is well known that this factor significantly influences the chances of therapeutic success. These first hours also offer the therapist a chance to assess intensively where the help-seeker currently stands in their life: What understanding of the world and their place within it does the help-seeker have? What or who do they think is responsible for their current situation? How well are they able to concentrate? To what degree can they be approached intellectually? How well developed are their abilities of introspection and self-motivation? What words and terms do they repeatedly use? Which channels do they prefer when making significant experiences or statements (visual, olfactory, auditory, tactile etc.)?

Furthermore, an assessment should be made of potential risks: How stable are the ego structures (see 3rd Fundamental of BPT)? In particular, how stable and developed are the abilities to test reality, tolerate frustration, ease their own burdens, control affects and impulses, form attachments, behave socially, self-reflect, introspect, and empathise? What level of ego defence structures and possibilities for self-stabilisation do they have?

The first assessments to be made after carrying out the anamnesis are important for deciding the details of the following treatment. They provide information regarding the ability of the help-seeker to safely negotiate crisis situations and the amount of support they need at these times. Furthermore, they also suggest how deeply the help-seeker should immerse themselves in visualisation exercises, how well they can let go, what their relationship to meditation is like and what forms of meditation might be the most suitable.

The stability of the client and the therapeutic relationship and the skills of the psychotherapist are all critical when it comes to deciding how much confrontation could be appropriate for the help-seeker. They also help to determine the appropriate balance between protection and forcing, and between encouragement and reining in.

The help-seeker's own ideas about the cause and nature of their illness are particularly important. What or who do they think is responsible for the current situation? What system of interpretation do they use? For example, do they tend to internalise or externalise responsibility?

The client's current social status and situation are also crucial: Does the help-seeker live alone and are they happy with this, or do they feel isolated and lonely? Do they have friends, relations, family? How do they value these people with whom they have an affinity? Do their social networks provide security and support? How reliable are they?

This thorough analysis is an important and essential measure. Professional observations and assessments have to be made and recorded carefully and used to constructively shape the therapeutic alliance. This also includes being open and transparent about the analysis, which means that a Buddhist therapist should talk about their observations and impressions with the help-seeker where appropriate.

As Buddhist Psychotherapists we should pay careful attention to the following aspects:
- With how much conscious awareness does this person live and function?
- How identified are they with their roles and emotional patterns?
- How strongly do they desire liberation?

The use of medication

At the beginning of therapy, it might be necessary to explain what types of medication could support BPT or interfere with the work. Here it is generally advisable to work together with an appropriate medical specialist.

Using medication (pharmacotherapy) should only be considered as a supporting therapy; for example, it could minimise psychological disorders. Treatment exclusively based on the use of psychopharmaceutical drugs is nowadays generally regarded as an error. If it is appropriate to use psychoactive medication to support the therapy, BPT insists on carrying out prior laboratory tests to determine individual tolerance and sensitivity. Although this test is as simple as any other blood test, it is still not routinely carried out. Each person metabolises (breaks down) chemical substances, such as medicines, at a different rate. A technical commission of the European Union has been recommending for years that a tolerance test be carried out *before* prescribing pharmacotherapy. Prof. Joachim Bauer estimates that approximately 30% of the population belong to the "intermediate metaboliser" group, who break down chemicals four times more slowly than others. And about 10% of the population are "poor metabolisers" who can take up to 100 times as long to break down medicines. These results imply that some 40% of all patients receiving psychoactive drugs are clearly or even massively overdosed. At the other end of the scale, about 2% of the population are "rapid metabolisers", whose detoxification capacity is so strong it probably breaks down prescribed medicines before they have any effect. In these cases the therapist could be forgiven for accusing the client of not taking their medicine!

Any treatment with medication needs to be discussed individually with the help-seeker at the beginning of every course of BPT.

Contact is important

In the initial phase of establishing contact, the therapist should make every effort to immerse themselves in a professional way in the world of the person sitting in front of them, to "learn their language", and do anything else they can to facilitate this initial contact with the therapy.

There are many therapists who consider it unnecessary or even unhelpful to explain the concepts behind their type of therapy, but BPT adopts the opposite attitude, carefully describing its Buddhist approach to therapy to the help-seeker during the initial phase. In fact, a basic understanding of the treatment concept can be considered an essential building block of the therapy, especially with regard to the integration of theory and practice. Other schools sometimes regard this as difficult, but practical instructions to overcome the gap between theory and practice are in fact one of the "recipes for success" in Buddhism and Buddhist Psychotherapy.

After a minimum of 3 to 5 trial sessions, individually agreed key points for the therapy should be written down and the main phase can then begin.

Conveying the Fundamentals of Buddhist Psychotherapy

This step deals with the question of how the course of treatment will develop and what needs to be considered.

The treatment concept in Buddhist Psychotherapy includes both individual and group sessions. The individual therapy sessions take place weekly and last about 50 minutes. Every help-seeker is also given individual exercises which they should practice *daily*. The group sessions include facilitated group discussions, which usually take place weekly, and instructions or Dharma talks from Buddhist Psychotherapists followed by group meditation, which can take place about twice a week. Regular participation in group sessions is of particular importance in BPT.

The Buddha's cousin Ananda once suggested that the spiritual community should make up at least half of our spiritual life; he is reported to have answered that active participation in a spiritual community does not make up half of our spiritual life but rather all of it.

This is one of very many examples which make clear that the Buddha himself and the Buddhists that came after him were strictly against withdrawal from the world in favour of concentrating exclusively on oneself. This still applies today. Of course, we concentrate a lot of effort on ourselves, but at the same time we are working for the benefit of all other beings. Neither self-sacrifice nor self-denial is highly valued; we are not self-centred, nor do we cloister ourselves away from the world. The Wisdom of the Middle Way is visible here and will accompany us often (especially as part of the 9th Fundamental of the BPT).

Tailored information

The BPT offers a very wide range of helpful ideas and views. On no account should the poor help-seeker be indiscriminately bombarded all at once with all of them. Rather, the theory should be introduced in a carefully selected and tailored fashion.

Right at the beginning, even before the treatment starts, the therapist should find out what aims the help-seeker has and they should take a look together to see how realisable they are. What specific aim would help-seeker like to pursue? Would they like to get rid of a conflict, fears, pain, addiction, depression etc? Is there a pressing need for clarity with regards to particular life situations? Or have they come looking for some meaning in their life? These aims should be written down with as many details as possible and immediately examined together with the client in a realistic and critical way.

Another important topic that has to be conveyed in the initial phase is an explanation of how physical and psychological problems arise. The therapist should present two areas in an integrated way:
1 Medical and scientific information
2 Approaches from Buddhism and the humanities.

Western medical and psychotherapeutic aspects of this topic are conveyed together under the heading of *psychosomatic* connections. There are no physical (= *somatic*) symptoms without mental (= *psycho*) and emotional ones and there are no emotional and mental changes without physical reactions (see 5th, 6th and 7th Fundamentals of the BPT).

The second point is dealt with during the whole therapy as the Buddhist teachings are conveyed by means of the BPT Fundamentals.

An important objective in the initial phase of the treatment is to make it clear to the client that the Eastern scientific (= Buddhist) and Western scientific (= psychosomatic) sides of BPT are in fact *one*. The Fundamentals of Buddhist Psychotherapy presented in this book can and should be used as a guideline for this.

As early as possible in their course of Buddhist Psychotherapy, help-seekers should develop a good understanding of psychotherapy and Buddhism. Of course, the therapeutic context will determine to a significant extent how this understanding can be developed: The exact nature of this "psychoeducation" will depend on whether the treatment or counselling takes place in a hospital, an outpatient institution, in private practice, as individual therapy or in a group setting. Buddhist Psychotherapy has been successfully tried out in all of these different contexts.

Individual therapy will allow for better tailoring to the needs of the individual, taking into account the client's personal background and wishes, whereas group situations place their own particular demands on Buddhist Psychotherapists. Group dynamics always have to be considered as do the individual levels of concentration amongst participants. The teachings provided have to be "easy to digest": Teachings are not provided for the benefit of the teacher—they should be adapted for the benefit of the listener.

Conveying relevant Buddhist teachings should be linked with presentations of psychological and medical backgrounds. Effectively linking Eastern-Buddhist and Western-medical-psychological resources has proved to be very successful and beneficial. In this way the effects of therapy can be very long-lasting with benefits for the help-seeker resulting in even greater well-being. In scientific terms this is an example of a positive *synergy* (synergy can be described as the case when the result is more than the sum of the individual parts).

Buddhism and science

Buddhism is itself a science. It is now considered to be one of the oldest and best-tested sciences of the mind. It has been and still is a source of inspiration for many Western humanities and the connection between Buddhist teachings and Western natural sciences is also now a firmly established tradition.

Buddhist Psychotherapy is one of a range of different examples of the integration of Eastern-Buddhist and Western-scientific approaches which are developing all over the world in many different subject areas. One of the best-known is the *Mind and Life Institute,* which organises regular meetings between a variety of scientists and Buddhist masters in order to promote international, interreligious and intercultural scientific exchange. The first such meeting was in 1987 and the Institute was officially founded in 1990. Each conference has a different current topic and some of the world's leading scientists from the relevant field meet with the 14th Dalai Lama and other renowned Buddhists in order to discuss the issues involved. Some of the topics covered in previous conferences include: emotions and health; cosmology; compassion; and dealing with destructive emotions. One of the tasks of these conferences is to fulfil the mutual desire to learn from the rich scientific and experiential resources of the other scientific culture. So the participants see themselves as both learners and teachers.

Western humanities such as psychology and psychotherapy and Eastern sciences of the mind such as Buddhism have some remarkable common features*. Both pursue the goal of reducing human suffering and providing assistance through insights into the human condition. Both concentrate more strongly on real life conditions than on transcendental powers in the world beyond. Both conduct research to find causes and solve problems.

In the past there were more fundamental *differences* between Western and Eastern sciences. For a long time, Western scientists were convinced that our brain is significantly formed by impressions resulting from experiences in early childhood and then remains so forever after. Buddhists, on the other hand, have known for many centuries that our psyche can transform itself very radically. Western science has now confirmed this with the discovery of neuroplasticity (the ability of our nervous system to adapt itself, see 5th Fundamental of BPT) and in particular through the use of modern imaging techniques, such as magnetic resonance imaging (MRI), which enable us to gain insights into how our brain actually works. These have shown that we are definitely able to fundamentally transform our psyche at the biological level of nerve cells even late in our life. What we think, what we regularly do, the issues we regularly concern ourselves with—all of this has a fundamental influence on our psyche/mind and our nerve cells. (We will cover this in more detail in the 5th Fundamental on the topic of our body and the 6th Fundamental about our mind.)

These relatively new results have had a major impact on neurological studies and our picture of humankind. They reveal and prove the extent to which we can change ourselves and illustrate the opportunities and potential available to us. This was obviously the perfect topic for the *Mind and Life Institute;* the 14th Dalai Lama has initiated and supported many studies on this issue in collaboration with renowned scientists. For example, advanced meditation

---

* Translator's note: This is reflected more directly in the German terms *Geisteswissenschaften* and *Wissenschaften des Geistes,* respectively.

masters were studied during specific types of meditation exercise by means of the electroencephalogram (EEG) and functional magnetic resonance imaging (fMRI). EEG can measure the strength of electric potentials between specific regions of the brain and fMRI produces a sequence of images illustrating the processes taking place in a working brain. One example of the results seen during these experiments was with meditation masters such as Yongey Mingyur Rinpoche, whose meditation was able to increase the activity in regions of the brain responsible for feeling happiness by up to 800%. This compares to beginner meditators, who were able to increase the activities in the relevant brain regions by only 10 to 15%.

This type of factual scientific information forms part of the theory conveyed during a course of Buddhist Psychotherapy. It is included in this book because experience shows that Western people in particular find it helpful as they develop their own connection to BPT and its exercises. Conveying this sort of information needs to be done in a careful, understandable, measured and client-centred way.

Psychoeducation and the danger of identification

Of course Western psychotherapy also appreciates the value of psychoeducation—explaining the nature of their illness to the patient—but often therapists interpret this in terms of a necessity for the patient to admit that they are ill. According to this approach, the help-seeker needs to realise that they *are* a person with illness X: I *am* an alcoholic; I *am* a depressive; or I *am* a borderliner. The ambivalence here is obvious: Information is good, identification can be a problem. Unfortunately we often find the disastrous equation "diagnosis = destiny".

In this book we will often return to the problem of taking on roles and identification. This tendency is constantly with us; it is inculcated into us very early in life: How often do children hear statements such as "You *are* a naughty boy" or "You *are* a stubborn girl" instead of the more accurate expression, "It annoys me when you *behave* in this way".

BPT has a completely different way of treating the issue of identification. A significant component of the Buddhist teachings are exercises designed to break down a whole range of different identifications. Nonetheless, good psychoeducation can be very useful for the help-seeker and we should respect this fact, taking the risks outlined above into consideration when providing it. The form and content of the psychoeducation should always be customised according to the competencies of the person receiving it; the middle way is also generally the right way here. For example, lightness and humour can play an important role when delivering the information. These are also essential when dealing with the basic Buddhist issue of suffering, which could otherwise become a very serious issue. Finding a good path together with the client is much easier if the therapist adopts an attitude combining seriousness and humour. Laughter is allowed—and desired. BPT should ensure that it lends support to the experience of elements such as humour, leniency, understanding, flexibility, appreciation, fun and enjoyment. Although "infotainment" is often a superficial combination of information and entertainment, presenting information in an entertaining way does not have to be superficial and can be a very effective way of conveying a message.

The basic desire of BPT is the wish to provide effective and lasting support for people who are searching for ways to end their suffering. This applies irrespective of the particular issue, and the aim should be made tangible to the client, ideally with the Buddhist therapist's characteristics serving as a role model.

Conveying the basic Buddhist principle of selflessness to people with problems of self-esteem

How can Buddhist Psychotherapists convey the core Buddhist concept of selflessness or egolessness to clients who have inadequate self-esteem, self-recognition, self-protection or capacity to draw their own boundaries?

Jack Kornfield makes a clear statement on this issue: "Both Western and Buddhist psychologies acknowledge the need for a healthy development of self." Is this not a paradox? One the one hand, we need a secure feeling of self to be a functioning unit but on the other, Buddhist teachings and Buddhist Psychotherapy both tell us that our feeling of self is an illusion.

In fact, it is not really a paradox. In a condition of weakness, self-preservation has to be the priority. Only when we strengthen our condition can we look more deeply with the power necessary to free ourselves. So first of all we need a secure sense of self and to have our resources on tap in order to proceed further and recognise that we are in fact able to achieve more than simple self-preservation and functioning. A good sense of self enables us to survive in and keep up with the cycle of life, but we can nonetheless remain trapped in this cycle of alternating happiness and suffering and ever more suffering. The final liberation requires us to free ourselves from our ego illusion.

Perhaps we can compare this situation with the virtual money of a stock-market speculator. Most of the time, he does not have any real money in his hands and simply hopes that the money exists somehow somewhere. His daily business consists of trading with this money—it is how he earns his living. So if this virtual money were constantly under threat and available in insufficient amounts, this would be a cause for constant worry. In a situation of weakness such as this, the trader would not be in a position to think about the virtual nature of this money—he would be too worried. However, on days when his (virtual) balance is more healthy he might be able to think more often about the real value and actual substance of money and might even come to the conclusion that money does not "really" exist, since it is actually just a "tool" that everyone has agreed upon.

Buddhist Psychotherapy focuses on the here and now

In the first and core Buddhist teaching of the "Turning the Wheel of Dharma", the significance of the present moment is emphasised alongside the Four Noble Truths and the Wisdom of the Middle Way: Use insights and wisdom in order to help yourself and others in the here and now.

We will take a closer look at this in the 10th Fundamental of the BPT but here we want to emphasise how seriously we should take this aspect during our psychotherapeutic work. The main focus should therefore be on a respectful appreciation of everything that is happening here and now. Processing past experiences is not obligatory but rather one aspect that only becomes relevant if things that happened in the past are preventing current progress. Here it is important to emphasise how careful we should be to neither promote the creation of new self-definitions and identifications nor reinforce old ones. Instead we should support the client in their careful reflection on any identification process which is happening; wherever possible we then help them to limit, weaken and stop it. For example, the therapy may bring the client back into contact with an old memory of a situation where they were a victim of certain circumstances or people. The role of victim needs to be respected, afforded its due significance and taken very seriously; then it has to be released and prevented from turning into a generalisation, where the client frequently considers themselves to be a victim. We human beings have a strong tendency to generalise. In this context we also have to be aware of the risk of unhealthy transference processes which could obstruct further therapeutic development for the help-seeker.

Team work based on the Buddhist image of humanity

In order to work as a team, the Buddhist therapist and help-seeker need to share the same quest. This implies making no distinction between a healthy therapist and an ill client. Suffering is universal and inevitable. Everyone is at their own individual stage on the path to liberation. Both therapist and client are studying Buddhist teachings and practice during the sessions and, above all, in their everyday life. There is an obvious difference here to most Western treatment methods, which generally assume a healthy doctor or therapist and an ill patient. The Buddhist image of humanity makes it clear that all human beings are equal, even if the therapist and the help-seeker do have differences. In fact, many different cultures share this insight, perhaps expressing it in terms of the divine spark within every human being; the Buddhist concept of inner nobility (see 8th Fundamental of BPT) is only unique in terms of its specific practical consequences for everyday life.

Before we leave the topic of the *form* and conditions of the therapy and move on to its *contents,* we still have a short summary regarding how to convey the theory, which we have called "The Four Benchmarks of Truth".

The Four Benchmarks of Truth

1. The first benchmark is rather general, pointing out that every aspect of the theory needs to be transferred into the language and way of understanding of the listener's culture. According to this, German Buddhist Psychotherapy would focus on different issues than Italian Buddhist Psychotherapy.
2. The second benchmark refers to the individual and points out that the person conveying the Buddhist teachings needs to adapt their choice of words and the scope of the teachings to the worldview and personal situation of the listener.
3. The third benchmark points out that Buddhist teachings are always given for the benefit and healing of the help-seeker, never with a missionary attitude. Teaching Buddhism should not be done simply for the sake of teaching and spreading Buddhism.
4. The fourth benchmark concerns a general issue, pointing out that conveying profound truths is still a core intention, even though these should be customised for each listener. Various contents of Buddhist theory might not be easily understandable at first, especially because some of them do not seem to accord with our everyday understanding of the world (which is often superficial). Nonetheless, these profound truths do need to be spoken openly and conveyed in a practical way.

Buddhism as a source

Buddhist practice is very diverse. During the 2500 years of its history, many exercises have been added and existing ones refined. They constitute an extensive pool of functioning strategies to reduce and

remove human suffering. In fact, all currently existing forms of psychotherapy have drawn their basic theories, concepts and ideas—and not least, their practical techniques—directly or indirectly from the ancient sources of the Eastern sciences of the mind, with Buddhism being one of these. Examples include:
- The concept of character and personality types
- The idea of an individual and universal (collective) unconscious
- The idea that ignorance or being unaware is a cause of suffering
- Dream interpretation
- The use of trance, hypnosis, relaxation and meditation
- A focus on the here and now
- The concept of systemic contexts, and
- Insights into the connections between perception, interpretation and the feelings that arise from this.

Balancing theory and practice

The twin aspects of theory and practice are extraordinarily important in Buddhist Psychotherapy. The exact balance between each of them should always be chosen individually for each help-seeker. This is never an "either-or" decision, but rather always a question of fine adjustment. We will also see that instructions concerning the theory or teachings should always be given *before* the start of practical exercises, according to the principle: Ensure secure foundations before building the practice superstructure.

All help-seekers have their own issues of concern and their own strengths which need to be recognised and used. Where one person might be better reached by means of rational explanations, the next needs much more practical instruction on how to behave. Some people need explanations first in order to open up to the possibility of an experience, others need to experience something with their own senses first before they can understand an explanation.

Marianne K had already read a lot of Buddhist books and meditated regularly for herself, but she was about to give up. She told us about various

Buddhist masters and could even quote some of them. She found the reports that she read very inspiring and was excited about the possibilities they described, but when she sat down to meditate she could not feel any connection to the things she had read about. The impression we gained from Marianne was that she was expecting to "jump" directly from the book into liberation.

The first therapeutic steps consisted of communicating a balance between theory and practice—between teachings and exercises. A large number of individual and group sessions in the initial phase served to help her develop a healthy practice, eventually experiencing meditation as a technique that could help her progress.

This Fundamental Should Convey the Following:

Buddhist Psychotherapy combines theoretical teachings and specific practical exercises. It needs active cooperation from the help-seeker, above all because the course of therapy is not restricted to a single weekly individual session, but rather comprises a weekly program of individual sessions, group sessions and group teachings with group meditations plus practical exercises for every day.

Now we are leaving the topic of the *form* and conditions of the therapy and moving on to its *contents*.

The 5th
Fundamental of Buddhist Psychotherapy

Recognise and Convey the Significance of the Body

> Mindfulness of the body allows us to live fully.
>
> JACK KORNFIELD

The physical side of being human has often been badly neglected in the humanities and in spiritual disciplines. To put it very clearly: We will never overcome our body in this life. We can only become happy *with* our body, never without body-oriented mindfulness. Even very advanced masters such as Shunryu Suzuki Roshi died from physical illnesses. So our body can never be "defeated" and a battle between mind and body will never produce a victor—only losers.

The 5th Fundamental of Buddhist Psychotherapy is dedicated to understanding physical concerns; we want to make it clear how helpful our body can be for us on the path to liberation.

This book deals with Buddhist *Psycho*therapy, so the reader would be forgiven for thinking that psychological concerns enjoy a *higher* priority than physiological ones. We will however see how problematic this segregation into the purely physical and purely psychological can be. The explanations in the 5th and 6th Fundamentals are intended to make the equal value of both aspects clear. Even those of us without any medical education can still observe how our various mental states (such as anger, fear or sadness) never appear without accompanying physical reactions. This shows that mental states are influencing our body, so we should also be able to consciously influence our physical condition by means of mental activities. We have also all experienced how physical activities can alter our mental states: examples include playing sport, taking drugs, sexual activity or asceticism. So changes can clearly be brought about from both sides—mental and physical.

Mental training can be used to bring about healthy mental states such as loving-kindness, joy, love and compassion, which will also have positive physiological effects. In the same way, physical exercises, such as breath training, various more active forms of meditation and mindful work, can bring about healthy mental states. When we take a closer look at all of these methods we often find that the distinction between physical and psychological aspects becomes blurred.

Another reason to pay particular intention to integrating both of these aspects is the fact that the body is no longer "sacred" for many people. It is often treated as something that simply has to function and is really only given any attention when it makes itself obvious through pain. Consider this: How does your left foot feel at this moment? If your foot is currently doing its job without pain, this question might seem very trivial, but this is an example of mindfulness and we will see how valuable mindfulness can be—especially mindfulness of the body.

The Buddha himself emphasised in many of his teachings how valuable the body is and how important it is to ensure that it remains healthy and unharmed. The significance of the body is mentioned in his core teachings about the Middle Way (see 9th Fundamental of the BPT). In one of the teachings given during the Buddha's lifetime (119th Sutra in the Collection of Middle-Length Discourses), the Buddha's disciples are discussing something which he had said: "Isn't it amazing, friends! Isn't it astounding! The extent to which mindfulness immersed in the body, when developed and pursued, is said by the Blessed One who knows, who sees, the worthy one, rightly self-awakened, to be of great fruit and great benefit."

The monks then address their teacher on this issue and ask him how to develop and cultivate mindfulness of the body. He explains that we can achieve this by means of:
- Meditation
- Awareness in the here and now
- Discerning, analytical observation of our body

- Awareness of our impermanence and mortality.

We need to observe our body in a mindful and completely honest way and then fully accept it. To illustrate this, the Buddha offers the following image: [A monk] sits, permeating the body with a pure, bright awareness. Just as if a man were sitting covered from head to foot with a white cloth so that there would be no part of his body to which the white cloth did not extend; just so, the monk sits, permeating the body with a pure, bright awareness. There is nothing of his entire body unpervaded by pure, bright awareness. So our body deserves our full attention.

The term mindfulness will be used many times in this book. It plays a key role in Buddhist exercises and on the path to liberation which we want to follow (see especially 6th Fundamental of BPT on our mind).

The Body and Mindfulness

Mindfulness practice is one of the core aspects of everyday Buddhist life. In this regard, our body is particularly indispensable because exercises designed to cultivate mindfulness start with perception exercises on the *physical* level.

The Buddha taught the *Foundations of Mindfulness* very clearly in the tenth sutta of the Middle-Length Discourses with a brief and clearly structured four-step process:

The Four Foundations of Mindfulness
1) Body
2) Feelings
3) Mind/Consciousness
4) Dharmas (Mental Objects)

Looking at these four steps, we can see that, when it comes to the questions of how we are or what we want, we can find the right answers more reliably by feeling than by thinking and, in turn, more reliably on the physical level than in our feelings. In other words, the Buddha showed us that we can increase our mindfulness (careful attentiveness) with the help of our body; we can find out more about our current state in unclear situations by paying attention to our body first.

We will explore a range of exercises which help us to cultivate our mindfulness (see also 6th Fundamental of BPT). We cannot emphasise this enough because help-seekers will often ask us how they can best get started and arrive at good decisions. So we always begin with mindfulness of the *body* and let our body signals lead us to important answers and impulses.

Our knowledgeable body

Buddhist science distinguishes a range of subgroups in our consciousness. For example, it distinguishes between our body consciousness and our mind consciousness.

Often our body seems to know more than our thinking mind, such as when my fingers "know" where the letters I want to type are on my computer keyboard much more quickly than my mind does. In fact, I really could not tell you the location of the keys for L or O on a computer keyboard. Nonetheless, when I am typing, I am often amazed how quickly my fingers find the right keys. So our body really does deserve our careful attention since it is an infallible yardstick that can often reveal more of our current state than our rational mind can.

When we have gained the ability to recognise and neutrally observe our *physical* sensations (mindfulness of body), then we can take the next step and turn to the associated *feelings*. After this we move on to the appropriate *thoughts*, before expanding the whole process to include *mental objects*—and therefore all phenomena in the world of appearance. This teaching about the Four Foundations of Mindfulness is synonymous with the instruction to fully perceive our corporeality or physical nature, as is the core Buddhist teaching of the value of the present moment—the desire to be as fully as possible in the here and now.

We can only be anchored in the present moment if we are fully present in our body. Our (rational) mind can move through time and space effortlessly, instantly and spontaneously going anywhere it wants to, whereas our body always has to remain in the here and now. If we allow our minds and our body to be separated too often and for too long this can lead to considerable feelings of tension on both the physical and mental levels. This then leads to various types of mental calls for help and to physical warning signals, both appealing to us to re-establish the unity of body and mind as quickly as possible.

Many psychotherapists have an educational background in psychology but not in medicine, so the physiological aspects of a problem might not be apparent, understandable or significant to them. So it seems indispensable for Buddhist Psychotherapists to study the foundations of psychosomatic (mind-body) connections and also to develop a comprehensive understanding of the inseparability of physical and mental-psychological-emotional processes. Once they have internalised this for themselves, they can convey this to the help-seekers. Additionally, many psychotherapists would be advised to cooperate intensively with colleagues who have more medical or clinical experience.

The Buddha tells us how necessary it is to train our powers of discerning, analytical observation regarding our body, in addition to our more meditative mindfulness practice. So we need to deepen our knowledge of relevant physical processes and get to know our body much better.

Our Body: Equality and Neglect

It would actually be more correct to call Buddhist Psychotherapy "Buddhist Psychosomatics" since the latter term provides a more accurate and comprehensive description of how this form of therapy understands humanity.

The term psychosomatics is not an invention of modern Western holistic therapists. In ancient India there were already teachings conveying the understanding of *namarupa* (Sanskrit: *nama* = name, mind; *rupa* = form, body; *namarupa* = mind-body = psycho-soma).

Many schools of therapy, philosophy and humanities and representatives of the medical sciences still insist on making an artificial distinction between mental-psychological aspects and physical ones. Some doctors are even heard to express this in a very direct way: "Does the patient *really* have an illness or is it *just* psychological?" An attitude such as this can be seen to be at least a few decades out of date if we take a look at the current state of scientific knowledge.

At the other end of the spectrum, a wide range of spiritual and psychotherapeutic schools strongly favour everything mental-psychological and tend to neglect the physical. Paying attention to the body has overtones of (forbidden) pleasure. This phenomenon can be traced back to ancient times; there are ancient Hindu ascetic practices that fully neglect the body, trying to subdue and overcome the worldly aspects of life. Ascetic purification exercises were indeed very necessary as preparation for particular beneficial and healthy sacred rituals; they made use of practices such as fasting and sexual abstinence. However, in many cultures and at many times they took on an extreme character, becoming over-emphasised and more important than the other elements of the rituals. Physical concerns and desires were demoted and disregarded.

Western cultural roots also shared these tendencies. In Christian cultures, for example, sexuality became a taboo and the body was regarded as debased, leading to extreme practices such as flagellation, mortifying the body in order to cleanse it by "fire" and liberate the "pure" soul trapped within.

The first natural scientists had to wait a long time before they received permission from the Church to dissect human bodies because religious authorities were anxious to protect the soul. Even when they relaxed the rules they still insisted on the very careful performance of the dissection, with punishment by burning at the stake for those who did not protect the human soul as required. The impure body—made out of blood, bones, bodily fluids (humours) and excrement—was considered to be a shelter for the sins, whereas the soul (Greek: *psyche*) was treated as being absolutely divine and pure. This medieval way of looking at the world still seems to influence the attitudes of many healers today: Medical doctors exhibit a fear of the soul or psyche, and counsellors, psychologists or psychotherapists seem to believe that the soul or psyche as a divine spark is the only crucial factor. The latter imply that all disease symptoms have a psychological origin and the body is nothing more than a means of expression for its controlling instance: the psyche.

So the importance of the body-psyche balance cannot be emphasised enough here. The Buddhist Wisdom of the Middle Way proves its general applicability and current relevance once again.

The Body and Its Limits

Humans have always used their body to expedite psychological transformation processes. Rites of passage or initiation incorporated exercises and techniques to push the body to its limits and bring about a particular step in mental development by means of these liminal experiences. Different cultures generally made use of a wide range of opportunities to attain these states: dance, ascetic practices, drumming, drugs, pain, physical exertion etc. Although ecstatic bodily experiences have been an important element in ritual since the beginning of the human race, they were generally built into a longer and carefully timed phase of fixed procedures (i.e. the ritual as a whole). It is also worth noting that liminal experiences important for psychological development were rarely attained using drugs. Increasing problems seen today regarding drug usage (addiction, early first experiences, heavy usage among young people) might be a sign that altered states of mind need to be anchored in a wider social setting and that physical and psychological needs both need to be more adequately catered for within the institutions that affirm our place in society, such as family and school.

As mentioned above, different cultures made use of very different methods to speed up mental processes in a targeted way in order to promote the desired psychological development. Classically Buddhist techniques focussed on retreats lasting many weeks or even several years where mindfulness practice is supported with a modest, reduced diet, early rising, long sessions of meditation, continual silence, mindful walking and meditative work. Enriching our psyche needs careful and patient work to reduce pleasure-oriented psychological and physical longings. Regarding dosage, we should always keep in mind the Wisdom of the Middle Way.

Our Body is Important

A very large number of modern medical studies have granted us many fascinating insights into our body and the way it works. These insights have demonstrated that very few of our physical aspects can be understood by comparing them to mechanical models and analogies. The most important systems in our body (nervous, organ, muscle, immune and endocrine systems) seem to interact and communicate with each other at a level of complexity we are only just beginning to grasp.

Being a science of the mind, the Buddhist tradition is based on an intensive training for the mind. Nonetheless, the Buddha made constant reference to the body and considered protecting the body from harm as more important than any meditation practice. As his monks set off to meditate and left an ill monk behind, the Buddha is said to have taken care of the ailing monk himself and clearly reminded the returning monks of the significance of caring for their own and each other's health. In other words, we cannot expect to achieve psychological development if we do not take care of ourselves and others, including our bodily needs.

These examples make it clear once again how close to reality Buddhism is: Keep developing yourself and make use of your achievements for the benefit of yourself and all others in the present moment.

Weighing up physical and psychological needs is not always easy. Even when we are dealing with only physical or only psychological needs, finding the right balance can be a challenge. When does carefully meeting physical needs become a pleasure? When do pleasures merge into desires? Where are the dividing lines between needs, desires, coveting and attachment? And when does a deep longing become an addiction? Walking these tightropes in everyday life is not easy and we often find that we oscillate wildly between control (e.g. abstention) and surrender (unbridled consumption). These processes always take place on both psychological *and* physical levels. We can hunger for something physically and psychologically; losing our sense of moderation and consuming uncontrollably can also happen on both levels. Our body is always affected, too, since there are no mental activities without physical reactions and no physical activities without mental reactions.

The Buddha's teachings were always based on his own experiences, and his teachings about the body were no exception. Tradition has it that in his youth he was a privileged noble enjoying all sorts of bodily pleasures and pampering; later in his life during his search for liberation he then almost pushed his body too far with extreme ascetic practices (including fasting and celibacy). In this regard, he gained an important insight as he overheard a musician talking to students about his stringed instrument—probably a form of lute. The musician explained that the string would break if too tight and would not produce any sound at all if it were too slack. This practical everyday situation helped the Buddha to recognise how he had been pushing his body to extremes. Returning to a "harmonic" balance was a significant step towards achieving liberation, and further similar experiences led him to develop his teaching of the Middle Way (see 9th Fundamental of BPT).

This important aspect of Buddhism is very helpful for us with regard to the relationship between body and mind. In particular we should try to be neither too tight nor too slack when it comes to the unity of the mind/psyche/soul and body.

Inhabiting our body

How do we inhabit our body? This sounds as if we live in our body in the same way that we live in our apartment or house. Although our body and our mind/psyche form a unity, it often seems to be the case that we exploit our body as a tool. We would like it to function as smoothly as possible, look perfect and serve us for many years without wearing out or ageing. We often do not want to—and in some cases are not allowed to—respect our physical limits. Many necessary activities—especially those which are job-related—seem possible only if we treat our body like a machine. In cases like these it can even pose problems when someone does develop an increased sensitivity towards their physical needs. In Buddhist Psychotherapy we take a very detailed look at practical situations of this kind and train appropriate alternative ways of behaving.

People who have lived through very traumatic experiences sometimes report how their body and mind separated during the crisis. Others tell us how they felt as if they were subject to "remote control" or standing next to themselves and observing themselves from afar. These unusual behaviours can be seen both as abilities and as problems—or symptoms of problems. If such difficult periods persist, this separation can become chronic and it would then appear to be very important to re-establish the unity of body and mind with appropriate treatment.

This sort of splitting also occurs in a minor way as a symptom of everyday stress; often the body is still busy with one particular activity but the mind has once again moved on a few steps further. If this occurs frequently or the moment becomes an extended period of time, it can be regarded as an unhealthy separation of our mind and body consciousnesses (see also 6th Fundamental of BPT).

The risks of "rarely inhabiting" our body are described in Buddhist teachings with the following image: If the master is not at home, uninvited guests will enter. If we treat our body mindlessly then we are not very aware and the master (mind) is not really at home (in the body). All sorts of uninvited guests will then come in (symptoms of excessive burden or strain).

An important aspect of Buddhist Psychotherapy is a component which psychologists call "psychoeducation": conveying information and knowledge about the help-seeker's situation. So we will make every effort to convey the relevant information about our mind, our body and the basics of psychosomatics (Sanskrit *namarupa*) to the help-seeker in a way appropriate to their prior knowledge and educational background.

Namarupa: The Significance of Psychosomatics for Buddhist Psychotherapy

Each client has very personal reasons for deciding to undergo a course of psychotherapy. Sometimes the key points are psychological, mental or spiritual factors, sometimes the focus is more on the body, and in many cases it is a combination of these—in other words, psychosomatic problems. Even if the client's description of their situation does not immediately reveal any concomitant physical/somatic symptoms, a Buddhist Psychotherapist will nonetheless pay careful attention to this aspect, especially because many of the following therapeutic measures include one type of physical exercise or another.

During the initial session(s), the therapist carries out a detailed anamnesis which includes the body and any physical symptoms (see 4th Fundamental of BPT). In addition the help-seeker receives an explanation—adapted to their educational background—of the most significant aspects of the crossover and interplay between physical and psychological processes. Important signals are set here for future understanding on the part of the help-seeker. These initial explanations determine how deeply they will find their own personal connection to this approach, so it is important for the therapist to succeed in clearly bringing home the measurable effect that mental training can have on physical processes and how physical exercises can influence our psyche. The help-seeker should also be able to satisfy him- or herself that all of the exercises, topics and Buddhist foundations have a measurable scientific basis.

One major component part of Buddhist Psychotherapy—and of Buddhism—is its focus on the issue of how human beings function. This is exactly the issue covered by psychosomatics, so one individual session—or more efficiently, a group session—should be used to convey psychosomatic basics.

The introduction to our psychosomatics should clarify several important points:
How do our body and our mind work?
We, our mind and our body: Are these one, two, three or more things?
Mental and physical training changes our brain (neuroplasticity).
Every mental, psychological and physical sensation and activity is precisely measurable.
Is our rational mind still our servant or already our master?
What forms and shapes us?

How do our body and our mind work?

When dealing with this and the following questions, the therapist needs to consider how they can best convey the information. Many people can remember facts much better and deal with them more easily if the information is presented in a *visual* way. As therapists we also need to make it very clear *why* we are doing what we are doing or explaining what we are explaining. It is quite likely that the help-seeker in front of us is one of many people who get nervous when it comes to medical or psychological issues. Perhaps they do not think that they are intelligent enough to understand certain information. So it is important to find the right way of speaking, to openly address any fears, and to do anything else possible to help them approach the issues at hand more easily.

Basic, underlying and necessary information can often be conveyed by means of a simple image which the therapist can draw on a flip chart or piece of paper. For example, in Figure 1 we can see a head with various structures that are intended to portray our brain. During the course of our evolution, our brain has changed significantly and today it is very different from the brains of other, less developed mammals. Nonetheless the line of development was never interrupted, which means that the evolution from reptile to small mammal to ape to human can be described as a continuous development of the brains. Over millions of years the small reptile brain increased in size and complexity, evolving into a mammal brain.

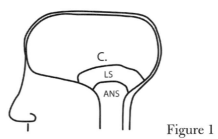

Figure 1

C. = cerebrum
LS = limbic system
ANS = autonomic nervous system

In Figure 1 we can indeed see a type of reptile brain: The area labelled ANS (autonomic nervous system) corresponds to the sort of brain which reptiles still have today. It controls elementary survival mechanisms (hunger, thirst, reproduction, digestion, circulatory system etc.) and basic feelings (tension, well-being, fight-or-flight response).

In creatures other than reptiles—mammals—the brain developed further. In Figure 1 this corresponds to the area labelled LS (limbic system). Mammals have a reptilian brain plus an extra "superstructure" which regulates emotional concerns in a more sophisticated way, enabling social structures to evolve. (Social structures can also develop without a brain as we can see with many types of insects and their colonies.)

The area labelled C in Figure 1 refers to our cerebrum. Apes, monkeys, whales and dolphins exhibit a similarly well-developed cerebrum. In humans, the cerebrum accounts for about 80 percent of the total brain. The brain itself accounts for only about two percent of our total body mass but is responsible for approximately 20 percent of our total daily energy consumption.

Modern imaging techniques (MRT, fMRI etc.) allow us to recognise quite clearly which areas of the brain are being used during particular activities, but its incomprehensibly high degree of complexity has so far prevented us from accurately mapping the whole brain. We can determine approximate regions where our language centre is located, visual memories are processed or physical movements are controlled, for example, and we also know which regions control the activity of our heart, digestion or emotions. However, a wide variety of basic human procedures are only possible when very different areas of the brain work together. And there are other phenomena, such as consciousness, which we assume to be related to the brain but for which we have yet to develop any feasible models regarding how they function or where they arise.

From this initial introduction to the topic we can see that some of our reactions might well be physical instincts—reptilian behaviour. And other reactions which are directly emotional might be coming from the level of lower mammals—so to speak. The possibilities which our cerebrum and cerebral cortex open up for us could then be described as representing our truly human potential so it seems only natural to appeal to everyone to actually take advantage of this complex organ we have evolved. Nonetheless, this potential and the related abilities can be used in both positive/constructive and negative/destructive ways, so it is essential to take a closer look at the background.

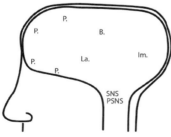

Figure 2

P. = personality
B. = body

La. = language
Im. = images
SNS = sympathetic nervous system
PSNS = parasympathetic nervous system

Figure 2 is a simple diagram designed to help us do this. Let us begin with a few specific examples. If we move our right hand, electrical impulses are set off in the nerve cells in the region of the brain indicated with a B (for body). Now let us think for a moment about our living room: What does it look like? Is there a sofa? What colour is it? What do the walls of the living room look like? Are there plants or pictures in the room? What do they look like? The images that occur in our brain in response to these questions arise in conjunction with electrical impulses in the regions of the brain indicated by Im. (images) in Figure 2.

Of course there are no nerve cells or groups of nerve cells where an exact image of an object is stored. Some nerve cell systems provide information about the edges or outlines, others about colours and contrasts, others about straight lines or curved surfaces etc. This means that the visual memories arise through a creative process bringing together different types of information, which in turn must mean that our memories are never precise. Instead they represent the product of a multiplicity of preconditions. So we have to be very careful when we are dealing with memories, especially in psychotherapy. This also corroborates our cautious approach to the phenomenon of identification (especially with the past), which Buddhism had already recognised.

When we speak, electrical synapses can be detected in our language centre, which is labelled in Figure 2 with La (for language). So far all of our examples have dealt with functions which we can also consciously control: I can voluntarily move my arm, think of a specific memory, or open my mouth to speak. By doing this I activate the appropriate region in my brain and this is further supporting evidence for the potential effect of physical exercises on psychological processes.

However, there are also functions we do not normally consciously control. Most people could not carry out the following orders: Stop your digestion immediately. Double your heart activity. Reduce your stress hormones by 20 percent. Fall asleep immediately. Lower your cholesterol level now. Begin to sweat. So it becomes clear that very significant physical functions—especially those necessary for survival—cannot be controlled voluntarily (with the exception, perhaps, of a certain degree of control over our breathing).

These important procedures are controlled in "lower" parts of our brain; these are further back towards the brain stem and older in a phylogenetic sense. We cannot influence them directly and only in some cases can we influence them indirectly. Our autonomic nervous system (ANS in Figure 1; SNS and PSNS in Figure 2) controls functions essential for life. This system can be activated by external influences (dangerous situations, conflicts with other people, sports etc.), inner processes (self-reproach, negative expectations, negative memories etc.) and all of our mental states. Soothing or reassuring external or internal conditions activate a particular area of the autonomous nervous system: the parasympathetic nervous system, which is indicated in Figure 2 by PSNS. Threatening or apparently threatening external or internal conditions activate a different area of the autonomous nervous system: the sympathetic nervous system, labelled SNS.

If the sympathetic nervous system is activated we generally have a high level of tension and stress. This "control centre" then triggers the following measures:

- Blood vessels become narrower which increases blood pressure. This effect is similar to increasing water pressure by standing on a garden hose.
- Blood values (glucose/sugar, lipids/fat, oxygen) increase. Now we are programmed for stress. Muscles need nutrition (sugar, fat and oxygen) which the tissue makes available. Another reason for the increase in blood pressure is to ensure that these nutrients are delivered quickly to the muscles. So if our doctor says,

"Your cholesterol levels (blood fat) are too high—please do not eat so much meat", and we follow this advice but continue to have as much stress as we did before then we will also continue to have high blood fat values.
- Tissue acidity increases. So we could say that stress makes us sour in two ways: physiologically and psychologically.
- Stress hormones (e.g. adrenaline) are released.
- Digestion is slowed down. Blood is "borrowed" from the digestive system and pumped into the large muscle groups.
- Immune system activity is reduced. If our immune system would really swing into action at the same time as our sympathetic nervous system, this might possibly result in the immune system attacking our own body. This is one of the reasons why prolonged stress increases our risk of infection and makes us significantly more susceptible to illness.
- Unconscious muscle tension increases. We can consciously control our muscles in part (e.g. biceps) but some muscles are controlled unconsciously. We all have an unconscious muscle tension in our neck—without this our head would hang to the side. Stress increases total muscle tension, which is why we often run around with our shoulders pulled up high when we are stressed, resulting in stress-related tension in our neck and then pains in our head.

This is only a selection of the physical reactions to stress—i.e. to the activation of the sympathetic nervous system. As mentioned above, this activation is often triggered by all sorts of external stimuli. For example, some people react with feelings of stress and panic if they see a large dog but this very same dog would trigger feelings of joy in others. This makes it extremely clear how significant our own experiences are. These experiences are all stored within us. Sometimes we remember something consciously, and on other occasions a particular situation, statement or smell might remind us of something, reactivating a memory involuntarily. Depending on the characteristic of this memory, our autonomous nervous system will react with a particular level of stress; in the case of neutral memories it will not react noticeably.

There are various reasons why these processes are very significant for us. There does not seem to be a genuinely balanced relationship between the sympathetic nervous system and the parasympathetic nervous system. This leads to the question of whether it might be possible to improve our own ability to control these structures. So we need to get to know these control centres very well. Of course the presentation in this book is a very simple one and we have only concentrated on our *central* nervous system—our brain—although our whole body has many kilometres of nerves running along its lengths.

Figure 3 illustrates our main nerve pathways. Again, it is simplified and can only suggest the fractal nature of the myriad of fine nerve tracts.

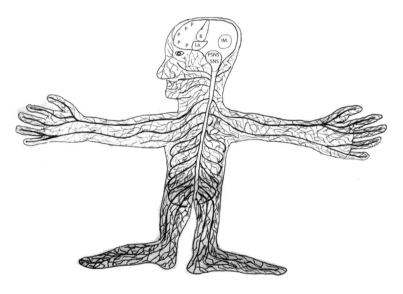

Figure 3

Our nerves transmit electrical signals in the millivolt range and we can interpret the contents of these signals as information (see also the 6th Fundamental of BPT on the topic of our mind). And in addition to this electrical information, there is a significant exchange of information occurring on a chemical basis in all of the tissues of our body by means of substances known as *neurotransmitters*. Our physical organs are coated with nerve fibres to receive electrical information and a protein layer for sending and receiving particular neurotransmitters.

If we cut out a piece of our tissue from any part of our body it is full of chemical and neuronal information units. We will find both nerve tissue and a variety of chemical transmitters. So if we consider this piece of flesh, is it a part of our physical nature or body? Of course it is. But we can also ask the question: Is it a part of our psyche or mind? The answer here also has to be yes. These examples and explanations should make the following points clear:

- Everywhere in our body we find neurons (nerve cells) and neuronal connections.
- Everywhere in our body, electricity is following measurably and functioning as a carrier of information.
- Everywhere in our body there is electrical energy and electrical potentials.
- Everywhere in our body—in all of our tissue—there are chemical transmitters.
- Everywhere in our body an exchange of information is taking place 24 hours a day.

Our attention can change the electrical charges in various regions of the body including the brain. This perception of inner electrical fields can be used as the connecting link between our physical body and our endless mental areas. By training our attention to strengthen either our expanded awareness or our single-pointed concentration, we can bundle our energy and direct it into particular parts of the body in order to transform and release blockages.

These issues are some of the most exciting aspects which have come to light through the establishment of connections between

Buddhist and neurological sciences. The opportunities for mutual influence here are presented more extensively in the 19th Fundamental of BPT.

In Buddhist Psychotherapy the training helps us to pursue the goal of making the processes in our mind-body more transparent. The Buddhist approach is based on a profoundly scientific and strongly empirical attitude. We want to recognise and understand in order to be able to act in a better and safer way.

Most of the time we experience and go through our inner processes as a victim: Our reactions seem to be automatic as we become sad or depressed, lacking in drive or strength, angry, scared, annoyed or irritated. Is there really something controlling this? Is it the situation which triggers something in us? Or is there somewhere, perhaps a region in our brain, where our ego arises and takes control of everything like the captain of a ship?

We, our mind and our body: Are these one, two, three or more things?

This might seem to be a nonsensical question because out first instinct assures us that we are obviously one person with one body, one heart, one intellect, one personality and so on. However, if we take a closer look at this issue we come across some fascinating insights which contradict the experience we have every day.

It is actually a fact that modern research into the brain has confirmed the lack of a critical node anywhere in the brain which gives rise to the ego or self. Neuroscientists divide our brain into various regions in much the same way as we divide a geographical area into regions on a map in order to maintain a better overview. Our whole brain is divided into "lobes" (frontal, parietal, temporal and occipital lobes) and personality structures are located in *all* of these lobes; in other words, each of these lobes includes areas that are activated when we become aware of part of our feelings of self. As can be seen in Figure 2, these personality centres (labelled P) are distributed throughout our brain. Neurophysiological research describes the ego as *modular*. This means that the ego is not one fixed unit. Instead, it is a fabric made up of different modules which are spread over all of the brain's lobes. Depending on the acute needs, various parts of this ego fabric are activated: I pay heed to my conscience (ethical self); I remember something from the past (autobiographical awareness or self); I am aware of my body (body awareness or perspective self); I carry out an action (action-planning self, self-attribution of actions); I check where I am in time and space (orienting self); I think about myself (self-reflecting awareness) etc.

The nerve structures which create this range of aspects making up our sense of self are located in different places throughout our cerebrum, but there is a higher density of planning and ethical functions in the regions close to our forehead and temples. These have been identified by means of imaging techniques such as fMRI and MRT and also by examining people with brain injuries. One case which enjoyed a great deal of attention in neuroscience journals was that of Phineas Cage, a railway worker in America whose skull was pierced by an iron rod in an accident. Miraculously he survived this terrible injury but the loving family man he had been turned into a self-centred, ruthless, irritable and often aggressive person after the accident, which destroyed several areas of his frontal brain.

There are also reports which go in the other direction; for example, brain damage transformed one long-term criminal into a sensitive and artistic man. The British neurologist Oliver Sacks has described a variety of similar, fascinating human fates.

Examples such as that of Phineas Cage are not cited to prove that our psychology is fully determined by our physiology but to underline the importance of avoiding premature judgements. Many current conditions deserve a deeper, holistic examination. Sometimes disasters can change our life in very drastic and incalculable ways. Even without such drastic events, we human beings are much better described in terms of a dynamic process and not a static state or condition. Every experience we have can change our life regardless of whether it is an accident or not and how dramatic or not it may be. And changes within us are also brought about by a wide variety of smaller, even unnoticeable, causes.

The interdisciplinary field of human biology has shown us that many important processes in our body are subject to cycles during different phases of the day. These include blood pressure, temperature, sleep, digestion, attentiveness, level of activity and hormones. These continually changing factors are very important control instances within us and determine how we feel, our moods and our state of mind—without mind training and mindfulness we have no chance of controlling them. So it is logical to conclude that in the present moment we are definitely not the same person as we were four hours ago. We can also observe changes in our basic personality within a very short time when we interact with different people: Perhaps we are very patient and considerate in the company of a small child but these healthy characteristics suddenly appear to be beyond our reach when dealing with certain other adults.

So we are slowly gaining an insight into the dynamic and flexible—or even, deceptive and inconsistent—nature of our sense of self. As we search for this, we find nothing fixed, reliable or substantial because there is no "ego core" in our brain. These neuroscientific research results come very close to the Buddhist understanding of the illusion of the fixed self. Both Buddhists and neuroscientists assume that our sense of self is merely a somewhat helpful but unstable construction that, upon closer examination, has no real existence.

Mental and physical training changes our brain (neuroplasticity)

We have already seen above that such basic structures as our sense of self can change. Old sayings such as "You can't teach an old dog new tricks" or "You can't shift an old tree without it dying" were considered to be true for a long time but a critical look shows us that although they might be true for dogs or trees, they are not generally true for human beings.

Until fairly recently we could only conduct brain research by dissecting the tissue of dead brains. However, we are now able to directly observe brains as they are working so we now know that new experiences and learning lead to changes in our neural structures.

Neural pathways that are used more often become stronger and form new connections with each other. For example, in the brains of young people considerable neural growth has been found in the region responsible for controlling the movement of the right thumb. This neural growth has been observed in the era of mobile phones: Young people use their thumbs particularly often to write text messages.

Neurological examination of the brain

We now have methods at our disposal to directly observe activities in our nerve cells. These methods include magnetic resonance imaging or tomography (MRI/MRT); electroencephalography (EEG); and electrode tests (directly in the brain). We can also conduct clinical monitoring of neurological deficiency symptoms caused by accidents, strokes and metabolic diseases etc. So we benefit from a great deal of data which our computers can analyse and evaluate.

Reinhard Olivier, a mathematician, has voiced very justifiable criticism regarding the ways in which we interpret this data. Much of the interpretation cannot be conclusive because the sheer complexity of the interactions between our neurons inevitably makes the picture obscure. For example, regions of the brain which consume particularly high levels of energy (such as sugar and oxygen) are assumed to be the most important. Reinhard Olivier questions whether those who speak the loudest are always the most important. He points out the enormous relevance of "places of silence". This book is not the place for a more detailed presentation of the fascinating discussion. However, we can draw the Buddhist conclusion that all of our truths which we express in words are relative and that the inherent nature of all things is impermanence. The current state of scientific knowledge is exactly that: current. We work with what we have but we do not get stuck in it.

Our brain remains a "mysterious" place which refuses to give up its secrets easily. So let us respect the provisional nature of our knowledge and try to explore the reality behind it.

How quickly does our brain change?

An American experiment took ordinary citizens and scanned their motor cortex (the region of the brain responsible for our movements). Then they were taught a very simple finger exercise and told to carry this out a few times a day with their left hand. Five days later another computer scan of the brain was made and showed a clear increase in the number of neural connections in that region of the brain. This is impressive evidence of the speed with which our brain can adapt itself on the physiological level.

This advantage has some noteworthy consequences: On the one hand, it guarantees us good chances of being able to change ourselves in a very fundamental level including underlying structures of our brain (through regular training); on the other hand, however, it means that bad habits are also deeply "ingrained" and might not be all that easy to change. Neuroscientists often compare this phenomenon to a snow-covered mountain: The mountain symbolises our brain, whose form and structure are generally fairly solid. Each behaviour is a skier leaving their tracks in the snow. Habits are then symbolised by deep tracks where the skiers always stick to the same course.

We can create new tracks by carrying out new activities but it is not always easy to get out of the existing tracks. So it is often easier to form a new habit—create a new track in the snow—than it is to change the old one. Nonetheless if we frequently use the new tracks these will also become stable and the old ones will slowly crumble or be covered up by the wind. This explains why it is difficult to simply give up an old habit without finding a replacement. If we want to change or avoid something we really need an alternative: a new "track" or activity. Of course, these metaphors heavily simplify the situation but this simplification allows us to convey the information in a catchy and understandable way.

It is hard to imagine anything more complex than our brain. Normally there are some 100 million neurons (nerve cells) in a human brain. Each of these tiny cells can form tens of thousands of even tinier "branches" (dendrites and axons) resulting in a network of more than 100 trillion connection points which can then form an astronomically high number of different combinations of connection patterns. Neuroscientists report that there are more connection possibilities in our brain than atoms in the universe! This miracle of complexity deserves our utmost respect and appreciation. In fact, this is one of the reasons why many Buddhists refrain from taking drugs.

The human brain is a unique organ, greedily eager to learn. It consumes almost 20% of our daily energy and never stops its activity (even at night). It reacts to every external stimulus and every internal process. Every thought, experience, memory, perception, new stimulus, physical action and learning process changes its patterns of connection. This process—known as neuroplasticity—is never-ending, from the small-scale, everyday occurrences to larger, higher levels of being and becoming human through to phylogenetics (development of species).

For example, fish only have a few nerve cells for the recognition of colours or to regulate their coordination and balance. In their habitat they simply do not need these, which is why the appropriate nerve fibres never had to be formed. In comparison, apes and monkeys live in habitats which are clearly more diverse. Here colour recognition, balance and coordination are essential for survival, which is why these competencies also manifested neurologically. To put it very generally: External experience creates internal connection—life creates inner life. Life = connections. Without life there are no connections since the lack of stimulation leads to the death of nerve cells.

No matter how talented and motivated a fish may be, there is no possibility of turning into a monkey. Humans, however, have a highly complex, programmed-to-learn brain which we can choose to feed or starve. This is much more than just a scientific detail that is interesting to know. It shows us and proves that we can use targeted training to achieve fundamental changes at the mental-emotional and physical-physiological levels. We will also see that the line separating these two levels becomes ever more diffuse.

It also clearly shows us something that Buddhists have known for centuries: If you constantly repeat something, it shapes you, your character and then also your fate. And another Buddhist principle has also been confirmed by this research: the enormously high relevance of mind training. Neuroscientists have been able to prove that the stimulation of our brain and the desired training of new neural connections can be achieved by training—whether physical or mental. In other words, even if we are learning something that has a physical aspect, we can change our brain in the desired direction while sitting still and intensively imagining the changes we want to bring about.

The fact that targeted training has a direct effect on our nerve cells is a fascinating insight. In addition there is a whole range of further important effects that can be achieved through mental and physical training. Here in the 5th Fundamental on the topic of the body we should not neglect to mention that physical stamina training leads to measurable changes, mostly increases in neurotransmitters (e.g. dopamine, serotonin, noradrenaline). These are capable of taking over basic control processes in our body and influencing such systems as emotional regulation, stress management and control of our attention.

Of course, these connections between body and mind were recognised by ancient cultures a long time before they were confirmed by Western scientists. Today, these ancient systems of body-mind training are also available to us in the West—for example, yoga and tai chi.

Developing our potential, and its limits

For a long time, people were told that classical music had positive effects on the development of the brain in small children. This led to many children being "blasted" with this type of music. It should, however, be clear that any sort of "monocausal" or one-dimensional thinking such as this will not lead to any lasting effects. There are no miracle CDs, pills or books which can turn us into better or more intelligent people. This needs a much broader, multimodal programme.

There are certainly sensitive phases in our lives which are particularly suitable for learning something new and where we are more receptive than in other periods. For example, learning a foreign language is much easier when we are six years old and the results will generally be better than for new languages learned when we are 60. Nonetheless, it is still completely possible to learn a foreign language well at this age. Learning "new tricks" in old age, however, can be more difficult if we have not kept up this habit; if we remain interested, open and motivated all of our life then we will find it easier to take in new information when we are older, too. Mental degeneration in older people is not the result of some automatic process where everyone becomes less intelligent with age. Rather it is often a sad consequence of a monotonous life buying the same things in the same shops, eating the same food at the same time every day and always talking about the same topics. This is indeed the best prescription for the slow death of brain cells.

We do not have an inexhaustible capacity to catch up on or make up for things we have missed. For some abilities there are critical or sensitive periods and if these are not used, deficits arise which are difficult to compensate. We have all heard of sad examples where children were trapped in families that treated them in a terrible or even psychotic way with lasting consequences for their human development. There are reports of children who grew up in complete isolation, locked in a basement, without communication or positive contacts. One such child was only rescued from their imprisonment at the age of 13 and even after many years of counselling was only able to develop very limited social and communicative abilities. This child's language abilities never progressed beyond primitive sentences such as "shop go apples buy". In a similar case where the child was discovered earlier—at the age of six—they were able to articulate full complex sentences after one and a half years (see John J. Ratey).

These examples also clearly show how important social experiences are for us. Language abilities can only develop if other people communicate with us, and, in a similar way, social skills such as compassion and kindness can only grow stronger if we actually experience them ourselves.

So we need to conduct a thorough analysis of our skills with consideration of our early experiences to gain a clear picture of where we can and should work on compensating for our deficits. In doing so we should value our great potentials and also our limits.

Every mental, psychological and physical sensation and activity is precisely measurable

The statement simply has to be repeated in all of its precision. As help-seekers or therapists, when we come into contact with different professionals in the healthcare sector we will repeatedly come up against the attitude that tries to categorise help-seeker's problems into "real" (= medical) and "imagined" (= psychological) symptoms. However, even a cursory investigation of current neurological research (such as the brief description above) suffices to understand that every thought and every feeling corresponds to electrical and chemical activity in our nerve system and is therefore measurable. There is not one square millimetre of our body tissue which is free of nerve fibres and chemical information carriers (neurotransmitters).

> We need to understand and be able to convey to the help-seeker that *namarupa* or psychosomatics is not a particular psychological illness or special type of treatment. Instead it is a term referring to the way that humans work: *Every* human being functions psychosomatically.

Is our rational mind still our servant or already our master?

What names do we want to use for the inner voices within us? Rational mind, intellect, mind, consciousness, ego, the "I"? We will discover more about this tricky issue in the 6th Fundamental of BPT on the topic of our mind.

The mental activities which we want to take a closer look at here can probably be brought together under the term "rational mind". It might be appropriate to pause for a moment and feel our gratitude for the gift of our rational mind. It assists us, protects us, alerts us to many things in daily life and enables us to carry out our profession and everyday activities in an efficient way. It is our rational mind which helped us to achieve a certain level of ingenuity and establish ourselves as the dominant species on this planet. In fact it has also made it possible for us to leave the planet. There is an endless list of advantages which our rational mind has given us.

However, we also need to pay attention to the side-effects and shadow side of our rational mind. Phrased provocatively, we could claim that there has been a "silent revolution" and our servant or assistant has steadily taken over and became our master. We have not even noticed because it did this with its usual cleverness and efficiency.

If the reader reacted sceptically to the previous paragraph, let us now try to present some evidence. Put this book aside for a moment and tell your rational mind to remain silent for five minutes... You surely know what will happen: Our mind never stays silent. Even if we ask it to concentrate on one very important thing, we often notice how difficult this is. Our mind is like a clever little monkey: always active, always running around and always looking for the next banana.

We do have strategies (generally unconscious) which we have developed to manipulate and calm our mind. These techniques are worthy of closer consideration especially because many of them have a very self-destructive nature.

What do we do to appease our rational mind? One strategy is to keep feeding it bananas. We make sure that it has continuous input: television, books, magazines, internet, telephones, communication, exercise, work, hobbies, distractions, alcohol, drugs and much more. How many minutes of the day are left over if we subtract all of the activities listed here? For many people, we are left with a few minutes just before we fall asleep. And even then we suffer from one of many endemic problems: sleep disorder, unease, ruminations etc.

Another "scourge of the mind" is described vividly by Eckhart Tolle: Our conditioned mind drives us away from the present moment—out of the only moment which we can truly live in. Our mind has a predilection for worries, thoughts and plans—either in the past or the future. How difficult is it for most of us to remain in the here and now?! We need to realise that we only have a real chance of joy, satisfaction and peace in the here and now.

We will discover that concentrating on the here and now is one of the cornerstones of Buddhist exercises. The Buddha had good reason to include the significance of the here and now in one of his main teachings: the *Sutta of the Turning of the Wheel of Dharma* (see 10th Fundamental of BPT).

If we find it difficult to bring our mind into a calm state in a healthy way in order to stay in the here and now, we need to recognise that this is not really our mistake, weakness or inability but rather that the human mind generally functions this way. Of course, this also has an underlying physiological basis. Our mind is a very active organ with extremely complex tasks and functions. One piece of evidence for this can be found in the inability of any computer to map all of our brain activity. This complexity is constantly and actively maintained; our brain consumes some 20% of our total energy even though its mass (1-1.5 kg) is very small, relatively speaking. The brain can be compared to our heart muscle: Both work constantly for our whole life, whether we are awake or asleep.

The basic concept of Buddhist Psychotherapy is to value the advantages of a functioning rational mind and use them carefully whilst applying patience and regular daily mind training to rein it in, guide it and repeatedly bring it to rest. If we can understand how our mind works then we can also have a chance of freeing ourselves from unrealistic goals such as switching off completely or attaining lasting peace. The relevant techniques will be described more fully in the 19th Fundamental of BPT.

Despite the amazing abilities and complexity of our body, especially our central nervous system, we should be aware that this nervous system has adapted itself to the conditions of its surroundings.

We need to realise that its basic function is controlling our body and putting elements of our surroundings into context: dark clouds are a sign of bad weather, a fierce face in front of us indicates anger, pain in one place means this, noises in another mean that, etc. Our brain is set up to make these connections very well, even if it is not possible to come to the right conclusion all of the time. Our brain is (unfortunately?) not set up and has not been trained to see the world as it "really" is. Our brain works at a relatively superficial level, not a profound one. We are good at developing hypotheses but we are not good at gaining fundamental, profound insights.

These mental qualities are often limited by our brain structures. By manoeuvring and training our minds in a more targeted way we can expand the structures in our brain, in turn allowing our mind to change. This is a fascinating reciprocal interplay which clearly illustrates the fact that our mind and our brain are not identical. There is as yet no clear answer to the question of whether our brain gives rise to our mind/consciousness or whether our mind "uses" our brain in order to manifest itself.

What forms and shapes us?

This question is of great significance because knowing how we became what we are would quite probably give us knowledge of how we can change. Of course, a vast range of explanations have already been proposed to answer this elementary human question. The two most famous models were subject to fierce debate for decades: *nature* versus *nurture*. On one side, our genetic make-up is considered to be a significant factor explaining why we develop in a particular way. The supporters of the other side claim that the environment in which we live has the most significant influence on us. Of course, both of these models (and combinations of them) have a great deal of supporting evidence. And many more explanatory models have been proposed, including those specific to a particular culture or religion.

Within this 5th Fundamental of BPT, which concentrates on physical aspects, we will focus on physical approaches in order to understand a little more about how our physical disposition determines (in part) what we will become. Further relevant explanatory models dealing with mental aspects will be described in the 6th Fundamental of BPT.

Which physical conditions are determined by our nature? On the one hand, there are *general* genetic factors affecting every "healthy" person, and, on the other, there are *specific* conditions which we have to consider which we inherit from our family. The *general* factors determine such common aspects as having two arms, two legs, one heart, two lungs and the sense organs we need to see, smell and hear. The *specific* factors determine skin, hair and eye colour and our specific predispositions for particular diseases as well as our temperament (in part).

Epigenetics

It used to be assumed that only relatively fixed characteristics can be passed on from one generation to the next. However the relatively new science of epigenetics is challenging this with examples of how experiences can also be heritable. This branch of biology studies how and to what extent our genetics can be changed through external influences and whether these changes are then passed on. We have known for a long time that external circumstances can "switch on/off" particular sequences of genes. For example, the temperature of the water decides whether particular species of frog grow up to be male or female. External influences cause specific proteins to be built which are able to activate or deactivate particular sections of DNA strands. Recently a Dutch study provided evidence of significant health risks in children and grandchildren of people who had suffered from extreme starvation for a long time. This shows that at least some forms of experiences can be inherited. So it appears that we are shaped by the experiences of our ancestors as well as our own—a concept of transmission which was long regarded as unthinkable by Western scientists. We can recognise signs of a very deep interconnection between people of different generations.

However, these insights also provide evidence that we are actually even more unique than we previously believed. Even identical twins have more genetic differences than thought: Although their genetic material itself is almost identical, it is "switched on" in very different ways.

Buddhism offers concepts which appear to overlap with these new scientific insights into the coexistence of interdependence and individuality. Above all, Buddhists have always regarded all phenomena as "compound". This means that everything which exists is put together subject to a multiplicity of interconnected preconditions. So this ancient science of the mind is characterised by a deeply systemic understanding of the world.

Genetics and interconnection

Analysis of genetic structure, especially comparative genetic analysis of different peoples, has shown how humans evolved in Africa and spread out to populate the whole world. Fascinating evidence has been provided to show that all humans (the species *Homo sapiens*) living today can be traced back to a relatively small group of people who left Africa some 100,000 years ago in the "second exodus". Compared to the development of other species this is a relatively short length of time so it is fascinating to discover these common ancestors. We have already seen that humans are, physiologically speaking, almost identical; now we could say that we are virtually identical on the family level.

Since the family tree of our human development is only part of a much larger family tree for all species on this planet we naturally have to carry over this concept of interconnection and apply it to all other living beings.

This great and comprehensive connection shared by all humans concerns the deeper structures of being human so it is in no way a contradiction to observe that we are all unique beings on a more individual, superficial level. Once again, modern Western science and Buddhist science appear to confirm each other.

Now we come to another, very important physical aspect: the signals of our body—what our body tells us.

The Messages our Body Sends Us and the Secrets it Divulges

Although we may not be aware of it, we are all very good at interpreting the body language of other people. During scientific experiments, photos of people exhibiting a range of facial expressions (smiling, angry, disgusted, scared etc.) were shown to participants from a wide variety of different ethnic groups (Africans, Asians, Native Americans, Eskimos, Aborigines etc.). Independent of their background and race, all of the people were able to quickly and correctly interpret the facial expressions of other people. We unconsciously make use of this phenomenon every day: When we meet another person, an inner check starts that shows us how we should react to the other person and what they say. Without this information, the words alone would often be insufficient to understand. For example, take the phrase "That's really funny": In order to know whether this is a genuine compliment or meant ironically, we need further information such as the facial expression, the tone of the speaker's voice or the writing before and after the sentence to understand the context.

It is also important to be able to interpret our *own* body language. We know today that our body sends an uninterrupted stream of signals to the central nervous system regarding location in time and space, posture, condition, level of tension etc. (Of course, distinguishing between body and central nervous system is just a useful construction here.) Why do we perform mental arithmetic better with our mouth closed than with a sagging jaw? Why do we feel worse if we are bent over than when we are standing upright? For our nervous system, walking around all day with sagging shoulders is information equally as significant as the appearance of an unidentified spot on our skin. Every piece of information is interpreted and assessed (Where did it come from? Does it represent a threat?). Our bodily posture and our mental/emotional "posture" are generally in agreement (congruent) and influence each other. If we are buckling under the weight of sadness, maintaining an upright posture can be as effective as taking an anti-depressant. Taken together, all of our physical aspects are therefore particularly important for our work during Buddhist Psychotherapy. These connections will become even clearer in the 19th Fundamental.

The Body in Western Psychotherapy

Earlier Western cultures had their own healing techniques for the mind, emotions and soul but we generally only trace the roots of psychotherapy back as far as Sigmund Freud and the discipline of psychoanalysis which he initiated at the turn of the 20th century. One rule which developed very early in the history of psychoanalysis was the "Rule of Abstinence": The psychoanalyst shall refrain from any form of encroachment on their client. In other words it was forbidden to have any non-therapeutic contact, especially physical contact, with the client. This abstinence rule did not develop without a reason: Many psychoanalysts carried out other examinations on their patients, including gynaecological examinations, and some even started sexual relationships with them. Physicality within the therapy developed into a problem for many psychotherapists and this was probably the reason for the taboos which developed relating to bodily concerns and in turn a tendency to neglect the body within Western psychotherapy.

One undisputed pioneer and trailblazing scientist in the field of mind-body connections was Wilhelm Reich. He recognised many fascinating links between psychological and physiological processes. For example, he described "character armour", which referred to blocked, frozen emotions which become fixed in various groups of muscles. His theories made it possible to justify physical measures within psychotherapy and psychological interventions for physical complaints. Bioenergetics and a variety of other body-oriented schools of psychotherapy trace their roots back to Wilhelm Reich.

Raymond G is himself a doctor and wonders whether his painful tenseness has a physical or psychological cause. As an internist he is well acquainted with his body's needs so his therapist introduces him to the basics of mindfulness, since mindfulness of the body is the first step in this awareness training (see 6th Fundamental of BPT). Raymond is advised to continue taking his body seriously. Mindfulness meditation—initially guided and then alone—helps him to become more aware of where in his body the pain arises, how it feels and whether or not this pain changes. Individual therapy sessions then provide the opportunity to go deeper into the sensations and process the feelings and thoughts associated with them. After a while Raymond no longer considers it so important to distinguish between "physical" and "psychological".

This Fundamental Should Convey the Following:

A desired change for the better, a transformation or liberation/enlightenment: None of these can be achieved working *against* our body or if we *ignore* it. In fact, the very idea of *having* a body appears to be a naive or superficial way of looking at reality, so we have to look deeper, understand the insights we gain, and convey these to the help-seekers. We *are* our body. However, it is not true to say: We are *only* our body. The consequences of misinterpreting this complex reality can be seen in intellectual, religious, spiritual and psychotherapy circles, where the body is the subject of disdain, neglect or other unhealthy attitudes and practices. Without our body, we would not be able to experience this world at all. Our body can ground us, is helpful in many other ways and is the source of many pleasures. Our body also shows us our limits and provides for many forms of suffering.

As Jack Kornfield describes in his book *After the Ecstasy, the Laundry,* we will never be able to keep hold of a lasting experience of enlightenment or liberation. Rather, we have to learn the path of practice to enable us to reach our goal anew time and time again. In particular, it is our body that repeatedly brings us back down to earth. So during the psychotherapeutic and spiritual processes we learn about the value of our body and its significance for our daily practice. We recognise its value but do not get attached to it. We appreciate our body but do not identify ourselves with it. We internalise it as the basis providing us with the feeling of security but do not get stuck here. Our body will definitely not last forever. And perhaps it is already warning us of this fact, appealing to us to develop our mind because at the physical, material level we will sooner or later lose everything.

We now move on to the topic of the mind in the 6th Fundamental of Buddhist Psychotherapy. Although we are moving *on,* we will see that in fact we are not moving *away* from the topic of the body.

The 6th
Fundamental of Buddhist Psychotherapy

Recognise and Convey the Significance of Mental States

> The mind is the source of all experience,
> and by changing the direction of the mind,
> we can change the quality of everything we experience.
>
> YONGEY MINGYUR RINPOCHE

> It is our mind, and that alone, that chains us or sets us free.
>
> DILGO KHYENTSE RINPOCHE

We want to gain the most comprehensive information possible about our mental activities in order to have a sure sense of our strengths and weaknesses. This knowledge should then enable us to carry out our daily practice with more awareness.

The Terms

First of all, we really need to take a closer look at the terms and concepts* we use in this context (such as mind, consciousness, and psyche). Each of these has its own effect and way of working. In general, we all use a myriad of terms every day without really being aware of the full facts behind them. A term or label can make things simpler, but a false impression can arise if we then believe that the term has already explained everything we wanted to say.

---

* Translator's note: In this chapter, the word *term* is used to translate the German word *Begriff*, which actually covers the meanings of both *term* and *concept*.

Let us take the example of the term consciousness: Modern scientific research into consciousness has been very active for several decades, searching for a more profound understanding of this phenomenon. However, the question of how, why and where consciousness arises still counts as one of our greatest unsolved mysteries. Ancient sciences of the mind such as Buddhism have also dealt with these issues and given humanity a wide variety of insights and sophisticated models. Even if the final answers are yet to be found, it is essential to study this fascinating issue in more depth for many reasons, including the central role played by mind training within Buddhist practice.

However, before we turn to the Buddhist concepts relating to mind and consciousness, we still have to deal with a few linguistic problems.

The problem with the terms we use

What do we mean exactly when we speak about *mind*? Are we talking about the same thing as psychologists when they refer to the *psyche*? Or does the term *mind* overlap more with terms such as *intellect, intelligence, consciousness, spirituality, mentality* or *memory*? It becomes even more complicated when we ask ourselves whether Tibetans, Chinese, Indians, Britons, Americans, Germans and the French are all referring to the same thing when they use their respective terms? In other words, does each language have a word with the exact same meaning? If we look in a German-English dictionary under the entry *Geist* we will find a range of translations on offer: *spirit, soul, mind, intellect, wit*. Each of these English terms transports us into its own specific context(s) and associated meanings. And when we look in the other direction under the entry *mind* we find a range of German words covering concepts which overlap with English terms such as *sense, heart, soul, spirit, rational mind, intention, disposition, predilection* and *memory*. So there is a wide range of related concepts behind the field of related words we use in different Western languages. Nonetheless, in general we can find a clear distinction being made between mental/intellectual aspects on the one hand and feelings-based/emotional patterns on the other: head (rational mind) and heart/gut (emotions).

It is therefore very interesting to hear the Dalai Lama telling us that this distinction does not exist in Buddhism. All of these different experiences, whether *rational/mental* or *emotional*, are covered by Buddhists within one term, expressed in Sanskrit and Pali as *citta* and in Tibetan as *sems*. The Chinese and Japanese both use the term *xin* or *shin* to refer to these mental-emotional experiences.

So in these cultures, mental *and* emotional qualities are brought together in one term or concept and therefore seen as a unity.

From the viewpoint of Western scientists such as neuroscientists, too, the most realistic approach towards thoughts and feelings has been shown to be that of regarding them as a unity—or at least, very closely connected. Recalling memories, thoughts and knowledge never happens without corresponding activity in regions of the brain that influence our feelings, so these appear to add an emotional tint to purely rational experiences. The same also applies when perception creates new memories, thoughts and knowledge. Every one of our thoughts also has an emotional aspect; there are no thoughts which are not a little bit emotional. Of course, there are relatively "sober" thoughts and areas of factual knowledge where we do not sense our neutral emotional tension *as* clearly as when we recall information such as biographical memories (see also 7th Fundamental of BPT).

The distinction between thinking and feeling, *ratio* and *emotio*, reason and emotion, is not made in every culture. In fact, it could be regarded as an incomplete view. So we would do well to take a closer look at Buddhist knowledge, which makes these cultural differences clear and is being confirmed by Western scientific research. Where the Buddhist texts mention *citta* this is normally translated into English as *mind* (and into German as *Geist*), although we can now see that these translations are not completely accurate.

Another cultural difference is that Europeans could often be said to treat the mind as an independent *object*. An example of this is the assumption that our mind is located somewhere—such as in our head. Other examples might be when we say that our mind is *wandering*, that particular problems were *uppermost* in our mind or if we tell someone that they have been *in* our mind a lot recently. In contrast to this approach, Buddhists consider *citta* to be an *activity*. The Dalai Lama has suggested the term "experience"—here he is not referring to the concept of *having* experiences but the process of experiencing, as in every mental and emotional action or perception. In Buddhism there is no mind which is a type of *thing*, without contents. The mind is always an action acting on an object. In fact, *citta* can be translated as "that which acts on an object". So there is no mind without mental objects and equally there is no perceiver without the object of perception.

This might initially sound a little complicated, especially because our instant, unreflected basic feeling usually conveys the impression: Here I am, the others are out there; the world undergoes change but I remain constant. We normally feel separated from our surroundings and all of the things that we perceive to be "out there". At least, this is the normal feeling before we train our view with insight meditation.

A thought experiment

Let us imagine we had grown up in an infinitely large space without gravity and therefore have no experience of anything other than weightlessness and floating. This space was simply white and comfortably light with absolutely nothing in it. (Of course in this hypothetical thought experiment we have to assume that we need no nourishment and there are no bodily excretions!) It may not be easy to imagine something like this but assuming this scenario, let us consider the question: How would we—or how would our mind—develop without any form of input? We could speculate that we would become crazy. Or perhaps we would be completely silent and empty.

According to Buddhist models, a mind without contents is simply not possible. We can experience a very mild version of this inside an *isolation tank*. This is a soundproof tank filled with enough warm salt water so that we can float effortlessly. The tank is closed, allowing no light in. As another name for this tank makes clear—*sensory deprivation tank*—the reason for this experiment is to completely interrupt the flow of external stimuli to our senses. We have a situation where there is no input. Participants in such experiments report a range of very different experiences, but aspects that many have in common include dissolution of the body, Loss of a sense of time, and loss of control over thoughts. Without external input, our mind appears to almost completely lose track of its usual structure and way of functioning. Liminal or limit experiences are possible in this type of context because our mind does not sense its own limits without external feedback.

Experiences such as these can give us an approximate understanding of how inseparably connected our mind is with perceptions of our surroundings (including other people). For this reason, our mental states, thoughts and feelings can never be truly objective.

So now we have put forward and considered a number of different terms or concepts associated with mind. Using these as accurately as possible is important if we want to ensure that we understand each other correctly. In particular, we should remember that Buddhists do not differentiate between *good* and *bad* feelings; instead they distinguish between *healthy* and *unhealthy* states. In the same way, we do not differentiate between *emotional* and *intellectual* aspects but rather unite these as *mental states*. Then we can talk of *healthy* mental states, which we aspire to *cultivate*, and *unhealthy* mental states, which we should try to *overcome* (but not *avoid*, where this implies the risk of repressing them). Healthy mental states can therefore include *emotional contents* such as joy, love, kindness and compassion as well as *rational-intellectual contents* such as thoughts, ideas, words, memories or dogma and beliefs. Instead of speaking about *the* mind, it can also be more accurate to speak about our mental *states* and *contents*.

The torso twist—a useful exercise

When it comes to conveying the significance of the mind to the help-seeker, we need to do this in a vivid, practical and understandable way, so it is useful to have some practical exercises (see also 19th Fundamental of BPT). One such exercise is presented here: the torso twist. It illustrates the connection between mental and physical processes and should be carried out with the help-seeker early in the therapy. It can be performed at any time and needs no major preparation.

The torso twist

We stand upright with our feet firmly on the floor and shoulder-width apart. Our arms are raised to the side, parallel to the floor at the level of our shoulders. Now we twist to the right (left), rotating our torso as far as possible without moving our feet. When we cannot turn any further, we point our index finger straight ahead to note the spot. We return to the starting position, lowering our arms but keeping our feet in exactly the same position. We close our eyes and imagine twisting again. Externally, we remain perfectly still but in our mind we "move" through the same procedure again. We picture twisting as far as we can and repeat this imagined torso twist 10 times. Then we open our eyes, immediately raise our arms and twist "for real" in the same direction again. We see how far we can twist now.

Nine out of ten people are able to twist noticeably further when they repeat the exercise after the visualisations. This clearly felt effect provides valuable experience of how mental exercises can have tangible, measurable physical effects.

Perhaps it is the absolute simplicity of this exercise which makes it particularly impressive as a demonstration of the significance of mind training. Once we have performed the exercise with the help-seeker we can refer to it again and again, reminding us of the efficiency of mind training when we suggest this as an aid to deal with topics such as inner concepts, (false) expectations and judgements.

What Shapes Our Mind?

Models of explanation

In the 5th Fundamental of BPT above we learned about physical aspects which shape the development of our mind (genetics, epigenetic, neurology etc.). Of course, mental dispositions also shape this development and we are also influenced by systemic interactions between physiological and psychological factors.

Western scientists investigating the connection between mental and physical aspects put forward a number of meaningful arguments. In the womb we are already subject to external influences; stimuli in this prenatal period appear to shape our early psychological constitution. This refers to factors such as environmental toxins, noise and sounds as well as the behaviour patterns of our mother. The first post-natal years also see significant influences on our mental development. In fact, this should be fairly obvious since we would not have an ability to learn if we were not sensitive to our experiences in these early years. The major role played by these early influences is suggested by the observation that we learn foreign languages at this young age with much less effort and much more chance of speaking without an accent than if we try when we are older.

Psychoanalysts have published widely on the topic of formative childhood experience. They have also shaped our concepts of psychotherapy, so many people believe that undertaking psychotherapy involves working through our (horrible) childhood experiences before we have even a chance of healing. And the idea that a traumatic childhood is always the source of an acute psychological illness, such as personality disorder, can also be traced back to the psychoanalysts. Regrettably, it seems that it will take decades for us to see the social and healthcare sectors accept modern scientific explanatory models, such as systems and chaos theory.

According to the models developed by Eastern scientists such as Buddhist scholars, we come into this world with an infinite number of predispositions and potentials—described as *seeds* in our *storehouse consciousness*. The experiences we are subjected to or create ourselves determine which of these seeds are "watered" and sprout, and which of them are neglected and wither away.

So Eastern and Western sciences offer us common discoveries which reinforce the possibility of bringing about fundamental changes within us. The seeds/predispositions which we carry offer the potential for every imaginable version of the future—for better and for worse. Of course, some changes in behaviour are easier when we are young, but with patience and steady repetition of our exercises we can bring about tangible and permanent changes at any age. In this book we will often refer to the following Buddhist concept of personal development:

Intentions → Deeds → Habits → Character → Destiny

Even *apparently* firmly established systems such as our character can be changed by correcting the conditions which gave rise to them: The critical factors here are our *intentions*, which determine whether our *deeds* are healthy or unhealthy behaviour. If we frequently repeat particular deeds/behaviour, this establishes *habits*. These in turn form the foundations of our *character* and then our *destiny*.

Perhaps we are a little like the cats in a (morally very questionable) laboratory experiment who spent their childhood and youth in a large box whose walls were covered entirely in horizontal lines. Later in their life, when they were taken out of the box, they were unable to recognise vertical lines.

We can recognise the extent of the significance which the Buddha ascribed to mental aspects when we take a look at Buddhist considerations of the central elements which make up human beings. Here we are referring to the five "heaps" or "psychophysical aggregates" which constitute our personality—in Sanskrit *skandha*.

The Five Skandhas
1. Body, or form
2. Feeling, or sensation

3. Cognition, or perception
4. Mental formations, or impulses (often referred to by the Sanskrit term *samskara*)
5. Consciousness

We can see that there is *one* element corresponding to the body and *four* elements corresponding to the mind. This weighting is an indication of the importance Buddhists attach to mental processes but should not be misunderstood as the undervaluing of physical patterns. From a Buddhist point of view, the brain is simply a part of the body which the mind "uses" to communicate with the body. Our brain is *not* the place where thoughts arise. Thoughts arise in the (non-material) mind. There is still a lively debate on the issue of whether brain activity directly and always corresponds to consciousness activity, as is often assumed by Western scientists.

Western research on mind and consciousness

If we adopt the viewpoint of Western scientists regarding the issue of mind and consciousness, we immediately find a large number of completely unsolved mysteries, such as the fundamental question of how our consciousness arises. Scientific definitions of consciousness are purely *descriptive* and comparative. Lists are made of factors which have to be present if something is to be referred to as consciousness: cognitive abilities are active; our senses are in an alert state; emotional responsiveness. But *causal* conditions are not mentioned, since we still do not know what they are.

Many Western scientists assume that our nervous system produces consciousness much as our kidneys produce urine. However, they are not able to explain exactly how this process takes place. And there is actually still no proven causal connection between nerve activity in the brain and consciousness. The nerve cells we have are identical to those in other animals, including lower species such as jellyfish or snails which do not have a central nervous system. Although these animals have nerve cells, they do not exhibit signs of consciousness—this has only been recognised in humans and our close relatives among the apes. Science also claims without conclusive supporting evidence that consciousness is the result of a purely quantitative phenomenon: the size of our central nervous system. In fact, there is still a very vigorous debate on the issues of how to define consciousness or forms of consciousness and which other living beings exhibit it.

The issue of *intelligence* is similarly problematic. The significance of our external surroundings ("nurture") is no longer debated because it is now very clear that an African hunter-gatherer has to develop different forms of *intelligence* than a West-European city dweller. If we carry over this insight into the field of consciousness studies, we also have to concede that living beings in other habitats could develop other forms of *consciousness* which do not fit our definitions. So let us duly appreciate and respect the miracle of consciousness and once again acknowledge the limits of our knowledge.

How our mind works

If we accept for a moment the lack of models to explain the *causes*, we can take a closer look at the *descriptive* models of our mind in order to gain an approximate understanding of our mental resources.

Our mind appears to need two major components:
1. Memory
2. Consciousness

The structure of our memory store

Our memory is an extremely precious resource which is necessary if we are to fully use our mind. Many people suffering from dementia are still able to think but cannot store new memories; this condemns them to a certain degree of helplessness in our world.

The most common model of our memory divides it into different "stores":

1. Sensory or ultra-short-term memory: All impressions reach us via our senses. This sensory information is stored here temporarily (for a few milliseconds).

2. *Short-term or working memory:* The use of our working memory allows us to deal with information without having to remember it permanently.

3. *Long-term memory:*
   a. *Declarative or knowledge memory:* Here we find our semantic or encyclopaedic memory. It stores all of the knowledge we have learnt about the world. For example, this brain structure is activated when we hear the question: Where is Crete?

   Our *episodic* or *autobiographical* memory is also included here. It is where we store our personal information. This part of the brain is activated when we hear questions such as: What is your father's first name?

   b. *Procedural memory:* Regions of the brain located below the neo-cortex are used for this memory, which has details of sequences of learned behaviour or skills which we need to be able to carry out automatically without too much thinking, such as walking or riding a bicycle.

Memories are stories
Images, sequences of images and words are generally stored in a fragmented way. In other words, any particular memory is not stored at one particular point in the brain. Several different groups of neurons are coordinated when we remember eating a very tasty apple, for example: some neurons are responsible for contrast, some for colour, some for shape, some for taste, others for the concept of apple and others for the emotions associated with this experience. So the act of remembering does not involve retrieving complete pictures which are stored somewhere in our head; it is a process of compiling. In other words, it is a *creative* process.

Criminologists know about this difficulty and imprecision because of the role it plays in interpreting statements made by witnesses. And social psychologists such as Elisabeth Loftus have discovered that about one in four adults will develop a "memory" of events that never actually happened to them if they are asked the appropriate questions. She carried out a series of experiments where participants were given short narratives describing events from their childhood, written by close relatives. They were then asked to write down whatever they could remember about the event or to honestly say if they could not remember anything. One of the narratives was a story of how they got lost in a shopping mall as a young child, had to wait a long time until a relative found them and then cried a lot as they were reunited. One quarter of the participants were able to recall memories of this event even though the scientists knew from their prior research that this had never actually happened to them. Research such as this gave rise to the concept of the "false memory syndrome", which is subject to much debate within the field of psychotherapy. Therapeutic situations give rise to expectations and an emotional charge which can lead people to unconsciously put things together which never actually belonged together. In fact, these are the same abilities which allow us to create new concepts, ideas and art: All of us can probably "remember" (i.e. *imagine*) a green elephant!

The insights described above serve once again to underline is the importance for therapists of being very careful and discerning when listening to their clients. It also makes clear why Buddhists resist identifications, which tend to establish themselves as remembered identities within us.

Consciousness

Our brain works via the exchange of chemical substances (neurotransmitters) and electrical signals. This exchange takes place between individual nerve cells (neurons) and between networks of these cells. We have approximately 100 million neurons, each of which is able to form more than 10,000 connections to neighbouring cells, so the number of different possible connections is astronomically high.

Today we can demonstrate and measure both the chemical and electrical exchanges of information in our brain. For example, electroencephalography (EEG) uses electrodes placed on the scalp to measure electrical activity, recording voltage fluctuations in the microvolt range (direct measurements on the nerve cells give results in the millivolt range). The most common applications of EEG are clinical diagnostics and research issues in fields such as epilepsy, strokes, tumours, anaesthesia monitoring, psychiatric illnesses and sleep disorders. EEG measurements can give us objective indications of whether the brain being measured is active and whether the subject is focused, tired, in a deep sleep, dreaming, in a coma or dead.

EEG signals deliver very precise data on the level of activity in our brain. The brain signals recorded range in frequency between 0.4-80 Hz (Hertz = cycles per second). Researchers distinguish particular frequency ranges which indicate particular activity in the brain.

Gamma >30 Hz	high levels of cognitive performance
Beta 12-30 Hz	alertness, attentiveness
Alpha 8-18 Hz	light relaxation
Theta 3-8 Hz	deep relaxation, sleep
Delta 0.4-4 Hz	deep sleep

When the EEG pattern disappears completely, this absence of brain activity is classified as "brain death" (as compared to "clinical death" which is the cessation of breathing and blood circulation).

An important control unit

The most important structure for the achievement of alert consciousness appears to be the link between the thalamus and the cerebral cortex. The thalamus is situated deep in the lower layers at the centre of the brain (see 7th Fundamental of BPT) and is made up of various different thalamic nuclei. Nerve fibres connect it to the cerebral cortex and in turn to all other parts of the brain. In order for us to experience alert, concentrated states of consciousness this special connection has to vibrate at about 40 Hz.

We can use a more sophisticated EEG procedure to identify currently working *areas* of the brain through their electrical activity. The activity of different brain regions can also be identified by means of the nerve cell metabolism (oxygenation), as measured by fMRI (functional magnetic resonance imaging). These relatively new opportunities to observe the brain "as it works" have led to a whole series of spectacular results. For example, evidence has been provided of a phenomenon known as neuroplasticity (see 5th Fundamental of BPT), which concerns the enormous ability of our brain to adapt to new circumstances. If we train our brain it can lead to growth of new neural connections at all ages.

A corporate neuroscience analogy
The latest neuroscientific results regarding attention, memory and consciousness can be described using the analogy of a large company. This company is made up of a variety of departments (= brain regions) which work on very different tasks but are nonetheless connected to each other. It has a large number of active employees (= nerve cells) who are *constantly* communicating with each other—even at times when they do not have an immediate task to perform. Some of them compare data, others check old stock and others are talking to each other. When a new client appears, only a couple of employees initially react—everyone else continues their previous work. However, if the new client wants to buy something, many more employees suddenly turn their attention to him, comparing him to other existing clients, checking his wishes against current capacity, etc. Some employees concentrate on the financial opportunities, others weigh up the risks, and others might be looking for the possibility to close the deal quickly.

This analogy helps to make us aware of some remarkable processes in our brain:

There is constant activity. Nerve cells do not hang around passively, waiting for an input. Even without external stimuli, they are constantly in action and maintaining readiness. However, this can often be disturbing.

We can work in parallel. While we are reading, for example, we have other "departments" which are dealing with things such as bodily necessities, processing other structures and taking in additional information.

Our ability to focus our attention varies greatly. Depending on the internal debates taking place in the individual "departments" and the strength of the new clients (= stimuli), there is great variation in our attentional performance.

External and internal issues can be equally disturbing. It does not matter whether the cause of a disturbance is external or internal—the results can be similarly disastrous: a potentially dangerous client (stimulus) might be approaching our company (nervous system) or procedures within the company might be in chaos. Quite often our internal departments are so absorbed in their communication that we are not even aware of external situations. Or we experience them as an overload and then assess them incorrectly.

Who is in charge? Looking for the boss in this company throws up some interesting questions. Core structures such as the thalamus and hypothalamus do seem to play a significant controlling role but alert awareness appears to need *interaction* between the various areas, at a particular frequency (around 40 Hz).

The attentiveness of our inner company and its employees is constantly changing. Their experiences determine and influence the procedures for new transactions. We can only speak of "the company" if we take the many activities of the employees together: individual employees or departments are not enough. In fact, realising that it is this interaction which constitutes the company is a good way of describing the insights that many Western scientists have gained in their understanding of consciousness.

How Free Is Our Mind?

Our mind has material-physiological and non-material (psychological and spiritual) components, so it is subject to the influence of a multiplicity of very different factors, which we can divide into categories such as general and current:

- *General factors:*
  Genetic predispositions, family commitments, education, culture, status, intelligence, ego defence structures, mind training, life experience, etc.

- *Current factors:*
  Attention performance, alertness, concentration, nutrition, drugs, medicines, health, disease, motivation, arousal level, etc.

Seeing how long this list of influences is, we might be forgiven for beginning to doubt the idea of "free will". Indeed, this debate has never been concluded; there is as yet no final answer to the issue of the extent of our ability or opportunity to make independent, free decisions.

Critics of the idea of free will often cite the legendary experiments performed by Benjamin Libet which observed relevant brain activity *before* a free decision was made. Participants were free to choose when to push a button; the experimental design also allowed them to note the moment when they made this decision. EEG electrodes demonstrated the build-up of electrical charge in the motor cortex (the area of the brain responsible for moving the finger) before the decision to push the button. This "readiness potential" was taken by many scientists to be an indication that decisions are made and prepared unconsciously at the neural level without our noticing. These studies and their implications were subject to much debate in the decades to follow. Critics argued that all of the participants had already taken the basic decision to push a button when they agreed to take part in the experiment. This was probably a conscious process and could be the cause of the underlying readiness and activation in the brain.

Libet himself did not interpret his results as proof of our lack of free will. Instead he emphasised the interval available to us during which we can suppress the impulse that has already started. Interestingly, we seem to be significantly more active on an unconscious level than we thought. It appears that the unconscious even instigates actions in advance. However, this does not necessarily mean we should reject the concept of "free will" because, between the creation of this readiness potential in the brain and the carrying out of the action, there is still enough time for us to suppress the impulse and stop the action.

So our free will might actually be the freedom to stop acts instigated by the unconscious. We are, however, probably not fully free with regard to these spontaneous impulses, because they arise within us unconsciously.

Consciously making a choice or unconsciously following a pattern?

By now, the reader probably has an idea of how many factors manipulate our choice—either consciously or unconsciously. Furthermore, even if we think for a long time and make our decision about an action after long deliberation, the results can still frequently be seen to fit into a coherent and recurring (and often unhealthy) pattern. Perhaps we regularly experience this as a type of repetition: We might repeatedly come up against the same type of problems and conflicts or we might frequently encounter people or partners who resemble each other in a noticeable way. So we then sometimes ask ourselves, for example, why we always *choose* a partner with these particular characteristics. This puzzling habit becomes more understandable if we accept the fact that an untrained mind will never make a truly free decision and never really have a choice: Without deliberate mind training we simply follow a pattern which is usually unconscious. These patterns are often formed from our unquestioned identifications with our various roles and personality aspects and from our unreflected spontaneous emotions.

To summarise, we can conclude that without mind training, the vast majority of the decisions and choices in our life are governed by unconscious, unfree patterns.

Western science has made many discoveries in this field leading to many valuable insights, only a fraction of which we have been able to look at here. This glimpse should help us to understand these issues more deeply and as well as respectfully appreciating this information we also need to respect the gaps in our knowledge. In spite of our know-how, technology, money and efforts, there are still topics which are (and may forever remain) inaccessible to us as human beings.

We can, however, benefit from a consideration of the specialist areas where Eastern and Western sciences meet, from the combination of different techniques and achievements.

Meditation and Brain Activity

It is telling that there have been many studies into the issues of violence, hate and aggression but only recently have Western scientists taken a closer look at issues such as joy, compassion and kindness. With this, scientists can be said to have the whole range of human emotional or mental states under their microscope.

One element of these studies has been to compare Buddhist monks with many years of meditation experience and subjects without any experience of meditation. The Dalai Lama was a keen proponent of these experiments and personally selected eight of his monks for some experiments. The famous French Buddhist Matthieu Ricard also took part in the trials. In one series of experiments, the subjects had to lie in the "tube" of a CT or MRI scanner with the instruction to cultivate unconditional compassion within them— in other words, an objectless meditation with the aim of creating healthy mental states. As could be expected, the eight Buddhist monks recorded significantly higher levels of brain activity. Interestingly, this was in the gamma frequency range, which corresponds to high levels of attention. The researchers noted further that the amplitudes recorded were the highest ever seen in healthy people.

This shows us once again that meditation does not lead us into a sleepy state of relaxation but rather to the desired state of concentrated alertness and attention.

A further interesting result was the fact that the gamma activities of the Buddhist practitioners were significantly higher those of the test subjects even *before* the actual experiment began.

> This appears to show that experienced meditators are *persistently* more alert, more focused and more attentive.

These brain activities were higher in the frontal lobes in particular. This is a region which is believed to control resources that are able to compensate for negative thoughts and behaviours. The fact that the brains of the Buddhist practitioners exhibit differences compared to those of non-meditators both outside and during the experiment leads us to the conclusion that mind training enables us to achieve fundamental changes in our brain.

In the meantime, further experiments have shown that meditation has many other important effects relevant to our health. Meditative practice leads to obvious balancing effects in our autonomous nervous system—a region which regulates our stress symptoms and a multitude of vital physical factors such as blood pressure, blood values, digestion, sleep and immune system reactions.

> Our consciousness, emotions and mental states and our physical constitution can all be changed fundamentally and permanently by means of regular meditation practice.

So targeted training allows us to consciously influence the fundamental processes within us, such as consciousness, feelings and physical symptoms.

Desired Mental States

In addition to the core Buddhist aims of gentleness and compassion, Buddhists particularly aspire to achieve an alert and calm mind able to relax into wakefulness, concentration and mindfulness. We discovered above that targeted meditation training can lead to a very high level of concentration, attentiveness and alertness both within the meditation itself and as a lasting mental state. Perhaps this can be usefully compared to an experienced athlete, whose resting heart rate is persistently lower than that of an average human being.

So Buddhist meditation has very little to do with relaxation, sleep, hypnosis or "switching off". In fact, it brings about mental states that are the opposite of these—alert awareness. Connected to these are further core Buddhist attitudes such as concentration and mindfulness.

The distinction between concentration and mindfulness is important. The foundation for both is general attention—in other words an alert state of consciousness.

Attention →	Concentration
	Mindfulness

What is attention?

Our attention can vary considerably and is dependent on our state of consciousness. We already saw above that we can use EEG to gain an approximate indication of various different states of consciousness. The higher the brain frequency is (measured in Hertz), the greater our attention.

What is concentration?

Concentration is a bundled, focused form of attention. We direct our attention onto *one* object, much like the narrow beam of a torch. At high levels of concentration this can lead to a connection so strong that it (almost) creates a unity between the concentrating subject and the object in focus. In other words, in a highly concentrated state we almost merge with the object we are looking at.

What is mindfulness?

Mindfulness is one of the key tools in Buddhism and Buddhist Psychotherapy. So it is particularly important to develop a good understanding of mindfulness.

If we analyse the English term used by internationally respected Buddhist teachers such as the Dalai Lama, Thich Nhat Hanh or Tulku Lama Lobsang, we can see that it has something to do with *mind* and *full*, perhaps indicating that we should do something with the whole of our mind. As is the case with many terms and concepts translated from one language and culture to another, one word is often not sufficient and brings with it associations which are different to those in the original teachings. So we need to take a much closer look at this key concept in order to decipher its real meaning.

Mindfulness refers to a wide type of attention, as opposed to the bundled, focused attention that is concentration. Chögyam Trungpa also called it "panoramic awareness". This reminds us of our distinction between two forms of *attention*: the targeted, pointed *concentration* and the rather uniform, voluminous *mindfulness*.

In Buddhism, mindfulness is one of the significant qualities needed to achieve liberation. One of the most important classical Buddhist scriptures on liberation is the *Satipatthana Sutta-Foundations of Mindfulness* (the 10th sutta in the Middle-Length Discourses). Furthermore, mindfulness is also presented as a significant factor in the Four Noble Truths which can help us to gain liberation in everyday life. And the Buddha also listed Seven Factors for the attainment of enlightenment—of which mindfulness is the first.

Mindfulness is the key which opens the doors to further physical, mental and spiritual development and it is a pre-requisite for any implementation of the insights we gain on the path. Mindfulness helps us to put theory into practice. So mindfulness is a foundation which we build upon in Buddhist Psychotherapy: firstly during meditation and then extending it into our everyday life. Without a stable foundation of mindfulness, it is much more difficult to move on and work on our insights in order to progress towards liberation. Without mindfulness we will never be able to correctly implement any of the many techniques we learn.

Since this concept is difficult to understand with only one English word, let us explore it from many different angles.

Approaches to mindfulness could be:
- attention without concentration
- clear view without judgement
- observation without decisions

- acceptance without resistance
- self-recognition without identification
- circumspection without fatigue
- perception without attachment
- turning away without resistance
- awareness without analytic thought
- experience without preconception
- experience without analysis
- presence without fixation
- alertness without urge to act
- calmness without lethargy
- sensing without ego-centredness
- acceptance without being indiscriminate
- embracing without smothering
- recognising without categorising
- tolerance without indifference
- wisdom without arrogance
- introspection without vanity
- effortlessness without aloofness
- taking an interest without taking over
- activity without effort
- thinking without being too intellectual
- force without violence
- caution without restraint
- behaviour without confusion
- attitude without negativity
- compassion without partiality
- caution without fear
- guiding thread without tangles

Mindfulness is the means and the end at the same time.

Mindfulness is the key to both our recognition and our realisation.

Mindfulness is not a technique. It is an attitude but far more than just an attitude.

Mindfulness is not only a characteristic but rather a Buddhist virtue. Like all Buddhist virtues, it is less of an abstention and more of a practical instruction (see 20th Fundamental of BPT on the topic of Buddhist virtues).

Mindfulness always refers to the equality or inseparability of mindfulness for oneself and mindfulness for all other beings.

Mindfulness is the struggle against mindlessness or carelessness. Shantideva referred to this in his metaphor of thieves (disturbing emotions) lurking constantly waiting for a lapse in attention of the guards (mindfulness) so they can break into the house (mind).

If we cease to be alert when we relax, our mind (house) can easily be overwhelmed (broken into) by unhealthy thoughts or emotions (thieves) so this is why we consciously practice mindfulness during meditation and not relaxation. Exercises in mindfulness are also a very good remedy for compulsive worrying.

The Buddha himself made the special importance of mindfulness very clear. He taught the *Foundations of Mindfulness* as a clearly structured four-step process, with practical instructions for its implementation:

The Four Foundations of Mindfulness

1. Body
2. Feelings
3. Mind/Consciousness
4. Dharmas (Mental Objects)

Based on these Four Foundations, the first Buddhist instruction is: Pay attention to the signals coming from your *body*. Watch out for any possible tension or feelings of pressure and also pay attention to physical desires. When we start to do these exercises it is helpful to concentrate only on relevant physical signals and sensations and not to let any associations arise in the form of images or thoughts.

Before we move on to the second step and place our mindfulness on our *feelings*, we need to have a clear sense of our body and physical sensations. Our physicality can help us and therefore deserves something in return. Mindfulness of the body also means taking care of what we expect from our body, how we nourish it and whether we are subjecting it to any toxins. So we are mindful what our body gives us and what we give it.

Our *feelings* now have priority ahead of our *thoughts* or our mind (which constitute the third step). They also need and deserve an equally thorough mindful observation. For our feelings, too, we should take care to listen to what they are telling us and be careful of any emotional coarseness we impose on them. Dealing with our feelings deserves a great deal of attention, which is why the 7th Fundamental of BPT is devoted to this issue.

Again, when we start these exercises it can be very helpful to restrict our concentration to the qualities of the feelings without paying attention to any associative images or memories which arise.

Focusing on our *mind*—or our *thoughts*—only becomes part of the exercises after we have learnt to mindfully appreciate our physical signals and the qualities of our feelings. Without mind training, both our feelings and our thoughts depend strongly on our prior experiences, habits and character. We have to learn how to go through these entanglements by means of mindfulness. At the beginning this will only be possible with assistance, such as the framework provided by Buddhist Psychotherapy.

Mindfulness also goes beyond feelings and thoughts, to *mental objects* or phenomena. With the fourth step in our mindfulness exercises we gain insights into higher principles or constituent factors (*dharmas*) such as dependent arising and the nonexistence of things. The assistance we are provided with during Buddhist Psychotherapy will allow us to experience these ourselves.

It is important always to be aware of what these four foundations can convey to us but also of their limits. We should not read anything into them which does not belong there.

Although we repeatedly emphasise the great value of mind training in our life, this is a good opportunity to clearly emphasise the key role that our body plays here. When we deepen our mind training with meditation and mindfulness exercises (see 19th Fundamental of BPT) we will increasingly experience how intensely connected the mind and the body are with each other—like the two sides of a coin. We will often encounter profound interactions between the two and discover that deeper practice of the Four Foundations of Mindfulness often leads to the dissolution of the boundaries between body, feelings, thoughts, mind and dharmas.

Mindfulness in Western psychotherapy

Mindfulness as a beneficial attitude has often been recognised and taken up as a significant therapeutic approach. For example, Sigmund Freud encouraged psychoanalysts to adopt *"evenly-suspended"* or *"free-floating"* attention when listening to the free associations of their clients. With the term *Sensory Awareness,* Elsa Gindler and Charlotte Selver played a particular role in integrating the concept into Western psychotherapy models in the first half of the 20th century. The beneficial effects of mindfulness have also been recognised by and integrated into many other forms of therapy, such as:

- Mindfulness-Based Cognitive Therapy (MBCT) from Segal, Williams and Teasdale
- Mindfulness-Based Stress Reduction (MBSR) from Jon Kabat-Zinn
- Dialectical Behavior Therapy (DBT) from Marsha Linehan

Exercises on mindfulness have also been incorporated into the treatment of ADD/ADHD and body-oriented psychotherapy such as that from Ron Kurtz. And in Gestalt therapy, the overlapping concept of *awareness* is one of the fundamental units used to implement a therapy.

As was already mentioned in the Introduction, behaviour therapy (BT) is also now discovering mindfulness. So this core Buddhist principle is now enjoying recognition from one of the most important schools of therapy (alongside psychoanalysis and depth psychology).

The Buddhist Science of the Mind

Now we come to the Buddhist concepts of mind and consciousness. We always have to bear in mind the subtleties involved in different concepts and translations, as mentioned above. We have taken a brief look at Western sciences, getting to know the insights they have gained and the limits they face, and now we will introduce a selection of the experiences gathered over many centuries by the Eastern sciences. We will see clearly that there are both similarities and differences.

A long time before Western neuroscience, Buddhists distinguished a range of levels of consciousness. They recognised that our consciousness can basically be presented in four forms.

Four Forms of Consciousness
1. Mind Consciousness
2. Sense Consciousness
3. Storehouse Consciousness
4. Manas Consciousness

(Sometimes Buddhists speak of eight consciousnesses when the five subcategories of sense consciousness are listed in their own right.)

Mind consciousness
Our mind consciousness is the first form of consciousness. It incorporates our thinking, working mind. In the mind consciousness we can plan, make judgements, consider and complain.

Sense consciousness
The sense consciousness is made up of our five senses. Each of these has its own form of consciousness:
> Eye consciousness (seeing)
> Ear consciousness (hearing)
> Nose consciousness (smelling)
> Tongue consciousness (tasting)
> Body consciousness (touching/feeling)

We can often only have accurate experiences if a selection of sense consciousnesses work together, but ways of filtering these are open to us. And one particular feature worth mentioning is that individual forms of sense consciousness take in information below the threshold of our mind consciousness and thus are able to process this "unconsciously". This explains our ability to carry out an action such as walking, with our eye consciousness checking our steps, while our mind consciousness is busy with completely different matters. For the vast majority of the day, these processes are running in parallel without our really noticing. Our body functions, drives a car, walks up steps, repairs something: Sometimes our mind is present in these activities and sometimes it is brooding over something completely different.

Each of our *sense consciousnesses* interacts with three respective components in order to work properly:

- the healthy *sense organ*—eyes, ears, nose, tongue, body
- the external *sense object*—that which we see, hear, smell, taste, touch
- the *contact* or *sense impression*—seeing, hearing, smelling, tasting, touching

Storehouse consciousness
Also known as the substrate consciousness, this is where we find all our experiences and memories as well as all of our potentials (seeds), whether we have lived them out or not. This consciousness is regarded as inexhaustible, which makes it very clear that we have

every chance of cultivating, developing and realising absolutely any human characteristic we can imagine.

This consciousness is home to our destructive tendencies as well as our positive characteristics; sometimes they are hidden and sometimes open. Whether or not any of these aspects is activated depends on a multiplicity of influencing factors from the other forms of consciousness.

Simply by reading this page, new seeds are being added to our storehouse consciousness. It is able to take in this new information and store it but it is not a purely passive-perceptive consciousness. The information entered (seeds) is evaluated and processed. This evaluation and processing can take place in the mind consciousness or in the storehouse consciousness alone. In fact, decision processes can take place at the level of the storehouse consciousness unobserved by our alert mind consciousness. For example, one of our sense consciousnesses, such as our eye or nose consciousness, might provide information to our storehouse consciousness about a market stall selling fruits which look or smell very good. This then gives rise to a feeling such as a desire which in turn propels us towards the market stand or leads to us stretch our hand out towards the fruit. Our mind consciousness hardly plays a role in this process. And this fact is the source of frequent problems related to our limited or lacking free will. However, looking at it from another angle, it represents a huge potential which we can take advantage of by means of our insights and mind training.

So our mind, sense and storehouse consciousnesses all take in information about the world around us. These influences are planted in our storehouse consciousness, have an effect on the seeds stored there, and manipulate new experiences and decisions. So it is obvious that we have to be very careful how we "feed" ourselves or let ourselves "be fed". We have to carefully recognise how these processes take place, where the strengths lie and where the difficulties are lurking.

It may not be possible to remove the bad seeds in our storehouse consciousness, but we can use mindfulness exercises to train ourselves how to distinguish more effectively between the healthy and unhealthy seeds within us. We can also learn how to cultivate the healthy seeds and weaken the unhealthy ones.

Our storehouse consciousness is full of all sorts of positive and negative potentials; in other words, both wisdom and folly are present in latent form here. The presence of both in one store is a source of conflict, leading to many different contradictory impulses, insecurities and fears—states of tension. These want to be released. All of this causes our storehouse consciousness to create a new form of consciousness: our manas consciousness.

Manas consciousness or self-illusion consciousness
In this consciousness we find our self-consciousness or ego illusion. This makes it a significant component of the emotional linkage of the different consciousnesses. Our manas consciousness interacts intensively with our storehouse consciousness.

This consciousness does not serve the function of understanding or recognising the world. Instead, it forms because of our pressing needs to calm and control (among other functions). Although these are helpful functions, this consciousness also has some very considerable disadvantages because it is the source of many different types of attachment, resistance and ignorance: the sources of our suffering.

The structure presented here offers possible explanations for many of our everyday experiences. It explains how our mind consciousness can frequently go wandering, losing itself in time as it speculates about the future or broods over the past. During these periods without "supervision", the storehouse consciousness quietly continues its work, aided by the sense consciousnesses—psychologists would say "unconsciously". The results can be either healthy or unhealthy for us.

This applies to each of the forms of consciousness: Without targeted mind training, such as that which we perform as part of Buddhist Psychotherapy, their processes can be both a blessing and a curse. The blessings are very obvious if we consider the variety of uses possible; this is where we find the qualities of enjoyment, intelligence and learning.

We have to take a look at the costs in order to really take stock and find suitable alternatives where appropriate. Our mature yet untrained consciousnesses have reached a state where they "lead their own lives" in an undisciplined way which often provides us with more pain than pleasure. This includes the excessive tendency of the sense consciousnesses to lead to attachments and become confused by the mind and manas consciousnesses. (The pattern of confusion is generally more accurately described as being the result of the interaction of all forms of consciousness.)

This may all appear to be very theoretical, but we have to consider it because of the necessity to experience and discover as much as possible about ourselves and the way we work. Nonetheless, these studies should not be carried out for their own sake. The knowledge we gain needs to be implemented practically in the form of targeted self-protection measures, more balanced exercises and the most realistic and effective strategies for cultivating the positive seeds in our storehouse consciousness: identifying, promoting, maturing, protecting them and seeing them grow to fruition. This core aspiration of Buddhist practice can be more easily developed if we know ourselves well and are better able to assess our individual peculiarities.

We need courage and strength if we want to dive into our fascinating yet complicated inner world. So it can be advisable to seek out the courage and strength of an accompanying therapist, who can provide valuable support in our attempts to eradicate all our false beliefs and set our mind on the path of becoming lighter and freer.

Our fixed thought patterns and our own opinion

Without specific mind training, we are generally trapped in the tight confines of habitual thought patterns. As if we were trapped in a sect with its restricted reference system, we create closed models of explanation which apparently provide logical justification for why we should behave in a particular way or why we should feel like this and not like that—although we then often suffer because of this. So we need to dig out and remove our "sect mentality". If we look more carefully we might be able to see how tight, restricted and habitual our thought patterns frequently are. After all, we are probably a member of many "sects": family sects, clique sects, friend sects, colleague sects, sport sects, culture sects, belief sects etc. And furthermore, if we listen carefully within us, we can hear a wide range of dominant voices, feeding us opinions, assessments and comments and thus manipulating our mental states.

A meditation teacher once said, "Our rational mind is a good servant, but a bad master."

So we have to develop a more precise knowledge of our mind, study and tame its processes, and exercise more effective control over it. There can be no real doubt that our mind functions effectively and successfully. However, this truly efficient organ does tend to lead its own life in unsupervised moments, which does not always lead to healthy results.

The power of our mind has many aspects. One of these has been called the placebo effect.

Placebo—or the power of mind

The placebo effect unfortunately has a bad reputation. In medical research, the placebo effect is the decisive threshold which a particular medicine has to exceed in order to be considered effective. Subjects in an experiment are given a placebo (for example, a harmless sugar pill with no active ingredients) and told it is very effective medicine. In general, an effect is actually seen in 30-50% of the subjects. This phenomenon is called the placebo effect and it is fairly easy to understand why a new medicine has to show results exceeding this: Otherwise we could just give everybody sugar pills! Although many doctors look down on this with derogatory comments ("That is *just* a placebo effect"), it is worth asking why we do not highly value something that has a positive effect for 30-50% of people. And there are no conclusive answers to the fascinating question: How does the placebo work? Patients suffering from pain are given a sugar pill or vitamin pill with no active ingredients and then told that their pain will decrease—and in up to 50% of the patients this does actually happen!

So in reality the placebo effect is a wonderful process demonstrating the power and efficiency of our mind. And what is more, we can achieve this effect *without* special mind training. So how effective can it become if we regularly strengthen and train our mind?!

Mental attitude

In the 13th Fundamental of BPT, on the topic of ignorance, we will discover more about the many limits and restrictions our rational mind is subject to and become even more convinced of how we need to cultivate much more mindfulness and modesty in this regard. Step by step we are developing a deeper understanding of the variety of forces at work within us, helping us to recognise and understand why our mindfulness and awareness so badly need to be cultivated and strengthened.

Claudia L is a sociologist and very academically-minded. Being "stuck in her head" also had a physical expression: She generally let her head hang very low. This led to painful tension in her neck during meditation exercises. For Claudia, however, these pains provided her with the first opportunity to really feel the connection between her overly intellectual nature and her physical symptoms. She already had some knowledge of the relevance of mental processes, but the mindful integration of the mind *and* body which Claudia was able to experience in later meditation sessions as a unity became a focus of attention for her during her therapy.

This Fundamental Should Convey the Following:

In our culture and language, there are very many related terms and concepts such as mind, will, consciousness and intellect. And there are many more in other cultures and languages. So we need to be very sure that we know what we are talking about.

We have at our disposal a mind that can be very helpful to us in many regards but which can—in unsupervised moments—lead its own very risky life. We have received a lot of information explaining how our mind is constructed and how it becomes effective. In particular, this 6th Fundamental of BPT should have given us many incentives to adopt mind training.

Certainly, many of the details appear to contradict our initial everyday experience. For this reason, in Buddhist Psychotherapy comprehensive explanation is not enough: We need practical exercises to gain our own sense-based experience.

The 7th
Fundamental of Buddhist Psychotherapy

Recognise and Convey the Truth About Our Feelings

> Love is the only answer to hatred.
>
> DILGO KHYENTSE RINPOCHE

As we consider the 7th Fundamental of Buddhist Psychotherapy we will make a number of discoveries about our feelings and their effects on our mental states. Looking at the 6th Fundamental we already heard that our feelings are inseparably connected to our mental events, so when we treat feelings and mind as two separate things in the following discussion, this is simply an artificial distinction that serves to help illustrate particular facts more clearly.

The 7th Fundamental is particularly important for many people seeking our help because they generally only even consider psychotherapy after a long period of suffering from painful feelings, such as sadness, fear, anger, frustration or despondency. Wanting to get rid of pain as quickly as possible is, of course, a perfectly human reaction, so many people will come to Buddhist Psychotherapists seeking quick and effective relief from their negative feelings. This applies to every form of therapy, but Buddhist Psychotherapy in particular offers us the chance of *permanently* liberating ourselves from unhealthy feelings (see 1st Fundamental of BPT).

A stable therapist-client alliance is necessary if we, as Buddhist Psychotherapists, want to pass on the necessary teachings on how to deal with our feelings. One reason this is so necessary is because there are important aspects relating to how feelings arise which contradict the rather superficial everyday understanding of the issue.

There is hardly anything that is more *ours* than our feelings. We experience them intensely, they appear to give our life meaning, and very often they even keep us alive. What we read or hear might be interesting, but what we feel and experience emotionally creates a significantly more powerful access to learning and life experience. We experience a situation and the relevant feelings arise by themselves quite naturally; and we consider this to be the way things are. Our life experience shows us, for example, that we *automatically* become angry because someone has provoked us or we *automatically* become scared if we find ourselves standing on the edge of a cliff. We can be sure of these re-actions. And although we often suffer because of such emotional reactions, we generally do not question them. This is, however, exactly what Buddhist Psychotherapy does.

We will hear how BPT is clearly more critical than other types of therapy when it comes to our feelings. For example, many other therapists teach their clients: Trust your feelings. Pay attention and find out what causes positive feelings and what leads to negative feelings. Try to develop positive feelings and avoid negative ones. Buddhists, as we will see, have some interesting insights to work with here and take a very different approach. We will also discover that Western scientific research is confirming these insights.

We will concentrate primarily on the most important topics relating to our feelings:

1 How do feelings arise within us?
2 How long do feelings last?
3 What do our emotional reactions look like?
4 How can we deal with our emotions practically?

How (and Where) Do Our Feelings Arise?

If we look at the simplified illustration in Figure 4, we can imagine a ring of nerves above the sympathetic and parasympathetic nervous systems—this ring is our limbic system or feelings centre (indicated in Figure 4 by LS). It is located relatively low down in our brain, which is interesting when we consider the issue of conscious control of our feelings: The lower areas of our brain structure, situated closer to our spinal cord, are all older (in evolutionary terms) and less sophisticated or less accessible to conscious control. For example, the autonomous nervous system (SNS and PSNS in Figure 4) cannot be controlled by an act of will (see 5th Fundamental of BPT).

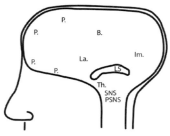

Figure 4

P. = personality
B. = body
La. = language
Im. = images
LS = limbic system
Th. = Thalamus
SNS = sympathetic nervous system
PSNS = parasympathetic nervous system

Neuroscientists have been able to confirm something that Buddhists have known for many centuries: a distinction between initial feelings and subsequent emotions. When we perceive something, the first sensory impression initially stimulates a type of basic control unit found in the deeper levels of the brain: the thalamus (Th. in Figure 4). From here, the impulses are forwarded directly to the limbic system (LS in Figure 4)—this is our feelings centre. This means that the first input stimulus occurs without rational interpretation. It does not yet lead to the "mature" emotions, instead creating a diffuse emotional basic pattern that in turn leads to a tension, which can be positive, negative or neutral. After this, the higher regions of the brain receive the stimulus and interpret it based on previous experiences. This takes a few milliseconds. Only then do the emotions arise, which we perceive as anger, sadness, fear etc. Buddhists refer to these initial tensions as primary feelings and the latter as secondary emotions.

Primary feelings become secondary emotions

A Primary feeling	B Evaluation		C Secondary emotion	
–	individually	+	+	e.g. curiosity, anticipation
	individually	–	–	e.g. fear, anger
+	individually	+	+	e.g. happiness, contentment
	individually	–	–	e.g. greed, craving
~	individually	+	+	e.g. calmness, serenity
	individually	–	–	e.g. boredom

Any specific situation creates within us (A) a tension which is either uncomfortable (-), comfortable (+) or neutral (~). These are our primary feelings. Depending upon our previous experiences, these are interpreted individually and (B) evaluated. Only then do we experience (C) a secondary emotion, such as anger, happiness or boredom. For example, if we are walking through the park and a stranger approaches us this might trigger (A) an uncomfortable tension (primary feeling). This is perceived, compared with previous experiences, interpreted and evaluated (B). Based on this, a secondary emotion then arises (C) which will be correspondingly negative (e.g. fear of the stranger) or positive (e.g. curiosity about the stranger). This whole process happens within milliseconds so it is hardly possible to be aware of it in detail without a specially trained power of attention.

> This makes it clear that we create our emotions ourselves, based on our prior experiences.

Although we will be taking a very close look at the positive and negative primary feelings in column A, the importance of the often neglected neutral feelings (~) should be emphasised here. Unfortunately there is a tendency to assume that they all fall into the category of "boredom", but if we pay careful attention we recognise that a better understanding of this category helps us to experience the healthy effects of calmness and freedom.

So our prior experiences shape our current experience of the world as strongly as our individual preferences and personality patterns, which have a direct effect on our interpretation scheme. However, current external influences are also important: In one experiment, subjects received an injection without any detailed explanation of what effect this might have. The subjects were divided into two groups and each group waited in a different room. One group encountered an angry person and the other a euphoric person. Even though they had all received the same injection (adrenaline, a natural stimulant found in all humans), some subjects became angry and others euphoric—exactly corresponding to the external circumstances they encountered.

Experiments like this appear to show that we do not only have one single *automatic* response to a particular stimulus; the emotion we develop depends on our own way of interpreting the situation we find ourselves in, which in turn depends on both external references and internal factors such as our prior experiences.

Emotions therefore appear to be more ambiguous than we might often want to believe. Our individual ways of interpreting stimuli vary from day to day, from mood to mood and from situation to situation. Nonetheless, we can also recognise typical patterns or tendencies for each person.

Let us remind ourselves of the Buddhist model of character formation (see 6th Fundamental of BPT). According to this, our *intentions* lead to our *deeds*. Repeating these creates *habits*. Our *character* develops from these and then in turn shapes our *destiny*. So if we experience or initiate particular repetitions, this plays a significant role in the development of our habitual patterns and formation of our character or personality. If we apply this understanding to our issue of the interpretation of basic feelings, we can see that we should take a critical look at spontaneous (mis-)interpretations and also start looking for reaction patterns which are typical for us. Here we can make use of the character typology (grasping, aversive, confused) derived from the Buddhist teachings on the Three Poisons or Three Unwholesome Roots (see 8th Fundamental of BPT).

The BPT psychotherapeutic process for working with emotional reaction patterns always happens in a particular order:
- Firstly, we have to train ourselves to become aware of the very quick, generally spontaneous and unconscious way these reactions arise, from the initial stimulus through the diffuse primary feelings to the secondary emotional reactions.
- Then we cast a critical light on the patterns of interpretation, which manipulate our emotions.

The therapeutic path in each situation often involves taking a couple of steps backwards, as if we are rewinding the film in slow-motion, from C to B to A, in order to take a closer look at the process. This can help us, for example, to realise that anger (C) is a secondary emotion. We observe this emotion within us, without condemning or even evaluating it. (After all, there have been many situations in life when our anger was actually helpful.) At this point, we become mindfully aware of our thoughts and urge to evaluate or judge (B), which in turn "feed" our emotions.
- Then we continue the slow-motion rewind and explore our primary physical feeling (A). Regular practice helps us to smooth out the jerkiness of the picture as we rewind, providing an ever clearer insight into the processes at work.
- Eventually it happens so smoothly that our spontaneously and unconsciously arisen emotion (C), such as anger, dissolves almost as quickly, leaving perhaps nothing more than (A) a tingling in our stomach and a slight tension in our shoulders or neck.
- Continued mindfulness practice then allows us to become aware of how these, too, change and dissolve.
- Later, we can conduct a more profound analysis of the character patterns which lead to our habitual interpretation tendencies.

These facts are extremely important but often quite difficult to convey. In fact, we have to be extremely careful in our efforts to cultivate and strengthen *personal responsibility* (assuming complete responsibility for our own emotions and actions). It is important to appreciate that this whole area touches on related issues such as guilt and failure, as well as aspects such as self-control, our capacity to exert influence and self-efficacy.

It needs to be noted here that 99% of all situations we encounter in our everyday life present us with an opportunity to assume personal responsibility, and it is important that we do so. However, this cannot be said to apply in exactly the same way in extreme situations such as natural or man-made disasters, the death of a loved one or experiences of violence. Nonetheless, at a basic level, exactly the same inner evaluation processes do take place.

We generally believe that our emotions *simply* arise within us *automatically*. According to this view, we are actually just the perceiver (and in many cases, the victim) of our emotions. If this is the case—and if we do not carefully control the process of emotional development described above—then it follows quite naturally that we only really experience the unhealthy end product: for example, anger, sadness or fear. This in turn easily leads to identification: I *am* angry; I *am* sad; or I *am* scared. However, once we have begun to intensively pursue the path of insight described in this book, we then take a more self-critical look at this process. Perhaps we are not quick enough to catch the process in action but nonetheless we are still able to come to a different conclusion about the end-product: I have created my anger/sadness/fear myself and strengthened it with angry/sad/fearful thoughts.

Step for step we become able to interrupt these previously unconscious processes earlier and earlier. After a period of patient training and practice, we will be able to perceive our physical tensions in a more sophisticated way and learn how to carefully control their further development, ensuring they end up in healthy emotions.

Similarly, we generally believe that our feelings are mostly created by external circumstances. Of course, this is blatantly true for the pain that arises if I hit my thumb with a hammer. However, here we are referring to emotional reactions to a pre-existing pain (see 11th Fundamental of BPT on the topic of our suffering). With specific mind training, we can experience the truth behind the idea that our own thoughts further worsen the pain of an arisen unpleasant experience. For example, we suffer a defeat, which of course is an unpleasant experience in itself, but then we add to this in the form of the accusations levelled by our "inner judge".

Of course, there are examples which appear to be clear situations where suffering is inevitable, such as the death of a family's only child. The parents are inconsolable. But what happens if we change the situation: The parents have ten children instead of one. Are they just as inconsolable? It might be very uncomfortable to ponder this question, but it does serve to suggest that even in apparently clear cases, our emotions are very dependent on ourselves, our life circumstances and our thoughts.

Even if it is not always possible to keep this rapidly developing process in check, we can understand that there is another chance to ensure a healthy result: A negative feeling does not inevitably mean that the end result is negative.

Emotions are not positive or negative— they are healthy or unhealthy

The Buddhist concept of the connection between feelings and emotions as described above explains why Buddhist therapists do not categorically devalue negative feelings or aspire towards positive ones. In fact, in Buddhism and in Buddhist Psychotherapy there is no judgemental distinction made between positive and negative emotions. Instead, we distinguish between *healthy* and *unhealthy* emotions.

Positive feelings such as enjoyment quite often lead to problematic habits such as attachments, neediness, longings and even addiction, in turn leading to a variety of further conflicts and suffering. In a similar way, negative feelings such as anger can actually be helpful for us and other people (e.g. for protection and defence) or usefully serve us in activities needing determination, courage and energy. Of course, this is only true if we *deal with them carefully and mindfully*.

A further example shows how the same emotion (desire) can be regarded as both an *unhealthy positive* emotion and a *healthy positive* emotion. The former could be the desire for status symbols which might feel good in the short term but in the medium or long-term create further suffering. An example of the latter could be the desire to help others, leading to healthy circumstances.

> It is impossible to categorically describe most emotions as good or bad, right or wrong. For this reason, there is no reason to suppress any emotions at all. Nonetheless, every emotion should be monitored to check for the conditions that led to it arising—i.e. our patterns of interpretation—and its possible healthy or unhealthy effects.

An important component of our therapeutic training will be to actively strengthen healthy emotions and transform unhealthy ones. In the 19th Fundamental of BPT we will learn how to carry this out.

In addition, it is worth noting here that one of the first and very significant phases of the BPT consists of training how to distinguish between healthy and unhealthy emotions. If we can thoroughly understand, internalise and implement this distinction then we can set off on the path of liberation from this aspect, drastically reducing the frequency with which we experience unhealthy conditions and increasing the speed with which we can transform them. After this we then stop aspiring to healthy emotions, resulting in a condition of liberation from the polarities. Adopting the approach of *having no intentions* can then consolidate itself in our life in a healthy way. This means that we are increasingly free of the pattern of thinking in terms of two categories; we no longer experience good or bad, praise or criticism, winning or losing, affection or rejection, peace or conflict etc. Freedom from these category pairs is a profoundly joyful serenity free of the compulsion to evaluate or judge (see 1st Fundamental of BPT).

How Long Do Emotions Last?

After learning how our emotions arise, the second major topic is the duration of emotions or how they are maintained. As with the first topic, the theoretical background is not easy to convey, but in Buddhist Psychotherapy we do not simply have to accept these facts at face value—we receive instructions to help us experience them for ourselves (see 19th Fundamental of BPT).

Normally we have the impression that we feel an intense emotion for a long time. We might feel angry for hours or the whole evening and we sometimes feel sad for days or weeks. And the feeling of being in love—we want this to last for months! However, Buddhist teachings and neuroscientific experiments give similar insights into this topic suggesting a much shorter lifespan.

As a biological level, the perception of feeling needs chemical messengers (neurotransmitters, peptides etc.) and electrical potentials (in the millivolt range) in special areas of our brain—and other organs, too. These chemicals and electrical voltages can only be maintained by our nerve cells for a relatively short time. Without new input, they both decline rapidly. So at the most, an emotion can only last some 20-30 seconds.

However, this decline generally does not appear to take place, with emotions often remaining tangible for a very long time. How can this be consistent with the biological reality described above? The fact is that we keep our emotions alive. If we were to take any particular emotion and regard it in a genuinely neutral way, we would discover that our emotions level out and "burn up" after a short time. Our thoughts, too, quickly move off in a different direction.

In practice, however, our thoughts strengthen our emotions. For example, when we experience an annoying situation, a negative tension arises within us. This is followed immediately by our interpretations and the feeling of anger. Our rational mind now calls up previous similar or related experiences and based on these it starts to produce new angry thoughts, continuing this for a long time ("What is he thinking of? Wait, I'm not going to let him get away with that. If he does that again I'm going to let him have a piece of my mind. How could he...? I've always been so polite and now he does that! That's outrageous!") This chain of thoughts keeps provoking the emotion anew and keeps it alive.

A healthy way to deal with our emotions

Buddhist Psychotherapy can help us to learn an alternative approach. Of course, we will still experience the initial situations and feel negative tensions arising within us. However, since we are now aware of how our emotions arise, we can react mindfully to the thoughts which are beginning to seed within us. Now we observe where the strongest tensions are in our body. We breathe mindfully, consciously and regularly. We take great care not to "pour oil on the fire" of our emotion (in the above example, our anger). By means of mindful observation, we sap the energy of the chain of thoughts which previously arose unconsciously. We will then notice that our physical tensions are also changing and decreasing. (For more details see 19th Fundamental of BPT.)

Readers might react to this portrayal with a sceptical "Yes, but ..." or even annoyance because we cannot imagine that other types of reaction are possible. Or we might protest that our reactions are simply the way they are and we are entitled to react in this way. In Buddhist Psychotherapy we take a long and deep look at this topic, including the very frequent observation that people prefer to assert their "rights to suffer" and stick to the approach they know rather than adopting a new path and suffering less. Of course, taking a new path is full of risk and uncertainty—this is why we need support and experienced therapists. On our own and without mind training we are hardly able to observe our emotions in an analytical yet non-judgemental way.

Practice helps us to control our predispositions

Although we all have a wide range of very different predispositions, none of these (even a predisposition to violence) is present in such a way that it makes the bearer a "victim" of their genetics. Many of our predispositions manifest themselves automatically in all healthy people, for example, the predisposition to the ability to see. From the moment of our birth onwards we have eyes, optic nerves and a complex nervous system that is able to interpret impulses from the optic nerves. In a similar way, we also have many further predispositions which manifest during our development, adapt to the circumstances we find ourselves in and are then available to us.

There is also a wide range of attitudes or predispositions which are only present as *potentials*: We are born with predispositions to speech, walking upright, showing compassion, behaving ethically etc. If these potentials are never fostered they will never manifest. Although almost everyone grows up in an environment that fosters the potential to speak or walk upright, it is not unknown for people to grow up in environments where compassion or ethical behaviour are absent or undervalued. So it is not unusual to need special training to "catch up" in our development of some of these healthy mental states.

What Do Our Emotional Reactions Look Like?

It is to be hoped that we all have particular ways of responding to our emotional reactions in different situations. However, it is worth taking a closer look at these processes in order to check for repetitive behaviour patterns.

The question we should ask ourselves here specifically relates to our typical reactions or personal behaviour spectrum when we feel under pressure. There are generally both physical reactions—such as strong heart beats, pressure in the stomach, neck tensions or perspiration—and corresponding psychological tensions—experienced as accompanying emotions resulting from our interpretation patterns as described above.

Much of this is positive but there are numerous negative physical-mental-emotional states which we would like to be rid of. Without specific mind training, such as offered by Buddhism and Buddhist Psychotherapy, we generally try to achieve this by means of stress-

and tension-reducing self-help techniques—some of which themselves are not completely healthy.

What self-healing techniques do we usually apply if we sense pressure and a "storm brewing within us"? As psychotherapists we can start by working with our clients to make a judgement-free list of all the possibilities. The most common ways of behaving when people feel under pressure can be put into two categories: introverted or extraverted traits.

Depression	Aggression
Introversion	Extraversion
Examples of "swallowing" feelings: silence withdrawal/being reserved going to bed brooding alcohol medicines cigarettes food/sweets	Examples of "letting out" feelings: arguing/shouting hitting sport/jogging chopping wood working going for a walk cleaning shopping

The two columns represent contrasting strategies for dealing with inner pressure. In the left-hand column, the pressure is kept within. These processes can be interpreted as depressive because one of the characteristics of depression is that everything is "swallowed". Depressive people become more and more reserved, lose their drive and express themselves less. The opposite of depression is aggression. This describes a process and not a permanently angry attitude. Here the energy is let out directly.

Are we able to freely decide whether to react in an introverted or extraverted manner in a particular situation? Or do we tend to generally choose the same type of reaction? The decisive aspects here are our personality and character styles, our current psychological and physiological constitution and current external factors.

The inner pressure cooker

A couple of metaphors might serve to help us understand these inner processes better. Since we often make use of simple, visual examples in Buddhist Psychotherapy, it is worth reminding ourselves that these images are not chosen at random; they are based on scientifically measurable psychosomatic processes. The intensity of arousal patterns in our autonomous nervous system can be measured exactly. Nevertheless, scientific facts are often less memorable than everyday examples, so here we make use of the pressure cooker metaphor.

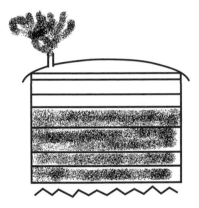

Figure 5

As its very name suggests, the pressure cooker is the most obvious example to take if we want to talk about feelings of pressure. In Figure 5 we see this pot on a flame. The flame illustrates the range of external stress factors, such as being pressed for time. The pot is never empty—our life is never empty of experience. Together with the help-seeker, the therapist can explore which uncomfortable things are filling our inner pressure cooker and how quickly it fills up. Does it take weeks, days, hours or just a couple of seconds? Does the speed at which the level rises depend on the individual acute experiences of stress? How high is the level now, exactly? The steam escaping through the valve illustrates our stress symptoms. What do these look like in detail? Strong heart beats, unease, nervousness, perspiration, indigestion? Do we first feel these symptoms when the level is already very high? What can we do to notice the rising level earlier?

Frequently, we do not even notice that the level is rising. Or we may notice it but ignore it, even if it is painful. And even if we do not completely ignore it, we often do not take it seriously enough. We convince ourselves that we just have to hold out and keep suffering a little longer, since the future will hopefully be better.

So let us return to our pressure cooker. It is interesting to remember that the current situation is dependent on many years of external and internal influences. Our inner pressure cooker looked very different during our childhood, as illustrated in Figure 6. We can see that it used to have a range of different valves at different heights on the body of the pot.

Figure 6

As children we were able to scream immediately when we were angry, laugh when we were amused and cry when we were sad. This whole palette could sometimes unfold in only 10 minutes: from anger to humour to sadness. But then we were "brought up". Many of us were brought up to be "seen but not heard". We were brought up to be well-behaved pupils, sitting silently on the school benches. We were brought up to talk calmly and rationally ("There's no need to shout."). We were brought up to keep ourselves under control. Much of this advice may well have been helpful or at least well-intentioned but it often meant that we had to close our pressure valves—especially if a strict regime was used to enforce and teach these rules of behaviour. So how many valves are still open and can be used today? If we only have a few valves or if our inner level is often very high, it can be very difficult to practice the mindfulness we so desperately need. We then have to resort to emergency measures which in turn often have negative consequences for us or for others.

As well as the stress reactions to let off pressure already mentioned—symbolised by the cloud of steam—we also use up tremendous amounts of energy simply keeping the inner pressure cooker intact. Many symptoms of exhaustion can be traced back to the energy we had to use to "keep ourselves together"—to stop the pot exploding. Many people simply do not have a clue what they can do when they feel how high their inner level is and how dangerous it could be to even touch the pot. This will then give rise to dangerous "vicious circles": If pressure is let off at this late stage it is experienced as an eruption and explosion, which often has very negative consequences. These create the impression that letting off steam is negative or dangerous, which in turn increases the tendency to look the other way and not let off steam, even when the level in the pressure cooker is still in the early stages of rising. Which then increases the magnitude of the eruption when steam is finally let off, and so on.

Our "alarm" buttons—the power that others have over us

If we are walking around with an inner pressure cooker in this condition, we generally notice a further peculiarity: Red buttons begin to form on its (our) surface. One wrong word from another person, the (wrong) person looks at us in the wrong way, a minor disagreement—all of these were then become the proverbial last straw. Our button is pressed. The alarm sounds and the pot explodes.

This gives other people a great deal of power over us; it makes us very dependent on them. Anyone can shake us up at the touch of a button—with one wrong sentence. Do we really want to give other people so much power over us?

We are thirsting for freedom from these dependencies.

This illustration serves to help us become aware of our own, often unconscious, patterns of reaction and hopefully also to encourage us to take up introspection. Our attention should definitely be directed to our inner constitution as well as our external concerns. In this regard, we should once again make use of the Wisdom of the Middle Way and its practical techniques (see 9th Fundamental of BPT). Here we will simply mention the relevant points and refer the reader to the practical instructions in the 19th Fundamental.

In the table above we saw the two columns with very extreme examples of strategies for how to deal with inner tension: depressive and aggressive traits. Now we can add a third column by taking the Middle Way.

Depression	The Middle Way	Aggression
Swallowing		Letting out
Examples:	Examples:	Examples:
Remaining silent	Mindfulness	Arguing/shouting
Withdrawal	Breath	Hitting
Going to bed	Letting go	Sport/jogging
Brooding	Relaxing	Chopping wood
Alcohol	Meditation	Working
Drugs		Walking
Cigarettes	Dialogue to clarify the situation	Cleaning
Eating/Sweets	Searching for a solution	Shopping
etc.		etc.

Of course, the whole spectrum of possibilities is always available to us so we can also remain silent or even argue but we will increasingly internalise a way of dealing with situations without inner resistance, attachment or negativity and with more joy, compassion and care for ourselves and others.

We have to find out how to achieve a healthy and flexible way of dealing with our inner tensions. Some differences in this regard are expressed in a very polarised way in the following West/East table:

Western way	Buddhism
Let "it" out	Middle Way is healthy Emotions are impermanent Be mindful, critical and alert with your emotions
Trust your feelings	Feelings, even positive ones, can mislead us
Arguments (e.g. in partnerships) can: • create intimacy • be a sign of passion • show that we are not indifferent to the other person	Unhealthy patterns are fallowed when we argue

How Can We Deal with Our Emotions Practically?

The four underlying secondary emotions which we most commonly suffer from are anger, sadness, fear and pain. Having studied this 7th Fundamental well, we now have a range of insights into suitable ways of dealing with our emotions. In the 19th Fundamental we will receive practical instructions about how to use these insights as practical tools in our process of transformation.

> Buddhists apply the Four Principles of Transformation (RAIN):
> 1) Recognition
> 2) Acceptance
> 3) Investigation
> 4) Non-identification

When we feel emotional reactions rising within us (whether fear, sadness, anger or pain), we should (1) *recognise* that these are *our* emotions which we are feeling. Nobody else created them for us. Of course, we like to blame others but this 7th Fundamental should have made it clear who carries the main responsibility: we do.

We do not dispute the current situation, we do not dither, we do not get tangled up in additional (self-) reproach: we (2) *accept* it. This does not mean at all that we simply "hold out" passively, stuck in our problems. Rather, we put an end to unnecessary additional suffering.

We carefully look inward, remaining very alert to our inner processes. We (3) *investigate* our thoughts and check the external and internal conditions.

In particular, we do not let ourselves be reduced to any fixed roles or patterns. There is (4) *no identification* with roles which compel us to burden ourselves and others with unhealthy and negative behaviour (see 13th, 16th and 19th Fundamentals of BPT).

If we apply these principles step-for-step we will increase the frequency of the occasions when we do not produce any further unhealthy thoughts that make our emotions more negative than they are or maintain them for longer than they naturally occur. For example, our negative primary feelings will not be fed and strengthened by angry thoughts; the feelings can then "burn out" by themselves. We can feel them as physical tensions, breathe into them in a balancing way, draw out their negative charge and let them ebb away. In this way, fear, sadness and anger can simply dissolve and our pain will not become excessive.

The crux of it all: pain

This feeling is very elementary and has a special, manifold significance (see 11th Fundamental on the topic of suffering).

We can distinguish between physiological, psychological, and biographical pain. Nonetheless, these different versions of pain are very often experienced as a single, indistinguishable bundle, with a particular characteristic such as dull, shooting, excruciating or stabbing. We will get to know some very effective measures and exercises to combat pain when we take a look at the 19th Fundamental.

Mary H comes to us because of some very difficult relationship problems. She feels attacked by her partner on an almost daily basis and is hardly ever able to calm down afterwards. Really, she ought to split up with him, as she says herself, but at the feelings level she is still very attached to him. She finds it particularly distressing that her partner knows her so well but can nonetheless still be so ruthless with her, hurting her on a daily basis with his inconsiderate words. If only he could stop doing this!

Mary needed quite a while before she could accept this Fundamental of the BPT. She examined her "alarm buttons" and gradually she was able to assume more responsibility for her own feelings. In particular the exercise which will be described later using the self-instruction "I let my feelings burn out" was very helpful for her. Mary reported using every social situation as a chance to practice this exercise during the initial period of therapy. This gave her chances to observe her emotional reactions and get to know her old automatisms. Becoming less emotionally dependent on others was a benefit which she found to be particularly helpful.

This Fundamental Should Convey the Following:

We recognise that it is *our* interpretations and *our* experiences which turn our spontaneous primary feelings into the secondary emotions, such as anger, sadness and fear, which so often lead to suffering for us or for others.

We recognise that *we* keep our emotions alive with *our* untamed mind. It has to be made patently clear that we are always talking about *our* emotions. They belong to no-one other than *us*. *We* are responsible for them!

We recognise that it can be necessary to train the development of wholesome emotions.

It is a fundamentally important milestone in our therapeutic work if we can recognise and truly understand how our feelings and emotions arise and develop, and how they can be controlled and modified. Once we have recognised, understood and internalised the fact that each of our emotions is nothing other than a form of tension within us, out of which we form something ourselves (the emotion) then we really have taken one significant step towards liberation.

Our goal is often a calmer mind, but surely not at the cost of sacrificing our feelings. We can achieve liberation *in the midst* of our emotions and not by trying to deny them.

Recognising, internalising and implementing these facts with regard to our emotions leads to liberation and enlightenment.

The 8th
Fundamental of Buddhist Psychotherapy

Recognise and Convey the Truth of Our Inner Nobility

> See the inner nobility and beauty of all human beings.
>
> JACK KORNFIELD

This Fundamental of Buddhist Psychotherapy examines the "statement of principles" concerning the view of human beings which underlies the approaches taken by Buddhism and Buddhist Psychotherapy. The high value placed on life and all living beings becomes clear with a presentation of the concept of the Inner Nobility at the heart of every human being. So here we are posing the question: What can we find *behind* a person's facade and their functional processes?

The Western View

Western psychotherapists assume that there are relatively fixed personality and character structures called ego functions. These are not present at birth; they form during childhood and only become stable during late puberty—provided there are no disturbances. Many psychotherapists only consider the ego functions to be stable in "healthy" people. According to this viewpoint, there are many sources of disturbance which can occur during the whole period of development from birth until consolidation in late puberty. It is therefore the disturbances which are decisive for the degree of stability of our underlying personality structures—our foundations.

The Buddhist View

Buddhists have a fundamentally different view here: They do not even assume that we human beings have a fixed personality and a solid self. These are illusory, according to Buddhism. This viewpoint then states that we have inner qualities which are more or less immune to negative influences. Surrounding this core are various layers and patterns which we carry within us; some of these are helpful and some less so. They can also be seen as containing bundles of problems and false perceptions. All of this can be experienced if we patiently perform particular exercises, enabling us to penetrate ever deeper through these layers of wrong perceptions, reaching areas imbued with personally and universally healthy qualities. We will also see how these experiences render tangible our own value and the high value of all life.

The structures we reach when we have penetrated through the various personality patterns and protection layers can be referred to as our Inner Nobility.

What Is Our Inner Nobility?

The American meditation teacher Jack Kornfield, who trained for many years in Buddhist monasteries in Asia, tells the tale of a large clay Buddha statue from a monastery in North Thailand which attracted pilgrims for hundreds of years. Unfortunately, the cracks in its clay surface became deeper and deeper so it was deemed necessary to undertake repairs. As a monk shone a light into the cracks to determine the extent of the damage, he discovered that the clay was only a thick layer surrounding a solid gold Buddha statue. Quite probably, at some point in history the gold statue had been covered in clay to "hide" it from plunderers. Now that the clay has been removed, the gold statue in its full glory has become an even greater site of pilgrimage for visitors from all over the world.

From a Buddhist point of view, we assume that *every* person has this gold core within them (Inner Nobility*) with different layers of clay being applied to protect it from a very early age. At this point we should warn the reader that this metaphor does have one disadvantage because it suggests that we can find a *solid* core within us. So we should not try to search for a fixed, solid structure but instead remember that the gold here stands for a *non-material* quality within us.

This Inner Nobility is our internal source of power and our gateway to liberation. It is a symbol of our inherent value and the value of all life. Unfortunately, we human beings feel driven to protect this core quality. This process of self-protection begins at an age when we cannot yet speak and therefore do not have the opportunity to store our memories as language. So these early self-protection measures are no longer accessible in the later stages of our development.

This process affects *every* person—not just children who suffer trauma at an early age. Every infant has the very early experience that not all of their needs will be fulfilled immediately. Their environment can also trigger many fears; this is understandable when we consider the limited capacity of an infant to react. So in this way, protective layers are formed in *every* person in infancy because of the need for security and to reduce their fears. As our development progresses, these can then express themselves in very different ways, depending on the interaction between the experiences of the growing child and youth with their genetic predispositions. For some very fortunate people, these protective layers might not need to de-

---

* *Translator's Note:* The term "noble" or "nobility" also has to be understood in its Buddhist context. Translators and teachers have often discussed how to translate the original term ariya and the reader is referred to this discussion. The word is a common word but, especially in Britain, the immediate association for "noble" may be a class of persons distinguished by rank. In BPT we are using it to describe a quality which everyone possesses, so it can perhaps better be understood as a form of "excellence". Many scholars in fact assert that Buddha used the term ariya in that sense.

velop very strongly, whereas for others they have to form one upon the other, much like the annual rings of a tree (Figure 7).

Figure 7

In the short- and mid-term, these protective layers reduce our pain and fears but in the long term they turn into our "prison walls", preventing us from clearly perceiving and making contact with ourselves and the external world. In some cases, the thickness of these layers leads to people feeling isolated, emotionally restricted and almost numb to feelings. Very often we then undertake more or less unconscious self-healing attempts. In particular, high alcohol and drug consumption can be interpreted as one of these helpless attempts to tear down our inner walls and regain access to the feelings of connection and happiness created by contact to our Inner Nobility. However, these attempts are doomed to failure. They poison our minds and our body and only create vicarious satisfaction; this might appear to be almost what we are looking for but does not really closely resemble it in any way at all.

Our layers of protection have very significant consequences for us and also for our contact with the external world: For many people, their interaction with others could be described as "clay covering to clay covering". Since we cannot immediately recognise the Inner Nobility of another person, we have to understand that all of their personal characteristics, interpersonal conflicts and problems are located in or on these layers of clay. That is why we mistake this clay surface for our human essence. So we need to constantly remind ourselves that all humans carry this Inner Nobility within them when we are in contact with others or taking a deeper look within ourselves.

> This Buddhist understanding of our Inner Nobility, if we can internalise and realise it profoundly, is sufficient alone to lead to respect and lasting peace with ourselves and others.

Buddhism and Buddhist Psychotherapy can help us to penetrate these layers of clay, gaining access to them and loosening them, becoming more aware of them and eventually making them more flexible or even removing them.

The corresponding image of humans

Many psychotherapists are taught that our personality only develops very slowly as we grow up, hopefully gaining stability, health and uniformity. These developing personality structures correspond to the skills and functions we learn as we grow up, such as the ability to test reality, control our impulses, tolerate frustration and judge other people in a stable way. According to this model, these functions or structures make up our character and our self.

This theory would suggest that we are not born with an inner core but first have to form it. So if there are disturbances in infancy—for example, any form of stress—this inner core does not have a chance to become firm and stable. This compares to the Buddhist view which we have already described, where disturbances only affect the *outer* "layers of clay" but not the "gold" at the *core*—the essence or Inner Nobility which makes us human. From a Buddhist point of view many of our delusions, problems and conflicts result from this false opinion that we are made up of only these outer layers. This opinion prevents us from seeing our core of Inner Nobility. This point of view does seem to offer a plausible explanation for problems of low self-esteem, feelings of isolation and abandonment, and the issue of self-alienation. It might also help to explain the common feeling of being separate from nature, and even xenophobia. If we can regain access to our Inner Nobility, we will also gain a new experience of our own individual life energy and universal sensations such as all-encompassing interconnection.

Inner Nobility and a Variety of Personalities

There is much in common between the Buddhist and Western views of human character and personality, but there are also some clear differences.

The Western psychotherapy model

Many Western psychotherapists learn a model which could be described as a process model. The quality of the personality structures or ego functions can be ascertained relatively well by observation, test procedures, self-description and description by others.

How effective are our ego functions? In other words, how effective are our abilities of frustration tolerance, delayed gratification, reality testing, self-protection, affect regulation and impulse control, flexibility, ability to form attachments to others, social behaviour, self-reflection or introspection, anticipation, empathy? How stable are our object relations—for example, how stable is our evaluating perception of people close to us?

According to this model, if a person's ego functions are almost completely impaired then psychotic (i.e. manic, schizophrenic) symptoms occur. If these personality structures are less damaged, but still extremely unstable, then personality disorders manifest. Depending on the severity of the damage, these could be schizoid, borderline, avoidance, dependent or obsessive-compulsive disorders. If the structural disorders are not so severe or in cases where the level of ego functioning is adequate, the disturbances can be called personality trait accentuations instead of personality disorders. For example a person could be said to have an accentuated obsessive-compulsive personality trait. If the personality structures are relatively stable the conflicts are treated using the notion of neurosis. Neuroses can be considered as a type of "diversion" which arises because our culture very often does not permit drives to be satisfied directly.

This model places every human being somewhere on the scale between schizophrenic psychosis, personality disorder, accentuated personality trait and neurosis. The ego functions listed above are the crucial factor in determining a person's position on this scale—their level of (un)happiness.

So in the opinion of many *Western* psychotherapists, these ego functions form the inner core of a human being.

The Buddhist model

In contrast, Buddhists consider the disturbances in the ego functions to be located in the *external* layers. From a Buddhist point of view, every human is basically whole, healthy and good. Unfortunately, at a very early stage we lose our access to this wholeness, healthiness and goodness—in a sense, we can say that we lose our way.

> According to the Buddhist model, a person can be suffering deeply yet at the same time completely healthy on the inside.

This assumption of basic healthiness and goodness makes Buddhism and Buddhist Psychotherapy considerably different from Western models of illness and human personality. Buddhist Psychotherapy considers itself to be a type of navigation system which we use to find our way again and rediscover our Inner Nobility—our true healthy being. One of the main tasks of the Buddhist therapist is to facilitate contact between the help-seeker and their innate inner qualities. So in a way, the help-seeker does not learn anything really new. Instead, they rediscover a connection to something that was always there but where the contact was broken at a very early age.

Namaste

In our Western culture, only very few people are declared to be holy and these saints are generally only canonised many years after the end of their lifetime, during which they exhibited their extraordinary behaviour. Imagine a society where everybody is holy! How different would the internalisation and realisation of saintly values be in such a society?! And what effect would this have on our life together? In a sense, this is exactly what Buddhism is trying to achieve. And this is also reflected in the Indian greeting "Namaste!" which can be translated as "I bow to the light within you" or "I bow to the divine within you".

Different Buddhist personality styles

When we as Buddhists think about our established personality traits, we have to bear in mind that we are not referring to our innermost foundations but to the auxiliary structures which have formed *on* or *in* our protective layers. In this way, many centuries before the birth of psychoanalysis, Buddhists recognised that people can develop relatively stable personality styles at a particular level of functioning. It needs to be noted that these should carefully be understood as *dispositions*, which we can use as "tools" as we go through life. However, we *are* not our tools. We *are* not the same as our personality aspects or personality styles. They are just functioning units located on our *outer* protective layers.

The three different Buddhist temperaments or personality types are
- Grasping personality
- Aversive personality
- Confused personality

There is no ranking for these three types; each of them has its own special features, strengths and weaknesses.

How can we recognise our own personality type?
Jack Kornfield presented us with an example to illustrate this typology. Imagine you are invited to the housewarming party of a close friend. You enter the house for the first time. What are the first things you notice?

Is your attention drawn to the attractive wall colour, the comfortable sofa and the large living room with its cosy fireplace? So you tend to look first at the attractive things and make comments about these? Then you probably belong to the *grasping* personality type.

Is the single glazing in the windows the first thing you notice? Your attention is immediately drawn to the small size of the kitchen and the neighbouring house, which is much too close? Can you quickly assess the disadvantages and deficits? Then you probably belong to the *aversive* personality type.

Or perhaps you arrive a little late and are so overwhelmed by all the new impressions that you do not really notice the details of the house at all. You are mainly interested in your friend, not their house. So you probably belong to the *confused* personality type.

The *grasping* temperament is aware of much beauty but this love of nice things brings with it the risk of attachments, clinging, entanglement and longing. Negative things tend to be suppressed.

The *aversive* temperament is very discerning but can tend towards pessimism, isolation and aggressive behaviour. Here, positive things tend to be suppressed.

The *confused* temperament seems to be very unattached but can also appear to sink into chaos. External stimuli are often suppressed.

Since Buddhists do not consider these personality traits to be our inner core, they can be brought into conscious view and made useful by means of discipline and mindfulness. However, like their Western therapist counterparts, Buddhists also accept that these strong dispositions are generally not completely transformable. A grasping personality will generally remain basically different to the aversive temperament, but the former can develop into a free, conscious aesthete and the latter into a free, conscious, constructively critical person. And the confused temperament can become a free, conscious, open-minded person.

Our core
and our sense of self

So Buddhists have notions of relatively fixed personality traits but they also claim that the ego, self or "I" is an illusion. Are these two views compatible?

According to Buddhism, our Inner Nobility should not be understood as a solid core. We do not really have a firmly established, stable, permanent self, although we do permanently appear to perceive this "I": *I* want..., *I* think..., *I* have... etc.

This feeling of "I" or self begins to form very early. We begin our lives without ego functions; we do not have any abilities to perceive or set boundaries. We are directly connected to the world: If the surroundings are funny, children are amused, too; if everything around them is tense, they become tense, too. Perhaps this dependence is not all bad, but we do appear to experience it at least as ambivalent because we soon develop a desire for control and our survival instinct starts looking for possibilities of protection.

As protective layers are formed, a feeling of success develops in parallel and then, building on this, the beginnings of the sense of self: *I* can do this, *I* have this or that effect, etc. Children take extreme pleasure in proving or discovering their self-efficacy—their capacity to bring about effects in the external world. And this in turn leads to more feelings of self. Strengths and weaknesses are experienced. This leads to a variety of identifications. *I am* a boy/girl. *I am* good/bad at maths. *I am* a talented/poor athlete. *I* have..., *I* belong to..., *I* love..., *I* hate..., *I* will..., *I* avoid..., etc. This process gains momentum and, unless it is treated with conscious mindfulness, becomes a lifelong end in itself.

If we sit down and try to list all of our identifications we might be surprised at the length of the list. It should include both our obvious roles and the beliefs and convictions connected with them: employee, mother of my son, daughter of my parents, partner, patient, woman, American, Christian, customer, athlete, friend, colleague and many more. Looking at this list we may begin to understand what Buddhists mean when they claim that the self or "I" arises because of identification and is kept alive through identification.

When we begin to give up one identification after the other, our ego (sense of self) decreases steadily. Even if I just weaken the identification "I am a hard-working employee", I will probably experience a slight reduction in stress and pressure and be able to relax a little more.

There is a Buddhist motto: No ego, no suffering.

It is well worth studying these connections in more detail, especially if we are working with patients suffering from extreme problems of self-esteem and self-image and who have previously thought much too little about their ego or sense of self.

Complementarity of Inner Nobility

Another important aspect is the experience of complementarity with regard to our Inner Nobility—we experience it as having two apparently contradictory characteristics.

Complementarity is best illustrated using the example of light. Depending on how we measure it in an experiment, a ray of light can be experienced either as a wave function or as a stream of particles. In other words it has both a material and a non-material nature. Our Inner Nobility also exhibits a complementarity because it has both an individual and a universal character. Depending on how we access it, we will feel intensive bliss as an *individual* or, if we pursue the path further, we will experience the *universal* quality within us. One way of interpreting this is that we feel the sensation of connection more clearly as we reduce the dominance of our perception of our (imaginary) self.

The many facets of our personality

As we presented in the 5th Fundamental on the topic of our body, modern research into the brain has confirmed that there is no clearly identifiable single place in the brain where the "I" or sense of self arises. Scientists describe the ego as a subjective perception comprising many processes taking place at different places and in different structures in our brain. This means that the ego or sense of "I" is not a fixed unit.

To put it in a nutshell: There is no uniform, permanent personality. This might not be easy to understand, particularly because we do not experience ourselves as "compound" or composite (made up of parts). We generally consider ourselves to be one person or personality. However, if we look more carefully we can recognise many different personalities within us. Perhaps we are always a very patient person around children but quite different when we are at work.

Very drastic personality changes have been observed as the result of injuries, accidents, shock and trauma, as well as other liminal experiences.

There is no convincing evidence for the belief in a lasting personality that always remains the same. For example, the science journalist Judith Rich Harris reports that pedagogical studies have shown how measures introduced in schools to improve social behaviour were effective at school but had no effect at home. This shows that we manifest our different personalities in different contexts.

Up to now there have been no studies which convincingly explain how a personality develops or how it develops exactly the way it does. There are indeed numerous studies which claim to demonstrate links between all sorts of early influences and later personality traits but the quality of the causal connections discovered can at best be described as weak. Nevertheless we believe—we want to believe—that we and our fellow human beings show signs of a fixed personality because we imprudently hope to be able to find support in something fixed and stable: a constant personality. For the same reason, even therapists are surprised when by chance they meet one of their depressive patients in the street—in a good mood and dressed up to go out.

Emotions also exhibit this variable nature even though we believe they have a degree of permanence. From the description given to us by our clients and from our own experience we know that we feel acute emotions over long stretches of time. However, although we appear to be sad the whole day, angry for hours or in pain for years, as we saw in the 7th Fundamental an emotion can only last for 10-30 seconds before the next feeling takes its place.

We are engaged in an unceasing attempt to avoid suffering and keep hold of happiness, so what would be the best strategy to secure lasting peace and happiness and eliminate suffering? This was exactly the question which Siddhartha Gautama set out to answer over 2500 years ago. He found the solution after he spent many years learning from other teachers and experimenting with his own ideas. The Buddha had to stand up to a wide range of tests, temptations, troubles and problems before his inner liberation—and after it, too.

Mike V needed a while before he could talk about his problems of self-esteem. In a sober, factual way he listed his many deficits and weaknesses. Differences which he perceived between himself and others were always interpreted self-critically. For Mike it was very healing to recognise that under the surface we really are all very different and that his assessments were almost always correct. Intensive meditation, guided at first, helped Mike gain access to the deeper aspects of our human existence. He gained a very strong sense of our basic needs, our physical processes and our inseparable interdependence as the foundation of being human. At this level, Mike was no longer aware of any significant differences and deficits. Becoming aware of his Inner Nobility—and that of all other human beings—was a key experience for Mike. For the first time ever, he was able to bring together his doubts and his longing for positive self-esteem.

This Fundamental Should Convey the Following:

We and all other human beings carry an Inner Nobility within us. This needs to be recognised, experienced, respected and appreciated—for ourselves and for others.

This Inner Nobility is like a golden core. It needs to be protected very early in life and this leads to the formation of protective layers which can, depending on the difficulties experienced, have different strengths and characteristics in different people.

All conflicts and problems are on or over the external protective layers—not in the core. They do not have the power to influence the Inner Nobility. It needs to be remembered that this golden core is a symbol for the high innate value of every life. It does not mean we really have a solid, permanent core.

The 9th
Fundamental of Buddhist Psychotherapy

Recognise and Convey the Wisdom of the Middle Way

> The middle way is found between all opposites.
> Rest in the middle.
>
> JACK KORNFIELD

The Wisdom of the Middle Way is one of the central teachings which the Buddha recognised some 2500 years ago and then passed on to his disciples. As a teaching it is one of the easiest to convey; as a philosophy it is certainly very reasonable and can be understood quickly; yet as a method it requires diligence to implement, as we shall see.

The Buddha spent the first years after his enlightenment conveying the contents of his first teaching to the people he met in northern India.

The famous teaching of the *First Turning of the Wheel of Dharma* **contains three significant statements:**
- Follow the Middle Way
- Use the insights to stay in the here and now and help yourself and others
- Understand the Four Noble Truths

In the following Fundamentals we will take a detailed look at these three elements because they represent the main building blocks of Buddhist teachings and can therefore also be considered as the foundation of Buddhist Psychotherapy.

The teachings on the Middle Way will be presented here in the 9th Fundamental of BPT. In the 10th Fundamental we will deal with the insights concerning staying in the here and now and using this to help yourself and others. The teaching of the Four Noble Truths will be covered in the 11th and 13th to 17th Fundamentals of BPT.

Following the Middle Way

His search for liberation from the ongoing experience of suffering led the Buddha-to-be to follow a range of different paths for many years. Legend has it that before he set off on his quest, Siddhartha Gautama led a life full of material riches and dedicated to pleasure. As he began his search for liberation he rejected this completely. He was able to benefit from the rich treasure of experiences already gained by Indian culture and studied with various meditation masters (Alara Kalama, Uddaka Ramaputta) who taught him the useful techniques he needed for a deep meditative absorption. However, he recognised that these important techniques, as rich and profound as they were, could not lead him to complete liberation. We should take careful note of this fact and understand that we, too, should not exclusively rely on meditative techniques. The other building blocks of Buddhist Psychotherapy should be studied and practiced equally seriously.

As his spiritual search continued, the Buddha-to-be is said to have lived ascetically until his body almost collapsed. In other words, he consumed less nourishment than his body actually needed. This phenomenon can be found in all cultures: When people set off on a mental-spiritual path they are often tempted to neglect their body and its demands or even to consciously spurn it. The physical aspects of life are often regarded negatively, fearfully suppressed, avoided or even demonised. For Siddhartha, this strategy brought him to the edge of death but not to the destination he was seeking: liberation.

So neither a life of pleasure nor an ascetic life had been free of suffering. Recognising this helped him realise that the path to liberation was not to be found in the extremes. According to legend, the Buddha-to-be overheard a musician tell his student, "If you tighten the string too much it will break but if the string is too slack, it will create no sound." The musician was talking about his lute but the Buddha-to-be realised that the message applied to him and how he was treating his body: Not too strong, not too weak, not too much, not too little-stay in the middle. Our body and our mind should be looked after with both *care* and *moderation*. This is the Wisdom of the Middle Way, implying that we should not pursue any extremes.

This insight might appear to be very straightforward but in practice (in everyday life) it is a never-ending tightrope walk and serves as a permanent touchstone of our alertness. We are constantly called upon to check what the right measure may be in the present moment for us and for all other sentient beings.

Einstein once said that a good theory should always be simple. This theory can be expressed very straightforwardly: Stay in the middle. And despite this simplicity, it is a powerful tool to help us to assess all of our efforts and can be found reflected in many other aspects of the Buddhist teachings. For example, the Middle Way indicates a realistic strategy we can follow to liberate ourselves from unhealthy aspects of life. It would not be realistic or very "human" to aim for the extreme solution of eradicating basic mental states such as sympathy, anger, sadness, joy, fear, love and impatience so that we never feel them ever again.

If we speak of freedom we are normally talking about freedom *from* something. But this is not the case in a Buddhist context:

> The Middle Way means we are not seeking to liberate ourselves *from* all our mental states and feelings; we are seeking to liberate ourselves *in the midst of* all our mental states and feelings.

All of our feelings remain there: respected, perceived, mindfully recognised, seen through, understood and dealt with in a calm way.

If we can liberate ourselves in this way *in the midst* of all human concerns, this means we have put an end to our dependence on external factors. No longer does anyone have the power to dampen our spirits permanently. Our "buttons" or sore points are protected, no longer raising an automatic, unconscious alarm. If we can reach this condition, we have liberated ourselves in the midst of all our feelings without dissociating ourselves from them.

No hate, but no indifference either.
No craving, and also no avoidance.
No attachment, but no aversion either.
No grasping, and also no pushing away.
No gluttony, but no fasting either.

This should not be understood as favouring the adoption of "coolness", by which we try to disguise our feelings. Instead, we are talking about putting an end to dependence: ceasing to hold tightly onto something and realising that we can indeed let go. This reflects the essence of Buddhism-liberation from unhealthy mental states (see 1st Fundamental of BPT).

Opening ourselves up to this possibility requires much insight and courage. Are we really ready to free ourselves from life's drama? From the ups as well as the downs? Or do we still need life's rollercoaster rides?

Leaving the Middle Way

If we have not yet found the path, we will still experiment with many aspects of our lives, including some important ones. Our youth is a particularly good example of this, being a period where we still have to gain many experiences. Quite often this is a period when we "try out" a range of extreme positions regarding such issues as fashion, opinions, political views, drugs, criminality, sexuality and music. This may be quite natural but it generally does not solve our fundamental task of finding an appropriate, healthy middle way. Even if our young body allows us to perform many extreme actions—including damaging our health by ignoring our body's limits to achieve demanding (occupational) goals—we will, before long, feel the physical and psychological consequences. These are inevitable if we ignore the appropriate middle path over a long period of time. Obvious consequences of leaving the Middle Way include addictions (alcohol, cigarettes, hard drugs, medicines, games, food, sex, shopping) or a wide variety of physical and psychological reactions to stress and overload (circulation problems, obesity, chronic pain, sleep disorders, obsessive brooding) and of course certain "ascetic practices" (anorexia, depression, tendency to withdraw, avoidance traits, escapism, suicide).

We will cover the inevitability of suffering in the 11th Fundamental of BPT, but even without further explanation the reader can probably already understand that our life will always have an aspect of suffering. This is not due to any mistakes we have made or other people's weaknesses: Life inherently gives rise to occasional suffering. Some problems, such as old age, illness, death and all sorts of loss, are simply inevitable.

So we need a great deal of courage and skill to go through life in the best way possible. It would be helpful to have some guidelines, and this is exactly what the philosophy of the Middle Way offers us. However, this path is often enough actually the more difficult one. Extreme rules such as "we are not allowed to do this, that is forbidden, this is poisonous, that is punishable" are actually clear instructions telling us precisely how to behave. In comparison, the guidance offered by the Middle Way is somewhat vague, so it poses more problems when it comes to the exact details of how to implement it in a specific situation: "Not too much, but not too little; not too tight, but not too slack; not too ambitious, but not too lax." To actually apply this guidance in a constructive way we need mental training such as mindfulness practice.

The Worldly Wisdom of the Middle Way

The Wisdom of the Middle Way is in fact not just worldly but universal! Traces of this teaching can be found in the philosophies of many cultures in all eras.

For example, let us take a look at the ancient Greek story of Daedalus and his son Icarus. According to the legend they wanted to escape from Crete by sticking feathers onto their body with wax and flying away. Icarus flew too high and too close to the sun we could say that he left the Middle Way. The wax melted in the heat of the sun, he lost his feathers and crashed fatally to the ground. His sad father Daedalus survived by remaining on the Middle Way, flying neither too high nor too low.

Icarus embodies youthful, exciting but often dangerous wantonness and also the general human characteristic of wanting to test our limits and go beyond them, as expressed by the Nobel Prize-winning astrophysicist Subrahmanyan Chandrasekhar: "Let us see how high we can fly before the sun melts the wax in our wings."

Blessing and curse are often more closely related than we think. Modern science, for example, has given us the blessing of useful medicine but also the curse of nuclear weapons. Perhaps here the Middle Way might offer some assistance for a path that is often extremely one-sided and rational.

So to fly through our life we need to maintain the right altitude and therefore need an instrument to tell us when we are flying too high or going too far. Buddhist Psychotherapy offers us a wide selection of exercises to help us find and stay on the Middle Way.

This worldly wisdom can also be found in other religions. Islam describes itself as *ummatan wasatan*, meaning the Middle Nation, following the middle path. In Judaism there are a variety of rules covering different areas of life such as the first years of life, marriage, food, prayers, religious holidays and the duties of a Jew; one of these is conducting their life on the "middle way".

As practical guidance, the Middle Way is applicable to many aspects of our everyday life: what we eat, going to the gym, the medicines we take, our relationships and our professional lives. Too much of a particular thing can kill us, too little of another has no effect. We always need to find the right balance and dosage.

In its very name, the Wisdom of the Middle Way makes beautifully clear that it is not a static condition but a *path*. It even suggests that we will never reach a permanent, static condition of enlightenment or liberation where we can rest on our laurels. Instead, we will always be on the way—a path that will hopefully be a middle one and will nonetheless always require our constant attention. It needs to be noted that this path is not a strenuous mountain footpath but a *spiritual* path with special features. For example, reaching our destination on the path will never be achieved by over-exerting ourselves. We will not find freedom by doggedly fighting our way forwards. Instead we have to recognise and acknowledge the following paradox: The Middle Way does not lead away from our current location to a distant, future, ideal destination. It can be better understood as leading us from there to ourselves. By stepping onto the path we are already—for this moment—at our destination. We are already on the path and will stay on it until a moment of ignorance, attachment or resistance once again leads us astray.

The Middle Way in Buddhist Psychotherapy

An important part of Buddhist Psychotherapy consists of providing specific assistance to help each individual help-seeker follow the Middle Way. Together, therapist and help-seeker uncover the areas of life where the "right measure" has been exceeded and find practical examples of what the Middle Way could be in each specific case. Another Buddhist teaching can be used as guidance here to cast light upon the areas of life that need a closer look: the fourth of the Four Noble Truths. It shows us eight areas of everyday life where our insights need to be implemented, summarised as the Noble Eightfold Path (see 17th Fundamental of BPT).

The Noble Eightfold Path
1. Right view
2. Right thought
3. Right speech
4. Right action
5. Right livelihood
6. Right effort
7. Right mindfulness
8. Right meditative concentration

In each of these eight areas we can use the Wisdom of the Middle Way as the measure, continually checking to see if we can find and establish the right balance as it applies to that particular aspect of life.

Memory aids

The paths we take in life are often winding and even tortuous, characterised by distractions, demands, burdens and false turns. In our hectic everyday lives we often do not even know if we are coming or going. So we should accept the fact that we will stray from the Middle Way many times. And when we stray, we then look anew for the balance and right measure.

As well as continuous mindfulness practice, some memory aids will also be useful in the initial stages of our Buddhist practice to help us remain on the Middle Way or find our way back more quickly. We need to regularly interrupt our daily routine, even if this is only for a few minutes or seconds. Fixed times may help us to keep a regular check on our current situation and other forms of reminder may help us to return quickly to a state of mindfulness.

Images, illustrations and presentations that do not use words often help us to understand better. Figure 7 below is an example. Some of the people we work with therapeutically are lacking in healthy criticism and insufficiently aware of possible dangers; they insist on focusing exclusively on everything that is positive (illustrated by Pos in Figure 7). We should encourage them to identify and take a closer look at critical aspects of their life. However, other help-seekers (illustrated by Neg in Figure 7) are over-critical, full of resistance and generally very negative. These should receive instructions for exercises such as expressing gratitude for things they see and receive, or trying to first see the good in everything. They can perform these exercises for a certain period of time.

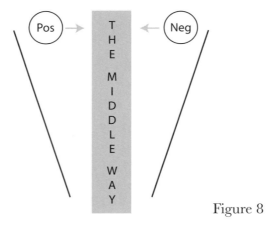

Figure 8

This figure clearly illustrates that the instruction to try out enforced gratitude and positivity for a while will not turn a person who always makes things difficult for themselves or treats everything as negative into a naive optimist! Instead, they will hopefully oscillate with slowly reducing amplitude between the extremes of overly positive and overly negative, landing eventually in a stable pursuit of the Middle Way.

Andrew B is a competitive athlete and defines himself fully in terms of his athletic performance. So he initially applied this same, successful strategy to his "Buddhist training program", aiming for rapid success. Andrew's frustrating meditation experiences at the beginning unsettled him. Although he could intellectually understand the teachings on the Wisdom of the Middle Way, he found them difficult to apply. So he found it helpful to receive clearer explanations of the *intentions* behind this philosophy. This approach enabled him to define his own differing intentions for different situations and to cultivate sophisticated strategies that helped him to find his own Middle Way in a non-sporting context. Applying this wisdom to his athletic activities was an aspect which was best postponed until later in his therapy.

This Fundamental Should Convey the Following:

The Wisdom of the Middle Way can become an important and indispensable navigation aid to keep us from careering off into extremes. During our Buddhist Psychotherapy we will process our tendencies towards a range of extremes, including excitability, nervousness, kicks, drama, tensions, excesses, uncontrolled boundary testing and constantly pushing ourselves to our limits.

On the Middle Way we do not seek freedom *from* our feelings but rather freedom *in the midst of* all our emotions and concerns.

To remaining on the Middle Way is to be in balance. Maintaining a balance is maintaining health.

Let us remind ourselves once again that the three main components of Buddhist teachings and of Buddhist Psychotherapy correspond to the three significant elements in the famous teaching of the *First Turning of the Wheel of Dharma:*
- Follow the Middle Way
- Use the insights to stay in the here and now and help yourself and others
- Understand the Four Noble Truths

In addition to the Wisdom of the Middle Way, there is a further important instruction to guide our behaviour: Every insight, every experience, each life impulse happens only in the present moment, the *here and now*. Focusing on and appreciating the present moment-mindfulness in the *here and now* are two core Buddhist exercises and therefore also form a central element of Buddhist Psychotherapy. They will now be presented in more detail in the 10th Fundamental of BPT.

The 10th
Fundamental of Buddhist Psychotherapy

Use the Insights to Stay in the Here and Now and Help Yourself and Others

> Let one not trace back the past
> Or yearn for the future yet-to-come.
> That which is past is left behind
> Unattained is the yet-to-come.
> But that which is present he discerns
> With insight as and when it comes.
>
> THE BUDDHA

The main message in this 10th Fundamental is one of the three significant elements in the Buddha's famous teaching known as the *First Turning of the Wheel of Dharma*. It underlines a further essential Buddhist concern: Buddhism appeals to us not to indulge in escapism but rather to remain very aware and present, fully in the here and now.

This appeal has a range of different aspects. For example, as briefly mentioned already, it emphasises that we should focus our efforts on the here and now in our everyday life and not on sometime and somewhere in (heavenly) spheres beyond this world. Another very important aspect of this statement is the clear desire to give us courage and spur us on: We can achieve all of our goals in the here and now!

> The Buddha himself clearly emphasised this. He expressly stated that every human being already possesses all of the skills they need in order to reach the goal and to liberate themselves in the present moment.

There is, nonetheless, a certain amount of effort, patience, wisdom and practice required. The present moment anchors us in this world. It puts the experience and progress we make in a nutshell by appealing to us not to become fixated on other-worldly or future goals but instead to ensure that we apply them in the here and now for ourselves and for the benefit of all other sentient beings. If we disregard the concerns of the present moment, none of our apparent successes will actually have a true meaning.

Many gruesome deeds carried out in the here and now are justified by appealing to our desire for a better future; there were and there will be brutal actions which take place in the present moment but are intended as sanctions for things that happened in the past. These deeds are very mistaken and cannot bring about healthy change.

Only being in the present moment can enable us to create healthy benefits with the greatest possible mindfulness and respect for ourselves and all other sentient beings. If we act now in an unhealthy way or base our actions too much on the past or the future, we will lose our connection to the true life of the present moment. The Buddha repeatedly exhorted his disciples to respect and take care of each other in the present moment in addition to performing their meditative practice. For example, if someone was ill, caring for them was more important than any meditation or teaching.

Buddhist Teachings Are Holistic

This short sentence "Use the insights to stay in the here and now and help yourself and others", reflects the entirety of the Buddhist teachings. Within it we can recognise various aspects which Buddhism values highly: life itself, being fully present, being in *this* world, interconnection, compassion, living in the moment, mindfulness and respect for oneself and for others. This property of being *holistic* is something we discover time and time again as we study Buddhism: The whole is already contained in the part.

The Buddhist teachings and practices are comparable with an ocean in their complexity and richness. So we would do well to recall their holistic nature when it comes to accessing and understanding them. Whichever aspect we select, when we look at it in detail we will always find reflections of the whole. The Buddha himself used the metaphor of an ocean to refer specifically to the issue of liberation by emphasising that wherever we choose a drop of the ocean to taste, it will always taste of salt, just as each and every aspect of the teachings has the one taste of freedom.

Furthermore, we should not forget that the Buddhist teachings as a whole have also been described as a type of raft. The teachings are not intended to be learnt for their own sake, becoming a set of rules to memorise. Just as the raft serves a specific, practical purpose, the teachings serve to help us overcome the river of life's suffering and reach the other bank—liberation.

Buddhist Psychotherapists should frequently check that both they and their help-seekers are still in touch with reality. Buddhist teachings or BPT should never be used as justification and support for distancing ourselves from the world and its concerns. Actively taking responsibility for ourselves and also for others is an issue which has immediate significance and relevance for us. At times it may well be necessary or desirable to incorporate retreats into the psychotherapeutic process of the BPT, but these should be considered very carefully—including consultation with those close to the help-seeker. Retreats for fixed periods are indeed considered essential in Buddhist practice but these too are not undertaken for their own sake. Any progress and insights achieved during these retreats are only of real value if they can be applied and realised in "post-meditation" time—in other words, in everyday life. As we progress through this book we will encounter this strong emphasis on a realistic, practical approach many times in the descriptions of BPT.

Here and Now!

Although the following example is gruesome, it is useful to make a valid point. (Carefully selected use of shocking images such as this may help us to create lasting impressions in the minds of the help-seekers.) If a frog is placed in a shallow pan of water and the pan is heated slowly, the frog will remain in the water until it boils and the frog dies, even though it could have jumped out. However, if we place a frog in a pan of water that is already hot, it will immediately attempt to jump out of the pan.

If we think that frogs are probably particularly stupid then we would do well to consider whether we ourselves have stuck around in situations that were unhealthy for us: "OK, just two more hours then I can go home"; "Well, one more day and then it'll be the weekend"; "I only have to stick this out for three more weeks and then I'll be on holiday"; "Just this evening, but from tomorrow ..."; or "Well, just one more time".

Our goal is all too often in the future. Not now, but later. We are often no longer aware of the possibilities for influence we have now. We have lost sight of them. So we console ourselves with the illusion that it will be possible to improve something later: Once I do X or buy Y or change a few external things Z... only then will I be able to make improvements. Not until I own that particular car; once I have lost 5 kg; as soon as I get that job; not until I have saved a certain amount of money; only when... etc. Any time except *now*! This disastrous approach can cost us many years. We are not very different to the donkey constantly pursuing the carrot dangling in front of its nose but never reaching its goal.

Another driving factor is our rational mind (see 6th Fundamental of BPT), which is constantly moving around in time. It is either producing thoughts about things that already happened or creating worries about what could happen in the future. Here we can acknowledge that this is a universal quality of our rational mind. It is not our mistake or a characteristic of us as an individual: It is simply the nature of the human mind to produce a constant stream of thoughts, ideas, old memories, future plans, daydreams and worries. We are generally not very aware of this if there are sufficient external distractions and stimuli but it becomes noticeable when we try to calm down.

.. We also pump ourselves full of input, tasks and duties. Often running the risk of overload, our attention is consequently drawn incredibly strongly to external affairs. Other people demand our attention and we also let ourselves be distracted.

Vicious circles

This often results in truly vicious circles. We have many tasks so we take less time for ourselves, we suppress disturbing thoughts and memories, we make a strong effort to do things better in future, we work more in order to reduce our anxiety about further setbacks, we overstep our own performance limits to achieve this, we now have even less opportunity to take time and look inwards, we feel our inner tension even more clearly, we consume more intoxicating substances, we are constantly in action, we become more and more restless... At some point our body and soul simply go on strike.

So there is a wide range of factors which drive us out of the present moment and keep us busy thinking about the past or the future. It is said that time is precious, but actually time is not precious because it is an illusion—it is not real. Only the present moment is really real and therefore precious. We can only live in the moment—in the here and now. We can never experience anything outside of the here and now. And we can never do anything other than in the present moment. Past and future are actually constructions of our rational mind.

We need to take a closer look at what is being created in the past (1) and the future (2).

1) The past lends us an identity—although it is mostly false or incomplete. We are not what we have experienced but nonetheless we believe we are what we can remember. We have already described how creative—and therefore not objective—the compilation process of remembering actually is. So it should be clear how carefully and cautiously we need to deal with memories from our past. In particular we will still often have to deal with the problematic process of identification. Although the chains between memories and self-image appear to be very logical, we have to loosen and slowly release them. For example, if we think we are such a miserable person and have to be this way because of what happened to us in the past, then we have fallen into the trap of identification.

2) The future gives us (mostly deceptive) desires and hopes. We dream of achieving something particular or owning something because we believe we will then really feel good. These dreams in our head cause us to overlook the life that is happening here and now.

There is a famous quote from Michel de Montaigne which has been echoed by famous authors and statesmen: My life has been full of terrible misfortunes, most of which never happened.

The particular quality of the present moment has perhaps now become clear. But how do we bring ourselves back into the present moment? After all, we get distracted so often, the future is so uncertain and a source of worries, and there is so much in the past to regret or quarrel about.

Practical help

In the old days we would tie knots in our handkerchief to serve as a reminder for something important, so perhaps we can adapt this technique to remind us to frequently return to the here and now. Of course, Buddhist Psychotherapy encourages each help-seeker to work out their own, individual solutions but there are some tried-and-tested methods we can introduce here.

Most of us are never without a mobile phone. We could set a reminder function to vibrate every two hours, for example, and return to the here and now when we feel the signal. Dedicated apps with similar functions are available for many smartphones.

- We can paint a small dot on our wrist. Whenever we see this dot we remind ourselves of the present moment.

- We can consciously choose a specific item of jewellery and wear this for a set period to remind us to be mindful.

- We can choose a specific category of object which we encounter in our everyday life (postcards, statues, stones, posters) and use these as a reminder. Anything can serve to bring us back into the present moment.

- The meditation teacher Thich Nhat Hanh also tells us that any signal can be used for this purpose: the peal of church bells, the telephone ringing, the doorbell, a dog barking etc. We can choose to interpret anything like this as a welcome reminder call. We should be grateful for these noises even if they appear to disturb us because we really do need these reminders.

Initially, these helping hands might seem annoying because they have the effect of showing us how often we are worrying about the future or ruminating over the past instead of remaining in the present. Nonetheless, soon we will more rapidly be able to adopt the position of inner observer, notice that we are not in the here and now, and then return to the present. If we now notice that we are thinking about the future, then actually we are already back in the here and now!

Victor G has been suffering from sleep disturbances for months due to obsessive worrying. During the day, he tells us, he feels permanently "charged up"—restless and busy. Every available minute is used for planning and reckoning. In the evening he would like to wind down and go to sleep but his mind just keeps working.

Victor was introduced to the principle of "here and now" and was given a range of different "homework" which forced him to focus on the present moment many times a day. In bed and as he was trying to fall asleep, Victor performed mindfulness exercises to help him remain aware of the here and now. Simple breathing meditation was particularly useful for this. During the initial and transition phases, he still suffered from evening restlessness, so he made use of the BPT's *Chair Exercise*. As soon as he noticed that he was wide awake in bed he was to get up immediately but not start any action such as watching television or reading a book. Instead, dressed simply in his pyjamas without any extra warm clothing, he sat on a normal chair (not an armchair or sofa). The exercise then consists of consciously registering every *current* sensation. Victor soon noticed that it was uncomfortable and cold sitting on a chair at night. After ten minutes he was generally exhausted. Back in bed he felt *in the here and now* the cosiness and warmth of his bed. He then often fell asleep fairly quickly.

This Fundamental Should Convey the Following:

Buddhist Psychotherapy should not be studied or carried out for its own sake. Nor should it be used as a justification for escapism or a means to create a new identification. Attachments need to be recognised and then steadily removed without replacing them with new ones (not even Buddhist ones!). Every change in ourselves should be carefully and critically examined to ensure that it benefits many other sentient beings. What this means for each individual needs to be worked out on a case-for-case basis. Personal growth should never be allowed to turn into increased narcissism. So *"Thou shalt love thy neighbour as thyself"* but also *"Thou shalt love thyself as thy neighbour"*.

Practising Buddhism does not put us in any sort of privileged position. Should we become stronger, we should strengthen our help for others.

We live only in the here and now. Memories from the past are often deceptive and create identifications that tie us down. Worrying about the future also uses up valuable life energy and distracts us from the only important moment that there is: the present moment.

The 11th
Fundamental of Buddhist Psychotherapy

Recognise and Convey the First Noble Truth of Suffering

> There is suffering.
> There is the cause of suffering.
> There is the end of suffering.
> There is the path to the end of suffering.
>
> THE BUDDHA

As we have already heard, the Buddha summarised his experience of enlightenment in three significant insights which he taught in the *First Turning of the Wheel of Dharma*. The 9th Fundamental of BPT covered the first of these—the Wisdom of the Middle Way—and in the previous Fundamental we looked at using the insights to stay in the here and now, while being of benefit to both ourselves and others. So now we turn to the third insight: Understand the Four Noble Truths.

The Four Noble Truths

The Four Noble Truths cover both avoidable and unavoidable forms of suffering or dissatisfaction. They exhort us to acknowledge the suffering, provide us instructions on how to deal with it, and show us how we can bring it to an end. The Buddha's teachings on these truths provide us with practical measures to carry out in our everyday lives.

Buddhism is still often wrongly perceived as a pessimistic philosophy focusing on suffering and claiming that we all lead lives full of dissatisfaction or even pain. We will discover below that this is definitely not the case, but let us start with a very simple example that should show us how wrong this misunderstanding is. The countless number of Buddha statues which can be found all around the world have a fascinating characteristic in common: They never portray a suffering Buddha—he is always serene, smiling and equable.

The fact that human life is linked with unavoidable suffering is probably common knowledge for the majority of readers. So Buddhism should not be accused of being overly negative simply because the first of these four truths "states the obvious". And the real significance of the Buddhist teachings can only be seen when we move beyond the first truth: We then hear the optimistic message that we have the capacity to take a good look at the causes of suffering, act accordingly, and find liberation.

The Four Noble Truths

1) The truth of suffering: What role does suffering play in life?
2) The truth of the causes of suffering: How does suffering arise?
3) The truth of liberation from suffering: What can we do about suffering?
4) The truth of the Right Path for our practice: How do we implement this?

The Buddha spoke of twelve permutations or modes concerning the Four Noble Truths: There are four truths and each has three phases or rounds. The first round comprises recognition and understanding of this statement about reality. The second round is to deepen this by internalising the message and applying it. And the third round is the realisation that comes from having implemented the message in everyday life.

Once again, we can see the holistic character of Buddhism within this core topic: If we explore any one of the Four Noble Truths very deeply then we will recognise that it contains the other three. Acknowledging, understanding and profoundly realising one truth automatically leads us to the other truths. For example, accepting that there is suffering and internalising this insight automatically shows us the way to change it and liberate ourselves from it.

What needs to be done?	The Four Noble Truths
1. Recognise and Understand 2. Contemplate and Internalise 3. Realise and Implement	1. The truth of suffering: What role does suffering play in life?
1. Recognise and Understand 2. Contemplate and Internalise 3. Realise and Implement	2. The truth of the causes of suffering: How does suffering arise?
1. Recognise and Understand 2. Contemplate and Internalise 3. Realise and Implement	3. The truth of liberation from suffering: What can we do about suffering?
1. Recognise and Understand 2. Contemplate and Internalise 3. Realise and Implement	4. The truth of the Right Path for our practice: How do we implement this?

When conveying and studying this topic, it needs to be borne in mind that this is one of the most central Buddhist teachings and needs to be conveyed as authentically and correctly as possible within the framework of Buddhist Psychotherapy. Alongside the concept of Inner Nobility, it provides the fundamental understanding of how BPT views human beings (and their therapeutic treatment), so as therapists we need to convey this understanding to the help-seeker as early as is appropriate.

We will now move on to look at each of the Four Noble Truths individually, beginning with the first one. The general issue is obviously suffering, which we need to evaluate and liberate ourselves from. So how does Buddhism (and BPT) regard suffering? Are we indulging in some sort of pessimism or even masochism? Do Buddhists really believe there is something called karma which is the cause of all suffering?

Suffering is universal and inevitable

The suffering we will hear about has to be divided into two categories: unavoidable *pain* and avoidable *suffering*. We are making the distinction: *Pain is inevitable, suffering can be avoided.*

Suffering is our reaction to painful experiences. We are using the term *pain* here to refer to more than just physical pain (such as the reaction when I hit my thumb with a hammer) because the Buddhist understanding of this concept is wider*, comprising three types of unavoidable pain:
1) Life's pre-programmed experiences of pain
2) The pain of discovering impermanence
3) The pain arising from ignorance.

Life's pre-programmed experiences of pain
There are many different experiences of pain which are universal because it is certain that we will all experience them. These range from the shock of *birth*, through the negative experiences caused by *illness* and the problems of *growing old*, to *death*. The definition of pain here also includes the pain of knowing about these types of pain.

The relevance of very early traumatic experiences surrounding our *birth* has been confirmed in research conducted by development psychologists, obstetricians and various schools of psychotherapy. As far as *illness* is concerned, its likelihood can be reduced by adopting a healthy lifestyle but it cannot be prevented completely. And even if we remain healthy, we will be confronted with the illnesses of the people around us. There does not appear to be anything we can do to completely prevent this; even very advanced meditation

---

* Translator's note: As the online version of the Pali Canon explains: *'No single English word adequately captures the full depth, range, and subtlety of the crucial Pali term* dukkha. *Over the years, many translations of the word have been used ("stress," "unsatisfactoriness," "suffering," etc.). Each has its own merits in a given context.'* And it is with this in mind that the author here chooses two (*pain* and *suffering*) to emphasise a useful distinction. For the wider meaning of the original Pali term it is perhaps best simply to look in the very teaching referred to here, the *First Turning of the Wheel of Dharma*, where Buddha himself defines the concept for us: Birth is dukkha, aging is dukkha, death is dukkha; sorrow, lamentation, pain, grief, & despair are dukkha; association with the unloved is dukkha; separation from the loved is dukkha; not getting what is wanted is dukkha.

masters such as Suzuki Roshi can develop serious or fatal physical illnesses such as cancer.

Even if we do not fall prey to the obsession with youth prevailing in our Western cultures—instead experiencing *getting older* as a positive process of becoming mature—ageing itself cannot be glorified. There are two sides to the story: the wisdom we gain with age is balanced by natural phenomena that are very painful and difficult to compensate for, including the inexorable approach of *death*. We see our parents die, our older relatives and then our friends—and perhaps even our children. These are all painful life experiences and there is no certain protection against them.

The pain of discovering impermanence

Buddhism defines further inevitable sorts of pain, including the fact that everything which arises will at some point pass away. There are no objects in our world which arise from themselves. Everything comes about as part of a highly complex interaction. A tree, a person and even the sun, the moon and the Earth require many different external conditions to be fulfilled if they are to continue to exist in their current form. There is no way that all of these necessary factors can remain constant for a long time, so decay (or change) is pre-programmed. We can see this easily as a mayfly progresses from birth to death within a day. The process was less rapid but is now visible for the Pyramids and we can be sure that it is even true for the stars: They are decaying, even if it is not as obvious to us.

Physicists' investigations into the natural laws governing our universe also confirm this underlying impermanence because there are natural forces leading to decay. For example, the fourth of the fundamental forces (also known as fundamental interactions) governing the elementary particles of nature is the "weak interaction" which leads to atomic decay. (The other three fundamental interactions are electromagnetism, strong interaction and gravitation.) Then there are the laws of thermodynamics where the concept of entropy and the second law of thermodynamics describe the tendency of any system towards dissipation and dissolution. So it seems that nature does not include permanence; the very "nature" of nature is constant transformation, dissolution of forms and continual transition. Change is the only constant.

We will take an even more detailed look at this and hopefully be able to show in an experiential way that it is *form* which passes away but not *consciousness, mind* or *energy*—whichever term we prefer.

The pain arising from ignorance

The third, very basic, aspect of pain from a Buddhist point of view is the ignorance that we suffer as human beings who are yet to awaken. We may indeed have some degree of understanding of the concepts mentioned above but as human beings who are yet to liberate ourselves we have not truly understood or internalised them, which leads to us repeatedly re-entering the cycle of pain.

This human weakness can be explained in terms of our nervous system: We were simply not created to recognise and understand the world as it really is—our faculties are only sufficient for grasping basic connections relevant to survival. In fact, as human beings we have always been very good at this: dark clouds—watch out for rain; fierce face—watch out for the danger of violence; tracks in the earth—predator or prey; etc. This survival strategy was very successful but now simply does not know when to stop. We are constantly trying to order all of our sensory impressions into these types of connections: That is good/bad for me, right/wrong, friend/foe, boring/interesting etc. So we are drilled to evaluate and assess our environment but not to understand it at a very profound level. Of course, this has advantages but it also leads us to repeatedly make painful mistakes.

Avoidable suffering

We have now analysed the *unavoidable* pain—the pre-programmed problems in our life—so let us move on to *avoidable* suffering, which has a completely different quality. We are referring to our individual reactions to the range of unavoidable types of pain. The Buddha provided us with an example: We are struck by an arrow (unavoidable suffering) and in reaction to this we shoot another arrow into ourselves (avoidable suffering). What does this refer to? How do we react in painful situations?

A documentary film featured an interview with a man who had survived a plane crash in a wild, uninhabited area. He explained that most people who experience an accident like this do not die because of starvation, thirst or attacks by wild animals. No, most crash victims die of shame! This wise survivor explained that in difficult situations most people no longer consider which measures would be most effective but waste a lot of time and energy worrying about why they ended up in this situation, what they must have done wrong, why other people always cope better than they do, etc. In other words, in the wake of a first painful situation (= unavoidable pain) we ourselves produce a second painful reaction (= avoidable suffering). This often takes the form of self-doubt, self-judgement, resistance, anger or defiance.

The first step in our consideration of the First Noble Truth should be to recognise and understand. The facts, logic and theory might often seem easy at first but how does this continue in practice? We need to be particularly self-critical, especially if we feel we are within our rights, such as in the case of "righteous anger". Once again, we need to remember that the essence or basic intention of Buddhism is liberation. As mentioned above, the first step of this path is always recognition and understanding. On a rational level, this step can be taken relatively quickly. But for the next step of deepening and internalising our understanding we have to experience, recognise and name the distinction between unavoidable pain and unavoidable suffering many times in the course of our everyday life.

This second step or round of deepening and internalising the understanding of these truths can be achieved using a wide range of different techniques if we carefully choose the one best suited to each current situation and the particular issues that each help-seeker has. Of course, conveying information about the issue of how feelings arise (psychoeducation, see 7th Fundamental of BPT) is recommended here, but in no way is it sufficient. It is indispensable for everyone to have their own practical and sense-based experiences of every Buddhist insight we convey.

Western psychotherapy has many different methods which can be used here to facilitate the personal experiences of the help-seekers. And classical Buddhist techniques such as mindfulness meditation are suitable, too. In general, we are aiming to enable a deceleration in the automatic, unconscious emotional reaction patterns that otherwise take place very quickly. There is a form of healthy, self-critical doubt which can be encouraged here: Perhaps my spontaneous reaction is only *one* possible reaction amongst many. Useful methods include the exercise known as *Sacred Inner Moments*. It involves consistently "pressing the pause button" before every answer, action or decision. Performing this exercise regularly is good training; frequent repetition is necessary if we want to loosen up and break down established habitual behaviour patterns.

Really internalising the First Noble Truth liberates us from many illusions and concepts which we torment ourselves with, such as the desire for perfect parents, the perfect partner, or the perfect boss etc. If we really believe that everything always has to happen "smoothly" and in the "right" way, we might need to acknowledge that we have become idealists or perfectionists. If every disturbance is interpreted as a mistake then we run the risk of crumbling under our own false ideals.

The First Noble Truth helps us to acknowledge and understand that painful occurrences are completely normal. This might then enable us to become aware of our judgements and rein ourselves in. Developing increased serenity in this way is a very practical implementation of this First Noble Truth.

In order to avoid any possible misunderstandings it needs to be noted that this acknowledgement or acceptance of the existence of suffering in the world is in no way to be understood as passively "putting up with it". If I am stuck in a difficult situation, I need to mobilise all my energy in order to get out of it. However, there is no reason to create additional avoidable suffering with denial, complaining or any other unhealthy emotional reaction. In other words, we are not being exhorted to "put up with" suffering and injustices. We are being given suggestions how to limit suffering and, in particular, how not to create additional suffering.

The Differences between Western and Buddhist Views of Suffering

Whereas Buddhists consider suffering to be a phenomenon affecting *everybody*, many people in the West—including therapists—consider suffering to be the result of faulty metabolism in the brain, learning wrong behaviour patterns at an early age and/or some error that occurred etc. Some form of mistake or accident must have happened at some time and somewhere because suffering is not "normal". This is related to the opinion that most people are generally healthy with a more or less small proportion of the population suffering from some form of illness and needing treatment.

Unfortunately, these ways of thinking are all based on a monocausal understanding of the world. This means that for any particular phenomenon—for example a conflict or a dominant, negative feeling—there has to be one clear cause. This model in its pure form is almost 100 years out of date and has been clearly revised by systems theory and chaos theory. However, these more modern approaches have been taken up only very slowly or not at all in the fields of social sciences and health care. So many doctors and therapists are still working with an outdated, monocausal model whereas Buddhist concepts of humans and our environment have been deeply systemic for over 2500 years.

Of course, many occurrences are indeed monocausal. If I hit my thumb with a hammer it will hurt. That is simple. However, these simple models generally only work for isolated and limited examples. More complex systems, such as human behaviour, the dynamics of larger groups, the human body, physical sensations, perception and chronic illnesses, cannot adequately be described using these simple monocausal models. Even what appears to be an easy question such as "Will it rain tomorrow?" demands an answer which considers many different factors. A simple "cause and effect" description does not work anymore. Non-linear calculations are used, incorporating systems and chaos theory. In fact, it should not be surprising to realise that human behaviour is just as difficult to predict as the weather!

In spite of this, there are still many therapists whose main focus during the treatment is to find *the* event(s) in the past which triggered the troublesome symptoms. Having found something to blame, this then needs to be processed and after this the problem should (at least theoretically) be solved. In practice, however, it often looks very different. In fact, many patients are seen to strengthen their identification with their deficient self-image and "faulty" biography. Going through something again and again generally leads to it becoming more firmly established—this also applies to the undesired aspects of our self. Alternatives and possible solutions are described in this book.

More modern Western models:
Systems theory and chaos theory

The model proposed by chaos theory is not actually chaotic. Instead, it attempts to calculate apparently differing interactions between a wide range of different conditions. Chaos theory is based on a systemic understanding of everything. Complex calculations are used to determine not chaos but probabilities. One assertion made here is that even small, apparently insignificant causes can have large effects and lead to significant consequences. This effect is often known as the *Butterfly Effect* because of the theoretical example used where a butterfly flapping its wings in one part of the world could lead to significant effects in the weather elsewhere due to the chaotic connections and systemic links at play. A similar, although more linear, effect is known as the *Domino Effect*, where one falling domino within a tightly packed system can have dramatic consequences.

Applying such models leads us to the conclusion that it is possible for very serious human and interpersonal problems to arise *without* there necessarily being a serious cause. They equally imply that small and short interventions in a therapeutic context can lead to significant results.

It needs to be clearly emphasised that these models do not concern a simple process of adding up small details. They concern systems with particular sensitive dependencies and conditions which often contain exponentially developing subsystems. So the small components do not simply accumulate. Rather, they serve as a type of key or starting signal.

Models of this type have long gained full acceptance in scientific circles but we find it difficult to carry them over into our practical work. We human beings really do prefer to keep it simple.

Western cultures' views on suffering

Times of crisis and difficulty or when life deals us a tragic blow often bring our otherwise hidden personality aspects and patterns to the surface, clearly revealing our deeper attitudes towards life, including our approach to suffering. Many of us believe these forms of suffering are signs that something has gone wrong or that we are being subjected to some form of divine punishment. Suffering in Western cultures generally carries with it a connotation of being unjustified, inappropriate or exceptional—not the normal situation.

Indeed, difficult situations such as those just mentioned lead many of us to turn away from the world and/or God because we believe we are the victims of some sort of injustice: We have tried our best to do everything right so any form of punishment (suffering) would be wrong and unjust.

Would it be an exaggeration to claim that our culture predominantly defines itself through being strong, successful, youthful and materially wealthy? The more you have, the more you are! So our culture appears to promote the view that if you are suffering then either you have done something wrong or you are the victim of circumstances: If you try hard enough, struggle, or work hard then you will have good chances of success or an easier life. If we do everything "right", we will not have to suffer.

Suffering is turned into a taboo. We even create "ghettos" by excluding people who are suffering. After all, our culture deems these people to be part of a relatively small minority.

At least, this is the defensive lie we tell. But we need look no further than our Western model of health and illness to see how shallow this lie must be. We can either be healthy (one option) or we can have an illness (thousands of options). So the chances of being continually healthy and therefore without suffering are very low. We might easily ask ourselves the question if anyone in our society is really healthy at all when we read the statistics from highly developed or over-developed countries regarding the rates of suicide, criminality, addiction (alcohol, nicotine, hard drugs, soft drugs, sleeping tablets, tranquillisers, painkillers), chronic illnesses, psychosomatic illnesses or interpersonal conflicts. And how many of us can claim that we have never suffered a loss, an injury or some other sad occurrence?

In the 18th century, the German philosopher Gottfried Leibniz coined the term *theodicy* (from Greek *theo*—god and *dike*—justice) as he considered whether the existence of a benevolent God was compatible with the presence of suffering in the world. How could an omnibenevolent God allow us to suffer? In the centuries that followed many answers were sought and given.

The Buddhist answer is not only much older but also convincing in its simplicity: Suffering is inevitable in this world. Having read the considerations above, we might have to admit that the Buddhist view has a certain justification. However, let us remember once again that Buddhists do not stop here with this somewhat negative description. They move straight on to provide practical solutions.

Dorothy F quarrels with herself and the world. Particularly in the evening, she would spend a lot of time making complaints and judgements in her thoughts. At the beginning of her therapy, she was asked to make a list of as many recent painful situations as possible. The therapist then worked through this list together with Dorothy. The primary reason for this was to make a rational distinction between the initial *unavoidable* pain and the secondary *self-inflicted* pain. This was of great help to Dorothy, who could then begin to treat current problematic situations in a more discriminating way. She was able to increase her own awareness of what she was doing to herself. This experience of self-responsibility was a relief, even if she still had plenty of work to do during the therapy to deal with her inner censors.

This Fundamental Should Convey the Following:

We can recognise and internalise the fact that there is suffering in the world and in our life which we *cannot* avoid.

We can recognise and internalise the fact that there is suffering which we *can* learn to avoid.

We will encounter problems and troubles every day. Our task is not to get entangled in them. Instead, we should recognise that these occurrences are perfectly normal and then we can smile (even if only inwardly), take a deep breath and try to solve the problem without producing any additional problems.

We will frequently encounter suffering in the future so it is important to prepare ourselves now, rather than just sticking our head in the sand.

The Second, Third and Fourth Noble Truths can all provide further assistance to help us give up *avoidable* suffering and, as we progress, to alleviate and let go of the *unavoidable* suffering.

In the next Fundamental of BPT we will begin to investigate the causes of our suffering. The three main causes identified by the Buddha were ignorance, attachment and aversion/resistance. We will dedicate one Fundamental to each of these, but first we will take a look at an issue which can also be understood as a cause of suffering. It is a concept which the general public immediately associates with Buddhism but which is often misunderstood: *karma*.

The 12th
Fundamental of Buddhist Psychotherapy

Recognise and Convey the Significance of Karma for Our Suffering

> Intention is the seed that creates our future.
>
> JACK KORNFIELD

When we consider the causes of suffering we frequently come across a concept which has now become quite well-known: *karma*. Unfortunately there are many misunderstandings surrounding this term which often lead to insecurity and resignation, especially if karma is falsely interpreted as irrevocable fate.

Karma Is the Law of Cause and Effect

Is karma really responsible for everything which happens to us and others? Does karma allude to an irrevocable fate? What does karma mean exactly?

Karma is a Sanskrit term which we can translate as "cause and effect". Everything that happens has a cause and every cause has an effect. Our actions are governed by particular causes and lead inevitably to effects or consequences which in turn serve as causes for further deeds.

Karma is not an esoteric, spiritual, religious or philosophical concept but primarily a term based on rational references to things that are factual and observable. Everything around us can be understood as "cause and effect" in this way—or can we find an example of an effect (an occurrence) that happened without a cause? The concept of karma is very comprehensive and diverse so we can see how sayings such as "everything is karma" arose.

Very often karma is cited primarily as *consolation* for someone experiencing some form of interpersonal situation which may be uncomfortable. According to aspects of the concept of karma, an unfortunate situation is not unjustified or coincidence but has very practical causal conditions. For many people it can be consoling when they realise this.

This understanding of karma also means our capacity and opportunity to create or influence current conditions is necessarily a capacity or opportunity to create or influence new causes for everything that is yet to come. If only we can recognise and understand the causes and conditions, then we have the opportunity to sow the seeds of healthy future alternatives.

Thousands of years before Sigmund Freud and the psychoanalysts, Buddhists came to the conclusion that what we represent (or what we are) today is dependent on what we previously experienced: We are the way we are today because this or that happened yesterday. The scientific aspect of karma can thus be enriched by an important psychological component: Prior causes are shaping and characterising us, our minds and our actions. Taken further, this implies we are currently experiencing everything in a uniquely "distorted" way; we each have our own pair of tinted glasses and thus perceive our surroundings individually, based on our specific prior experiences. Our karma clearly determines the way we now perceive and react.

Nonetheless, this also means that what we will become tomorrow is determined by what we do today. The current moment becomes very relevant—once again, we encounter the significance of the here and now.

So karma is actually the opposite of a simple belief in fate. The concept clearly illustrates the mechanism of action in our environment and within ourselves. There is no effect without a cause. Seen this way, everything functions according to karma; after all, we cannot imagine any event that arises without a cause.

This principle does not necessarily only apply to external affairs. Kant provided evidence that we human beings cannot think outside of various principles—causalities such as cause and effect, or space and time. Let us try to imagine any object, such as an elephant, existing outside of space or time. It is impossible. And an elephant cannot arise without a cause. So it really is impossible for us to think outside of these categories. Although we are basically very creative and can apparently imagine anything we want to, there are in fact limits. Our imagination is not free. We carry these categories such as causality, space and time within us.

For a long time we believed that only the external world functioned according to these mechanisms. Kant clearly showed us that we ourselves approach the world with these inner mental preconditions. In the 6th Fundamental of BPT on the topic of our mind we have already discovered how intensive the interactions between our mind and our environment are. Buddhism shows us that this inseparable networking and linking means that there is no essential difference between ourselves and the world. Therefore, karma (the law of cause and effect) must be universal and its effects must be felt everywhere.

So we have discussed the definition of karma as a general law of cause and effect. One version of this is using the term karma to clarify the consequences of our individual behaviour. This version goes beyond the simple principle of cause and effect, particularly because the conditions of the causal relationship have to be analysed in a more sophisticated way.

According to the law of cause and effect it is practically impossible not to behave in a karmic away, since each of our actions will have some form of consequences—even if only very weak ones. There are, however, particular causal conditions which need to be fulfilled in order to create a clear effect such as a change in destiny.

Does Karma Influence Everything That Happens?

It is indeed common to find books and very advanced masters making the very provocative statement that everything we experience occurs due to the karma we accumulated in our own past and present lives. This message is intended to offer some consolation for suffering people, helping them to accept the situation they find themselves in and giving them courage to become active regarding their future.

The concept of karma can also be applied to larger systems such as a family, a city, a country or a planet. However, many people are outraged at the idea that victims of natural disasters or crimes could be partly responsible for what happens to them because of their karma. In fact, expressed like this, we are dealing with a partial misunderstanding of the concept of karma because the teachings make it clear that there has to be *intention* involved.

Karmic actions always have three stages
1) Intention
2) Action
3) Completion or fulfilment

For an action to be considered as karmic there has to be intention, followed by performance of the action, and, finally, completion of this action. If we take the above example of a natural disaster, we can see that there is no *intention*. Many negative things can happen to us but this does not mean we are experiencing negative karmic effects. A natural disaster can be considered karmic, in the sense of karma describing a process of cause and effect, since every natural phenomenon does have its cause and does illustrate the effect of the cause.

However, this is not related to *our* human karma because nature does not have an intention. In other words, when we are affected by a natural disaster, it is not relevant to pose the question, "Why is this happening to *me*?"

When we are clearly the actor, what karma do we then create? The decisive factor here is also our intent. Let us consider a situation where one person is using all their strength to press down the rib cage of another person lying on the ground: What is their *intention* for performing this action? Are they a paramedic trying to save the person's life? Or is this part of a fight and an attempt to injure the other person?

When it comes to our own actions and examining our own intent, it can often be much more difficult than we think. Ignorance, suppression and delusion all cloud our view. Sayings such as "The road to hell is paved with good intentions" or "Hell is full of good intentions, but heaven is full of good works" reflect the fact that even well-meant actions can lead to suffering. Sometimes we are not in a position of complete clarity regarding our intentions, but we can still check what possible consequences our actions might have. If suffering arises because of our deeds this may well be a sign that deluded intent was playing a role.

The first stage of the karmic process has another special implication: "Bad karma" has already been created if we have bad thoughts (intents) without actually carrying out the action. Nonetheless, if we stop ourselves before going through with the intention (second stage), at least we only create one-third of the bad karma. So Buddhists would not completely agree with the claim that "thoughts are free", since the Buddhist concept of karma does imply that thoughts have karmic effects—positive and negative.

The Power of Thought

Buddhists consider a thought—an intention—to have a considerable effect: If we think through an intention, then we are performing the first of the three karmic stages listed above. On the negative side, this means that our negative thoughts are sufficient to create negative karma for ourselves. But on the positive side we can harness this process for the benefit of ourselves and all others. Positive thought, such as a prayer, blessing or helpful wish, is also the performance of the first karmic stage and therefore creates "good karma". Of course, it is even better to perform the second stage as well and carry out the healthy action in order to achieve even more benefit.

We can reduce the creation of bad karma by interrupting the process before any of the stages. Interrupting our thoughts (the first stage) is quite an advanced skill but we are generally able to interrupt a process (i.e. stop before the third stage of completion) when we notice that our action could have negative effects. And with some mindfulness training we will increase our ability to "catch" a negative intent before we even start to put it into action (second stage).

If the reader has doubts about the power of our thoughts in this regard, we recommend reading about and trying out the *Torso Twist* exercise described in the 6th Fundamental. This clearly demonstrates the connection between mental and physical activities and the power of thought.

We Can Improve Our Karma at Any Time

The really good news is that even if we do not manage to interrupt the process before the third stage and end up completing a (negative) karmic action, we can still change its effects. For example, we might get caught up in our automatic reactions and perform a malicious act, hurting somebody. Even though in the heat of the moment we acted maliciously, we can still approach this person afterwards, apologise sincerely and perhaps perform some sort of atonement. In this way we can develop a deeper relationship to ourselves and also to the other person. And this in turn has a positive transformative effect on the previous negative (karmic) action.

We need to note here that a targeted analysis of our intentions is a major component of both Buddhism itself and Buddhist Psychotherapy. We have already been introduced to the process involved: Our *intentions* lead to our *deeds*. Repeating these creates *habits*. Our *character* develops from these and then in turn shapes our *destiny*. So it can be seen that in the long run our motivation or intention determines our destiny.

Can any of us claim that all of our intentions so far in this life have been good? And our actions? No, that would be too idealistic. So what will happen because of our bad karma? Is it too late to escape a negative destiny?

Baking a cake

In this regard, Jack Kornfield has given us an easy-to-understand example which we reproduce here in its essence. Imagine two elderly ladies who both want to bake a cake. One of them lives in the countryside, has a very old kitchen and an oven which she has to fire up manually. Her cupboards are somewhat bare and she barely scrapes together the ingredients she needs, which are no longer very fresh. The other woman lives in a modern city apartment with a high-tech kitchen and she goes out to buy all the necessary fresh ingredients at her local organic retailer. It is clear that one of these ladies clearly has less advantageous starting conditions. But who will bake the most delicious cake?

We do not know for sure. The prior conditions (karma) do *not* completely determine the end result. We do have clear opportunities to influence the results ourselves. Whatever the conditions we are subject to and whether these are the result of good or bad karma, we can influence our life now. Admittedly, sometimes this is easier said than done. Nonetheless, if we appear to be lacking something we need to be happy, if we or others are not perfect enough, or if our current conditions seem to be inadequate, we should remember the two old ladies and their cakes.

In other words, the message is: Do not quarrel with the past—become active and improve the future for the benefit of yourself and others.

In Buddhist cultures the concept of karma is almost inextricably linked to the concept of rebirth, with many people placing great importance in accumulating good karma for their next life. Since many of us in the West are less sure about the issue of rebirth, Buddhist Psychotherapy makes a clear statement on this issue:

It is not really important whether we believe in rebirth or not. If we do, then we make every effort to lead a good life now in order to have a better life later. If we do not, then we make every effort to lead a good life *now* in order to have a good life now. Whichever way we look at it: It is always about the here and now.

More about Causes

Of course, as a precise science of the mind, Buddhism has a much more sophisticated view of the processes related to cause and effect than the simplified version presented above. In particular, there is the issue of many results which arise without intentional action, such as accidents, injuries, natural phenomena and disasters.

Buddhism has a range of explanations for how changes and other events come to happen. For example there are the Five Aspects of Cause and Effect, the 12 Links of Dependent Arising, the 24 Types, and the Four Conditions. We do not want to look at all of these in detail in this book, so as an example we will present here the Five Aspects, which describe everything that happens in terms of not more than five categories of cause.

The Five Aspects of Cause and Effect, or Five Orders *(Niyama)*

1) The natural order of non-living matter. This covers causes of occurrences such as earthquakes or vehicle breakdowns.

2) The order of living matter. We might think of our modern science of biology when regarding this category. It explains the causes relating to plants, animals etc.

3) The natural order of mind or consciousness. It is worth emphasising that this category covers unconscious acts (such as a clumsy mishap or bad luck) and that the next category generally applies to conscious actions.

4) The natural law of karma or action and result. This covers causes related to conscious, intentional actions (see above).

5) The order of dharma or natural phenomena. This category covers causes beyond the world we are able to experience.

The fact that karma is only one of the five orders should make it clear that Buddhism does not consider everything to be a direct result of karma. It also shows that Buddhism considers karma to be one form of natural law (like other scientific laws) and not a form of divine retribution. As we saw above, an action is only deemed to be a karmic action in terms of human karma if it fulfils one or more of the three specific stages listed. Nonetheless, these do apply to the majority of human behaviour, so karma can indeed be considered as a general principle of cause and effect in this regard.

Lewis T is a chaplain and increasingly convinced that we cannot exercise any control over our own destiny. He tells us that he often feels a great helplessness because of all the problems he hears about and also because of the difficulties he experiences in his own relationship. He has the impression that pressure, stress and atrocities are all on the increase in our society. In fact, it all seems so bad that everything feels meaningless and he is losing his belief that the world is good at a fundamental level.
Lewis' initial contacts with Buddhism were very difficult for him, particularly because he found the idea of karma very frightening. By working through this Fundamental together with his therapist, Lewis was able to gain a more sophisticated understanding of the opportunities for self-efficacy. In particular, deciphering the individual elements of his destiny and looking for causal intentions helped Lewis to find ways to become active again.

This Fundamental Should Convey the Following:

Karma is a continually active mechanism of cause and effect working at a deep level and deserving our constant attention. Our intentions and deeds are of elementary significance because they have incalculable consequences for ourselves and for others.

The wisdom of karma should help to console us because it shows that we have not been thrown carelessly and randomly into a chaotic universe in which we are helpless to escape our suffering.

Understanding the process of karma enables us to acknowledge our own responsibility, our possibilities for self-efficacy and our opportunities to influence the future.

By training in mindfulness we can increase our ability to exercise a positive influence on karma at every moment and therefore improve our future in a positive way. Karma is flexible and can be modified at any time.

So it is now hopefully clear how the concept of karma, for example as the cause of suffering, should be understood within the wider context. This enables us to move on to the Buddha's insights about how suffering arises. These were taught as the contents of the Second Noble Truth.

The 13th
Fundamental of Buddhist Psychotherapy

Recognise and Convey the Noble Truth of Our Ignorance

> Delusion misunderstands the world and forgets who we are.
> Delusion gives rise to all unhealthy states.
>
> JACK KORNFIELD

Now we turn to the *causes* of our suffering. Ignorance or delusion is one of the three causes of all *avoidable* suffering (alongside attachment and resistance/aversion), as described by the Buddha in the second of the Four Noble Truths.

Again, we have to emphasise the distinction between unavoidable pain and avoidable suffering because these two have very different causes. As we saw from the First Noble Truth (see 11th Fundamental), pain cannot be avoided and this pain is almost bound to become the cause of further suffering. Our birth is an example of unavoidable pain, as are ageing, illness and death. In fact, even just noticing these can be equally painful.

Additionally, in the previous Fundamental we found out that we ourselves create a very large part of our suffering due to the natural law of cause and effect (karma). In this Fundamental we now take a closer look at how and why we create our own suffering.

The three causes of avoidable suffering are
1) Ignorance
2) Attachment
3) Resistance/Aversion

These three causes give rise to a wide range of mental states. In the middle column of the following table three randomly chosen examples are listed which could arise from the respective causes. In the third column, the three most extreme examples are listed, which could arise if other negative emotions increase their intensity or strength. These three columns present different intensities for the concepts known in Buddhist teachings as the Three Poisons.

The three causes	Three examples	Three extremes
Ignorance →	Naïveté →	Delusion
Attachment →	Pleasure →	Greed/addiction
Resistance/aversion →	Critical thinking →	Hate

For example, ignorance can express itself as naïveté or, in the worst case, bewilderment and delusion. Feelings of attachment can give rise to pleasure but extreme forms of attachment include greed and addiction. Aversion may express itself as criticism but if intensified this can lead to hate.

In the following two Fundamentals we will deal with *attachment* and *resistance* respectively. Here, we will look at *ignorance* as a cause of suffering and before we proceed it is important to note that these three causes of suffering can be presented with their counterparts: three causes of healthy mental states.

The three causes of healthy mental states are
1) Love
2) Mindfulness
3) Generosity

Sometimes taught as the Three Antidotes (to the poisons), these three can be causes for all positive mental states. By cultivating healthy mental states we automatically reduce the incidence of unhealthy mental states because, according to the Buddhist view, the two cannot exist in the same moment.

> We will repeatedly hear this Buddhist admonition: A critical focus on unhealthy mental states is useful but it is equally important to actively cultivate healthy mental states.

In the following consideration of ignorance or delusion as one of the three causes of our suffering, we will see that Western and Eastern sciences confirm and complement each other in their statements on this issue. Translating the Buddhist concept with the term *ignorance* poses the risk of misunderstanding it as a lack of academic knowledge. Western culture and science still place a great emphasis on accumulating factual knowledge. We seem to believe that we will completely understand the world one day if we just study hard enough and collect enough details. This approach has indeed led to many very remarkable and helpful results, so it is very tempting to follow it. But we should also remember a range of very unhealthy effects. From medicine to weapons technology, we are faced with very mixed blessings resulting from a lack of guidance in science (or adherence to the guidance we do have). Whilst recognising that the basic motivation of most science is to make life easier and better for humanity, we do have to pose a very serious question: Are these really improvements, or merely changes? For example, even poor people in highly developed countries are living lives far more luxurious than a medieval nobleman. We have citrus fruits and exotic spices, as well as a good healthcare system. But how many poor people here really feel like nobles?

Ignorance of What?

If we make a distinction between accumulated facts and genuine knowledge then we can also distinguish between educational deficits and the concept of ignorance: In a Buddhist context, we may have gained the highest academic qualifications but still remain deeply ignorant. So if we are not talking about a lack of encyclopaedic knowledge, what are we ignorant of?

Ignorance itself, according to Buddhism and Buddhist Psychotherapy, can be considered as having three forms. These in turn give rise to a wide range of mental states, including naïveté, uncertainty, confusion, illusion and confusion and even delusion and madness.

The three forms of our ignorance are
1) Ignorance in the form of inattention
2) Ignorance in the form of denial
3) Ignorance in the form of misperception of reality

Ignorance in the form of inattention

The first form is perhaps the easiest version of our ignorance to understand and relate to. Without mind training we generally have a relatively limited attention span. This can vary considerably, depending on how interested we are in the current issue, our state of mind and body on the particular day, our general ability to concentrate and our individual interests.

Are we the type of person who walks along with their gaze fixed two metres in front of them? Or do we more actively take in our surroundings? Are we consciously in the here and now as often as possible? Or do we get trapped in worries about the future or brooding about the past? As we are reading, could we say what colour the wall behind us is or what the lamp above us looks like without looking up from the book? Sitting on the train, do we know what the person next to us looks like? There are certainly times when we can answer these questions more easily and others when it is more difficult.

Our attention or concentration is like the beam of a flashlight: We target it onto particular things in our surroundings and certain features of our surroundings attract it. The beam is generally quite tightly focused, so we do not take in other nearby features, which it does not illuminate even though they are there. The sunrise may be particularly beautiful today, but if we are in a hurry to catch the tram we will not notice it. A friend is calling us from the other side of the street but we are engrossed in conversation on our mobile phone and do not hear them. In other words: We shut out a large part of our surroundings.

Ignorance in the form of denial

The second version of ignorance reveals aspects of ourselves which we might prefer to avoid. So it is much more difficult to convey, and as help-seekers we might also find it more difficult to accept. For this reason, it can be advisable firstly to consider the topic theoretically before moving onto the actual issues being experienced by the help-seeker.

Denial covers both an active mechanism and an unconscious mechanism of "not wanting to believe it". From a psychological point of view, denial belongs to the unconscious psychological defence mechanisms used to maintain our psychological stability. This is a universal process which affects us all but it always has a very individual character.

Generally we try to shut out anything that could pose a danger to our apparently stable self or decrease our self-esteem. Our self considers these contents to be a threat so it is necessary to create a safe space if we want to take a look at them. Therapy can offer a suitable space for this self-critical process once we have established a trusting and stable therapeutic working alliance between the therapist and the help-seeker.

Ignorance in the form of misperception of reality

This third aspect is also a universal one since it can be found in everyone. We are referring to the common limits of our knowledge about our own nature and our environment. We need to take a more detailed and self-critical look at how we perceive ourselves and the world, including the filters we apply in the form of prejudices, fixed opinions, automatisms and unconsidered assumptions—all are used to give us a (false) sense of security. With the help of this 13th Fundamental we will be able to see how these illusions arise very early in our childhood, grow as we grow, and then become something we consider to be perfectly natural.

As humans we have an extremely complex nervous system. During the course of our evolution we have developed highly refined abilities to recognise context and connections, evaluate events very practically and make all sorts of generalisations which are useful for our survival. The advantages are obvious and are perhaps the reason we have come to dominate this planet so very effectively. Nonetheless, this pressure to generalise inevitably leads to mistaken assessments. The ability to look behind the scenes does not seem to have been so important for survival so we generally do not have a built-in ability to look deeper and see the "thing-in-itself". It is therefore not surprising, from a Buddhist point of view, that our way of perceiving reality is actually an "ignorant" *mis*perception.

Our focus here is on ignorance as a cause of our suffering. By understanding this more clearly we can hopefully then reduce our ignorance and in turn our suffering, so we are now going to take a comprehensive look at our misperception of reality with reference to the basic Buddhist principles of selflessness, impermanence, emptiness, interconnection, compassion, epistemology, perception, and thoughts and feelings.

Eight areas of the misperception of reality as an aspect of ignorance

1) Ignorance of impermanence
2) Ignorance of how painful emotions arise
3) Ignorance of emptiness
4) Ignorance about our self or ego
5) Ignorance about compassion
6) Ignorance of the limits of our cognitive faculties
7) Ignorance about our perception
8) Ignorance about our rational mind

These eight areas are closely related to each other and in some cases overlap. In particular, impermanence, emptiness and the limits of our ability to perceive and understand the world interact directly with each other.

247

Our ignorance about impermanence

The belief in the permanence or continuity of the things that surround us is one of the main sources of our suffering.

An example of the illusion of continuity is that we are (too) quick to believe that the behaviour we observe in a person at any particular moment can tell us everything about their personality—in other words, we believe they have stable, continuous personality traits. This could be seen in a socio-psychological experiment where the participants were told they would all take part in a test, that one of them would be chosen randomly to be the test leader, and that this leader would be given the instructions to remain strict and aloof as they perform this role. The supposed test was then carried out with one of them in the role of the leader. Afterwards, the participants were asked to imagine meeting the person who played the test leader in a supermarket by chance the next day. How would this person behave? The overwhelming majority firmly stated this person would also be "strict and aloof" in this private context. Of course, this questioning was the real experiment (not the supposed test they all carried out). In spite of the fact that all of the participants had been told in advance that this randomly chosen person would be *following instructions* to be strict and aloof, they still believed that these apparent personality characteristics would show up outside of the experiment.

This clearly shows our human propensity to generalise very quickly. We experience something and all too often we tend to believe that the condition we have perceived once will then persist. Imagine you are a therapist who has an appointment one morning with a person who appears to be suffering severely. Later that day you meet them by chance in the street and they are all dressed up to go out with friends. You would probably be a bit confused, wouldn't you? This is because we like to believe in constancy: A person suffering from depression should logically behave depressively for 24 hours a day!

There are many facets to our understanding of constancy. Over 2000 years ago the Greek philosopher Heraclitus made his famous statement "No man ever steps in the same river twice". Although the stream at the end of our village is always there and always flows towards the same river, if we take a closer look we will see that it is a different stream every time we look: The water has flowed past and never comes back to flow past again.

Our ignorance of our own impermanence is illustrated by a classical tale from the Buddha's lifetime. A woman came to the Buddha with her dead child, inconsolable in her grief and hoping the Buddha could perform a miracle and reanimate her child. The Buddha recognised that a direct, theoretical explanation of our impermanence would be inappropriate and incomprehensible in this moment of grief, so he claimed that to perform magic such as this he would need a special ingredient: mustard seeds from a household that had never experienced a death in the family. The woman ran straight off into the village to find such a family. She knocked at every door and the people wanted to help, but at every house they told her that they had lost relatives. After searching for a long time she slowly began to understand the message: Death comes to everyone; nobody can escape it. Death is not a mistake; it is inevitable and natural that we cannot hold onto something or someone forever. Nothing has absolute existence.

To take some examples from our everyday life: If we buy something new and exciting then we can hardly imagine ever losing it. We love somebody and want to preserve this state forever. Maybe we have a good job and want to keep hold of it for the rest of our working life. The ground under our feet is firm and solid, so we believe that this is naturally and unalterably so.

Misperception with regard to impermanence also concerns our emotions and their impermanence. The earlier Fundamentals should be studied to help recognise this. When an intense emotion, such as anger, love, pain, happiness or fear, arises within us, we can hardly imagine that this feeling will pass. If someone asks us how we felt yesterday, we often remember that we were sad or in a good mood or tired *the whole day*. If we develop a feeling of panic, we immediately have a very strong impulse to flee or distract ourselves.

It is very rare for us to actually realise that this emotion that we feel is only temporary and will soon change. In fact many people find it very annoying to hear that the average duration of a particular emotion is less than one minute. We normally do not experience the truth of this because we prematurely turn away, distract ourselves or prolong the emotions with our secondary reactions. However, if we do actually concentrate our attention on an emotion as it arises and hold it there (see 19th Fundamental of BPT), we will experience for ourselves that it is actually impossible to be scared for 20 minutes, for example, or be continually angry for even 10 minutes. Perhaps the emotion repeats itself anew, and, if we let ourselves be distracted, this feels as if the particular emotion has lasted for a long time. But if we remain undistracted, we can observe the process. Then we can interrupt it and by interrupting it we can observe and understand it in even more detail.

We will need to take a more detailed look at *how* we can stay with a particular emotion by means of mindfulness. It is not the same as dogged perseverance, which traps us in a cycle of unproductive, self-tormenting brooding. We are generally responsible ourselves for keeping unhealthy mental states alive by means of our unconscious mental activities. Closer observation allows us to recognise that, for example, our thoughts nourish and strengthen the feelings; a feeling of anger would quickly dissipate were not for angry thoughts, the feeling of sadness needs sad thoughts in order to persist, etc.

There is a Native American tale of an old man who tells his grandson that there are two wolves fighting within his stomach: an angry grey wolf and a gentle white wolf. The young boy is curious, looks carefully at his grandfather's stomach and asks him which of the wolves will win the struggle. The wise old man replies: The one I feed.

Very often it can feel good to believe that everything surrounding us is firm and stable and will exist for a long time (if not forever). The ground we are walking on is safe and secure; our insights and knowledge seem to be just as secure. We might have an inkling that this is not a perfectly accurate description of reality but we are reluctant to let go of our illusion.

Impermanence can also be experienced symbolically. During special Buddhist practice days, retreats or seminars, whole groups of monks or practitioners spend many hours of detailed, patient work creating very elaborate mandalas made of colourful sand. Hundreds of hours of intensive concentration are often put into these creations. They are unique, harmonic, deeply moving and almost miraculous works of art. And then, at the end of the retreat or practice days, they are brushed away and destroyed. For those present, it can be a dramatic and very real experience of the connection between concentrated effort and the ultimate ineffectuality of our efforts. The preparation of the mandala itself serves to practice meditative concentration; its destruction is a reminder that transformation is always around the corner. Everything, including beauty, ceases to exist. We cannot keep hold of anything. Our focus remains fully in the here and now.

This is an exercise we can also practise for ourselves. We start to draw or paint an elaborate mandala (there are even ready-to-use designs for these) and work on it every day, for example by dedicating an hour every evening to it. When the mandala is finished, we will tear it up or burn it. As we carry out this "destruction" we pay careful attention to all the emotions and thoughts that arise. (In this 13th Fundamental we also discover that every act of apparent destruction is actually always a transformation.) Internalising the insight that nature's inherent characteristic is always impermanence can be a very frightening experience for many of us. On the other hand, this insight may also be felt as a slight relief, since everything negative is also impermanent. Whenever we are suffering or experiencing difficulties we may be able to relax a little if we remember that nothing lasts forever.

Our ignorance of how painful emotions arise

This form of ignorance actually refers to almost all significant processes within us. We will take our emotions as a practical example since we have already had a good introduction to this topic in the 7th Fundamental of BPT.

As we already know, our *intuitive* understanding of how emotions arise is often deceptive. We see a large dog and naturally feel fear within milliseconds. Our boss summons us—of course we instantly feel symptoms of stress. These perfectly understandable reactions appear to suggest that we are completely dependent on the situation we find ourselves in. But are our emotions really only spontaneous and automatic reactions?

We are often fully convinced of the correctness of our emotions (even when we are actually mistaken). Very early in life we learn the simple stimulus-response pattern. Boiling water means scalding and pain. A smiling face means someone to hold us and feelings of happiness. We learn to trust our emotions (most of the time). Indeed, many psychotherapists today still promote this message relatively indiscriminately: We should trust all of our emotions.

Of course, we are not saying it is necessary to *mistrust* every emotion that arises. Nonetheless, it does seem appropriate to take a more discriminating look at this issue, as we did in the 7th Fundamental. When desires arise within us this might be felt as a pleasant tension; if we then move on to fulfil our cravings, we often feel happy (at least for a short time). Or we might experience an anger ("righteous fury") that appears to be helpful in certain situations, providing us with extra strength to defend ourselves, for example. However, in both of these situations, an indiscriminate acceptance of these emotions rarely leads to permanent solutions for our problems. Both positive and negative emotions can lead us into difficult situations. We need a very clear mind and a high level of mindfulness and awareness in order to really determine the consequences of our behaviour.

A range of causes, such as predisposition, current health, and our body's natural cycles, will determine which one of the three primary feelings—a positive, a negative or a neutral feeling—is activated within us by a particular situation. Then our automatic evaluations immediately take over, emerging from the depths of our experience. For example, the sight of a stranger may activate an uncomfortable tension within us. Our interpretation then leads to the secondary emotion; this may be either "Who is that? They might be interesting" or "Who is that? A dangerous stranger?" According to Buddhism, the same applies to an initially pleasant feeling which, after interpretation, may develop into either positive or negative secondary emotions.

We also need to be aware that we generally tend to avoid neutral feelings. Unconsciously we often experience these as boring or "useless waiting around" and prefer to experience strong stimuli which take us out of this neutral condition. With increasing mindfulness, we would do well to take this as a starting point and learn how to experience neutral feelings more as peace and quiet, reining in our tendency to look for the stronger stimuli.

The information presented here is intended to help us develop a deeper understanding of previously unconscious processes within us. It is indispensable to recognise the extremely high relevance of our mental processes and the importance of working to become steadily more conscious of how they occur. Awakened people are much more conscious in this regard. Without this awareness we are nothing more than puppets of our own history, shaped by our experience and trapped in the patterns of our automatic evaluations. To avoid continually re-creating our familiar patterns of experience we need to place greater mindfulness on our evaluations, judgements, opinions and interpretations.

Our ignorance of emptiness

A further misperception is the belief that we possess a self (an "I") that is independent of others and relatively stable. And that the other things around us are equally independent of us and stable. The Buddhist concept of *emptiness* (Sanskrit *shunyata*) states that this is not true: In Buddhist terminology, saying that something is *empty* is the same as saying it has no independent existence—it is empty of independent characteristics or "empty of self". But what does this really mean?

The principle of emptiness of all things, or interdependence, is often illustrated with the example of an ocean wave. The wave exists for a certain period. We would be entitled to believe in its individuality and if we look closely enough we are sure to discover that it is unique. Nonetheless, it originates only in dependence on many other factors, such as currents, water properties, salt content, temperature, the phase of the moon, the Earth's rotation, tectonic movements and the non-linear influence of other waves. The wave is not empty in the sense of being empty of water. It is, however, empty of self in the sense that the wave does not exist independently of the ocean—it has no independent self. That is what Buddhists mean when they talk of the emptiness of all objects.

Just like waves, we humans also need a whole selection of prior conditions to be fulfilled in order to become who we are today. We can take the crest of the wave as a symbol for the very *individual* aspects of being human, such as nationality, religion, looks, fingerprints, genetic predispositions, profession and lifestyle. The deep base of the wave is then symbolic for the *universal*, common aspects of all humans: Metabolism, organs and sexual reproduction are identical, and our need for sleep, food, protection and security are also extremely similar. If we proceed to an even deeper level, we have features identical or very similar with all mammals including instinctual behaviour, nourishment and digestion. Continuing deeper within the wave, we have many things in common with lower species of animal such as cells made of the same types of proteins and similar nerve cells. When we reach the level where we can see that in common with plants we also need nutrients, warmth and sunlight and we also have a common "will to survive", then we should be able to recognise that we are no longer talking about a part of the wave that is clearly identifiable as the individual wave (individual species) we started with, but is now just as much part of the whole ocean (all forms of life). So it really is not a contradiction to acknowledge that we have both a unique identity and a universal interconnection.

Another everyday example used to describe emptiness and interdependence is a simple wooden table.

- The table was brought to the place where it now stands. For this, it needed vehicles, fuel, drivers and all of the factors that these in turn needed for their existence.

- The table was constructed. This needed wood, glue, tools and carpenters. Again, all of these also need other factors in order to exist.
- The wood came from trees which were felled and processed. This needed lumberjacks, chainsaws and vehicles, as well as everything these need for their existence.
- The trees were planted. This needed older trees, earth, sun, rain and insects. Again, all of these also need other factors in order to exist.

Furthermore, even the most basic of these factors are dependent on the climate and other global conditions.

Of course, this really only presents the "tip of the iceberg", but it should suffice to help us understand that absolutely *everything* in our world is subject to this principle of complete interdependence with *everything else*. The table is *empty* of any properties that only exist in it and therefore make it independent. A table has nothing that is inherent to it alone, since there are no specific properties that only this object possesses or only exist in this object. However, the table is *full* of many other properties and factors such as forest, earth, rain, sun, wood, carpenter and hammer, which demonstrate its interconnection with all other things. All things are *empty* but at the same time *full*. Every object is a *compound* object—a composite of many other factors and conditions—and impermanent because this complex composition cannot remain unchanged.

This emptiness of self also applies to us as human beings, and we are also full of the factors of interconnectedness. Take a look at your hand. Like your body as a whole, your hand is actually more than two-thirds water. (The person we love is 70% water?!) Where do you think this water came from? Did you drink it? And before that? It came out of deep springs, from rain, from water vapour, from rivers and from the Earth's oceans. Maybe these very water molecules in your hand were previously the habitat of a fish deep in the ocean. Maybe they were previously part of the hand of another person (many of us find this idea somewhat off-putting). We all perspire and our sweat evaporates, contributing to the moisture content of the air around us (which we need to survive). These cycles do not only concern water. So we only need to consider a few essential factors of life such as oxygen, beneficial bacteria or carbohydrates to realise how deeply interwoven all living beings on this planet are.

The deeper we look, the more signs of our interconnection we experience and the more clearly we recognise that we too are composite beings. We, too, are empty of the factors that would define us as independently existing and therefore we are empty of an independent "I".

Our ignorance about our self, "I" or ego

The Buddhist insight into the emptiness of all things and therefore also the illusion of an independent "I" or self is one of the most difficult insights to convey.

It appears to be a very clear contradiction of our everyday experience, where we clearly experience a dominant self or sense of I. However, we can see parallels to another basic insight: the fact that the Earth is a sphere. If we think about it, our everyday experience seems to contradict this, too: We clearly walk around on a flat surface—so the Earth must be flat! Sometimes we really do have to look deeper to uncover the truth.

The philosopher René Descartes was one of the most famous representatives of the Western philosophical tradition and is particularly well-known for his sentence: I think, therefore I am. As we will see the I is very tricky and cleverly establishes itself within us, making us believe that it has a solid, continual existence. It appears logical to claim "I think, therefore I am", but perhaps it would be more accurate to restate his conclusion as "Thoughts exist, therefore thought is". Perhaps it is our I which then tricks us into believing that thought cannot be separated from a self and therefore the existence of thought proves the existence of I.

Even if we perceive people to be far more individual than waves in an ocean, the existence of a person is actually just as dependent on many factors as the existence of an individual wave is. The sense of self or feeling of "I" is a feeling of separation, of being separated, and therefore contrary to the feeling of "we" or interconnection. But our life is actually a result of innumerable prerequisites that were necessary and are necessary for our survival, so there can be no denying that we are part of a very complex network.

We are dependent because there is nothing within us which would allow us to exist independently. We are *empty* of properties which would grant us independent existence. So this logic dictates that we do not have an independent I or self. Our basic, underlying nature is interconnection. This in turn shows us that compassion is a basic component of our existence.

These considerations lead to the question of whether it is preferable to aspire to a healthy sense of self or to the lack of sense of self: a healthy ego or egolessness. From a Western point of view, a weak ego is a sign of a problem—perhaps even a psychological disorder. From an Eastern point of view, a less-developed ego seems to be desirable. The Buddhist saying "No ego no problem" is often disputed here in the West, but this clash of views is actually based on a lack of mutual understanding. Buddhists make this statement on the assumption of an ideal normal condition: a healthy, stable ego which every human develops as they grow up. So Buddhists are not promoting "underdeveloped" egos but rather pointing out that even "fully developed" healthy egos still continue to create problems and suffering.

If we are supposed to reduce or break down our ego, does this lead to a void? Is there something missing afterwards? Should we replace it with something? As our practice leads to a deflation of the sense of self we will notice that this process enables a connection to a much greater whole. So rather than experiencing something "missing" we feel enriched. Of course, in Buddhist Psychotherapy we receive careful instructions and accompaniment for these experiences to ensure that we stay on track in a healthy way.

The principles of emptiness and egolessness are often consciously or unconsciously misused in order to rationalise escapism, along the lines of "Nothing really exists, everything is just a dream". Jack Kornfield's comment on this phenomenon is: If a Zen student argues that everything is just a figment of his imagination, their Zen master would hit them sharply with a stick and ask them, "So, was that just a dream?"

To conclude this section, it seems an appropriate place to briefly mention the Buddhist concept of death and rebirth. What happens when the wave "dies"? Examining the metaphor above, we can see, for example, that none of the water molecules making up the wave actually disappear or cease to exist. Everything that existed before—including its interconnections with everything else—still exists after the "wave" has "died". It is left to the reader to complete the transfer of these ideas onto the example of a human life.

Nonetheless, there are no fixed dogmas in Buddhism. You could follow the above argumentation leading from the principle of emptiness and interconnection to a belief in rebirth; you would probably then make every effort to lead a good life now in order to have a better *next life*. However, if you do not believe in rebirth then the insights into interconnection and the way feelings and emotions arise combined with an emphasis on the here and now would still lead you to make every effort to lead a good life now—in order to have a good life *now*.

So whether we start with the principle of interdependence and emptiness or with the principle of maintaining a focus on the here and now, we still end up seeing that we should lead a "good life"; in other words, we recognise the importance of compassion as an essential building block for our existence.

Our ignorance about our compassion

The term compassion is often mistakenly assumed to mean the same as pity. However, in a Buddhist context these two terms are very different. Indiscriminately showering someone with feelings or looking down on someone in an unfortunate situation and offering them a handout are not expressions of compassion in the Buddhist sense of the term. Instead, compassion is considered to be a very profound and essential understanding of the mutual, systemic interdependence and interconnection of all beings which the Buddha recognised 2500 years ago and which has also entered into the world view of many Western scientists in recent years. For example, climatologists are engaged in a very lively debate on the effects of mutual dependencies.

True compassion is an *active* approach to life with an awareness that we should help other living beings directly and indirectly—and that we are able to do this. It is more than empathy (the ability to feel the emotions of a person we are with) and it is certainly not the same as being passively overwhelmed or infected by the emotions of someone close to us.

Compassion is a mentality or attitude arising out of a deep understanding of the *interconnection* of all the things around us.

Within this understanding we see that we are not a separate or isolated being but rather an integrated and inextricably linked part of an infinitely networked world. Every one of our actions has innumerable effects on everyone else and therefore on ourselves as well. This leads a Buddhist to the conclusion that there is an imperative to act (in the most compassionate way possible).

The Buddhist understanding of *virtue* is also an *active* approach demanding positive action. The virtue of being honest involves more than just not committing dishonest deeds; an honest person actively works for truth and the rights of all other living beings (see 20th Fundamental).

This contrasts with a very common attitude in our culture where a virtuous person is someone who does *not* do something: A virtuous person does not steal, does not kill, does not lie, does not consume drugs etc.

Having read all this, some readers will undoubtedly sympathise with those who claim emphatically, "I'm having such a hard time. How on Earth am I supposed to look after others as well?!" This is in fact an expression of our ignorance of the nature of our interdependence. With a little less ignorance, we can turn it around and recognise: "Actually you are having such a hard time because you are not sufficiently interested in other people." Our feelings of connection with others are signs of a healthy mind, whereas our feelings of isolation are often a symptom of unhealthy mental states.

There is also a biological basis to our connection. Fundamental biological processes such as the way nerve cells function are almost identical in all living organisms. Many of the components necessary for life, such as the enzyme cytochrome C, which is an essential component of our metabolism, are identical in all living beings from primates to yeast. The genetics of our closest relatives, the chimpanzees, are 99% identical to ours. This 1% difference means that we are closer to them than two species of gibbons are to each other (6% difference). Unfortunately this wonderful principle of connection has had a gruesome side effect: Legions of animals have perished or suffered in experiments to gain information for the benefit of humans, including their use for experiments with new medicines.

There are so many consequences of our interconnection, both positive and negative, so it is worth considering it very carefully. If this insight into our comprehensive interdependence is the only one we choose to adopt from the whole selection of Buddhist teachings, it is still enough to make a huge contribution to a peaceful and non-violent way of living together. We could consider such ideas as the following: Because I like to buy very cheap products, there are many people whose jobs are cut; the high rates of interest I enjoy on my savings lead to banks and credit institutes to step up their exploitative activities in other, poorer countries; our freedom to drive anywhere we want is connected with ecological consequences all over the world. This list could be continued infinitely.

So it should now be clear that everything can only arise and exist dependently. This thing here exists because that thing over there exists. He is the way he is because I am the way I am. Others are the way they are because we are the way we are.

An exercise
We can try to make ourselves aware of this connection as often as possible by remembering a sentence such as "This person in front

of me is the way they are because I am the way I am. I am the way I am because they are the way they are." During the course of the day we can try this out on many different types of people. This will confront us with many of our tendencies to judge and clearly reveal our tendencies to manage the distance between us and others.

Experiencing this involves both compassion and an understanding of connection, both of which are very beautiful concepts that are difficult to put into practice. We often have very good reason for not liking someone; if they curse or threaten us, how is it possible to believe that they are the way they are because we are the way we are? To really adopt this attitude at an inner level involves gaining a truly deep insight into the nature of universal interdependency.

Are we an island?

The saying "No man is an island" may be well-known, but if we really want to combat our mistaken feelings of isolation and independence, we need to do more than just quote famous sayings. If we think about islands we can recognise that in fact they are not separate; underneath the water there is continuous land linking one "summit of an underwater mountain" to another. However, even this intellectual contemplation of the phenomena is not enough: Meditative contemplation and direct experience are needed to really internalise this insight, which can then lead us deeper into the truth of our life. Buddhism *is* rooted *in* the world; compassion should lead us to put our insights into practice in everyday life and assume ever more self-responsibility.

The most frequent obstacles to living out compassion are rage and anger; feelings of loneliness and isolation also get in the way. Rage and anger are examples of feelings generally accompanied by intense physical sensations and high energies, which can cut us off from compassion. We will discover more about this phenomenon, so here we will simply mention that dealing with anger really is a very difficult balancing act. Many psychological and psychosomatic symptoms arise because of an overly introverted attitude which can lead to us "swallowing" problems instead of "letting them out", although the latter in itself is also not a solution. In the 19th Fundamental of BPT we will discover more about how we can deal with difficult emotions in a mindful way.

Our ignorance of the limits of knowledge

We will now move from the general systemic level and go a little deeper into the details, treading the path of physicists and looking into everything that exists, asking what it is made of. Physicists continued the tradition of the natural philosophers, looking for the most basic building blocks of life and trying to find the ultimate answers. Technological developments led to historical successes, discovering molecules, atoms and then subatomic particles. Delving deeper into matter then required huge efforts, but these too were successful; phenomena were discovered which we now know as quarks, followed by superstrings. Interestingly, these theories do not imagine matter to be like a sandcastle, with tiny grains of sand piled on top of each other. Instead, the spaces between these tiny subatomic particles are extraordinarily large in comparison to the particles' size. Perhaps we can compare this to our solar system, in which the sun, planets and moons constitute a whole; the main characteristic of this whole is, however, distance, space or emptiness. Physicists' further investigations have also revealed that our superficial distinction between matter and energy is not as clear-cut as we think. Matter and energy can be regarded as equivalent. So it could be said that something non-material constitutes all material things.

This subject matter is highly complex, and even leading physicists cannot agree on all of the details. The extremely technical procedures involved mean that neither particle physicists nor astrophysicists can ever express their statements with absolute certainty. Furthermore, physics was very quick to recognise the "observer effect". At a basic level this reminds us that the question being researched determines the type of experimental design and apparatus, which in turn determines the type of answers which can be found. And on a more fundamental level it has been shown that the mere observation of a process actually influences the process itself.

Agreement has been reached that the journey deeper and deeper into matter will never end. In other words, the quest to find out what we and all other things are made of leads us further and further into "the void"—every new answer gives rise to many new questions.

So we run into difficulties when we look for anything solid in the depths of matter. And we also have problems finding confirmation of our idea that the things around us exist independently from us and others. Nonetheless, we are good at constructing a world around us. This apparent contradiction is less surprising when we realise that we do not have to profoundly understand this world we construct. It is sufficient for the model to "work".

Many readers will have played the following group guessing game. One person goes out of the room and the others choose a term which the first person has to guess when they come back in. They do this by asking 20 questions which can be answered with yes or no. Legend has it there was once a group which decided not to choose a term but to try and answer the 20 questions consistently and correctly anyway. This meant that only the first answer could be chosen randomly; for each further answer, the group had to think carefully to ensure that their answer did not contradict any previous ones. The 20th question was then, "Is it a crocodile?" and all the participants were surprised to realise that the answer had to be yes. The questioner had indeed found the correct answer (although there originally was none).

Critics of science could argue that scientific research sometimes works in a similar way to this game. Ever more questions in a particular direction are asked, special equipment is designed, and all of this then "ensures" that the right answers are found.

Science has certainly delivered some very fascinating discoveries but at the same time it reveals that we do not really understand some very important areas of our environment. We are pushing ahead into areas that open up more questions than they answer. Although scientists have become symbols of intellectual achievement for many people, it is actually these very scientists who clearly demonstrate the limits of our systems of knowledge and concepts.

Our ignorance about our cognitive faculties or powers of perception

It can be very difficult for us to realise that there really is a difference between the objects around us and our perception of these objects. We perceive a table by means of our senses (feel it, see it etc.) and then believe very firmly that this image of the table in our mind is identical to the object existing "out there". However, there are no objective objects; there are only *objects of our perception*.

Imagine looking at a snowy landscape. Do we really see the same thing as an Eskimo, who grew up in ice and snow? Or as an Australian aborigine, who has never seen snow before? If we look at the table, do we see it in the same way as a carpenter?

Actually, we do not really see anything objective, but simply interpret patterns of light on our retina (seeing) or electrical signals from the receptors in our skin (touching) etc. And the product of this interpretation depends on our prior experiences.

The image produced in our mind is not a 1:1 projection of the object because a multitude of different nerve cells with different tasks is involved, working together in a complex way. It is not a simple "photograph" but rather the product of a creative process putting together very many individual pieces of information to make a whole. The images that arise within us when we sense something are made up of more information than simply the impulses coming from the respective sense organ. So when we see something we see with more than just our eyes! Seeing is a very complex and creative process which takes place more in our brain than in our eyes (and the same applies to our other senses).

Objects actually do not have any fixed, unchangeable properties. We recognise an apple whether it is small, irregular and green or large, smooth and red. An apple can have different colours and these can change. A mouldy, brown, rotting apple is still an apple. And we would still recognise an apple if it were 1m in diameter and made of concrete! The taste of different apples can vary from bitter to sour to sweet. So shape, taste, size and colour are not fixed. Nothing is constant and nothing defines an apple. We simply have a variety of concepts of what an apple is. This also applies to everything else which we perceive. Basically, we interpret sensory signals, compare these to existing concepts in our mind and develop an idea or opinion.

This is a further demonstration of how all objects are compound or composite. Nothing has a fixed existence. Everything is changing all the time. Nothing exists for itself.

Neurological casuistry (case-based research—most doctors describe the people seeking their help as "cases") has shown us that one of the main activities in the brain serves to construct connections and contexts—in other words, to integrate. A very famous neurologist is the British professor Oliver Sacks, who has described scientific insights into neurological disorders in several entertaining books, including *The Man Who Mistook His Wife for a Hat* and *A Leg to Stand On*. Professor Sacks' "clinical anecdotes" describe a wide range of people with neurological anomalies due to accidents, metabolic disorders or tumours. He describes vividly how these disturbances at a biological level in the brain lead to problems such as the disintegration or fragmentation of our perception. Physical sensations or perception schemes that were previously coherent cease to be so. For example, someone may experience their own arm as a foreign object or no longer perceive objects as a fixed whole but as a continuously changing, flowing process.

A related topic is that of optical illusions. Most readers will be familiar with these and the issue is well-documented so we will not consider it in detail here, but it does show us how susceptible the creative nature of our perception makes us to misperceptions.

The nature of the things that we recognise around us is characterised by impermanence. They have no independent existence; they are without self; they are compound, arising through the interaction of numerous other factors; they can only be understood and explained in terms of these interdependencies. This argumentation should make clear that we never see the things around us as they "really" are. Instead we perceive them according to our prior experiences and sensory conditions. In fact, although the range of sensory frequencies we have researched around us is extremely wide and diverse, our powers of perception are rather limited compared to many other animals. There is an endless list of information from our surroundings which we are not able to perceive, such as x-rays, radiation, short and long waves, radio waves and natural ground radiation.

Looking deeper shows us that although our experiences and perceptions seem to be so certain and reliable, they are in fact anything but certain.

Our ignorance about our rational mind

Our rational mind is extremely precious and appears irreplaceable, so it is natural for us to be worried about "losing our mind" or "not being in our right mind".

There was hardly a time in human history when our individual access to knowledge was as extensive and rapid as it is today. However, this privilege has given rise to at least two problems: Firstly, we are bombarded with an almost permanent input and secondly, this accentuates our rational mind's own dynamic characteristics and tendency to create identifications.

We have already considered our deceptive perception of a constant feeling of self. Many, if not all, readers will agree with the statement that we did not come into the world like this: In the beginning there was no *self* or "I". There were probably only the three primary feelings: positive, negative and neutral.

The discipline of developmental psychology has developed a very sophisticated way of describing how the experience of self then develops. To put it very briefly, our very first pre- and post-natal moments in life are experienced as complete symbiosis with our mother. However, after that it is impossible for any mother to be available for 24 hours a day and perfectly meet every need of an infant, so our life necessarily leads to situations which we experience as tense, threatening, painful or scary.

Even in a very small infant there is a general instinct or survival principle which tries to reduce tension and restore balance. Attempting to do this without our parents' intervention (or even as a response to their actions) highlights the fact that this infant is separate from its environment. Its slowly developing rational mind forms an idea of self during this process of understanding and controlling the interactions between itself and its environment. We begin to store experiences that provide us with information about a self: If *I* do this, that happens; if *I* smile, a smile comes back; if *I* cry, *I* often receive food or attention.

Later, identifications are formed as concepts are learnt or developed: I am a girl/boy; I can do this well that, I cannot do that well; I should do this more often because it makes me feel good; I should not do that very often because it makes me feel bad. Our power of reasoning (our rational mind) continues to form and become more sophisticated. Our sense of self becomes more stable and permanent.

The previous Fundamentals have already described how there is no fixed, single location in the brain that is home to a sense of self. Brain researchers understand our ego to be a network comprised of structures located in all regions of our brain. So there is no independent, stable ego. Instead, there are many different ego activities: I pay heed to my conscience (ethical self); I remember something from the past (autobiographical awareness or self); I am aware of my body (body awareness or perspective self); I carry out an action (action-planning self, self-attribution of actions); I check where I am in time and space (orienting self); I think about myself (self-reflecting awareness); etc. This all happens in very different regions of the brain and in a relatively stable way. Everybody behaves according to their character, but our behaviour also depends strongly on our situation and mood.

So our hardware (our brain) does not contain a fixed ego centre, and our software (our behaviour) does not exhibit stable or consistent ego properties. We have conducted a fairly sophisticated search for our ego or "I" so we should now be slowly coming to the conclusion that we have once again fallen victim to a form of self-deception.

Originally, our ego and our rational mind were intended to be tools to help us survive in this world. However, a "silent revolution" steadily took place without our noticing. Our rational mind took control. It created identifications, and these accumulated, leading to the situation in which we believe that we are identical with our rational mind and the sense of self. We *are* the tool.

The identifications suggested to us by our rational mind took on a life of their own. I *am* a hard worker; I *am* a bad person; I *am* right; I *am* a victim; I *am* an anxious person; I *am* helpless. The roles took over and we began to believe that we have to behave accordingly, repeating these behaviours, establishing them and lending them a fixed structure.

Incessant activity on the part of the rational mind is needed to maintain these suggestions. Our mind never stops. Buddhists often compare it to a little, restless monkey hurrying here and there. Goethe put the following words into the mouth of his figure Faust: "When, to the Moment then, I say 'Ah, stay a while! You are so lovely!' Then you can grasp me: then you may, Then, to my ruin, I'll go gladly! Then they can ring the passing bell." We have all become Faust, driven by our rational mind, always moving on restlessly, never being aware of the moment, our focus is always on the next step.

Our rational mind seems to find it very difficult to stay in the present moment. It apparently suffers from a compulsion to create time and busy itself with the past or the present. This fact itself would appear to lend the present moment a particular significance. So it seems appropriate for Buddhist teachings and practice to highlight the key role played by the here and now: Use the insights to stay in the here and now and help yourself and others (see 10th Fundamental of BPT).

In addition to creating time (i.e. past and future), our rational mind also loves to keep itself busy with thoughts and worries and with an inexhaustible "drip feed" of constant input. What would happen if we turned this off? No TV, no telephone, no computer, no Internet, no book, no newspaper and no action: just sitting quietly. We would be alone with our rational mind. And this is initially very difficult.

So we can see that our rational mind is a very helpful tool that has developed a life of its own. Each one of us is much more than the sum of the different identifications our mind offers us. Are we just our body? Or are we just our brain?

And where does this possessive pronoun "our" (or "my") come from anyway? By now we should have begun to understand that our ego (which can possess something) is not completely identical to some psychological or physiological aspect of us as a living being. The ego is nothing more than a construction of our rational mind which should serve us as well as possible in particular situations. However, our real existence should not be reduced to this. This can be particularly difficult to grasp or experience because it does not correspond to the superficial experience we have in everyday life. To help us come to terms with this, we should remember other common examples which show us that our everyday experience is not a reliably calibrated measuring instrument. Does our everyday experience correspond to the fact that we are standing on the surface of a planet rotating on its own axis with a surface speed of over 1500 km/h (plus the speed with which the planet is travelling around the sun)? The way we perceive the world has developed to ensure our survival—no more and no less.

To summarise: The insight into no-self (breaking down the illusion of ego) and the many limits to our knowledge, perception and cognition form a central element of Buddhism which is very difficult to understand and convey. In a therapeutic context it is particularly important to choose the right moment for this, especially to take into account the current state of the help-seeker. For people lacking the necessary balance and strength, other structures which provide stability and security are needed first because the concept of egolessness would otherwise be overwhelming.

Ignorance and Connection

We have seen that our ignorance pervades many areas of our life. Just how valuable it is to be able to admit this cannot be appreciated highly enough. And admitting our ignorance can also enable a fundamental relaxation in our attitudes, particularly because we realise there are no longer any fixed opinions which we have to defend.

Help-seekers who have not previously studied the Buddhist teachings should be encouraged to become familiar with the practical implications rather than focusing on the theory. This means that we as therapists show them a constructive way to deal with unhealthy mental states and difficult emotions. As mentioned above, the Buddhist way of doing this is a three-stage process: (1) *Recognise and understand,* (2) *Contemplate and internalise,* (3) *Realise and implement.*

Of course, the task of *rationally* considering the deficits of our *rational* mind is anything other than straightforward. So Buddhist Psychotherapy has a range of practical exercises on offer to assist the process. We need to find the strength to acknowledge that we persist in our unconscious, unknowing or deluded states despite—or in many cases because of—our power of reasoning.

If we want to consider the issue of our ignorance it might be advisable to check if we have understood the basics of the Buddhist teaching on the Three Marks of Existence or Three Seals.

The Three Marks of Existence are
- Impermanence (*anicca*)
- Unsatisfactoriness, or suffering (*dukkha*)
- Non-Self, or dependent arising (*anatta*)

As was described above, we first have to understand and internalise the fact that everything is in a constant state of flux. Nothing is permanent; everything is continually changing. Change is the only constant.

We need to give up our idealism; it is unrealistic and therefore mistaken. We should relax: There is no perfect job, no perfect partner, no perfect whatever. Unsatisfactoriness is not an error. It is part of our nature.

All living beings and all the things we come into contact with are compound phenomena. In other words, they arise dependently. Nothing can arise or exist without prior conditions.

The Buddhist views of interdependence, interconnection, impermanence and emptiness really do need to be understood, internalised and put into practice.

As a type of summary, we will now take a look at the term *interbeing* which was coined by the Vietnamese Buddhist master Thich Nhat Hanh. This concept includes all of the significant Buddhist factors regarding impermanence, connection, life and death, rebirth and emptiness etc.

Interbeing

Thich Nhat Hanh uses this term to clearly illustrate how inseparable and connected we are. In his teachings he often uses very practical examples of this. The book you are reading now has a certain weight so the longer you hold it the more clearly you will feel it. Look very closely at this page: Is it smooth or a little rough? We can feel it if we run our fingertips over the page. We can feel the paper. We can see the colour of the ink. Where does this ink come from? What is needed to make ink? Which country was this ink made in? Under what conditions? The fibre in the pages was previously part of the trunk of a tree. Where did this tree stand? What type of tree was it? Who felled it? If we delve deeper into the mystery that the material aspects of this book represent, we come into contact with paper, printing ink, wood, trees, sun, rain, earth, lumberjacks, sawmills, paper factories, workers, suppliers and much more. We could say that the whole cosmos is within this little book. Thousands of prior conditions come together in order for us to be able to hold this book in our hands. This is a very practical example of what we mean in Buddhism with the terms *dependent origination* or *interdependence*. Furthermore, this book has nothing unique and defining for this book: It is *full* of paper, ink, wood, tree, sun and rain but *empty* of anything that is not shared with anything else. There is nothing that is only typical of "book". The book is a compound—comprised of numerous other materials and conditions. This applies to everything in the universe, including human beings. So the book is also a practical example of the Buddhist understanding of *emptiness*.

When the book burns

Inspired by Thich Nhat Hanh's teachings we can now imagine taking a box of matches and setting fire to this book. It would burst into flames, transform and heat would arise, as would light, smoke and ashes. The contents of the book would not burn; they would continue to exist. The smoke might rise into the clouds, giving rise to rain, which would water some trees, which would then be used to make paper for more books. The ashes might end up in the earth and then become nutrients for more trees.

Before we strike the match, where is the flame? When the book has fully burnt, where did the flame go? If the conditions are right (oxygen, a spark, combustible material), a flame can reappear and if the conditions change, it disappears. The flame needs oxygen; trees produce oxygen. Trees also produce combustible material. Fire produces ashes which act as fertiliser for more trees (and thus more combustible material).

We are taking a flame as a symbol here for any other phenomenon, but in particular for our mind. Everything continues to transform, subject to a constant flux of change. This inextinguishable connection between us and all other things around us is the meaning of Thich Nhat Hanh's term *interbeing*. Within this understanding, there is no birth and no death; there is only the eternal process of becoming and passing away.

Here in the 13th Fundamental of BPT we have been documenting various aspects of Buddhism as a science of the mind and its appeal to us to acknowledge and investigate our ignorance and to commit ourselves to reducing it, shining the light of awareness into the darkness of our ignorance. The active definition of the term "virtue" in Buddhism encourages us to be active in our quest for more profound knowledge and not to be content with just limiting our ignorance.

Thich Nhat Hanh refers us to the Eight Great Realisations, which can help us to attain enlightenment and liberation:

1) All dharmas (phenomena) are impermanent and empty of independent self.

2) More desire brings more suffering.
3) A simple life leads to more peace.
4) Only diligent practice leads to liberation.
5) Ignorance is the cause of birth and death, samsara, the endless wheel of life and therefore: suffering.
6) Poverty is the cause of negative thoughts. Generosity is important.
7) We live in this world but we should not get caught up in worldly matters.
8) We are not struggling solely for our own liberation but for that of all living beings.

Wolfgang Z speaks very openly about how obsessively he has to clean and control everything. Wolfgang takes his duties and, indeed, everything in his life overly seriously. In his course of Buddhist Psychotherapy, the first teaching he can really grasp is about mindfulness. Wolfgang considers it to be very important to behave carefully, respectfully and mindfully and can carry over these thoughts to other aspects of mindfulness. Since the first foundation of mindfulness is mindfulness of the body, in his first meditation sessions, Wolfgang is instructed to imagine situations where he can clearly sense his compulsions. The next step is to focus his attention on any physical reactions (tensions) during these obsessive phases. This is then followed by guiding Wolfgang through the further foundations of mindfulness: becoming aware of *emotional* aspects (fear and anger) and *mental* reaction patterns (fear of losing control, desire for stability).
Wolfgang realises that his compulsive actions give him a sense of security, but this has problematic aspects because it is partly based on a misperception of stability and permanence.

This Fundamental Should Convey the Following:

During BPT the many forms of ignorance, such as inattentiveness, denial and misperception of reality, have to be studied and analysed very carefully, allowing each help-seeker to gain an individual understanding and intensive personal experience of them. The basic aim is to look for the liberation which is an end to our ignorance.

We now move on to describe two further important causes of suffering: attachment and aversion. There is constant interplay between these two and ignorance.

The 14th
Fundamental of Buddhist Psychotherapy

Recognise and Convey the Noble Truth about Our Attachment

> To take for permanent
> that which is only transitory
> is like the delusion of a madman.
>
> Kalu Rinpoche

> No ego, no suffering.
>
> (Buddhist saying)

So now we turn to another cause of our suffering: attachment. This is one of the three causes of all *avoidable* suffering and was described by the Buddha in the Second Noble Truth.

Attachment can reveal itself in very different ways: from the love of beautiful things and the desire for pleasure through to coveting, greed and addiction. In Buddhist usage, the term refers to every form of holding onto something (in thought or in deed), fixation, obsession, not letting go and "wanting to have".

When we are feeling good or experiencing a pleasant situation we often want to hold onto this, conserve it and avoid anything negative (for as long as possible). We believe that we can have exclusively positive experiences and maintain purely comfortable conditions if we do the right things and make the right effort.

This craving takes place on many very different levels. At the level of basic needs there are in fact many very essential and necessary desires: we need food; we need shelter; we need money. These things are necessary for survival and we generally do not have a free supply of them. Instead we have to obtain them somehow.

The Buddha recognised that we could prevent a lot of suffering by ensuring that everybody's basic needs for income, food and shelter are met. So we can see that the Buddha was already engaged in improving our *social* situation and not just mental-spiritual issues; many Buddhists have followed his example during the millennia since.

Desire is also fundamentally necessary for our survival at the emotional level. Without any form of desire, we would not seek a partner and ensure the reproduction of our species-this might actually be the basis for all other intense human mechanisms of desire. However, these mechanisms seem to have come off track in the highly developed Western countries because survival is no longer an issue for most of us; they now express themselves as the desire to possess or consume more and more.

The principle of attachment also pervades every other aspect of our life. We never want to lose the people we love; they should never be allowed to die or move on. We possess many beautiful and valuable items; these should never be allowed to break.

> A significant cause of our suffering and entrapment in the cycle of suffering is our attachment. The feelings associated with this can be both positive (enjoyment) and negative (greed).

Western and Eastern Views on Attachment

Western cultures tend to place a high value in pleasure and the ability to enjoy life as well as all other positive feelings, with the provision that nobody is harmed. The Buddhist view is that there is no essential difference between positive and negative aspects of attachment. Attachment is never something positive, even if it initially gives rise to enjoyment and pleasure. A true capacity for pleasure needs to include a thorough understanding of possible entanglements which can arise.

As far as Buddhism and Buddhist Psychotherapy are concerned, enjoyment and our constant search for more enjoyment can be compared with taking sedatives: We numb ourselves for a short time in order to escape reality, responsibility or the corresponding emotional reactions.

If this sounds "anti-pleasure", we need to reiterate that, if we want to liberate ourselves fundamentally, we are not freeing ourselves *from* pleasure but rather freeing ourselves *in the midst* of our pleasures.

Maybe we are like a small rodent trying to hoard food-our stockpile can never be large enough. But if we stop for a moment and look inwards, we recognise that everything can decay and perish. Somewhere deep within us we know that there is no such thing as absolute security.

So it is easy to understand that fear and attachment are connected. However, we need to recognise that hoarding (and our attachment to our possessions) will only really allay these fears in the short term and superficially. An example of this is the number of rich people who are still anxious and mistrusting, plagued by fears of losing what they have. In fact, like all other people, they know (or at least suspect) that sooner or later they will lose everything.

Everything is subject to change, nothing is permanent. If we take a deeper look at this truth we may be able to find some relief in it: Okay, whatever I am currently experiencing will not last forever. Worry, too, is not permanent, even if it is mercilessly pervasive, gnawing at our soul like an uninvited hungry guest constantly knocking at our door (often the case if we do not train our mind). If we can experience the relief that lies within the insight that everything negative is impermanent, then we also have to understand and internalise the fact that everything positive is also impermanent. The nature of our whole existence is impermanence, non-constancy and change. In fact, if this were not so, the world around us and we as humans would not even have been able to evolve.

So there is a type of desire which is necessary for survival-satisfying basic needs-and a multiplicity of "derailed" desires. How can we learn to distinguish healthy from unhealthy? In this context it once again becomes clear why Buddhists do not distinguish between *good* and *bad* but rather between *healthy* and *unhealthy*. Attachment and the corresponding suffering arise not only from bad desires, but also from good ones. The apparently good feeling of enjoyment or pleasure quite often develops into neediness, envy, jealousy, anger or even hate and injury. And sometimes, if we remain mindful, we can even gain a healthy power from an unhealthy emotion such as anger. So we need to understand that whether our reactions and corresponding physical or psychological sensitivities are positive or negative, the most important thing is to deal with them in a very mindful and critical way.

Which attachments do we have to give up?

In this regard, Buddhists often have very different opinions to many other people. From a Buddhist point of view, we should aspire to a condition which frees us from both bad *and* good experiences. We liberate ourselves from all positive and negative attachments.

Should we really liberate ourselves from emotions as nice as love, joy and happiness? What type of life would that be?

This issue is very often a source of misunderstanding, particularly because Buddhist literature itself contains very different statements which can even appear contradictory. Some Buddhist authors seem to be extremely fundamentalist in their approach when they talk of the goal as *perfect* or *absolute* liberation. In fact, it is very difficult to really know what they mean without receiving teachings directly from them.

Buddhist Psychotherapy follows the basic principle which the Buddha himself clearly explained as the *Middle Way:* Remain in the middle and avoid extremes.

With regard to liberating ourselves from attachments, this means that we do not liberate ourselves *from* our feelings but rather *in the midst of* them.

We are human, and human beings have intense emotions, so we should not lose contact with these. We naturally feel angry when we experience injustice and sympathy or compassion for people close to us. *However*, we do not let these feelings dominate us: We become free. This is the context that should make it clear why Buddhist Psychotherapists distinguish between positive and negative emotions in a different way to that of many other Western therapists.

It should have become clear by now that many positive emotional reactions can lead to various aspects of attachment. For this reason, in psychotherapeutic situations it is particularly important to be able to carefully contextualise positive changes and emotions, in order to avoid the danger of simply replacing an old identification or attachment with a new one. During a limited *transition* phase it might be helpful to use a new identification with Buddhist values to enable the help-seeker to give up an old identification (as a victim, for example). However, as therapists we are responsible for ensuring that this remains a helpful *interim* solution. In order to be able to do this we necessarily have to free ourselves of our identification with and attachment to our role as counsellor or Buddhist therapist. We may *have* this role but we *are* not the role.

The issue of dissolving attachments and the Wisdom of the Middle Way are directly connected with each other. We will see this repeatedly as we proceed in this context. Perhaps many of us, just like the Buddha himself, will initially tend to distance ourselves too much as we attempt to avoid the attachments and addictions we previously enjoyed. Very often we see an oscillation from one side to the other: After the attachment comes the phase of avoidance; as we notice this, we try to avoid the avoidance and become slightly attached, and so on. However, the amplitude of the oscillations reduces as we proceed, gradually finding our way back from the extremes to the middle way.

We should not be tempted to immediately throw away all of the possessions in our apartment that are not absolutely necessary. There is an old saying that encourages us to let material wealth into our house but not into our heart.

We do not slip from an old role straight into the next role-for example, becoming "a Buddhist" (or at least, what we believe a Buddhist to be). We avoid identifications and we avoid extremes.

We are okay the way we are but we still have to change something! This appears to be a paradox but we can discover its truth by means of meditation (initially guided), which can help us to feel the distinctions deep within us as we analyse and penetrate the protective layers we have built up around our core Inner Nobility (see 8th Fundamental of BPT). The goal consists of feeling life with all of its intensity but remaining mindful and aware, avoiding any identification with current or past conditions, i.e. with roles, status symbols or other desires. We free ourselves *in the midst of* everything that life offers us.

The Necessity of Liberating Ourselves from Role Attachments and Identifications

The stereotypical roles and the identifications which we took on, learnt or acquired as we grew up seem to have become a fixed part of us. They form our sense of ego or I. And for this very reason it is not easy to change them in the way we need to.

The previous Fundamentals of Buddhist Psychotherapy have delivered us a wide range of information about our patterns of behaviour, influences and roles as well as our predispositions and the seeds in our storehouse consciousness (see 6th Fundamental). We need to recognise and gain a genuine feel for our potential; here we need to carefully study the Fundamentals, attend Buddhist study events and have our own experiences (for which practice and, initially, also guided exercises are essential). When we have experienced and recognised that we always have a choice, then we have taken the first step and are ready to go further. We learn to make increasingly sophisticated distinctions and gradually become more self-critical and attentive when it comes to possible problematic identifications.

These changes will be reflected in altered ideas and sensations, such as: "I *have* a few troubles" instead of "I *am* annoyed"; "I *am feeling* sad" instead of "I *am* sad"; "*That is* frightening!" instead of "*I am* scared". We stop making statements such as "*I am* a coward", "*I am* so hot-tempered", recognising that although we might be scared or angry at this moment, these are not permanent states.

At some level, we allow ourselves to be scared or angry and we can change this. And anyway, everything changes of its own accord. All mental and emotional states are also impermanent.

I *work* conscientiously but I *am* not a worker. I *am feeling* angry but I *am* not an angry person. We also need to carry this process over into our ideals. I *work* actively towards a cause but I *am* not an activist. Even though this is an example of an identification that initially seems very positive, ultimately it limits us and ties us down.

Unless we look deeply, many of our identifications feel very good. This obviously applies to the positive identifications we seek out, but even when we are feeling bad (angry, frustrated, humiliated, insulted), our identifications support us in prolonging these emotions and suffering. This is an unhealthy form of acceptance; we feel pretty bad, even our body is registering painful stress, *but* we are justified in feeling this way. We are suffering but what does that matter—even if it kills us, we are right, and that is what counts. We persist in feeling our painful emotions, and most of the time we also exacerbate them.

When people curse, insult or humiliate us, we have the freedom to choose our own identifications. He called me an idiot—*Am* I really an idiot? Do I have to fight back to prove I *am* a fighter and not a coward? *Am* I really a persistently angry "bulldog"? Within us we have so many variations—so many alternative personality components. We really need to cultivate and promote them. Repeating old patterns will more firmly fix them; repeating new ones will help to establish them (see 5th Fundamental of BPT on neuroplasticity).

Identifications

There are numerous examples of how quickly we identify ourselves with something: with a range of different movie heroes; with purely invented characters such as those in computer animation films; and even complete strangers seem to have the power to force us into particular roles. They may only need to speak one sentence and we have already identified with the fighter or the victim within us.

Jack Kornfield illustrates this with an example: Can you feel the weight of the book in your hand? Let us imagine we *are* the book.

What would it be like to lie in a hand? What is it like to be the subject of such direct attention? What would it feel like to have such a nice cover? Would it feel different being a thick book or a thin book? How would we feel if someone threw us (as a book) on the floor? What would it be like to spend our time standing hidden in the second row on a dusty bookshelf in the corner? What does it feel like to be snapped shut? How would it feel to have pages ripped out of us? What would it be like to have our pages turned carefully and tenderly? How do we feel as a book?

Now let us completely remove this *identification* with the book. The book is simply a book. We can put it away any time we want. How do we feel now?

This was an example of consciously adopting an identification and then letting it go. In everyday life, adopting an identification unfortunately occurs unconsciously. However, with practice we can actually deal with all of our everyday identifications in the same way as we just dealt with the identification with the book. Once we have become conscious of them, we can let them go.

The deep biological roots of our Attachment

Our capacity to enter into another person's feelings and emotions (empathy) has very deep roots within us. In the deeper structures of our brain there is a region with special nerve cells called mirror neurons. These are able to mirror the experience of others as though we ourselves were acting or experiencing. In this way we can understand other people better and feel more secure in our contact with them. For example, if we have a direct experience of someone accidentally cutting themselves with a knife and we can see the flesh wound, we ourselves experience a sharp pain accompanied by all sorts of psychological and physiological symptoms, although nothing has actually happened to us. This phenomenon occurs with almost everything that can happen to people close to us or even those we are watching on television or on the cinema screen.

Once again, there are two sides to this coin-healthy and unhealthy. Our capacity for compassion is just as innate as our capacity to suffer with others and identify with them.

Compassion often turns into suffering

This deep physiological level of our mirror neurons can often lead to intense connections to others, sometimes of very short duration. This is one of many reasons for our difficulties with the issue of balancing closeness and distance. Our compassion can quickly lead us to have the same feelings of suffering as the person we are with. Important boundaries dissolve and the feeling of connection starts to go down the wrong path. We begin to identify ourselves with other people or with various parts of our personality. This identification generally takes place unconsciously so it is difficult to control. Additionally, there is generally more than one form of identification taking place and these can be very different. We begin to adopt various roles: we *are* the needy; we *are* the unlucky ones; we *are* the avengers; we *are* the watchdogs; etc.

We will be introduced to exercises which can help us to increase the level of awareness with which these identifications happen, enabling us to let go of them more quickly—just as we let go of the identification with the book in the exercise described above.

Material Attachment

A preoccupation with material objects or comforts is another aspect of our grasping which we can now examine briefly. If we look around our apartment, where do we feel strong feelings in our heart? When we see our neighbour drive past in a brand-new sports car, how do we feel? If our neighbour buys an elegant new designer handbag, how do we feel? If we have just bought a new tool or gadget and it gets seriously scratched on the first day, how does that feel? When we finally save enough money to treat ourselves to some new luxury, how do we feel? And in all of these cases, how long does this emotion last?

After asking ourselves these questions we may begin to suspect that the *objects* possess *us* rather than the other way round. Do our tools and machines command us to repair them? Does the clock give us an order: "Quick! Hurry up!" Does our sense of reason dictate that we get angry in a particular situation? If this is the case, surely liberation is very desirable?

To have or to be?

With his book *Zen Buddhism and Psychoanalysis,* Erich Fromm was one of the earliest authors to see a connection between Buddhism and psychotherapy. In another book, *To Have or to Be?* he concisely described the issue at hand here. He presented two paths. The first one is that of constantly wanting to "have"; our mind is persistently restless, it never quietens down, it always wants more, it wants to have more and it wants to possess more. A vicious circle begins: In order to placate our worries, we hastily acquire the things we need to be satisfied. However, there is never enough and then additional worries begin to arise—our possessions might get stolen or broken etc. The second path is the path of "being". This is where we find ourselves without status symbols to assist our identification. We do not have to achieve something or possess something; we are already fine the way we are. We already have everything that is necessary to be happy.

Who is the happiest?

Happiness and wealth have become very popular issues and form the subjects of some very interesting large-scale international studies. Some of these concentrate more on the gross domestic product (GDP) and others on the Human Development Index (HDI).

Here we would like to introduce another instrument: the Happy Planet Index (HPI). This includes the criterion of sustainability as well as satisfaction and life expectancy. To compile the index, studies are made of how happy people are, how old they become, and what level of resources they have to consume in order to live the way they do.

Readers might already suspect that the highly developed countries are nowhere near the top of the ranking list in this index, covering some 180 countries. In 2006, the first year of its compilation, the first 60 places were taken by countries such as Vanuatu, Columbia, Costa Rica, the Dominican Republic, Panama, Cuba and Honduras. Then we find Austria as number 61, Italy in 66th place, Germany at 81, France ranked at 129 and the USA near the bottom in 150th place.

So this index helps to make it very clear that material security and satisfaction with life do not appear to be connected in a healthy way. All of our efforts, aspirations and struggles to fulfil the desires that our inexhaustible market economy promises to satisfy do not seem to help us to be happy; indeed, they almost seem to prevent it.

So what would happen if we tried to change something regarding our continual attachment? If we take the opposite of "grasping" then we have to focus on "letting go". We will now look at one exercise for this; some more practical opportunities for "letting go" are described in the 15th, 16th and 19th Fundamentals of BPT.

A *letting go* exercise

Letting go is accompanied by unconscious fears so to investigate these we can carry out the following exercise with the help-seekers who come to us for Buddhist Psychotherapy. It is suitable for both individual and group sessions.

The help-seeker is instructed to sit comfortably and upright on their seat, to relax the body quickly, let their shoulders fall loosely, close their eyes, breathe regularly and naturally, and to ask themselves: What would I like to let go of? They should note the first thing that comes to mind, without censoring anything.

Now they open their eyes and immediately write down what they want to let go of (paper and pen need to be put near their seat before the exercise). In this exercise we note *one* aspect, not a whole list.

In the next step, they close their eyes again whilst grasping the paper tightly in their hand, balled up into a fist. Their concentration is focused on the aspect written on this paper. When they can see the issue clearly in their mind, they should stretch out their arm, aware that they are about to let go of what they have written down. The help-seeker should take a moment to mindfully observe the emotions that arise here. What emotions arise as we make the decision to let go but before we have actually let go? No emotion is unjustified or wrong; each one should be perceived and noted mindfully, without criticism.

Now the instruction comes: When we are ready we open our fist and let go of the issue.

What happens now is often very revealing. Each of us *feels* in our own body what it means to let go. Some people throw the paper far away from the body; some people simply let it fall to the ground. Others wait a long time, hardly able to keep their arm stretched out, because it is so difficult to really let go. And some become sad or annoyed because they cannot let go of this slip of paper (or the issue it represents). Or because they have to.

We will see that almost everybody releases their slip of paper sooner or later, but with a whole range of different emotions.

The next instruction is to remain silent for a moment and observe everything happening within them.

The help-seekers take back the slips of paper they have let go and then the exercise finishes with a demonstration by the therapist. We write our own issue on a slip of paper and hold this in our fist. We concentrate on our issue and stretch out our arm. If we want, we can rest our elbows on our thighs so that we can comfortably take a while to focus on the letting go that will follow. Now we demonstrably turn our fist so that the back of our hand faces *down* and then open our fist. In this way, as we let go, our slip of paper (and our issue) remains in our open palm and does not fall to the ground.

This simple exercise allows us to illustrate different aspects of letting go:

We do not only philosophise about the different aspects. Rather, we *sense* very intensely the emotions associated with letting go.

We gain a strong inner impression of whether we really can or want to let go of the issue we have chosen.

We gain an intense sense of everything which we associate with letting go. Before seeing the demonstration, almost all participants will open their fist towards the ground, revealing that they associate letting go with loss of control. With this misunderstanding (letting go = loss) it actually is sometimes reasonable not to let go.

The simple transformation of the exercise by opening our fist towards the sky clearly symbolises the simple inner transformation that can lead to a completely different understanding: We can be much more relaxed about letting go when we realise that it does not necessarily mean loss.

It is probably advisable to deal with these inner connections between letting go and loss in a very careful and subtly differentiated way. The simple exercise above can only serve as a quick introduction.

There is no single general strategy which serves as a solution. For some important matters it can indeed be sensible to "open our fist towards the ground" and really discard something in order to free ourselves from it. However, experience shows that this type of process can generally better be carried out as a *process* of *development* instead of *single dramatic act*. So it is almost always advisable to initially "open our fist towards the sky" in order to take one more look at the issues we want to let go of. Perhaps we might want to say a few more conscious words of farewell before we turn the fist down and drop the paper or issue.

Tamara J almost always has financial problems. Her shopping addiction can no longer be hidden. Buddhist Psychotherapy offers her a good opportunity to work with the background issues behind her addiction. The compulsive way she shops for brand-name articles; the intense, short period of joy she experiences after the purchase; the shame she feels after some time and when she looks at her bank statements; her feeling of failure: these have all become firmly established behaviour patterns. When she hears about the concept of attachment, Tamara thinks it was written especially for her.
At a practical level, she works with her therapist to develop a multifaceted treatment plan, integrating many areas of her life including the way she spends her free time. Tamara experienced a key moment during group

mandala painting. Hours and hours of painting created beautiful little works of art. As the group then proceeded to burn all of these pictures, this gave rise to many emotional reactions within Tamara. The following therapy sessions worked with these and she recognised a great deal about her attachment and her desire to hold on to everything.

This Fundamental Should Convey the Following:

Let us take a look at our life with a quiet, clear mind. What do we really need in life? What really has priority? What makes us dependent? Which things or people are we sure to lose after a while? Of all the things we have, which of them are all but certain to decay certainly decay?

We have to remain aware and mindful if we want to find the Middle Way and stay on it. We definitely need to prepare for this since we really cannot hold onto anything. If we do not carry out these preparations in time (mind training) we will suffer very much.

So the basic aim is this: liberation from our attachments.

The 15th
Fundamental of Buddhist Psychotherapy

Recognise and Convey the Noble Truth of Our Resistance

> Aggression is not essentially innate, and violent behaviour is influenced by a variety of biological, social, situational and environmental factors.
>
> XIV DALAI LAMA

We are now moving on to another cause of suffering: aversion or resistance. This is the third cause of all avoidable suffering, which the Buddha described in the Second Noble Truth.

The word *resistance* here covers many related aspects, such as aversion, negativity, refusal, denial, anger and hate. When we leave the Middle Way, we either drift off into naïveté and ignorance on one side or negativity and resistance on the other. Neither of these options is desirable. And resistance is just as difficult to deal with as the two other causes of suffering we have already covered.

Being in the right

There's no denying that the pressures of life are increasing, even in highly developed countries. Everybody frequently experiences situations where they feel powerless or helpless in the face of so much injustice and so many shortcomings and wrongs around them. If we then find ourselves in difficult conflict situations where we are certain that we are "in the right" then it appears almost impossible to stay calm. When we feel that we have behaved correctly and are in the right, this seems to be adequate justification for reacting to injustice with anger, resistance and refusal.

This pattern often shows through even more strongly when we are representing others, particularly our own family or children. Who would not do *anything* for their children? We are very certain that we *have to* fight for them. If we feel we are in the right, we struggle and fight on even when we are doomed to failure. We would rather die than give in.

These situations occur often enough and make it difficult for us to trust in the Wisdom of the Middle Way. At times like these we therefore need assistance from someone else (such as a teacher or therapist).

Our Michael Kohlhaas syndrome

A famous example of a fight for justice is given to us in the figure of Michael Kohlhaas in the novella of the same name by Heinrich von Kleist. He is described as someone who feels he is in the right and fighting for justice, but then loses and perishes. "Justice at any price" is indeed a common attitude; perhaps we all suffer from this to some extent. We frequently experience situations where we will definitely not yield or retreat. However, whether we cannot or do not want to concede, the result of our bitter resistance is often the destruction of what we were fighting for.

So is the solution to stop standing up for the things we believe in? Should we cease our struggle to achieve something we consider important? No. We continue to be committed to our causes with all our strength. We do not simply tolerate wrongs, abuse, violence and other problems. We actively stand up for justice. Nonetheless, there is a way to do this without developing resistance and hate. We can be active and committed in a careful, mindful way—without anger or violence.

Our alarm buttons

In this regard, we also have the phenomenon of the "buttons" which get pushed (see 7th Fundamental). Almost every person has these, some more visible than others. Something happens and either consciously or unconsciously we experience it as negative; this pushes our button. Like a red alarm button, it immediately sets off a strong reaction. Often it is a particular type of person who sets this off, and so we might think the problem has something to do with how they are. But if we cannot react other than by exploding or getting stressed, then these buttons are *our* sore points, not theirs. We cannot blame others for our reactions even if we are often completely convinced this is the case.

No-win situations

There are many areas of life where disputes only have losers—no winners. This is true of large-scale events, such as wars between countries, and at lower levels, too, such as within families or couples. Both parties have their good reasons for their position. However, the negativity connected with the "justice at any price" approach leads to injuries on both sides.

Many relationships unfortunately end in a no-win situation, with both partners equally claiming to be in the right and unwilling to yield at all. If we knew that there can only be losers, it would not make sense to start the game at all. But often we can only recognise what is happening when it is too late.

This book emphasises the alternatives to struggling or fighting. We are so accustomed to having to fight (whether the supposed enemies are external or internal) that we are hardly able to recognise how senseless our strategy is.

There are indeed many metaphors within the teachings of the Buddha himself which make use of imagery such as "being on guard" and "fighting our unhealthy impulses". The Buddha explains how we can wrestle down aspects of ourselves like a fighter or make use of physical efforts (such as pressing our tongue hard against our upper palate) to increase our awareness of undesirable thoughts and to resist them. In order to understand the use of this imagery correctly and to act upon it, we may need the advice of a teacher who can clarify the wider context and what each detail refers to. For example, metaphors involving resistance and struggle always need to be understood as part of a wider context with even more important calls to action, such as remaining on the Middle Way and maintaining mindfulness in the here and now for the benefit of ourselves and all living beings.

In the 19th Fundamental of BPT with its focus on practical Buddhist-therapeutic exercises and measures, we will be introduced to some very significant teachings and instructions that show us a very gentle way to deal with our inner and outer "demons", taming them and even transforming them into healthy companions without fighting them. Tsültrim Allione, an American Buddhist, describes a Tibetan Buddhist practice *(Chöd)* from the 11th century which demonstrates a successful way to avoid using resistance and angry struggle.

Human cultures are so strongly characterised by angry resistance and fighting spirit that it will be a great challenge for many help-seekers to cease their patterns of resistance. Adopting a critical stance is also made difficult by the sheer abundance of portrayals of (often successful) resistance in our novels, stories, traditions, legends and films. These standards and values have formed such a major part of our cultural heritage that they have become part of us. And this in turn means that we have to be very careful when we begin "triage and clearance" work. We will very quickly uncover the fears beneath these patterns and it will become very important to convey how much more courage is involved in *not* choosing resistance, instead opting for wise acceptance of what we find around us. Based on this and with a clear mind free of anger and hate, we can set off on the path of improving the conditions in our life and in that of all other sentient beings.

Of course, gender-specific expressions of resistance, opposition and violence can appear very different. For example, we need to be able to recognise very many varieties of violence. There is physical violence, such as beatings, and there are also more hidden forms of psychological violence such as withdrawing love, refusing to talk, exclusion, disregard and bullying.

It is helpful for therapists to be able to recognise and acknowledge how many people without mind training are condemned to unconsciously following a *pattern* rather than being able to make a real conscious *choice*. When we do reach the point where we strongly feel that we want to consciously change something within us by working on our patterns and striving for more self-control, then we very often encounter an inner opponent:

Our Psychological Resistance

Even if on the surface we have made a decision to change, strongly conservative aspirations and tendencies can still be found deep within us. We are using the word *conservative* here with its meaning of preserving existing conditions and limiting change as far as possible; this tendency suggests that there is no need to really reveal our desires and concerns. Self-protection mechanisms are at work, some of which are unconscious. However, others can be accessed consciously.

We have a very diverse range of psychological defence mechanisms putting up resistance against any information that might reduce our self-esteem. Wilhelm Reich was one of the first Western scientists to recognise and take a closer look at our psychological defence mechanisms and the corresponding physical muscular armouring. His book *Character Analysis* has been an inexhaustible treasure chest of deep insights into human psychosomatics for generations of psychiatrists, psychologists and psychotherapists. Clear and with many examples, it analyses the way our mind resists at physical and psychological levels.

Wilhelm Reich was a very critical thinker and developed a range of ideas which society at that time did not accept, and his life unfortunately came to a a tragic end. However, one of the students listening attentively in his lectures was the very young daughter of Sigmund Freud, Anna, who later published the book *Ego and the Mechanisms of Defense,* describing the unconscious psychological ways we defend ourselves. Readers are referred to both the excellent books mentioned here for a deeper understanding of these defence functions than we can present in the Fundamentals of BPT.

Examples of these unconscious techniques include sublimation, rationalisation, repression, denial, dissociation, reversal into the opposite, identification (with the aggressor), turning against oneself, isolation, pretending something did not happen, regression, projection and introjection. We will repeatedly come across these functions within ourselves and during our therapeutic work because we *all* make use of these aids. Sometimes they merely appear as psychological quirks which are not particularly problematic. Some of them might be more obvious and others take place in a more hidden away so we need to be particularly careful during the therapeutic process. It also needs to be clear that nobody is making a point of behaving in a resistant way. We are dealing with unconscious automatisms that arose to ensure self-preservation. We all have these self-defence mechanisms available to us; they are there to protect our vulnerable personality aspects.

In particular as *Buddhist* psychotherapists we should understand that our resistances and conflicts (as well as any other difficulties) are *not* our true nature. They are simply auxiliary constructions built by an auxiliary construction: our self or feeling of "I".

This self receives special critical attention in Buddhist Psychotherapy. Our unconscious measures do actually serve to protect our Inner Nobility in a certain way. We need to appreciate this; it is a process and quality which all of us have. Only then can we find the right speed and the right supportive space to uncover, illuminate and transform our defence mechanisms.

Resistance and boundaries

As important as it might be to have sufficient self-protection, the extent of our resistance can sometimes be very threatening. Ken Wilber offers a readily graspable description of this as a process of drawing boundaries in all important areas of our life.

At the first level, we draw boundaries within ourselves. Our own undesirable impulses, needs, ideas and aspects are denied and suppressed. We can describe this as creating a *shadow* which we fill with these undesirable aspects. We often project this shadow externally and can then reject or hate these suppressed characteristics in others instead of in ourselves. Wilber describes how this divides a whole human being into an impoverished *persona* and an unloved *shadow*. Counselling and conventional psychotherapies can perform valuable reintegration work at this level.

At the next level, the persona and shadow are split off from the *body*. We are no longer an integrated physical-psychological being; instead we become the owner of a body, which we use and which is required to function. Humanistic and body-oriented psychotherapies can be very helpful here.

At the third and last level, persona, shadow and body are split off from their *environment*. Now we experience ourselves as an isolated and separated human *organism*. At this level, holistic therapies, such as Buddhist Psychotherapy, are the most beneficial.

We can summarise the totality of the boundaries we create for ourselves thus: The *persona* is impoverished because more and more unwelcome aspects are suppressed into the *shadow*; we hardly notice our *body* anymore, except when it hurts or goes on strike; and the *environment* is perceived as foreign, separate from us as human *organisms*, sometimes threatening and sometimes to be exploited.

Our resistance creates boundaries

Our resistance separates us from our environment. This is the reason that many people suffer from feelings of loneliness and isolation. Our natural understanding of our connection with others and with nature dissipates. Many of us experience the "kick" of individuality as a thrill, but this narcissistic thrill comes at a very high price.

Concentrating and focusing on our differences is often found in the same context as strong fears. If we feel threatened we often instinctively look for things which are alien or which do not suit us—these can be regarded as the reason for our sense of threat. The polarities of resistance and attachment may exist within us in similar measure, in which case we often feel torn between the two. Or one may be dominant, shaping our character, perhaps making us aloof or clingy.

Our rational mind tends towards resistance

The abilities of our rational mind are clearly illustrated by the example of science, which generally functions in a very analytical way. Our dissecting mind is in control here. Everything is reduced, dissolved, subjected to impact, chopped up, ground up or blown up in order to try and find the answer in the component parts.

This suggests that our analytical mind is always in resistance, creating opposites, whereas our heart connects opposites, creates wholes and thus heals.

Breaking down patterns of resistance

Within Buddhist Psychotherapy we always develop very personalised solutions; there are rarely routines or standard methods which apply to everyone. Many very different measures have been developed to treat patterns of resistance in different areas of life. Exercises which have been proven to have a generally healthy effect are those dealing with gratitude and acceptance. For example, people suffering because of their patterns of resistance are given the *Giving Inner Thanks* exercise as homework: they mindfully register as many of their perceptions as possible and then consciously give thanks (silently or out loud) for each of these sensations, accepting them. If they get caught in a rain shower—express gratitude, everything is okay. If they have to wait in a long queue—express gratitude, everything is okay. If someone speaks to them harshly—express gratitude, everything is okay.

Suggesting this exercise is often met with objections such as this: But it is not really true if I say that everything is okay. So as the therapist we need to make clear that we are not recommending them to wear "rose-tinted spectacles" but rather conducting an exercise designed to break down established patterns of resistance which will then enable us to return to the Middle Way. The necessity of occasionally approaching one extreme in order to help break down the other extreme was already presented visually in the 9th Fundamental of BPT.

Faruk S developed a panic disorder three months ago and has hardly been able to leave his apartment since then. To some extent he recognises his situation as a problem that needs to be solved but he also rationalises his withdrawal as a sensible measure of self-protection in a world full of dangers and injustice. Faruk feels like an injured animal, retreating into the shelter of its cave in order to lick its wounds.

His therapy uses traditional behavioural therapy techniques for treating panic disorders, supplemented by BPT teachings on resistance and aversion. Faruk was able to trace his resistant side far back through his biography. He has been helped to work through many negative emotions that he experienced, especially those of rejection.

The appropriate Buddhist teachings have helped Faruk to take a closer look at the various aspects of his own personality and also to understand that resistance is not to be understood as his individual weakness, but rather as a mass phenomenon. During the weeks following these teachings, Faruk gained particular benefit from a range of exercises to practice letting go.

This Fundamental Should Convey the Following:

We recognise within ourselves and within others the natural resistances which actually developed to serve a useful purpose (self-protection) but often become one of the main causes of our suffering. We get to know our expressions of aversion and resistance and train new ways of dealing with them. We learn to accept more, in turn feeling more relaxed.

Giving up resistance does not mean passively and patiently tolerating everything that happens around us, including injustices and abuse. We can become active but without resistance in the form of annoyance, anger or hate.

The basic aim is liberation in the midst of our resistance and aversion.

This finishes our presentation of the Second Noble Truth on the causes of suffering. Before we continue on to the next Fundamental with its description of the Third Noble Truth on the *liberation* from suffering we will introduce a further aspect that can be identified as a cause of suffering.

The Buddha's teachings on the Second Noble Truth of the causes of suffering (ignorance, attachment and aversion/resistance) were amongst the first teachings he gave. As time went by, the search for the causes of human suffering led to further distinctions, resulting in teachings such as that of the *Ten Fetters* which obstruct us and prevent us from achieving liberation. They are a further development of the Second Noble Truth and also cover the issues of ignorance, attachment and resistance.

The Ten Fetters are
1) False belief in a self
2) Compulsive doubting
3) Attachment to rites and rituals as ends in themselves
4) Craving for sensual perception
5) Ill will
6) Passion for form or material existence
7) Passion for formlessness or immaterial existence
8) Conceit
9) Restlessness
10) Ignorance

We have only briefly listed the ten fetters here. Readers are encouraged to read the appropriate Buddhist literature for a more detailed understanding or to take a particular detail of this teaching and look at it closely, penetrate its truth, internalise it and put it into practice.

Once again we remind the reader of the need to remember this three-stage process (recognising and understanding, contemplating and internalising, realising and implementing) in order to ensure that conveying these teachings never becomes too theoretical. The Buddha himself emphasised the urgent necessity to carefully adapt our choice of words, topics and examples for each help-seeker. It might be advisable to quickly move on to an intensive study of the next two Noble Truths, since they emphasise the practical side, with instructions for active behaviour and the steps we can take towards solutions.

Nonetheless, Buddhist teachings do have a strongly holistic quality, which means that in each of the Four Noble Truths we can take any detail and find signs of the whole. So concentrating intensely on the First or Second Noble Truth may lead to individual solutions for some of us.

The 16th
Fundamental of Buddhist Psychotherapy

Recognise and Convey the Noble Truth of the Liberation from Suffering

> There are both healthy desires and unhealthy desires. Know the difference. Then find freedom in their midst.
>
> JACK KORNFIELD

> The basic nature of the subtle consciousness itself is something neutral. So it is possible to purify or eliminate all of these negative emotions. That basic nature we call Buddha nature.
>
> XIV DALAI LAMA

The Third Noble Truth deals with the issue of freedom or liberation—liberation from suffering. It answers the question as to whether we can do anything to counteract the suffering and causes of suffering identified in the previous two truths. The answer is a joyful one: Yes, there is suffering, but we can definitely free ourselves permanently from it.

> The Third Noble Truth comprises the essence of Buddhism with the fundamental statement: We can liberate ourselves from suffering.

The Buddha expressly stated that every human being already has everything they need to achieve liberation, right now. Thich Nhat Hanh expresses the same message very bluntly: There is nothing we have to do; enjoy your being, in the peace of your clear mind. In other words, the path that leads to liberation is the same as liberation.

So the path lies within or in front of us, but we still have to find our access to it. We have generally achieved our various successes in life by means of hard work and toil, so we might suppose that this strategy will be successful here, too. But we would be mistaken: Toil and effort will not liberate us; one of the main keys to freedom is the clear, wakeful and peaceful mind. To cultivate this will initially take patience and regular practice.

With any luck, most of the information and techniques conveyed here will not be completely new to us. In fact, we will probably often feel as if we are rediscovering something very clear that we already knew.

In order to put into practice the Third Noble Truth leading to liberation from suffering, we need to recapitulate what we have learnt up to now. The most important points concern two main Buddhist topics:

A) Knowledge of our Inner Nobility (see 8th Fundamental of BPT); and

B) The teaching of the First Turning of the Wheel of Dharma, which itself contains three significant elements:
1) Follow the Middle Way (see 9th Fundamental)
2) Use the insights to stay in the here and now and help yourself and others (see 10th Fundamental)
3) Understand the Four Noble Truths (see 11th and 13th-17th Fundamentals)

A short review of the Wisdom of our Inner Nobility

Recognise deeply your own innate value: Your infinitely precious life, symbolised by your golden core of Inner Nobility. The teachings tell us that if we searched the whole universe for someone who needs love, we would find nobody who needs love more than we do. We are inseparably connected with all other living beings and all of the other living beings also carry this precious core within them. So we and all others profit from this equally.

We can bow to holy people and holy symbols because they serve as a clear embodiment of something that we all have within us. We could also bow to a tree, since this tree lives with us, through us and from us; we also live through it and from it. Understanding our golden Inner Nobility creates mutual respect, non-violence, the insight of our inseparable interconnection with everything and everyone, and a very peaceful inner attitude.

A short review of the Wisdom of the Middle Way

We avoid the extremes. This also means, for example, that we do not completely change our life overnight simply because we discover Buddhism. We practice moderation in all affairs.

The Middle Way is fairly easy to understand but nonetheless very difficult to follow, requiring constant course adjustments as internal and external attractions and distractions lead us off the path. We live in a very complex and diverse world that has much to offer, especially in highly developed countries where we live in abundance (and even excess) 24 hours a day. So we constantly have to check if we are still on the Middle Way.

This path also means that we cannot generally exclude anything. We cannot say that liberated people are never annoyed, sad or scared. We can enjoy anything that our life offers us but we do not grasp onto it. We remain on the Middle Way. We live our life fully and liberate ourselves *in the midst* of our desires and problems.

A short review of the wisdom of remaining in the here and now for ourselves and for all others

Everything we achieve is achieved now and cannot be hoarded in the same way that a small mammal hoards food. In particular, we cannot take it into the world beyond. No, we recognise and feel the intense connection with all beings around us and do not lose ourselves in our ego's thoughts about our past or worries about our future (which is fully uncertain).

The need to be in the *here and now* is one of the most powerful principles we can adopt to achieve mental clarity and peace.

Our happiness and the happiness of all other beings is the most important thing—it should be our life's meaning. Happiness is experienced exclusively in the here and now. If I experience joy but begin to compare it with the past or worry about keeping it into the future, I step out of the present moment. My emotions and thoughts are no longer in the here and now and this generally destroys my happiness, often affecting the people around me, too.

A short review of the First Noble Truth

The First Noble Truth conveys the fact that we will always have to deal with two types of suffering: *unavoidable* pain and *avoidable* suffering (see 11th Fundamental of BPT). The best strategy is to initially free ourselves from the avoidable suffering, which is actually our individual reaction to prior unavoidable pain.

For example, ageing is *unavoidable*, as are the changes in our body which occur as a result. We often react to these with disappointment, frustration, annoyance, fear, worries or self-deprecating thoughts. These reactions are *avoidable* suffering. So we can see that the pain associated with *unavoidable* suffering can be greatly alleviated by freeing ourselves from our *avoidable* reactions. There are so many similar examples and listing them would make it very clear how many painful occurrences in our life there are which we have no influence on at all. It would be either superhuman or inhuman if we had no emotional reactions. So we need to be clear that our aim is not to cut ourselves off from these emotions but instead to liberate ourselves *in the midst* of them.

As we reach or slowly approach liberation, it will become easier to distinguish between these two types of suffering. We are not talking about blindly accepting everything that happens to us. Rather, we want to be able to mobilise useful reserves and resources when we encounter difficulties in order to cope with the situation in the most beneficial way possible. So this implies avoiding reactions that are not useful such as those which create additional avoidable suffering, including self-judgement, brooding, anger and fear. In this way, we save significant amounts of energy which can be utilised for overcoming real difficulties.

A short review of the Second Noble Truth

The Second Noble Truth identifies the three causes of *avoidable* suffering. Logically, this means that liberation can be achieved by overcoming these three causes: ignorance, attachment and resistance. The process we undergo here has three stages: recognising and understanding; contemplating and internalising; realising and implementing.

Within Buddhist Psychotherapy we ensure that one step has been established before we move on to the next. So we learn to distinguish the two types of suffering in order to recognise and understand which spontaneous emotional reactions we are experiencing. Then we intensively study types of emotional reaction in general. One way of looking at these reaction patterns is the system of three personality types (attaching, resisting and ignorant). The next two steps (contemplating and internalising, realising and implementing) are also gradual processes which can be learnt and put into daily practice using a variety of Buddhist techniques taught in BPT.

Breaking down identifications

We try to create some clarity regarding the various roles that we adopt in our life. How do we define ourselves? What do we determine for ourselves? What do we definitely have to work for? What patterns do we have to maintain at any cost? Are we victims, perpetrators, guilty, responsible, reconcilers, insecure, nervous, hot-tempered, hard workers, idiots, clever, believers, sceptics, atheists etc.? Do we identify strongly with our gender? If one of these roles is threatened or even just criticised, do we feel compelled to fight for it, become angry and hurt others?

It appears that one of many aspects of our personality starts to become dominant as a response to either internal processes (worries, complaints, desires) or external impulses (conflicts, dangers, losses). Supported by our rational mind, our sense of self very quickly—and generally unconsciously—activates a particular aspect of our personality. We see something beautiful and desirable; we immediately have to possess it (child personality). We are attacked; we fall into shock, unable to react (victim personality). We experience physical or psychological pain; immediately the world seems to be made up entirely of pain (pain personality). We hold firm, maintaining this aspect even if it threatens, attacks, activates or stimulates another personality aspect. In an untrained and therefore relatively unconscious mental state we experience a rather indefinable mixture of our sense of self, our intellectual or rational reaction, and our personality aspects (see overview "Unconscious Permanent Conditions").

When one of our numerous ego aspects manifests—for example our child or victim personality—then our rational mind immediately jumps on board. In an untrained and still unconscious condition, we (our *ego*) are completely identified with our rational mind and the roles we find ourselves in. This explains why even apparently positive roles such as Wise or Loving can become problematic, although we usually only recognise these problems when the roles are threatened or attacked. Extreme situations can drive us into one personality aspect and apparently cut off our access to any of our other aspects. If our family is in danger, we cease to have compassion for anyone else. If we enter the Victim role, there appears to be no more access to more mature aspects of our personality; we feel helpless, weak and needy and our rational mind confirms this with corresponding thoughts. The rational mind always delivers the "appropriate ammunition" for each role by unceasingly producing matching thoughts. If I am identified with the Fighter role, my rational mind will keep this armed with an endless supply of suggestions: "How could they?! ... Wait, I'll show them... What a nerve!... I'll get them back for that by..." In this way, the rational mind maintains and perpetuates each role and identification. Our rational mind likes nothing better than keeping busy like this. It finds it difficult to let go, preferring to brood, grumble, calculate, speculate, think,

Unconscious Permanent Conditions
Ego = Rational Mind = Role Identification: *Child* Personality
Ego = Rational Mind = Role Identification: *Victim* Personalityt
Ego = Rational Mind = Role Identification: *Pain* Personality
Ego = Rational Mind = Role Identification: *Fear* Personality
Ego = Rational Mind = Role Identification: *Sadness-Depression* Personality
Ego = Rational Mind = Role Identification: *Anger* Personality
Ego = Rational Mind = Role Identification: *Abandoned* Personality
Ego = Rational Mind = Role Identification: *Fighter/Avenger* Personality
Ego = Rational Mind = Role Identification: *Kind* Personality
Ego = Rational Mind = Role Identification: *Loving* Personality
Ego = Rational Mind = Role Identification: *Wise* Personality
Ego = Rational Mind = Role Identification: *Faith* Personality
Ego = Rational Mind = Role Identification: *Nationality* Personality
Ego = Rational Mind = Role Identification: *Family* Personality
Ego = Rational Mind = Role Identification: *Worker* Personality
Ego = Rational Mind = Role Identification: *etc.*

think and think some more. This is similar to the way our rational mind maintains and perpetuates our feelings and emotions.

Our initial aim should be to increase our capacity to distinguish what is going on. Buddhist teachings and practice give us the possibility to experience for ourselves that our ego and our rational mind are not identical. At first, we can establish an observer within us and strengthen, support and secure this as a lasting insight. This measure enables us (as our ego) to "look over the shoulder" of our rational mind as it carries out its activities. This step alone denies the problematic process of identification a significant amount of energy. As a quiet observer I can recognise when my rational mind once again tries to establish and fix one of the aspects of my personality (see overview "Ego as a Quiet Observer").

In this phase we will not yet overcome our role identifications. Instead we will observe how our rational mind eagerly jumps on each role and connects with it. The sensitivity we develop for this process as a quiet observer gives rise to the first small "gap", and this gap provides us with *room for manoeuvre*. Very gradually we can expand this gap moving on to the next interim aim of increasing our awareness and self-control. By becoming more aware we can open up to our self-efficacy and increase our future capacity to consciously change our role identification (for example, abandoning the Fighter role and adopting a kind personality).

During the interim phases, temporary *transition* identifications can be helpful. Perhaps we identify with Buddhist principles and precepts—our "Buddhist personality"—but we remain aware that the ultimate solution is not replacing old identifications with new ones, which will inevitably also force us into particular patterns. Our overarching aim is of course always *liberation*, which expresses itself here as overcoming all identifications.

We recognise our role identifications and let go of them. We liberate ourselves.

We free ourselves from the ballast of all the opinions, judgements and expectations which we apply to ourselves or others. For example, imagine a situation in the street where we see someone talking loudly to themselves (assuming this is not someone using a hands-free set for their mobile phone!) We can assume that some people do indeed suffer from this compulsion, talking constantly to themselves, and so we might feel compassion for them, or judge them, or have any one of many different reactions. However, have we considered the claim, expressed well by Eckhart Tolle, that we are not much different to these people? It might not be externally audible, but without mind training we also constantly hear inner "voices"

Ego as a Quiet Observer
Rational Mind = Rational Mind = Role Identification: *Child* Personality
Rational Mind = Rational Mind = Role Identification: *Victim* Personalityt
Rational Mind = Rational Mind = Role Identification: *Pain* Personality
Rational Mind = Rational Mind = Role Identification: *Fear* Personality
Rational Mind = Rational Mind = Role Identification: *Sadness-Depression* Personality
Rational Mind = Rational Mind = Role Identification: *Anger* Personality
Rational Mind = Rational Mind = Role Identification: *Abandoned* Personality
Rational Mind = Rational Mind = Role Identification: *Fighter/Avenger* Personality
Rational Mind = Rational Mind = Role Identification: *Kind* Personality
Rational Mind = Rational Mind = Role Identification: *Loving* Personality
Rational Mind = Rational Mind = Role Identification: *Wise* Personality
Rational Mind = Rational Mind = Role Identification: *Faith* Personality
Rational Mind = Rational Mind = Role Identification: *Nationality* Personality
Rational Mind = Rational Mind = Role Identification: *Family* Personality
Rational Mind = Rational Mind = Role Identification: *Worker* Personality
Rational Mind = Rational Mind = Role Identification: *etc.*

full of opinions, judgements, commands and rules. Of course, there are also respectful and supportive voices, but very often we suffer from this ongoing inner dialogue, dominated by our inner dictators, demons and censors. Within Buddhist Psychotherapy, we aim to identify and "get to know" them. We do not try to subdue them forcefully or repress them because this would only result in their finding another means of expression. By getting to know them and observing them, we initially gain a certain critical distance and conciliatory approach to ourselves. This procedure denies these inner voices a large part of their psychological energy.

No Mind

When these voices slowly become quieter and even silent for a few moments then we experience the state which Buddhists call *No Mind:* a fully calm mind (see 19th Fundamental of BPT). The practice of No Mind is central to Buddhism, representing a state of mind we should all aspire to. By means of patient practice we should be able to experience for ourselves how No Mind feels. Once we have experienced it for the first time, it will become ever easier to find our way back. Our access to this mental state will become increasingly unproblematic and quick. This is a further step towards liberation.

Letting Go or Accepting?

If we are grasping onto a branch hanging over a chasm, we certainly should not let go! Letting go should not be understood as a general strategy that applies in every possible situation. In the 14th Fundamental we were already introduced to various types of letting go. During Buddhist Psychotherapy we explore on an individual basis what each help-seeker associates with letting go.

Sometimes we will let go as if we were getting rid of a "hot potato", at other times we have to carefully place something aside, and at still other times we need to maintain permanent, concentrated attention whilst ensuring that we let go in an inner way. So whatever form it may take, letting go is always our attempt to create a relaxed and calm inner mental attitude. We are active and committed (for example, to fighting against injustice) while maintaining a relaxed inner approach that allows us to be free *in the midst of* all conflicts, desires, emotions, wishes and needs. With this basic attitude we can learn even to accept difficult situations that we cannot improve or change quickly.

In the Christian tradition we find the "Way of the Cross". Many Christians and many more non-Christians may well have asked why Jesus—who was a powerful figure—let himself be tortured and crucified by the Romans. The symbolism is probably much richer, but one aspect might be that he wanted to show us that bearing our cross can be a very high realisation. Struggling and lashing out is something that even small children can do. So we stop struggling. By becoming even more courageous we can come to peace. Taking the Way of the Cross is a very brave act. We accept our burden fully. Going this way is not a path of self-denial. We confront our suffering. We confront the world. With devotion and letting go we cease to put up resistance to life. We become active without hate or negativity.

Virtue

The basic principle underlying the entirety of Buddhism is always liberation. According to Buddhist views, we never produce something good solely by leaving out something bad. Instead we actually have to *actively* behave in a healthy way. So the Buddhist understanding of *virtue* does not only require us to stop doing certain things. Behaviour is only virtuous if it intensively and actively benefits us and our fellow beings. (More details on Buddhist virtue can be found in the 20th Fundamental.)

If we take a practical look at the three causes of all avoidable suffering (ignorance, attachment and resistance) it appears to be important to actively reduce our ignorance by taking interest in different issues, actively studying, listening to teachers and applying techniques of introspection. Equally, we actively reduce the effects of attachment and resistance at an appropriate speed for us by applying techniques that help us to stay closer to the Middle Way.

Dealing within Buddhist Psychotherapy with the causes of suffering requires a situation full of trust. It also means we have to take enough time for our practice. Every help-seeker is looking for rapid success but the best chances for lasting change do not come by adapting the teachings to meet this wish. It needs regular, daily, patient training. The emphasis on regularity is a well-founded instruction which has been proven to promote the process of forming good habits.

Letting go and forgiving ourselves and others are some of the most difficult stages on the path to liberation. They cannot and should not be forced. We keep concentrating on the appropriate exercises (see 19th and 20th Fundamentals of BPT) and try to mindfully be aware of the gradual changes which result from this.

Forgiving

Jack Kornfield tells a tale about the necessity of letting go and forgiving which relates the story of two prisoners who were tortured and abused by their prison guards. Upon meeting many years later, one asks the other, "And? Have you forgiven our tormentors?" The second former inmate replies, "Never! How could I ever forgive them?" The first man then looks kindly at his friend and remarks, "Well, it seems they still have you captive."

We might believe that forgiving someone guilty of an act means that they are never taught a lesson, or that a lack of punishment is the same as promoting the misdeed. Perhaps we think that forgiving is dishonourable because we are too soft. However, our focus should really be on how we behave towards ourselves. Self-torment, brooding and complaining, anger, stress and holding onto the past are all generally accompanied by uncomfortable or even life-threatening physical stress symptoms. They represent the three causes of avoidable suffering (ignorance, resistance and attachment) which we often exhibit so strongly one could believe we have been "branded" with them.

We described previously how our intention leads to a deed, our deeds form our habits, these in turn shape our character and this our destiny. We also learnt how the "butterfly effect" and chaos theory have shown that small elements can lead to significant effects in systems which comprise complex interactions and chain reactions such as this.

Forgiving and letting go can be applied in very different ways. For example, if we remind ourselves of the short duration of emotions, this gives rise to the possibility that mindful concentration on a prevailing emotion can reveal to us how the feeling dissolves "all by itself" (more details in the 19th Fundamental). Another important therapeutic example is letting go of our desire for rapid progress.

This can be encouraged by being very mindful of the first small steps in order to build up confidence and optimism, which then needs to be maintained as the initial wave of success ebbs and the next steps or successes appear to come much more slowly, or the process appears even to go into reverse.

Perhaps we can convey this to the help-seeker by means of the following metaphor. Imagine you are on a ship setting out from Hamburg; for the sake of this story, if you set a course of 270 degrees you will eventually reach New York. Because of the distance involved, if you set a very slightly different course, let us say 269 degrees, you will end up much further south, perhaps in the Caribbean. On the greatest journey that our life is, small changes in course can also have large effects. Every step counts and every detail deserves our attention. Small secure steps are much better than hurrying ahead rapidly and carelessly. This is something which cannot be emphasised enough and needs to be repeatedly addressed and supported by the therapist during a course of Buddhist Psychotherapy.

An emphasis on the small changes we can make now is also important because of the risk of demotivation posed by the presence of very advanced *role models* in the media. The Dalai Lama and other eminent Buddhists can be seen live at their events or experienced on DVD; bookstores are also full of their books. Additionally, Buddhist books often portray the goals of Buddhism in a very radical way, speaking of *absolute* and *perfect* liberation from all negative and positive aspects of life.

Liberation

Absolute and perfect liberation should perhaps be seen as a condition which we can return to again and again for a moment (assuming we practice regular Buddhist mind training) but which we can never preserve within us permanently. It is a great relief to find that many advanced Buddhist meditation teachers and masters talk about the goals of Buddhism in a thoroughly down-to-earth way (see 1st Fundamental of BPT).

We refer very often to Jack Kornfield. In his book *After the Ecstasy, the Laundry* he describes how arduous the path to enlightenment (liberation) can be, since enlightenment refers to behaviour and situations rather than a fixed state. His description makes it very clear that the condition of liberation in the here and now can be achieved again and again by everybody (and not just a few monks). A significant aspect when setting liberation as our goal is implementation—putting what we have achieved into practice in our daily life. Our quest for liberation or enlightenment is not only for our benefit but also for the benefit of all other living beings. We are not looking to come closer to our God or to dissolve into Spirit. We want to achieve a good life in this world in the here and now for ourselves and for all other sentient beings.

An old peace activist once said that there is no way *to* peace—peace *is* the way. Similarly, it can be said that there is no path *to* liberation—liberation *is* the path. Liberation is not, for example, the just reward for long years of painstaking meditation. We do not need to torment ourselves for years with the hope of achieving enlightenment *later*. Instead, we have to find a path from enlightenment to us in the here and now.

The whole process, from understanding through to carrying out the necessary steps, follows a very individual plan customised to meet each help-seeker's personal constitution and situation. This is why Buddhist Psychotherapy makes use of both universal and individual aspects and principles. In the 1st Fundamental, where we were introduced to the ultimate aim of Buddhist exercises (liberation), it was made clear that we are not working with purely negative definitions, such as aspiring for an *absence* of negative mental states. Instead, liberation was described as a varied condition which we can experience *in the midst of* all of our emotions. An additional *positive* definition describes the condition of liberation as the perpetuation of the *Four Illimitable Mental States:* loving-kindness, compassion, joy and equanimity. By repeatedly striving to return to these mental states, we establish a firm base for them which we can call up in critical moments.

Gabriella K is stuck deep in her depression. She sees no hope at all. She experiences an initial sense of relief when she recognises and understands that she *has* depression—instead of thinking that she *is* depressive. Her daily practice begins to stabilise and several times a week she attends the group sessions and group instructions with meditation. This daily and weekly structure gives Gabriella a sense of stability and a gentle increase in her motivation. In the individual therapy sessions she takes a closer look at her depressive moods and manages to transform them (more details in the 19th Fundamental of BPT).

This Fundamental Should Convey the Following:

The central message of the Third Noble Truth is this: Liberation is achievable for everyone—for yourself and everyone else—in the here and now.

The Buddha explained that every human being already has all the necessary capacities that they need for liberation. In the Second Noble Truth, he identified the three causes of suffering as ignorance, attachment and resistance. So it is logical to see that overcoming these three causes is a practical way to achieve liberation:

Liberation in the midst of our ignorance
Liberation in the midst of our attachment
Liberation in the midst of our resistance/aversion

The Wisdom of the Middle Way serves as a type of compass to help us achieve this (9th Fundamental).

A further guiding principle is the appeal to us to use our progress on the path to liberation in the here and now for the benefit of ourselves and all other beings (10th Fundamental).

Another very important aspect is the emphasis on the practical implementation and realisation of any progress we have achieved in our everyday life (17th Fundamental). From a Buddhist point of view, no real personal development is achieved if it is only present within our mind. We do not want our efforts to serve only ourselves;

instead, we should set out to benefit all sentient beings. This is a clear statement against escapism and in favour of an implementation suitable for everyday life, which makes Buddhism a very down-to-earth philosophy of life. This is exactly what the next Fundamental on the topic of the fourth of the Four Noble Truths will convey. It defines and describes the everyday areas in which we should put into practice our insights and progress.

The 17th
Fundamental of Buddhist Psychotherapy

Recognise and Convey the Noble Truth of the Right Path

> There is no separation between inner and outer, self and other. Tending ourselves, we tend the world.
> Tending the world, we tend ourselves.
>
> JACK KORNFIELD

> If you keep your body, speech and mind under control you will enjoy perfect tranquillity.
>
> SHABKAR

The teachings on the Right Path belong to fourth of the Four Noble Truths on liberation from suffering. This truth answers the question as to how we implement liberation in our everyday lives. The Fourth Noble Truth on the end of suffering is intended to show us how to realise what we have experienced and achieved in a practical way that is meaningful and healthy for both ourselves and others.

The Fourth Noble Truth is very sophisticated, showing us how to follow the Right Path in many different areas of our life. It might be argued that the name oversimplifies matters because it implies that there is *the one* path we should follow. We will, however, see that the path is very broad, offering comprehensive support in all the major aspects of our life. It is subdivided into eight areas and is therefore often called the *Noble Eightfold Path*. Listing these areas numerically from one to eight is not intended to imply a ranking or sequence. Once again, Buddhism reveals its holistic nature because the whole path is included in each of the eight points.

The process of following this path comprises the three steps we already know: recognising and understanding; contemplating and internalising; realising and implementing. So there are three subdivisions to each of the eight divisions of the path.

Buddhist literature covering this practical teaching contains a range of different phrasing and assigned meanings. One example is the name of the path itself, with some authors talking of the Noble *Right* Eightfold Path and others referring to the Noble *Perfect* Eightfold Path.

The Right Eightfold Path	The Perfect Eightfold Path
1. Right view	1. Perfect view
2. Right thought	2. Perfect thought
3. Right speech	3. Perfect speech
4. Right action	4. Perfect action
5. Right livelihood	5. Perfect livelihood
6. Right effort	6. Perfect effort
7. Right mindfulness	7. Perfect mindfulness
8. Right concentration	8. Perfect concentration

We can each decide if we prefer the adjective *right* or *perfect*. As is so often the case, we are dealing with a translation; the connotations of the original term include *complete, coherent, perfect* and *ideal*.

When the Buddha gave his teachings by turning the wheel of Dharma he immediately taught two further principles to help understand the Four Noble Truths: remaining in the here and now for the benefit of ourselves and others; and following the Middle Way. The latter is particularly helpful as we try to follow these truths. In fact, after explaining the Noble Eightfold Path in his masterpiece on Buddhist psychology, *The Wise Heart*, the meditation teacher and author Jack Kornfield actually summarises it by referring simply to the Middle Way.

These are the basic principles which also form the foundations of Buddhist Psychotherapy. In particular, when we are considering how far to set the goal posts we should definitely bear in mind the statements about the Middle Way and the call to use any insights for the benefit of ourselves and others in this world.

For this reason, it is perhaps worth considering whether it is advisable to use the term "perfection" when referring to this Fourth Noble Truth because of the effects this may have when it comes to putting it into practice in everyday life. If we are aspiring to achieve perfection, we need a great deal of serenity and patience. Would not it be very helpful to adopt a monastic, celibate life for that? This is not the primary target group for Buddhist Psychotherapy, but the term *perfection* can still be a source of motivation and help for many help seekers. If we choose to use it, we have to take a self-critical look at its meaning in order to make sure we do not get trapped in possible unconscious avoidance strategies, for example. If we discover that we are using this aim of perfection with an unconscious association with something that is not achievable, it might be advisable to formulate more realistic aims.

We will now move on to the descriptions of the eight individual points of the Eightfold Path. As we read these descriptions we can each ask ourselves how far we would like to integrate each of the points into our lives or how far we have integrated them already.

The eight aspects of the path are thoroughly holistic, just like the Buddhist teachings as a whole. Each of the aspects already contains the most significant information from the whole teaching. So the reader is encouraged to take any of the aspects which appeal to them, investigate it profoundly, talk about it with friends, acquaintances and ideally also with Buddhist teachers, and observe how this then leads to the recognition that the salty taste is present in each drop of the ocean. If we find one aspect of the teachings unclear or difficult to understand, then we can concentrate on other areas which address us more directly. We can approach the truth from any direction we want. The profound Buddhist insights will become accessible to us no matter which individual topics we study most deeply.

The Structure of the Eightfold Path

This teaching could be said to put our whole life under scrutiny. Looking at the Fourth Noble Truth, we can also clearly see that both Buddhism and Buddhist Psychotherapy do not have the focus on "the realms beyond"; they concentrate intensely on worldly, practical everyday measures.

The eight factors of life on the path are often categorised into three groups: wisdom, ethical conduct and meditative concentration.

The Noble Eightfold Path
Wisdom group
1. Right view
2. Right thought

Ethical conduct group
3. Right speech
4. Right action
5. Right livelihood

Meditative concentration group
6. Right effort
7. Right mindfulness
8. Right concentration

The Wisdom of the Middle Way serves as a yardstick and compass as we look for a measured and mindful way to implement the insights and progress in these eight areas of life. Each of the eight factors should be examined self-critically and illustrated step for step in cooperation with the help-seeker.

The Wisdom Group of the Noble Eightfold Path

1. Right view

We are unfortunately not born with the "right perspective" or "right understanding" so we have to develop it by studying Buddhist teachings and especially their basic building blocks. The famous teaching

of the *First Turning of the Wheel of Dharma* forms the basics of the teachings within Buddhist Psychotherapy and is therefore the foundation for our right view and insight. This teaching comprises the following points:
- the Wisdom of Middle Way
- the call to use the insights to stay in the here and now and help ourselves and others
- the Four Noble Truths

Having the right view is not just a simple knowing and understanding but rather a deeper recognition or insight. Typically for Buddhism, it also includes the realisation and practical implementation of our insights in our life.

Right view recognises itself and its deficiencies. We learn that there are both preconditions and limits to our knowledge and cognition. We are not a completely blank mirror which simply reflects the factual objects of our environment: What we know and perceive is subject to our prior knowledge and experience. For example, we cannot imagine that something exists without a cause, without time reference and without spatial quality. This preconditioning is also the reason why optical illusions and tricks work (both natural and invented ones). It also explains why one person may perceive and remember a particular situation completely differently to another participant.

Our capacity for cognition and knowledge is extraordinarily large, but is quickly exhausted when we engage in intensive scientific study. Recent developments in many fields have brought us an enormous growth in knowledge, but this only leads us to the somewhat frustrating conclusion that we will never be able to really comprehend the world "in itself". Nobel Prize-winning scientists resort to concepts that are beyond the scope of our normal imagination in order to explain real results from real physical tests. How should we imagine "parallel universes"? Or how can we picture the claim that our universe has more than four dimensions? And according to science, before the Big Bang there was a type of "supersingularity", which means there was no matter that could curve space and therefore also no space. How are we supposed to imagine "no space"?!

A metaphor might be useful here to illustrate the limits to our knowledge. Imagine a person who lives in a universe with two spatial dimensions plus the dimension of time. It is a flat world and we can imagine a stick-person as an inhabitant of this world. He has a piece of flat gold and puts it in a stick-house which he locks on all sides (for him). As a four-dimensional being, we have the advantage of being able to approach the stick house from a third spatial dimension and reach inside, stealing the gold. For our stick-victim, there will be no way of imagining how the theft was committed.

Whether we like it or not, we have to accept that we are subject to similar limits. The inability to think of more than four dimensions is just the tip of the iceberg as far as our limitations are concerned.

Using our senses to acquire more information, we can experience how limited these senses are: We generally need technical assistance to perceive most of the energy frequencies in our environment (light, heat, sound etc.) So we are constantly searching for new insights but our ability to find them is not without limits. It is a little bit like a drunken man searching for his key at night under a lamppost. A helpful passerby asks him, "Where exactly did you drop it?" "Over there," the drunken man replies, pointing to the doorstep of his house, "but it's too dark over there and I can't see anything".

The appeal to develop the right view should help us become very cautious and develop a reasonable self-criticism which takes into account that we can always make mistakes, that our views are often mistaken, that our prior experience often leads to preconceptions, and that we human beings generally cannot make any statements with absolute validity. When we know a lot, we begin to know how much we cannot know—to paraphrase Socrates. So the truth about the right view can also teach us to be humble, cautious and mindful.

Developing the right view is a real challenge, but the challenge can be met by means of the three-stage process we already know from our study of the BPT Fundamentals: recognising and understanding; contemplating and internalising; realising and implementing. And applying the Wisdom of the Middle Way is an effective way to analyse and counter our tendency to adopt extreme views, opinions, prejudices and judgements.

2. Right thought

Already we can begin to see connections between the eight aspects: it is obvious that without right view it is hardly possible to adopt right thought. Each detail has its own important value: This aspect casts light on the intensive training of the mind that plays a central role for Buddhists. Right view and right thought can only arise as the result of training which helps to dispel ignorance as one of our main causes of suffering.

As a science of the mind, Buddhism obviously concentrates on mental processes, culminating in the claim that everything is mind. Yongey Mingyur Rinpoche comments on this as follows: The mind is the source of all experience, and by changing the direction of the mind, we can change the quality of everything we experience and perceive.

As we read this book, what are we using to take in its meaning? When we look around us, where are we storing the experiences? When we plan what we still have to do today, what are we planning this with? Everything we know—everything we have ever experienced—has been taken in by our senses and put into an order by our mind. (There are perhaps some exceptions here, such as archetypical or inherited patterns, or as Buddhists would say, the seeds in our storehouse consciousness.) Because our mind interprets the world and thus plays a role in determining healthy or unhealthy reactions, it is very important to train mindfulness of mental activities.

Keep it simple

Our mind loves to simplify things and quickly establish routines, clichés and habits. As soon as we learn something, it becomes a sort of background knowledge. When we reach for a glass of water, the necessary thought and coordination processes take place automatically and unconsciously: stretch out our arm, form the hand into a grasping shape, grasp the glass, maintain our balance, etc. The way we are sitting or standing at this very moment as we read this book was most probably not consciously planned. This phenomenon pervades almost all of our everyday activities. We spend most of our time in automated, unconscious activity. And if our mind does make itself more clearly and consciously felt, it is very often only because it pesters us with complaints and worries.

Another example of the problems surrounding the control of our mind becomes clear if we try to let our mind to rest on one chosen issue for only two minutes. We can try it now: Think for two minutes about your left hand. ... How many seconds went by before some other thought forced its way in? We ceased to be the master or mistress in our own house a long time ago!

Much too much
Thich Nhat Hanh tells the tale of how on a stormy day he returned home to find he had forgotten to close the windows of his house. The wind had blown his paperwork all over the house. How many windows in our house (mind) do we leave open and how much wind (unhealthy input) do we let blow in? Our minds have an ever decreasing chance of being able to deal with this ever increasing rush of stimuli.

So it is advisable to carry out daily mindfulness exercises as well as implementing self-protection measures and slowly reducing our ignorance. A core feature of these mindfulness exercises is training our mind to remain in the here and now. A majority of our problems are perpetuated by our mind, such as worries about the past, or created by the mind, such as worries about what might happen in the future. A *here-and-now mindfulness exercise* can be practised at any time. It might even function right now: Can we actually concentrate *now* on this book without thinking about the past or future? And later, when we are drinking a cup of coffee or tea, does it become possible to only be aware of the cup, its weight and the warmth, aroma and taste spreading out from it?

The traditional definition of stress is this: Stress arises when the body is here and the mind is there.

We only notice how restless our mind is when we try to focus our attention on thinking. This is something we have to deal with a lot when we come to the topic of meditation. Of course, modern media are constantly feeding a superabundance of inputs into our mind, but the restlessness we experience is much older and could be said to be inherent. The electrochemical processes corresponding to our mental activities are dynamic—they are in constant flux. We often do not even recognise our thought processes because so much is automatic and happens at very high speed. We love routines and simplifications and in everyday life we are also distracted by a multiplicity of tasks. In fact, many of us could be described as addicted to distraction.

Everything comes from within
We often have very little access to our inner processes, so we believe that everything—good or bad—comes from outside. This is then reflected in our hopes for *the* right job, *the* right partner, *the* right medicine, the perfect holiday etc.

Jack Kornfield reports on a long-term study in which several thousand people were surveyed relating to their feelings of happiness. The survey was repeated after many years. It was particularly interesting to examine the answers of people who in the meantime had been very lucky—such as winning the lottery—or unlucky—such as suffering a serious illness or becoming partially paralysed. The study showed that people who had experienced significant external luck (good or bad) generally returned to their original level of happiness within two years. In other words, two years after winning the lottery, the person was just as happy or unhappy as they were before the win. And within two years, people who became paraplegic were also just as happy or unhappy as before their accident.

Our mind often leads us down dead-end streets and creates thought scenarios that might never happen but nonetheless keep us busy with worries now.

What we believe in
The story of the night watchman can serve as a sad example here. A watchman was employed to patrol the cold-storage rooms at a large

wholesale market. One night as he entered one of the older cold-storage rooms, the heavy metal door slammed behind him. This old steel door could only be opened from outside. The night watchman needed just a split second to recognise that he was trapped. He knew that nobody could survive a night at these temperatures. He wanted to be strong and dignified in his last moments so he took a wooden chest and sat upright on it. Very soon he noticed the cold creeping up his legs, his fingers slowly became numb, his forehead and face felt colder and colder. His fear and sense of hopelessness served only to increase the freezing feeling. He could very clearly feel the freezing cold spreading through his body and as morning came he was found dead sitting on the chest. However, the workers who found him were astonished because this old room had not been used as a cold-storage room for many years!

If we believe in something we quickly feel very secure with our new belief and tend to establish it, ignoring any contradictory information.

Our mind and our thoughts are very susceptible and have to be looked after very carefully. So we should respect them greatly and make best use of the possibilities we have to improve them. We will be able to master right thinking only if we respect our nature, according appropriate levels of value and respect to the drives within us. Right thinking does not mean that we assume absolute control, strangling and suppressing mental impulses and thoughts. Instead, it means that we carefully treat ourselves. Our mind could be our little monkey—often helpful but often annoying. We will never tame it by trying to throw it to the ground and dominate it. We have to respect its nature and its needs, remaining in contact with it, feeding it and occasionally caressing it.

Developing right thinking is also a challenge that can be met by means of the three-stage process: recognising and understanding, contemplating and internalising, realising and implementing. And using the Middle Way is also effective here as we self-critically respect our mind and its nature. We are not trying to switch off the mind but we cannot let it run around out of control.

The Ethical Conduct Group of the Noble Eightfold Path

3. Right speech

Speech, too, is directly connected with all other aspects of the Eightfold Path, especially because our speech reveals our mental attitude, view and thoughts. So Buddhism emphasises the value of what we say and how we say it as well as what we think and do.

Psychological and psychotherapeutic research proved a long time ago that psychological violence—such as verbal attacks—can be just as intense as physical violence. One detailed and well-developed approach for training respectful and peaceful communication is that of Non-Violent Communication, initially created by Marshall Rosenberg.

Unhealthy speech is a very reliable indicator for unhealthy and mindless mental states. We risk hurting other people with negative speech and we also risk perpetuating the pollution in our own mind. Repetition creates habits, and habits shape our character and destiny. So if we can make an effort to reduce and eradicate the expressions of negativity and unhealthy mental states in our speech then this will contribute to our further practice of reducing the negativity in our thoughts. This is a very practical approach because many of us find it easier to control how we phrase and express our speech than to directly control our mental activities.

Developing right speech is another real challenge that can be met by means of the familiar three-stage Buddhist Psychotherapy process: recognising and understanding, contemplating and internalising, realising and implementing. Once again, the Middle Way is also effective here; speaking in an open and honest way does not mean that we need to hurt the feelings of the person we are speaking to.

4. Right action

To start with we should reiterate the connection between all of the individual branches of the Eightfold Path: Right action cannot be treated as completely separate from right speech, right thought and right view, or any other aspects of the Fourth Noble Truth.

And when we talk about action we should also remember the chain of causality that is particularly relevant to the Buddhist viewpoint here: Our *intentions* lead to our *deeds/actions*. Repeating these creates *habits*. Our *character* develops from these and then in turn shapes our *destiny*.

So we need to learn how to recognise whether we are harbouring healthy or unhealthy intentions in every little everyday situation. Even positive situations that make us happy for at least a short time can lead to unhealthy results in the long term.

Actions which we often repeat are bound to shape us and our destiny. How do we spend our free time? What addictions do we feed? This Buddhist causality chain deserves a deep, self-critical and honest investigation if we are to really become aware of the long-term consequences. In fact, this causal connection between intentions and destiny could be expressed in a simplified way as an opportunity to "recreate" ourselves over and over again. The "only thing" we need to do is carry out selected *repetitions* in a disciplined way (see 5th Fundamental of BPT on our body and neuroplasticity).

Buddhism considers behaviour to have two important aspects: things we should not do and things we should do. The former overlaps with commandments from other traditions (*Thou shalt not...*) and the latter concerns virtuous behaviour. As we have already mentioned, Buddhists consider virtue to be *active behaviour* promoting positive outcomes rather than instructions about what we should *not* do. It means consciously committing ourselves to beneficial outcomes (see the section on Buddhist virtue in the 20th Fundamental of BPT).

2500 years ago the Buddha formulated five basic rules for lay people (those who are not monks or nuns) regarding things that we should gradually cease to do. The appropriate sets of rules for novices, monks, nuns and bodhisattvas have 10, 18, 36, 46, 227, 253, 311 and 364 rules, depending on the particular order and type of vows taken.

> **The Five Lay Precepts**
> 1. Refrain from deliberately killing or injuring living beings (including animals).
> 2. Refrain from taking anything that is not freely given.
> 3. Refrain from sexual misconduct
> 4. Refrain from lying and harsh speech.
> 5. Refrain from blurring consciousness by taking drugs.

Roles such as these can always be interpreted with a certain amount of leeway. Everybody has to decide for themselves which particular actions they deem to be appropriate or not. If we would initially like some slightly more detailed instructions on what to practice, then we can follow the guidance of avoiding the Ten Non-Virtues.

> **The Ten Non-Virtues**
> *The three unhealthy actions of the body*
> 1. Killing
> 2. Stealing
> 3. Sexual misconduct
> *The four unhealthy actions of speech*
> 4. Lying
> 5. Divisive speech
> 6. Harsh words
> 7. Gossiping
> *The three unhealthy actions of the mind*
> 8. Covetousness
> 9. Malice
> 10. Clinging to wrong views

These precepts can be seen to encapsulate the special spirit of Buddhism—respect for one's own life and the life of others. They are not rules upheld for their own sake but rather guidelines to provide support as we try to approach liberation. In particular, they should not feel like a corset restricting us and making us even less free.

Eric Fromm once said that we are accustomed to freeing ourselves *from* something but not to freeing ourselves *for* something. This means the freedom *for* responsibility, not the freedom *from* responsibility; using our freedom *actively* in order to make a decision *for* rather than *against* something.

Two further very important areas of right action are *Sacred Inner Moments* and *Non-Action*.

Sacred Inner Moments

We have already explained the problematic issue of automatism. The exercise *Sacred Inner Moments* is designed to counteract this process of acting too quickly and following unconscious patterns of behaviour. We try to increase our mindfulness and awareness by wilfully introducing pauses into our behaviour as often as possible. Thus becomes a particularly powerful practice when we apply it in moments where we have to make a decision. We stop everything we are doing for two breaths and direct our attention inwards. Only then do we continue with our behaviour. By practising in situations that are relatively free of stress or automatism we consolidate this ability and can then apply a *Sacred Inner Moment* whenever it is useful to make progress towards right action.

Non-Action

The next step in this context can then be *not acting*. This can either be a strategy within conflict (passive resistance), a gesture of composure, or a sign of respect for the limits of our own capacity to act. However, it should not be misused as a pseudo-justification for passive inaction. Non-action has many different faces and needs to be applied very carefully and effectively.

Practising right action is a real challenge that can be met by means of the three-stage Buddhist Psychotherapy process we are now very familiar with: recognising and understanding, contemplating and internalising, realising and implementing. Remaining on the Middle Way will help us mindfully avoid the extremes of blindly doing things for the sake of it or destructive lethargy.

5. Right livelihood

Not everyone has Buddhist parents to give us early guidance on how to study and train in order to earn a livelihood in an ethical way. And not all of us want to live a monastic life. So when we are introduced later in life to the wisdom of Buddhism and its guidance on how to live our lives, it can be difficult to adapt our occupation or professional activities.

The decision may be clearer for the small minority of us pursuing occupations that are directly connected to killing and harming: butchers, animal traders, fur farmers, vivisectors, drug dealers, arms traders or soldiers. For the rest of us, however, the situation can be more complex, especially in our advanced economies and when we consider the concept of interconnection. A baker is undoubtedly pursuing an honourable vocation, but perhaps he supplies bread to a nearby animal testing laboratory? Postmen perform non-violent work while wearing leather shoes. Not all of us can live on a vegetarian diet. And even if we make great efforts to ensure that we earn a right livelihood, our government takes our taxes and carries out many unethical activities that are beyond our control.

When we make progress with our mindfulness training, at some stage we will probably have to take some clear, practical decisions. Nonetheless, as much as we increase our levels of consistency and commitment, we remain aware of our inseparable connection with everyone else and all their deeds (healthy and unhealthy).

Of course there are stages to this process, so we can begin by implementing things that seem easier: no serious lies and then no small lies; no swear words, no insults, no provocations, no negative remarks, no judgements. To maintain our capacity to implement this mindfully, we can decide to cease consumption of mind-altering substances; we do not have to immediately stop drinking any alcohol or smoking cigarettes, but we can, for example, stop drinking when we notice we are losing control of our behaviour. In fact, as we make progress in our practice of meditation and mindfulness exercises, we generally find that we quite naturally develop an aversion to any substances that cloud our mind.

A meditator who trains sitting upright on a daily basis will get used to this and then discover they also walk with a more upright posture and, furthermore, naturally adopt an upright attitude in their life in general. Not stealing, for example, will then be understood in its subtler form of not taking anything that is not given to us, and this then clearly also becomes connected to the issue of not killing when we consider the taking of lives that are not given to us which goes on so that we may eat meat.

Whether we need to change our job completely is an individual decision that will depend on individual circumstances. Before taking a decision such as this, it is well worth remembering that often the issue is not *which* job we do but *how* we do it.

Use every opportunity to practice

Whatever we are doing, every activity can present an important opportunity for daily practice. Every burden and every form of professional stress can be used as an exercise. And we can learn to carry out every job-related activity we perform as if it were a sacred activity.

Right livelihood is a real challenge that can be met by means of the familiar three-stage Buddhist Psychotherapy process: recognising and understanding; contemplating and internalising; realising and implementing. In this regard the Wisdom of the Middle Way recommends that we carefully consider how to strike a balance between necessary compromises and adhering to principles. It is the path between total acceptance of our deeds, being fully aware of what we do and committing ourselves to necessary changes.

The Meditative Concentration Group of the Noble Eightfold Path

6. Right effort

The Buddha was and still is a very valuable companion on our path, who left us detailed theoretical and practical instructions that give us a chance to follow him. We gain hope by following in his tracks and sharing in his path. This path is well signposted but is still an exciting and sometimes strenuous adventure for each individual who embarks on it. We need the appropriate discipline combined with patience and a clear willingness to change, since the path is full of hidden dangers, pitfalls, temptations and distractions. We have to deal with our "baser instincts" in a new, mindful and respectful way, nourishing and cherishing them so we do not need to fear them anymore.

Another powerful inner opponent which we will need effort to overcome is the power of habit. Constant practice and repetition will wear it down. However, for many of us it is much more comfortable to remain in old familiar patterns, even if they are unhealthy and painful, than to set off into the unknown and new. To rid ourselves of old habits requires a great deal of motivation, perhaps a sweetener to get things started, and then plenty of patience and perseverance. New rituals and routines need a certain amount of time before they give us the same feeling of security as our old ones.

A well-known Christian prayer, now commonly known as the Serenity Prayer, expresses the wish for courage to change the things that can be changed and serenity to accept the things we cannot change. The prayer also asks for wisdom to tell the difference between these.

With regard to right effort we would also do well to remember the Wisdom of the Middle Way. We can apply this principle to almost all areas of life, and it should accompany us through the day like a mantra: Remain on the Middle Way. Not too much, not too little; not too strict, not too lenient; not dogged, not apathetic; not too quick, not too slow; etc.

When we are trying to decide what effort is right effort, we can let ourselves be guided by our emotions. Every unhealthy mental state could be an indication that we have left the Middle Way. Healthy states such as joy can be signs that we are on the right path.

The correct course cannot be determined in a universally applicable way. For example, while some of us should make more effort, others should reduce our activity. But even asking ourselves this question is a great start.

In addition to daily practice and other aspects described here, vows can be of assistance for people progressing along this path. In particular, for Buddhist Psychotherapists, taking the step of adopting a bodhisattva approach can be a very appropriate step in our Buddhist practice. Bodhisattvas are strongly drawn to serving all sentient beings and commit all their available effort and energy towards helping themselves and all other creatures achieve liberation. This represents effort in its mostly highly developed form. So it becomes clear that Buddhists do not understand right effort as the effort towards achieving success for ourselves. Instead, any personal progress we make is dedicated to the progress of all living beings. None of this teaching makes sense if we apply it only to our own effort for our personal success.

Right effort is also a real challenge that can be met by means of the familiar three-stage process: recognising and understanding; contemplating and internalising; realising and implementing. The Middle Way approach recommends us to avoid the extreme of forced and desperate action. Our effort should be the result of careful concentration and motivation.

7. Right mindfulness

This aspect of the path is also a milestone within Buddhist teachings and practice. Mindfulness is one of the major tools we have to help us find and follow the Right Path.

Right mindfulness can be an important link between theory and practice. Often, we very quickly gain an initial rational understanding of a subject, and mindfulness can then be a powerful tool as we try to bring reason and instinct together to create a harmonious whole. How many areas of our life are there in which we theoretically know what would *actually* be good for us but nonetheless behave very differently?

Thich Nhat Hanh offers us a helpful overview of the effects of right mindfulness:

1) Mindfulness helps us to achieve true presence
2) Mindfulness makes everything around us present

3) Mindfulness gives vitality to the object of our mindfulness
4) Mindfulness helps us to calm down
5) Mindfulness helps us to look deeply
6) Mindfulness helps us to understand
7) Mindfulness assists transformation

One problem often referred to is the difficulty of achieving and maintaining the necessary mindfulness in the midst of our everyday stress with its distractions, duties and burdens. Often we only really return to our body long after we have finished a busy working day. In other words, we spend the whole day subject to great pressure, without real self-awareness, but with a great deal of concentration on the stressors around us; we only really become aware of the internal effects of the day when we later experience symptoms such as pain, tiredness, sleep disorders or irritability.

Support is available in the form of the Buddhist sutta on the *Foundations of Mindfulness* mentioned in the 5th Fundamental.

The Four Foundations of Mindfulness
1) Body
2) Feelings
3) Mind/Consciousness
4) Dharmas (Mental Objects)

In particular for those of us who want to open ourselves to the power of our mind and spirit, the *body* is often regarded and experienced as troublesome. Our back aches, our stomach is hungry, our body is tired, etc. However, with mindfulness practice we value and respect it for what it is: our house, our home, our friend (who may not always be a good friend). Our body can give us very clear information in the same way as a thermometer. If our restless and perhaps ambitious or fearful mind wants to keep going on and on, our body can often signal to us to stop, telling us that's enough for the moment!

Using our mindfulness to become more aware of our *feelings* is the next step, then our *mind* and then the *mental objects* or all phenomena in the world of appearance.

The goal of achieving the most intense and comprehensive mindfulness possible is not always easy to implement. For example, there are certainly some jobs which can only be tolerated if we distance ourselves from them and turn our body into a "machine". But does this mean we should deliberately be less mindful because mindfulness could make an undesirable activity even more uncomfortable?

Of course, in practice it is a great challenge to perform undesirable activities with mindfulness. So we should begin our exercises with easier, more pleasant contents. With the greatest possible mindfulness we enjoy a cup of tea or coffee. Then we expand mindfulness to more and more areas of our life, perhaps initially our hobbies and the people close to us, progressing on to more difficult situations and people. As we put this into practice we will definitely experience a few surprises.

Mindfulness can lead us to take new paths; perhaps we notice when it is not necessary to quarrel or struggle and when we can simply accept our life's burdens. Furthermore, mindfulness is necessary to determine the right pace of life for each of us; the exercise *Sacred Inner Moments* is particularly helpful here.

Right mindfulness is another real challenge that can be met by means of the familiar three-stage BPT process: recognising and understanding; contemplating and internalising; realising and implementing. (More details on mindfulness can be found in the 6th Fundamental of BPT, among others.) The Middle Way approach recommends a practice of mindfulness that motivates us to maintain constant alertness without pushing us too much. Mindfulness gives us an increased awareness of where *our* middle is.

8. Right concentration/composure

Right concentration or composure is very similar but not identical to right mindfulness (see 6th Fundamental of BPT). Whereas mindfulness is a more dilated form of attention, the composed concentration referred to here is focused on one specific object.

We can practice general active concentration/composure by developing an alert understanding of everything around us. In an alert and conscious way, we see the things around us and take note of them. Everything comes and goes but we have no resistance or attachment. We perceive everything but do not judge it. Then we can practice selective composure or concentration by targeting our concentration on one object, without distraction, without a wandering mind.

> Alertness, concentration, mindfulness and awareness are important goals in Buddhism and Buddhist Psychotherapy. By achieving these, we can achieve liberation.

Right concentration is a real challenge that can be met by means of the three-stage BPT process we already know: recognising and understanding; contemplating and internalising; realising and implementing. The Middle Way recommends concentration which also allows us to relax.

Summary: The Noble Eightfold Path to end suffering is multi-faceted and concerns many different areas of our life. Each of the eight sub-paths is directly connected to all of the others.

Right view and right thought influence our right speech; this sheds light on our right mindfulness and right effort. In the same way, our right behaviour reveals our right thinking and right effort. Right concentration and right mindfulness can change our right livelihood, guide our right thinking, and influence our right view.

Erica R already has a lot of therapy experience but says that she has been unable to put much of this into practice. She reflects very often on her *thoughts*, she is in harmony with her *profession* and really feels quite *mindful* and *concentrated*. However, with regard to her *behaviour* and her *speech*, she still notices many weaknesses, particularly how easily she gets annoyed. Although she sometimes senses that she is reacting in the wrong way, it feels as if an unstoppable, unhealthy program is running within her. Despite this self-assessment, Erica agreed to take a fresh look at the eight areas of her life in order to find out which one it might be easiest for her to make practical changes in. During this detailed analysis, Erica recognised that there was a series of ambivalent and partially contradictory *thoughts* within her. This enabled her to recognise her personal strengths and pitfalls. In dialogue with other participants in the group sessions, Erica heard how others, too, often find it very difficult to remain on the Middle Way. Since her strict inner voices often go too far towards the extremes of discipline and judgement, she received the instruction to tell herself, quietly or out loud, as often as possible each day that what she is currently experiencing is good. Initially Erica was very sceptical (since it is impossible for everything to be good) but the exercise gradually helped her to come out of the "critic's corner" and into the middle.

This Fundamental Should Convey the Following:

Buddhist Psychotherapy includes all relevant areas of our lives because this school of therapy ensures a high level of practicality to complement its theoretical knowledge and specialist psychotherapeutic aspects. One of the cornerstones of BPT is to ensure that we take our progress in therapy and put it into practice in our everyday life for the benefit of ourselves and all others.

For this reason, therapist and help-seeker take a joint look at various aspects of our lives as illustrated in the Noble Eightfold Path: right view or insights, right thought, right speech, right behaviour or action, right livelihood, right effort, right mindfulness and right concentration or composure.

The path to end suffering is the Middle Way.

A milestone is reached

We have now completed our introduction to the most essential building blocks of the Buddhist teachings. Our intention was to develop an initial understanding of the famous teaching of the *First Turning of the Wheel of Dharma,* which contains three main statements:
 1) Follow the Middle Way
 2) Use the insights to stay in the here and now and help yourself and others

3) Understand the Four Noble Truths
These building blocks now form the foundations of our further progress.

The 18th
Fundamental of Buddhist Psychotherapy

The Teachings:
The Right Measure for Each of Us

> In the Buddhist scriptures it says that there is no difficult task which cannot be broken down into smaller, simple ones.
>
> MATTHIEU RICARD

The diversity and number of Buddhist scriptures available is quite considerable. As well as records of the original teachings, the scriptures also include experiences written down by teachers and masters as they put these teachings into practice over the last 2500 years. Buddhism does not have one superordinate body (such as the Vatican for Catholics), so every Buddhist country has its own schools, masters and teachers with their main focal points, practices and scriptures. Lineages developed as traditions of teaching and practice that can generally be traced back to one advanced master. Usually this master had selected particular issues for their own practice and that of their students, and the lineage continued to refine and develop these.

This process has been going on for a very long time so it is now impossible to say exactly how many texts constitute the complete body of Buddhist scriptures. This great variety ensures that everybody will find their own individual access to the teachings but some might run the risk of getting lost in the Buddhist library. Nonetheless, if it is used properly, the "library" will reveal its holistic nature: Choose one topic, look into it deeply, and in the detail we will recognise the whole (of the teachings).

In the previous Fundamentals of Buddhist Psychotherapy we frequently referred to the famous teaching of the *First Turning of the Wheel of Dharma,* comprising the core elements of the Middle Way, the Four Noble Truths, and the call to use the insights to stay in the here and now and help ourselves and others. These elements form the focal points of our work in BPT. Nonetheless, in this Fundamental we would like to offer an additional encouragement to the reader to study some further aspects of the teachings, which we will briefly introduce here. Upon reading this, some readers may well sound the alarm, fearing that the teachings are becoming too complex and too great in scope. We would like to reassure these readers that the teachings we conveyed in the previous Fundamentals are sufficient and have already covered the essence of the Buddhist teachings.

The Buddhist teachings are admittedly very comprehensive but they should never be the ultimate focus of our efforts. The Buddha himself explained that the Dharma is like a raft which we use to cross the river in order to reach the bank of wisdom and liberation. It is not the destination itself. The Four Noble Truths, for example, only have value if we can recognise them, internalise them deeply and put them into practice in our daily life. Anyone who does this will surely have a taste of liberation. But what this process actually looks like within any one individual's life cannot be prescribed in a general teaching; the destination has been described but there are as many different routes to this destination as there are different people aspiring to reach it. In order to reach an overall, universal goal we may have to first deal with our very individual, personal problems. So there will always be both individual and universal goals in Buddhist Psychotherapy. That is also one of the reasons why we would like to include a few further aspects of the Buddhist teachings in this book, increasing the chances of providing just the right aspects to as many readers as possible, enabling them to find their individual access to the central message. We often find that particular words or sentences resonate within us and thus become more easily memorable—allowing us to recall the meaning more quickly when we need it.

In order to decide which further aspects of the Buddhist teachings could be helpful for our work, we refer to the Buddha's own words. He explained that deep enlightenment can be realised if we internalise and put into practice the following three factors:

The Three Factors That Can Lead to Enlightenment
The Four Noble Truths
The Four Immeasurables
The Seven Factors of Awakening

The Four Immeasurables

The first additional set of factors we want to look at is sometimes also translated as *The Four Illimitable Mental States:*

The Four Immeasurables
1) Loving-Kindness
2) Compassion
3) Joy
4) Equanimity

If we can create these mental states within us then we automatically avoid every other negative mental condition because healthy and unhealthy mental states are mutually exclusive. For example, loving-kindness and hate cannot exist within us at exactly the same time.

Transforming our mental states

Transforming mental states is reported to be the 14th Dalai Lama's favourite technique. As the name of the technique makes clear, its purpose is to change unhealthy mental states into healthy ones without any external help.

We can only feel one emotion at a time. Although we sometimes have very confusing emotional conditions where we believe that we have a blend of different emotions, if we look deeper we will discover that certain constellations of emotions are actually not compatible with each other. During these complex emotional conditions, there may well be very rapid transitions between related emotions such as anger, annoyance and rage, but a change from anger to loving-kindness will certainly take a moment longer.

It is not possible to create loving-kindness and hate at the same time. A more likely outcome would be a new state in our mind, such as critical observation. Jack Kornfield expresses it in this way: When love meets suffering, it turns to compassion (for example). When compassion meets fear, the fear turns into another emotion.

We have already discovered that trained practitioners are able to create healthy mental states such as love, compassion, joy and equanimity so effectively that it can be recorded by MRT scans. We, too, can make use of patient training to stabilise our capacity to create healthy mental states; this will then enable us to weaken our unhealthy patterns, removing their power over us. It is advisable to perform many repetitions of our regular exercises and make use of quiet times for this training to ensure that we have a good basis and can act efficiently in times of emotional upheaval. If we wait until crisis situations and then attempt to transform our unhealthy mental conditions as untrained people, we will very probably fail. So it makes sense to prepare ourselves now because we can be certain that at some point in the future we will meet a problem or two.

Practical details for the exercises are given in the 19th Fundamental of BPT.

Self-control

The whole purpose of mind training is to increase our capacity for self-control when it comes to mental and emotional states which apparently arise within us automatically and uncontrollably. If we begin to feel negativity and unhealthy mental states, mind training allows us to intervene more and more to counter this; in particular when we learn to develop the Four Immeasurables. Love, compassion, joy and equanimity can be practised daily; we can incorporate them into our meditation sessions or we can practice directly in the course of our everyday life by applying such exercises as *Sacred Inner Moments*. For just a couple of seconds we sit upright, or stand straight or simply consciously improve our stance while walking, take a few conscious breaths, and smile. Our mind becomes calmer and we can concentrate on our selected immeasurable.

What does this condition feel like? Here we can apply the Four Foundations of Mindfulness, beginning by placing our mindfulness on our body, then onto our feelings and then expanding it onto our mind and mental objects. What does *equanimity* (for example) feel like in our body? How do we breathe when we feel equanimous? Regular practice should help to establish this element within us.

We can do the same with joy, compassion and loving-kindness. We practice *Sacred Inner Moments,* feel our breath, calm down and concentrate on our joy in life, the joy we feel regarding our friends or simply the joy of breathing. Or we select *compassion* to concentrate on and feel interconnection, sense our desire to support others and feel our empathy with them. We can also initially feel *loving-kindness* in our body, mindfully being aware of the sensations. At the beginning it is advisable to do this in relation to people who are close to us—those we love or like. Later we can carry over our loving mental states to people whom we do not know so well and then to people with whom we have few opportunities for personal contact. As we progress, we can also bring love to bear on people whom we do not like.

This one aspect of the Buddhist teachings—cultivating the Four Immeasurables—is itself sufficient for our studies and practice. If we can deeply recognise, understand, internalise and realise these qualities, we will have liberated ourselves from persistent negativity because the Four Immeasurables and persistent negativity are mutually exclusive. If we regularly practise and apply these mental states, we can call them up in situations where negativity and unhealthy mental states are brewing within us.

Learning to love is like learning to sail

If we find it difficult to create these healthy mental states in good times, then we will be completely overwhelmed if we have to do it in bad times. Matthieu Ricard compared this with learning to sail: Nobody chooses to have their first sailing lessons in stormy weather!

As part of the 7th Fundamental of BPT, we were introduced to the way our feelings and emotions function. So now we can apply this knowledge. We have understood that our emotions are often very deceptive and are influenced by many prior experiences; they are therefore by no means automatic, instead arising reactively. Knowing this, we can choose the appropriate daily practical exercises to develop a new way of influencing these processes and freeing ourselves of automatisms that are often unhealthy. We free ourselves from the power that other people appear to have over us and our feelings; we suffer because of the emotions they appear to trigger within us. Let us consider the example of someone cursing us: We can pause for a moment, look inwardly, practising the *Sacred Inner Moment*, breathing consciously and clearing our mind before allowing ourselves to experience a reaction. Our reaction will then be different; it might be a clear defence or an apology, but in any case it will be free from attachments and the compulsive retreat into a role.

Seven Factors of Awakening

The Buddha advised us to respect the Four Noble Truths and the Four Immeasurables, but he also added a third aspect: the Seven Factors of Awakening.

The Seven Factors of Awakening

Mindfulness, or remembering

Investigation (of dharmas), or analysis

Energy, or vigour

Joy, or rapture

Tranquillity, or relaxation

Composure, or concentration

Equanimity

When we take a look at the Seven Factors of Awakening, we find elements which we already know from the Four Noble Truths and the Four Immeasurables. The different components of the Buddhist teachings are linked to and interact with each other in the same way as the intricate cogwheels in a Swiss watch. Different people may find different constellations more to their taste or more meaningful in a certain way. Some people might find the interlocking structure of the Four Noble Truths too complicated and prefer the Four Immeasurables. Other people may find the order in which the Seven Factors are presented more logical or easier to remember and therefore more helpful for their daily practice.

The Noble Eightfold Path in Our Everyday Life

We can compile a helpful list to assist implementation of the teachings in everyday life by looking at the Fourth Noble Truth. By keeping this list with us we can refer to it and check our progress; some people may prefer to set a regular time for a review, others might use free moments such as short bus rides or waiting in line.

1) Is our view / our recognition clear, calm and pure?
2) Is our thought clear, calm and pure?
3) Is our speech clear, calm and pure?
4) Is our behaviour clear, calm and pure?
5) Is our professional activity clear, calm and pure?
6) Is our effort clear, calm and pure?
7) Is our mindfulness clear, calm and pure?
8) Is our concentration clear, calm and pure?

This list is designed to appeal to us to take a practical look at particular aspects of our life and the progress we are making at putting into practice some of the truths we have learned.

Watch out! Danger!

Positive mental states have been described above and now we briefly turn to a list of negative human characteristics which also deserves our attention, acting as it does as a sort of negative counterpart. Most of us will quickly recognise these aspects that often make our life so difficult. Thich Nhat Hanh describes them as the *Five Hindrances* that obstruct our path to liberation.

The Five Hindrances
1. Sensual desire
2. Ill-will, or malice
3. Torpor, or sloth
4. Restlessness, or worry
5. Doubt, or lack of conviction

These may appear to be five familiar companions and they are surely so well-known that they need no further clarification or description. They are like unwanted friends who insist on accompanying us, who do not understand the word goodbye, and who keep knocking at our door, whether it is convenient or not. We will learn to accept the hindrances the way we accept our old acquaintances. Of course, we do not hate them or get angry with them—what use can there be in trying to combat an unhealthy mental state with another unhealthy state? "Declaring war on war" is a strategy that can never work.

The First Noble Truth taught us that problems are simply part of life. Our own personal problems are not the result of a fundamental mistake we have made or a terrible destiny we have been burdened with. Problems are okay. Of course, they will never become our friends, but at least they can become our teachers.

With regards to the First Noble Truth, we also learnt to avoid adding to our problems (for example, sloth or torpor as one of the Five Hindrances) through the imposition of a further avoidable problem such as self-judgement, annoyance or frustration.

Buddhist Psychology

Now we have built up a good, solid foundation of Buddhist teachings. Further aspects regarding their practical implementation and the psychotherapeutic use will be presented in the following Fundamentals.

To recap, we have already met a very diverse and comprehensive range of Buddhist teachings:

- the Essence of Buddhism
- our Inner Nobility
- the Wisdom of the Middle Way
- the call to use our progress in the here and now for the benefit of ourselves and all others
- the Four Noble Truths
- the way that karma works
- the Four Foundations of Mindfulness
- the Four Immeasurables
- the Seven Factors of Awakening
- etc.

These teachings are very complex and so it is hardly possible or meaningful to try to summarise them at this stage. Nevertheless, it would appear useful to round off our body of theory a little. This can be done very nicely with the presentation of Buddhist psychology from Jack Kornfield's wonderful book *The Wise Heart*. He summarises it in just 26 principles.

When we come to carefully study these principles, we should compare them to the information we have conveyed so far. Many of the principles themselves seem very logical and easy to grasp, but a comparison can always be helpful, particularly for finding out how firmly we have grasped the theory.

Another indispensable aspect of Buddhist Psychotherapy is the interactive work in groups and individual sessions to deepen our understanding of the theoretical teachings. Only when we try to share or discuss our knowledge do we really experience whether we have understood and internalised what we have read. And this can be very helpful step towards the final stage of realising our insights in everyday life.

So let us now compare the 26 principles of Buddhist psychology with the 22 Fundamentals of Buddhist Psychotherapy.

The 26 Principles of Buddhist Psychology

1) See the inner nobility and beauty of all human beings.
2) Compassion is our deepest nature. It arises from our interconnection with all things.
3) When we shift attention from experience to the spacious consciousness that knows, wisdom arises.
4) Recognise the mental states that fill consciousness. Shift from unhealthy states to healthy ones.
5) Our ideas of self are created by identification. The less we cling to ideas of self, the freer and happier we will be.
6) Our life has a universal and personal nature. Both dimensions must be respected if we are to be happy and free.
7) Mindful attention to any experience is liberating. Mindfulness brings perspective, balance and freedom.
8) Mindfulness of the body allows us to live fully. It brings healing, wisdom and freedom.
9) Wisdom knows what feelings are present without being lost in them.
10) Thoughts are often one-sided and untrue. Learn to be mindful of thought instead of being lost in it.
11) There is a personal and a universal unconscious. Turning awareness to the unconscious brings understanding and freedom.
12) The unhealthy patterns of our personality can be recognised and transformed into a healthy expression of our natural temperament.
13) There are both healthy desires and unhealthy desires. Know the difference. Then find freedom in their midst.
14) If we cling to anger or hatred, we will suffer. It is possible to respond strongly, wisely, and compassionately, without hatred.
15) Delusion misunderstands the world and forgets who we are. Delusion gives rise to all unhealthy states. Free yourself from delusion and see with wisdom.

16) Pain is inevitable, suffering is not. Suffering arises from grasping. Release grasping and be free of suffering. (The Four Noble Truths)
17) Be mindful of intention. Intention is the seed that creates our future.
18) What we repeatedly visualize changes our body and consciousness. Visualize freedom and compassion.
19) What we repeatedly think shapes our world. Out of compassion, substitute healthy thoughts for unhealthy ones.
20) The power of concentration can be developed through inner training. Concentration opens consciousness to profound dimensions of healing and understanding.
21) Virtue and integrity are necessary for genuine happiness. Guard your integrity with care.
22) Forgiveness is both necessary and possible. It is never too late to find forgiveness and start again.
23) There is no separation between inner and outer, self and other. Tending ourselves, we tend the world. Tending the world, we tend ourselves.
24) The middle way is found between all opposites. Rest in the middle and find well-being wherever you are.
25) Release opinions, free yourself from views. Be open to mystery.
26) A peaceful heart gives birth to love. When love meets suffering, it turns to compassion. When love meets happiness, it turns to joy.

We can see that the BPT Fundamentals and their content can also be found within the 26 principles of Buddhist psychology as listed by Jack Kornfield. Both are equally suitable as a support for our daily practice. We can read them, meditate upon them and try to implement them.

We have very frequently referred to the practical exercises and psychotherapeutic measures which we will be introduced to in the following 19th Fundamental. It is important not to begin them too early or without the proper instructions.

Preparations

Tulku Lama Lobsang states very clearly that we have to clarify our mental constitution before we begin with Buddhist practice. So before we deal with the 19th Fundamental—the practical Buddhist-therapeutic exercises—we should have understood and internalised the previous Fundamentals of Buddhist Psychotherapy (1-18). We have to understand what our aim is and secure the foundations before we go on to start active training.

This means that we should have intensely studied the basics of Buddhist psychotherapy which have been presented so far: the Four Noble Truths, the Middle Way, the significance of the here and now for ourselves and others, the essence of Buddhism etc. If we have not completed this basic mental training, we will, for example, experience considerable difficulties during meditation. Progress may be slow or its direction unclear.

Keeping on course is of fundamental importance. The 1st Fundamental of BPT on the essence of Buddhism familiarised us with our destination: liberation from the cycle of life and suffering. It showed us what we can expect in the context of Buddhism and Buddhist Psychotherapy and what we can achieve.

Generally we consider a course of psychotherapy because we want to quickly rid ourselves of symptoms and rediscover the happiness we deserve. This process includes solving or clarifying problems and worries, irritations, conflicts and physical disorders etc.

Experience has shown that we seek out Buddhist Psychotherapy because we:
- are experiencing painful recurrences of an unhealthy pattern
- are suffering from an acute crisis
- sense a smouldering unease deep within ourselves
- would like to work on our spiritual growth, whether or not we currently have acute problems.

The latter point is a common reason for seeking out *Buddhist* Psychotherapy instead of another school. The 1st Fundamental of BPT on the essence of Buddhism immediately offers us a wider perspective.

The previous Fundamentals have conveyed BPT's suitability as a support in our aspiration to reduce or eradicate our individual, acute symptoms, but they should also have made it clear that it is only the more all-encompassing, universal goal of liberation that can help us to recognise how we really can escape the perpetual struggle between happiness and unhappiness. This outlook enables us to move beyond the goal of getting rid of characteristics we consider negative and promoting those we see as positive. A holistic transformation can indeed take place. All human beings always carry within them the potential to liberate themselves from Samsara, the eternal field of tension between happiness and unhappiness.

Happiness as tension? The 14th Fundamental on attachment explains what we will experience if we get stuck on the continuum between happiness and unhappiness.

We learn the Buddhist techniques included in BPT in order to regain our position as master (or mistress) of our own house. Our behaviour should no longer be determined by fear, anger, prejudice, addiction and greed but rather by our clear mind.

In order to achieve this we need to patiently continue with these techniques as part of our ongoing practice.

The First Noble Truth showed us that suffering is inescapable in this world, so the bad news is that we can never free ourselves permanently from every form of suffering. However there is also some good news: We can follow a clearly delineated Buddhist path that will enable us to completely eradicate many forms of avoidable suffering and loosen our grip on some other unavoidable aspects of suffering.

Another significant aspect which we have to consider with regard to therapeutic measures concerns the wisdom revealed by our *Innate Nobility*. The understanding of our golden inner core conveyed in the 8th Fundamental compels us to carefully and mindfully approach the inner protective layers which we built up around this core of nobility. One important aim could be to gradually break down these protective layers to let our "inner gold" shine through. Of course, we do not aspire to be completely without protection. However, our protection needs to be more flexible and brought back under our own control. This should lead to the desired effect of an increase in inner freedom, flexibility, empathy and self-control.

Changes

Some changes occur in a natural, almost pre-programmed way, such as physical maturation and ageing. Other changes are more susceptible to our direct influence, such as a change in hairstyle, an increase in muscles through workouts, or even a change of our appearance created by plastic surgery. We can also include inner changes brought about through our lifestyle or patient mind training, for example. Still other changes seem undoubtedly to be caused by external factors such as natural disasters, accidents caused by a third party or the experience of being a victim of violence.

Sometimes, however, it is more difficult to decide whether the responsibility for a change lies within or outside us. This can be the case in domestic or family conflicts. And another category of change could be those changes which develop unnoticed in a very gradual way for a long time before they become visible at some point.

One of the benefits of the practice of Buddhist Psychotherapy is the increase in our ability to initiate changes in a *self-determined* and *self-controlled* way. During the course of BPT we will soon recognise that our primary aspiration is no longer an *external* change. In other words, we do not necessarily have to change our family, our apartment, our job or our friends.

Tulku Lama Lobsang once summarised this message during his teachings as follows:

If you want a difficult life, try to change others.
If you want an easier life, try to change yourself.

So we can see first of all that we need to change ourselves, or rather our way of thinking. We will analyse the filters we use to perceive the world.

External changes are indeed often a result of this and they are significant, but generally we will see that they are nonetheless secondary. So we will be introduced to techniques which initially concentrate on creating changes *from within*.

Neuroscience has confirmed that we can change ourselves in a lasting way at a very deep level within our body. Our central nervous system can learn through a process where new neural connections are formed and existing ones become stronger if we actively repeat certain practices: neuroplasticity is the term used for this phenomenon.

Who is your teacher?

When we want to bring about changes, we may ask ourselves how these generally arise. What processes do we learn from? Which learning experiences have helped us to progress? We are not talking about mental arithmetic here but what we learn from our teachers. Many of our most intense, profound and character-forming life experiences were at the time very difficult for us; as human beings we often seem to learn the most from problems or solving problems. So, if they are not completely overwhelming, problems can be seen as our teachers. Without problems and obstructions we would make no progress.

Comfortable situations and a complete lack of problems can end up in stagnation. Good, enjoyable and comfortable things often give rise to negative conditions such as neediness, craving, dependency and addiction. Under certain conditions, suffering can arise from satisfaction—especially if this was achieved at the cost of others. Satisfaction can also give rise to dependencies and lethargy.

So problems will probably not become our friends, but they can certainly become our teachers.

In fact, the real problem consists of *not wanting* any problems. We can experience significant progress for ourselves and for others when we cease resisting the problems we encounter, accepting them without dispute or lament, and then actively trying to solve them.

Responsibility

Sometimes we hope to improve things by means of *external* changes. For example, we might believe that we will be happy if we have a pay increase, a quicker car, a larger apartment or more elegant clothes. These are typical signs of a *material* worldview.

If we recognise that we need to train ourselves, our mind and our body, these are signs of a *spiritual* worldview.

Of course, nobody can deny the great significance of the material side of our existence. We have to eat and drink and we need shelter (in the form of an apartment, perhaps). These are basic needs, but we should not confuse the foundations with the house. *Material* foundations are certainly necessary but are not sufficient for our happiness. *Material* deficiencies are usually quickly visible whereas *spiritual* deficiencies—such as can be observed in many population groups, particularly in highly developed countries—inhibit the development process in a way which goes unnoticed for a long time but nonetheless has tangible, unhealthy consequences in many aspects of life.

So we stop waiting for *external* conditions to change in our favour and acknowledge our *own* responsibility. Initially this leads us to work on inner transformation in order to effect changes, reducing the influence of external conditions. Then we move on to recognise the interplay between these and begin to provide the sparks for this process ourselves.

The issue of how much influence external conditions have remains controversial for many people. The influence cannot be disputed, but even in situations where this external influence is very strong, there is always individual room for manoeuvre. Otherwise, any particular situation would always see people behaving in a completely identical way, much like robots. So perhaps we can agree to phrase it this way: We often have significantly more influence on *our own* role and reactions than we might believe and certainly more than we have on other people and external circumstances.

We have to recognise our self-efficacy. This can mean that we stop making others responsible for our mental states (I *have to* be angry *because* my neighbour swore at me). It may well be true that many people generally have similar reactions in similar situations, but if we take a closer look we discover that we always have room for manoeuvre when it comes to our behaviour and our feelings. Only when we have understood this can we really open up to the possibilities of

Buddhist Psychotherapy. We have to understand this before further mind training, such as meditation, can really reveal its benefits.

Emphasising the importance of assuming responsibility for ourselves, we need to particularly highlight the aspect of *self-control*. We do not mean that we have to take the blame for everything that is wrong in our surroundings. Whatever has been done to us deserves to be respected and accepted, although, at the same time, we should not identify with what happened, nor should we lapse into judgement of ourselves or others, resentment, disappointment or any other unhealthy mental states and attachments which can trap us at times like these. Nor do we mean that we should want to or already be able to immediately brush off any problems as they arise. Nonetheless, very early on in therapy we should become familiar with the aim of letting go of many of our own ideas, opinions and judgements.

Forgiveness

We cannot force forgiveness or assume that it will be present, but it needs to be more than just words. In some cases, therefore, forgiveness cannot be a precondition for therapy but rather an *aim* which we envision and gradually approach.

Perhaps we already understand that our heart can forgive—it says, "yes". Our rational mind, however, often cannot forgive—it says, "no". Eckhart Tolle explains forgiveness as offering no resistance to life. In order to develop a liberated condition, it is essential to clear this hurdle.

The necessity of this should be clear from the insights in the previous Fundamentals of BPT and in the next (19th) Fundamental we will discover some exercises and practical instructions to put this into practice.

Preconditions

In his personal teachings, Tulku Lama Lobsang emphasises some prior conditions that are to be fulfilled *before* we begin practical exercises. Otherwise we would be sailing a ship without knowing the course we need to set and without access to a compass; in other words, we would end up drifting aimlessly on the vast ocean of the teachings and the ocean of our problems. The prior conditions taught by Tulku Lama Lobsang are described as the *Four Transformative Insights* which should always precede and then accompany our spiritual practice:

1) Recognise the high value of our life.
Our life and that of all sentient beings is very precious. And the current moment is valuable precisely because it is irretrievable. So we need to appreciate our daily life with regard to the value of the present moment—and be mindful of its impermanence.

2) Recognise that everything is subject to constant change.
The fact that we cannot preserve or conserve anything is not a problem or sign of inadequacy: It is the nature of all things. Everything is constantly changing and the more we can understand the processes going on around us, the more deeply we will recognise the extraordinarily dynamic nature of our world.

3) Recognise that suffering is universal.
Again, the fact that we suffer is not a problem or our mistake. It is simply a deep, natural process. The Four Noble Truths can help us here.

4) Recognise the influence of karma.
There are various prior conditions that influence us in the present moment. We should recognise this and act accordingly with regard to the effects we may have on our future.

Tulku Lama Lobsang considers these insights to be of considerable importance. They form one part of our spiritual path; daily practice is the other part.

We have to understand and internalise the Fundamentals presented here if we want to have an intense regular training because real progress is dependent on having a clear goal and the right understanding of the processes and topics within Buddhist Psychotherapy. Without understanding these we might end up sitting for a long time on our meditation cushions with, at best, a few comforting, pleasant visions and sensations or, at worst, hours of frustration (which in turn might lead us to us give up completely).

The Fundamentals presented here should have made it clear how Buddhist thought was developed and has been continually refined with the goal of reducing human suffering (and where possible, eradicating it completely). We in the West have only been able to benefit from this for a relatively short period of time. A few methods, such as meditation, have become relatively well known (at least, the term or concept has), but many ancient and effective Buddhist techniques have only become accessible very recently. Of course, the 19th Fundamental in this book does not offer enough space to offer a thorough description of all Buddhist methods, but we are able to give an overview and then concentrate on the details of those measures which have most relevance to BPT.

In this book we have often repeated the advice concerning the necessity of putting any insights gained into practice in our everyday situations. Every wisdom, every deepening of our understanding, every step of internalising is only completed by implementing it for the benefit of ourselves and all others in a convincing way.

Indeed, it is remarkable to see how BPT not only helps the individuals involved but also benefits the whole—through its conveyance of interconnection. Even if they initially come to BPT for very personal reasons, all help-seekers will come to recognise that all progress is progress for all. I do something for me and it benefits others at the same time. This was explained in the 13th Fundamental under the topics of compassion, interconnection and contexts.

The Buddha's "Therapy Instructions"

Of course, this was not the term that the Buddha himself used, but both the *Four Principles of Transformation* (see 7th Fundamental) and the *Five Methods of Mind-Training* (see below) can be understood as "instructions for therapy"; they both count as pre-conditions for the practical Buddhist-psychotherapeutic measures.

The Four Principles of Transformation
1) Recognition
2) Acceptance
3) Investigation
4) Non-identification

This and the following list present us with possible instructions as to the processes and sequences involved in the transformations we want to support within a course of therapy.

The Five Methods of Training our Mind
1) Recognition
2) Acceptance
3) Embracing
4) Looking deeply
5) Understanding

The first step—to *recognise* all the relevant issues—needs sufficient time and the appropriate degree of self-criticism. We may find this relatively easy: As the wearer of the shoe, it's easy to tell where it pinches. So this will do for the first assessment of the situation.

We are then often tempted to try to get rid of the pain as quickly as possible, but this is not the second step in a Buddhist approach. Instead, we *accept* the problem or issue. This does not mean that we remain completely passive; and it certainly does not mean we start to identify with the problem. Nonetheless, it indicates that we do not angrily or hatefully fight our problems as if they were enemies or a threat. Instead, we try to turn them into a friend or at least a guest who, unwelcome and uninvited as he may be, nevertheless deserves to be treated with respect. In the second list above, the *Five Methods*, this phase is elaborated further with the instruction to *embrace* the issue at hand.

The next step is to *investigate* or *look deeply* at the issue. This would hardly be possible with an angry attitude, so investigating with a clear mind obviously depends on the previous step of acceptance. This step also emphasises our non-passivity: We actively look at the issue to find new ways of resolving the conflict—the support provided in a course of therapy is very helpful here.

This process then leads to a deeper *understanding* of the issues. In fact, we gain not only a better understanding of ourselves but also a clearer view of the things and processes around us, recognising that all of these results are still part of a further, ongoing process of change and thus helping us to avoid the trap of *identification* and its accompanying attachment.

Understanding

If as therapists we want to successfully treat human suffering, of course we have to understand it. There is always a specific, individual background to suffering, but the Buddha clearly showed us that it has a general, universal aspect, too. His Four Noble Truths show us what is happening "behind the scenes": how suffering arises, and most importantly, how we can end it.

So we clearly need to understand the Four Noble Truths of Suffering in detail and internalise them. As an example, let us take the second truth identifying the three causes of suffering: ignorance, attachment and resistance or aversion. Logically, understanding this leads to the identification of a way to liberate ourselves from suffering by removing these three causes.

Every course of therapy should include therapy for each of the three causes of suffering:

Liberation from our ignorance
(and its 1000 forms)

Liberation from our attachment
(and its 1000 forms)

Liberation from our resistance
(and its 1000 forms)

The theory needed to back up these aspects of the therapy can be found in the 13th, 14th and 15th Fundamentals; the practical measures are described in the following pages, in the 19th Fundamental.

Understanding involves taking in a great deal of new information and learning new ways of looking at or dealing with issues. So we definitely need to be open to this; it is less a question of intelligence and more one of open-mindedness and healthy curiosity. this must be specifically mentioned here because generally we are quite "full up" with opinions, ideas, desires, hopes, worries, judgements and emotions which block our view and prevent us from seeing things clearly and with an open mind.

The need to let go, or: How full are we?

Sometimes the help-seeker sitting opposite us in our therapy session will keep asking us for clever advice although we have the distinct impression that they are already "full up" with fixed opinions, views, theories and information. In this case, even the most patient explanation of a new idea will be of no use. Instead, we should make use of practical exercises that do not need long rational explanations.

Even trying to describe what is happening to a help-seeker in this situation needs a clear example. Perhaps we could take an empty glass and a bottle of water. We tell the help-seeker that they used to be an (almost) empty glass, but they had many (painful) experiences. As we pour water into the glass we explain that it represents all the problems, worries, opinions, ideas and judgements that have accumulated over the years. When the glass is full to the brim, we make the point: Now we are sitting here together and want to add something new? More suggestions? More useful knowledge? Hopefully, it will then become clear how important it is to "let go", saying farewell to some things in order to make room for new ones (or to enjoy the empty space for a while).

Angela P finds it very difficult to calm down. She currently feels completely over-burdened. In the therapy session she expresses her fear of not being able to concentrate on everything she is taught. So yet another experience of being a failure is pre-programmed. When asked if anything taught so far was of particular interest, Angela mentioned the Four Immeasurables. She would dearly love to feel them, but she would have to put in a lot of effort before that would be possible.

So it was a pleasant surprise for Angela when she heard that she could forget about all the other contents of the teachings for a while and just concentrate on the Four Immeasurables. She began with some calligraphy, expressing each of the four in several different ways on small slips of paper. She posted these slips in different places so she would encounter them over and over again during the course of her daily routine.

Furthermore, Angela initially benefitted greatly from the guided objectless meditations, with different sessions each used to cultivate, strengthen and stabilise one of the Four Immeasurables. Very soon Angela could conduct the meditation herself without guidance, greatly enhancing her general ability to cultivate love, compassion, joy and equanimity.

This Fundamental Should Convey the Following:

Dharma teachings are as vast as the ocean. We will never exhaust them and we do not have to.

We concentrate mindfully on particular teachings, which our teacher, master or therapist selects in consultation with us, and work with them to gain as deep an understanding as possible.

Each individual aspect of the Buddhist teachings contains the entirety of their wisdom and power. It is not important to have read and remembered as much about Buddhism and dharma as possible. It is much more important to have understood, internalised and realised as much as we can.

Find the right measure of dharma. Dharma itself is not the goal. We should never lose sight of the real goal—our liberation.

The 19th
Fundamental of Buddhist Psychotherapy

Recognise and Convey Practical Buddhist Techniques

> Through my own experience, I know that the mind can be trained, and by means of that training we can bring about a profound change within ourselves.
>
> XIV DALAI LAMA

> Almost all Buddhist methods are designed for giving up unhealthy mental states and adopting healthy ones.
>
> JACK KORNFIELD

So now we come to the specific techniques, exercises and practice instructions for Buddhist Psychotherapy. Once again, we remind the reader that the exercises presented in this 19th Fundamental should only be carried out once the previous Fundamentals have been sufficiently understood and internalised. The exercises are not dangerous without this preparation but our efforts will not be very effective and this increases the risk of resignation and giving up, which would be very regrettable.

A helpful approach, which has been tried, tested and shown to be very practical, consists of combining teachings on one aspect of the Dharmic theory from the previous Fundamentals with an appropriate practical exercise. This way we discover the Dharma step for step and it encourages a progressive, growing integration of theory and practice. This proven approach avoids a common complaint of not knowing what to do with the new knowledge we have acquired.

In practice, this means that we always use elements from this Fundamental together with the other Fundamentals during the course of our work in Buddhist Psychotherapy.

The Therapeutic Measures in Buddhist Psychotherapy

We will now take a more detailed look at a specific selection of Buddhist techniques. Some of these produce very quick effects and others take longer, so some of them require a certain amount of patience before we sense the tangible and lasting effect they produce.

A practical exercise which conveys a personal, sense-based experience is generally much more effective than long explanations. One example of this is the *Torso Twist* presented in the 6th Fundamental on the topic of our mind. The reader may remember the exercise: We twist our torso as far as we can to the right or to the left, then we return to the centre and close our eyes. We repeat the exercise in our imagination ten times and then we open our eyes and repeat the exercise for real. We see how far we can twist now—much further.

For many people this little exercise is a very important experience that shows how quick and effective mental training can be. It is typical for Buddhist Psychotherapy because it provides a *tangible and comprehensible* demonstration of the wisdom we wish to convey. Human beings learn most intensely via their *own* senses and their *own* sense-based *experiences*, which is the reason why Buddhism has maintained a very practical approach for over 2500 years. If the few minutes it takes to perform the *Torso Twist* are enough to achieve such tangible effects, how much more can we achieve for ourselves and for others by means of ongoing training? The *Torso Twist* exercise can be referred to whenever we need to introduce other mental training exercises.

We now begin the main part of this Fundamental with the Buddhist mind-training technique that most people have already heard of: meditation. Of course, the technique is older than Buddhism; its roots are lost in the mists of time. When Siddhartha Gautama set off as a young man on his quest for liberation, he initially learnt meditation from other Indian masters who were part of a continuous practice tradition going back many centuries.

Meditation

The term meditation is so well-known it has almost become overused. Nevertheless, only a few people really have specific experience and are familiar with the clear practical steps it involves. After all, meditation is about more than just sitting cross-legged on a cushion with your eyes closed.

If we want to learn more about this topic we may ask questions such as the following: Is it is difficult to learn? Do I have to "switch off" completely? Can I do that? Will meditation finally give me the peace and quiet I've been longing for? Do I need to perform a feat of contortion to sit for hours on a cushion? Or is it only Indian gurus who can really perform this properly? My everyday life is so full and hectic—how can I integrate something like this? I am often very tired—won't meditation make me even drowsier? How often do I have to do it? And when will I notice the effects? If meditation doesn't work for me, does this mean Buddhist practice in general is not for me?

It would appear advisable to deal with these questions and expectations *before* we begin the practical exercises.

Meditation is just a *term*. This word is used to describe a practice and technique that is found in many different cultures, including those ancient cultures we disparagingly describe as "primitive". It can be found in many forms, including dance and drumming, invocation and shamanic journeys. The process of meditation is also to be found in all three main systems of religions:

- in the Western religions: Judaism, Christianity, Islam
- in the Chinese religions: Confucianism, Taoism
- in the Indian religions: Hinduism, Buddhism

The relevant terms we find there include: prayer, contemplation, invocation, absorption, meditation, composure, inner peace, yoga, mental training and focusing.

So meditation is very widespread practice. We can picture it as a way of "immersing" ourselves within ourselves. Since we actually only know ourselves relatively superficially, this is akin to diving into the unknown. Although we may believe that we are very familiar with ourselves, in fact we are only familiar with our functional surface layers. The reason we do not understand many aspects of our behaviour and thought is because we rarely go to any of the deeper layers. If we do explore these we generally experience a few surprises and some of our expectations are disappointed.

A list of common misunderstandings about meditation practice has been compiled by Mahathera Gunaratana, an internationally active Buddhist from Sri Lanka who has worked as an adviser on Buddhism at the *American University* and was president of the *Bhavana Society*.

Eleven Misconceptions about Meditation
1) Meditation is just a relaxation technique.
2) Meditation means going into a trance.
3) Meditation is a mysterious practice that cannot be understood.
4) The purpose of meditation is to become psychic.
5) Meditation is dangerous, and a prudent person should avoid it.
6) Meditation is for saints and sadhus, not for regular people.
7) Meditation is running away from reality.
8) Meditation is a great way to get high.
9) Meditation is selfish.
10) When you meditate, you sit around thinking lofty thoughts.
11) A couple of weeks of meditation and all my problems will go away.

Based on these misconceptions, we can devise a list of eleven aspects of meditation we should pay attention to:

Eleven rules for meditation
1) Do not expect anything.
2) Do not strain.

3) Do not rush.
4) Do not cling to anything and do not reject everything.
5) Let go.
6) Accept everything that arises.
7) Be gentle with yourself.
8) Investigate yourself.
9) View all problems as challenges.
10) Do not ponder.
11) Do not dwell upon contrasts.

The way of learning which we take in meditation is probably completely different to the learning processes we have previously encountered and gone through. It is common for people to have the firm conviction that only hard work increases our chances of success. But if we look at this list of eleven rules, it obviously indicates a very different approach. We want to learn something (how to meditate) but we should not expect anything or work too hard etc. So when we are conveying the art of meditation, this difference needs particular attention.

After dealing with the misconceptions and the points of good advice, we need to take another step and consider what we want to achieve with our meditation—or what it is possible to achieve.

As Venerable Gunaratana makes clear, meditation is not a form of relaxation. It is an ancient system of *active* mind training, during which the mind of the meditator remains very *alert* and *attentive*. In fact, a meditator is seeking to increase and stabilise his or her alertness and attentiveness.

The Fundamentals of Buddhist Psychotherapy have showed us how our problems arise and how we could deal with them, but knowledge alone is not sufficient. We need a form of practice suitable for our everyday lives that enables us to increase our influence in this regard. Some significant interim goals consist of using our attention, concentration and mindfulness to cast light on and clear up habits and unhealthy processes which were previously unconscious and unquestioned. For this, we will need a clear, calm mind. And this is the first task to learn in meditation: calming and clearing our mind.

> **Venerable Gunaratana lists five goals for meditation:**
> 1) Purification of mind
> 2) Overcoming sorrow and lamentation
> 3) Overcoming pain and grief
> 4) Treading the Right Path leading to achievement of eternal peace
> 5) Attaining happiness by following the Right Path

In this Fundamental we will be looking more closely at how to implement these goals.

Autonomy through meditation

Another goal which we may want to achieve by means of meditation is an increase in our self-control. Perhaps we are aware that our emotions develop "automatically" and even appear to possess their own logical intelligence. After all, we quite naturally become sad if something sad occurs. In the 7th Fundamental of BPT on the topic of our emotions, we had a theoretical introduction to the details of how they arise. So if we remember reading that mindfully observed emotions only have a relatively short duration, then we can always use a few minutes for a targeted meditation to let unhealthy emotions "burn out".

Research has shown that many people are relatively good at *creating* emotions such as anger, fear or sadness within themselves. While they were activating these emotions, their brains were being scanned, revealing the corresponding brain activity. Further similar computer scans then revealed that long-term meditation practitioners were particularly good at creating *healthy* emotions within themselves, such as compassion, joy and loving-kindness. One famous participant in these experiments was the French monk Matthieu Ricard, a former molecular biologist who has spent many years in Buddhist meditation.

Meditation practice allows us to tangibly experience how knowledge can be put into practice. This is reflected in the 2nd and 3rd of Ven. Gunaratana's goals: overcoming sorrow and lamentation, and overcoming pain and grief. The 4th and 5th goals remind us of the Fourth Noble Truth of the Eightfold Path, which will be easier to put into practice with the support of meditation.

How does meditation work exactly?
What do we have to watch out for?

As is often the case, generalisations such as "meditation" or "Buddhism" are not really helpful because they do not reflect the complexity of the issue at hand. There is a huge variety of forms of meditation. The most commonly known are probably silent and sitting meditation. Other versions include dynamic meditation, walking meditation, meditative dance, meditative listening, cleaning or cooking meditation, mindfulness meditation, meditation on koans (apparently unsolvable or meaningless questions in the Zen tradition), breathing meditation and guided meditations.

Each of these variants takes a wide variety of forms. For example, sitting meditation can look very different or have different contents. Some groups concentrate on the form—sitting *absolutely* still is important—and in others we are mindfully observing the signals of our body and avoiding pain—so mindful movement of a painful knee or "dead leg" would be allowed. Focusing on contents leads to even more variety and the goal of the meditation will be influenced very strongly by these contents.

Generally, however, the aim of the initial stages is always *Calming Our Mind* (which is usually very restless). The Buddha himself offered us a metaphor here, comparing our mind to a lake with many waves rippling over the surface. It is impossible to see the bottom or even look deeply into the lake. First of all, the surface has to become calm. Only then can we see more deeply.

Once again, we need to remember that in the Buddhist context, a calm and less excitable mind is nonetheless *alert* and *clear*. Meditation is neither a relaxation programme nor a tranquiliser.

The second aspect of meditation is *Looking Deeply*. Building upon a calm and clear mind from the first step, we can now look to the deeper levels and recognise with less distortion what is happening within us, in order to find a beneficial path for ourselves and for all others.

> The two aspects of meditation are: clearing and *calming our* alert *mind*, and *looking deeply.*

These two aspects interact with each other very strongly. When we clear our mind we can look more deeply; seeing the deeper levels then leads to more calmness and clarity in the mid- and long-term.

So now we have discovered a lot about meditation in general and can move on to a specific implementation. The meditation master Yongey Mingyur Rinpoche has given some very remarkable instructions for the implementation of meditation exercises. In his teachings and books he clearly describes what we should watch out for when we begin to learn and practice meditation.

The Seven-Point Posture for Meditation

1) A stable basis

Generally we sit on a meditation cushion on the floor. The basic idea is to sit in a comfortable, stable position. Experienced meditators can generally sit in a position known as the half or full lotus.

Half lotus: Our legs are crossed with both knees touching the floor. One foot rests flat on the calf of the other leg, the other foot rests flat *under* the other calf.

Full lotus: Our calves are crossed with both knees touching the floor. Our left foot rests on our right thigh. The soles face upward.

We can cross our legs in whichever way is most comfortable for us. Many will simply choose the common way of sitting cross-legged (often known as "Indian style" or "tailor style") and others prefer the position known as *Burmese style*. Here, both legs lie flat and bent at the knee, not literally crossed, but with feet and calves parallel and on the floor.

For some of us it is simply not possible to sit comfortably on the floor or a meditation cushion; of course, it is fine to sit on a chair. However, this should not have armrests. We should take care that our feet are firmly on the floor and our legs are parallel (not crossed). For people with short legs, a foot-rest is recommended.

2) Our hands

One hand lies in the other; both hands are relaxed (which means the fingers will be slightly bent and not stretched out straight). Our fingers are not interlocked as in prayer.

3) Our upper arms

Our upper arms are bent slightly away from our torso to allow a little space. Our arms and hands rest on our thighs. It is important for the hands to be cupped together, one resting in the other. We should avoid letting our arms hang to the right and left of our body since this would lead to painful sensations during the meditation sessions.

4) Our back and posture

This point is very important, since sitting *upright* is a significant key to success in meditation. We sit as if our spine was made of coins which we want to keep stacked in a vertical column.

When we refer to *posture* we are consciously using a term with more than one meaning: Our *attitude* to life and our *physical* posture mirror each other very often. Bowed down with grief or sorrow we will often find ourselves literally bowed down in a hunched posture, for example.

> During meditation, we practice maintaining an upright mind by training our upright physical posture.

In the 5th and 6th Fundamentals we were introduced to the connection between body and mind, so we can now easily understand how training our physical posture also trains our mind and vice versa; mind training can have positive effects on our physical constitution.

During meditation we remain alert, awake and mindful so we are much more likely to be aware of our body's signals and can quickly correct any unhealthy aspects of our posture.

Most of us initially have to train sitting upright for a while, so it helps to practice this outside of our meditation sessions, too. Every day, wherever we are sitting, we can try to sit perfectly upright. If we then notice pains, for example in the lumbar region, we should immediately change our position again and repeat the exercise later.

Even this very simple exercise of making a minor adjustment to our posture can be very significant and have a range of positive effects. People who start to carry out this type of exercise report that when they sit and walk in a more upright way, they can then breathe more easily and begin to feel much better in general. Furthermore, people around them also notice this.

The Royal Posture exercise
(adapted from Jack Kornfield)
We spend a whole day adopting the quiet dignity of a queen or king. In every area of our life, we maintain this *royal posture:* We sit upright and walk upright as if we were wearing a crown on our heads. We do not rush, we stride; we do not eat, we dine; we do not chat, we converse with dignity and respect. We remain aware and mindful of the effects this has on our emotions and the reactions of people around us.

---

5) Our head

Our head can be considered as a natural extension of our back. We take care to ensure that it sits straight on the top of our upright spine. We should pay particular attention to our chin, ensuring that it is directly in front of us and raised slightly; in this way we avoid the problem of a hanging head. However, we need to make sure that paying attention to our chin does not lead to us tipping our head forwards or backwards; our head should rest evenly on top of our neck.

It can be very useful to regularly look at ourselves in the mirror when we have adopted our typical posture. Very often we will discover that for one reason or another some aspect of our posture is wrong. Feedback via the mirror or our teacher is useful to check if our back, head, chin or shoulders are in the right position. Have we drawn up our shoulders too high? Are our shoulders too far forward? Are we pushing our chin out too much? Is our head tilting? Sooner or later we will notice any error in our meditation posture because it will produce pains. These pains and attention to our sitting posture provide us with valuable feedback about our attitude and posture to life in general.

> At this level, meditation is posture training and at the same time mind training.

6) Our mouth

We keep our mouth closed in a relaxed way. Our lips are not pressed together but our mouth does not hang open. It can be helpful to gently press the tip of our tongue onto our upper palate, just behind our teeth. This helps to alleviate the problem that sometimes arises when the flow of saliva leads to a frequent swallowing reflex.

7) Our eyes

Our eyes can remain closed. Reducing external stimuli by significantly reducing the amount of light reaching our retina leads to a reduction in external distractions, favouring inner processes. Additionally, our brain metabolism reacts to the reduction in light by releasing neurotransmitters such as melatonin, which also helps to calm us down.

Some people find it uncomfortable to close their eyes during group meditation sessions; this is not a problem at all. Instead, we can gently rest our gaze on a fixed point in the room.

Further aids and notes

In addition to the seven-point posture, there are some further helpful points to consider.

Our clothing

The key word here is *comfortable*. We should not wear any clothes which restrict us, cause pressure, bind or draw our attention to them in any other way. We should choose comfortable, loose and soft clothing. In particular, our trousers are important: If we want to sit cross-legged, they should definitely not be tight. And we take off our shoes when we meditate.

Our meditation cushion

The ideal height for the cushion is about 8 cm or 3 inches when it is compressed by our weight sitting on it. So when we are buying a cushion we need to do a "test sit" to check how much it compresses!

A blanket

We can use a blanket to keep us warm in group meditation rooms that are cool or unheated. And a folded blanket can also serve to prevent painful pressure on our legs if the floor is hard.

Our meditation room

Especially when we begin to learn and practice meditation, it is helpful to have a fixed place where we meditate, reserving a small space in our apartment or house for this and decorating it in a useful and motivational way. For some people, this might be a pleasant aroma from incense sticks or oils and for others it might be in the form of symbols such as mandalas or Buddha and bodhisattva figures. The space should, however, remain fairly simple. Interestingly, the attention and care we pay to these matters often reflects the attention and care we pay to ourselves and our welfare in general. Do we choose a place in the cellar or in our attic? Or is our meditation cushion in the corner of the living room? Is there a room only used for this? Of course, with a little patience and time we will develop our meditation practice to the extent where we can apply the technique anywhere and at any time.

Therapists and help-seekers should attend regular group meditation sessions (performed after teachings) in addition to their own daily practice at home.

Meditation time

Fixing the time for our daily practice is also very helpful as we begin to learn meditation since we will need a few weeks before our new activity establishes itself as a helpful habit. It is also best to fix the duration *before* we sit down. At the beginning, 10 or 20 minutes are definitely sufficient. Short, frequent meditations which we enjoy are much more helpful than longer sessions which we do not look forward to and probably cannot fit in our schedules as often.

If we begin over-ambitiously, convinced that we have to sit for hours and simply hold out during the inevitable physical and mental discomforts, then we will probably lose our enthusiasm just as quickly and give up. So, "less is more" is definitely a good motto at the beginning.

The right timer can also be very helpful to ensure we sit for the desired duration and do not have to worry about the time. There are special meditation timers and smartphone apps which display a countdown and signal the end of the session with a pleasant tone.

So we can see that there are many aspects worth taking note of in order to increase our chances of success.

The first meditation sessions

As help-seekers, we will probably carry out our first meditation sessions under the direct instruction of a teacher. So they can give us immediate feedback regarding our posture, for example. Furthermore, they will probably conduct the session as a *Guided Meditation,* which can help us to remember the important aspects without becoming confused or insecure due to the different issues we would otherwise need to concentrate on.

The first sessions will probably be kept short. The teacher will instruct us to watch our breath, breathing calmly and deeply from our stomach. After using this breathing to calm down our body and mind, we may then be instructed to watch any emotions and thoughts that arise. Here it is very important to simply accept anything that arises, taking the position of an *observer.* Just as if we were in our own private cinema, we watch our film, curious to see what will come next.

This point is important for many reasons. *Initially* we do not pay particular attention to any specific thought because the first steps involve learning how to calm down our mind and body. However, this does *not* mean that we relax fully; rather, we are continually alert and attentive. This first step leads us to learn how to tame our thoughts. Parallel to this, we remain mindful of the here and now. We regard and observe our inner processes in the present moment whilst also being aware of the things around us in the here and now, including noises or any of our own physical sensations. Many beginners report disappointment because they cannot switch off and start to pick up on every little noise around them; actually we should congratulate them and encourage them to continue being so alert!

So we need to say farewell to the common belief that meditation involves finding absolute peace. At the beginning, in fact, it will be the complete opposite. For perhaps the first time in our lives we will actually become aware of how many thoughts we have and how rapidly they come and go.

In the initial phase it can sometimes be helpful to visualise our inner zones of disquiet. For example, we can personify something within us provoking all these thoughts (a restless monkey, perhaps) or imagine a stormy landscape which we then work to calm down. This will help to achieve the clarity and peace we need for the rest of the meditation session. As we remember from the *Torso Twist* exercise described above, the power of mental visualisations such as these is quite considerable.

The *Counting Thoughts* exercise

We observe the flow of our thoughts, holding on to none of them, and curiously watching to see which thought comes next. It is important to let each thought pass without provoking connected thoughts or associations; meditation should not be allowed to become a directionless drifting in worlds of unconscious images. Daydreams, brooding, expectations, hopes and memories are all counter-productive.

A helpful exercise in this regard is that of *Counting Thoughts*. In order to support our attempt not to concentrate on the contents of thoughts, we simply give each thought a number, waiting for the next thought, given that the next number, and so on. At the beginning we usually experience a very quick exchange of thoughts, so we might reach higher numbers even in 10 minutes. This is fine. We then continue with this in the following days.

Characteristic aspects of beginning to learn meditation are:
- finding a regular meditation rhythm; integrating meditation into our life
- practising and establishing our sitting posture; carrying over our upright posture into our daily life
- training and stabilising our regular breathing from our stomach
- deeply experiencing the fact that meditation is not a relaxation technique but rather conscious perception of everything that is happening (which explains why at the beginning meditation feels like awareness of inner chaos)
- practising the exercise of counting our thoughts or our breaths

---

Becoming able to integrate these aspects into our life is in itselfn a great achievement.

There are numerous aides we can use for our meditation. Counting our thoughts is one of them. Concentrating on our breath and constantly repeating one or more healthy words (*mantra*) serve in the same way as a safety line which can quickly pull us back into position when we slip.

Meditation progress

With regular practice we will almost automatically develop access to the advanced aspects of meditation. We will discover that it becomes easier and easier to adopt the meditative posture. After a while, the upright sitting position will become very comfortable. And we will be able to clear and calm our mind ever more rapidly.

At the beginning we should practice at quieter, less stressful times. Once we have learnt to master meditation at these times, we can then move on to practice it during stressful phases of our day.

Elsewhere in this book we have already quoted Mathieu Ricard, the French meditation master, who pointed out that no one learns to sail in the middle of a storm. Beginners only venture out onto the water in calm winds. We first need to master basic sailing skills; otherwise we will quickly capsize when a storm comes.

Regular performance of exercises such as *Counting Thoughts* also provides us with a somewhat more tangible way of sensing our progress. As we continue our learning, we will most probably notice that the number of thoughts arising in a 10-minute period decreases. Our meditation progress becomes visible as thoughts arise less frequently. This exercise is also very suitable for people suffering from compulsive worrying or rumination.

No Mind

As our thoughts slow down, we may at some point become aware of tiny gaps between them: One thought passes and the subsequent thought does not appear immediately. These very precious, healing moments are especially valuable and deserve particular attention. We can enjoy these moments of having no thoughts, which are also known as *No Mind* or in Zen Buddhism as *satori* or *kensho*.

This experience can be strengthened. The No Mind condition generally leads to very pleasant individual sensations. As with all repetitions, repeating the exercises that lead to these moments will establish the practice and therefore also the state which ensues. In future, we will have easier access to No Mind, creating it more securely and quickly. Of course, we cannot hold onto this. We do not try to push away the next thought (which would be the end of the No Mind condition). In fact, we are still observing and curiously waiting for the next thought to arise. It is important to realise that we are not suppressing thoughts or feelings—we are letting them come and go.

The condition of No Mind cannot be created by means of "meditative performance". Just as the bud of a flower unfolds when the climate is warm enough, this condition unfolds when the prerequisites are right. So we train the creation of the right prerequisites (intention-free mindfulness). The unfolding will then occur and we can observe it.

> There are many levels of goals and effects we may wish for in connection with our meditation practice. As well as the moments of No Mind, the promotion of mindfulness, and support for more conscious behaviour, regular meditation practice should also help to develop, strengthen and cultivate a meditative way of living. This includes being able to quickly call up and then maintain a degree of calmness, serenity, mindfulness and clarity; in turn, our basic approach to life will become freer. we should notice the effects and our progress in our life as a whole, not just on our meditation cushion.

With regard to meditation practice, psychotherapists need to be very careful with and have a very good understanding of the aspects of boundary and ego dissolution. A secure diagnostic assessment is indispensable here. Although some therapists judge this type of boundary dissolution in general to be progress on the path towards egolessness, we have to be able to clearly distinguish between beneficial and harmful aspects for the help-seeker. Sometimes the healthy results of mind training can look very similar to the symptoms of the disturbed mind we find in people with severe personality disorders.

Meditation and emotions

As we progress further, we will also be able to call up the No Mind condition in times of emotional turbulence. As a meditation practitioner, our reaction to the appearance of emotional tension, such as anger, will be to adopt our meditative posture, breathe consciously and regularly from our stomach, clear our mind, and pay increased attention to our body. Where in our body is our anger manifesting? What does it feel like? What qualities does it have? Is our physical feeling one of pressure, stabbing, burning or tearing?

We then move on to the next step, which has two points of focus. Firstly, we maintain our observation of how this feeling is changing. Secondly, we clear and calm our mind so that we can observe any thoughts arising in addition to the physical sensations. These thoughts may then provoke secondary emotions. The aim here is, for example, to prevent angry thoughts nourishing and strengthening angry emotions, keeping them alive.

Progress in mindful observation will shed light on the intricate connections between our physical sensations and thoughts and the corresponding emotions. In particular, we can pay detailed attention to the thoughts which maintain our emotions, such as anger. We can become aware of our inner voice (see the section on *Chöd* practice below) and accept it. Then we can add an additional dimension by adopting the position of observer, which with draws the conscious energy from our inner (here angry) voice. The 7th Fundamental of BPT on our emotions showed us that an emotion actually only has a very short duration, unless we keep it alive with appropriate thoughts. By applying our attention as described above, the emotion loses its previously unlimited power and control over us.

So we can see that our daily life presents us with plenty of opportunities to train and apply the techniques we have learnt on our meditation cushion. Prior to starting our mind training, many of us are simply unaware of how often our own thoughts create a burden for ourselves and other people.

It is advisable to study the 7th Fundamental of BPT in detail and work through it in a very practical way with the help-seeker. We really have to learn to understand and internalise how our unspecific feelings become specific emotions which then cause so much suffering. We would like to let these burdensome emotions *burn out* and during BPT we can develop the appropriate self-instructions for this: "I let my anger burn out", "I let my fear burn up", "I let my sadness ebb away", "I let my pain fade away".

As therapists we need to use individual sessions with our help-seekers in order to help them become as familiar as possible with these techniques and develop specific instructions for daily life from their own experience. For most people, this process is very unfamiliar and even contradicts the experiences we have had so far in our generally *unreflective* life.

Switching

Learning to *Switch* is another step we can take towards liberation. Now *we* decide which aspects of us become activated or deactivated. In the 5th, 6th and 13th Fundamentals we already learnt that, although we generally experience ourselves as one fixed personality, this is not actually the case. In the course of just one day, we probably change our personalities several times, reacting to different situations according to our current state, either calmly, serenely and peacefully or rather with irritation and aggression. With an untrained mind, however, we do not control these changes ourselves. One or other of our personalities or roles automatically takes over, depending on the situation—and there is often then no way out.

In this context, *Switching* is the exercise of reassuming control. *We* decide which of our various roles we want to activate and we withdraw our energy from the others. We *switch* from an unhealthy role into a healthy one. For example, if we notice that in a particular situation we automatically become a victim (or a fighter), then we direct our attention to this process, *switch*, and thus change the whole dynamics of the situation.

In order to be able to do this, we have to get to know the roles which are most dominant within us, make them transparent, and enter into a dialogue with them so that we can gradually build up our control. We can exercise even more influence by means of the *Chöd* technique described below.

The time we need

Hopefully we will quickly develop a sense of progress in our meditation practice and its everyday applications, giving us hope, confidence and motivation. There are now studies showing that clear, positive mental changes take place very quickly—for example, after just *three months* of meditation retreat. In one such study conducted by Prof. Dr. Tania Singer together with Mathieu Ricard, it was shown that the participants experienced a measurable, significant increase in their attention span and attention flexibility, mindfulness, serenity and ability to deal with stress.

The speed with which the neural pathways in our brain change, grow, strengthen and become more sophisticated by means of training varies a lot. In the 5th Fundamental on the topic of our body a study was mentioned which proved that only five days' training was already enough to lead to significant growth in the areas of the brain being trained. Another very interesting detail of the study was the fact that it did not matter whether the training was physical or psychological: Both versions of the training lead to the same neural growth. Every person moves at his or her own speed and has his or her own very personal way of integrating new activities into his or her life. We need *patience* for ourselves and for all other beings. A patient and careful approach will give us far more than we can achieve by being over-ambitious and wanting to achieve as much as we can as fast as possible.

During our Buddhist Psychotherapy we will be introduced to a variety of different meditations using various images for meditation practice. In general, we can say that all types of meditation help to achieve increased self-control, mindfulness, concentration, influence over our emotions and clarity of mind.

Analytical meditation

When we can put into practice the aspects we have named so far, further perspectives, options and areas for the use of meditation arise. In *Analytical Meditation* we focus our mind on a particular issue. The first step is to create a clear and calm mind which does not attach or judge and which abides within us calmly and kindly. When we then use this foundation to analyse a problem, we initially act as an observer; we could say that we look over the shoulder of our own rational mind as it deals with the problem. Maintaining this observer role helps to withdraw consciousness energy from the brooding rational mind and it becomes quieter. It is only this quiet, clear mind which allows us to make truly healthy use of our analytical, rational intellect. For only then can we really make our own choices instead of unconsciously following automatic patterns.

In order to achieve a healthy state such as this we have to make a certain effort to look after ourselves. Mind training is just as important as our daily personal hygiene. Progress in mind training, however, is not something that happens "in a straight line". The progression is more wave-like, with phases of progress clearly being felt but followed by phases which feel like slipping back. These might be expressed as frustration, lack of motivation, fears or relapses into emotions we thought we had overcome. They might even lead to general doubts about what we are doing here.

Jack Kornfield describes these phenomena impressively in his book *After the Ecstasy, the Laundry*. Even meditation masters who have had insight experiences are still subject to these doubts and relapses. So the question is not *whether* problems will be encountered in our meditation practice, because this is certain. The question is *how* we learn to deal with them. Every practitioner will get to know their very own problems.

The most common problems we experience during meditation

Here we want to take a look at a selection of common problems experienced on the meditation cushion: pain, odd sensations, drowsiness, restlessness, racing thoughts, daydreaming, boredom and doubt.

Pain

If we experience physical pain, we should initially try to reduce it. We should not "hold out" and try to sit as long as possible while our mind is being "tortured" by pain. So we can consciously and mindfully loosen our muscles or change some of the conditions such as our clothing, caution or posture to relieve the pain. However, the next step is to investigate our pain. How can we assess it? Does it reveal something about our posture? Does it disappear if we mindfully correct our posture? Can we have a positive influence on our pain through further mind training or by means of breathing exercises? These aspects can be discussed with our Buddhist psychotherapist.

Odd sensations
The most common example of a strange sensation is the feeling of numbness in our legs when they "go to sleep". This is something we will encounter very often in our initial phases but is really a simple consequence of our "chair and sofa culture": In the West we long ago lost the habit of crouching or sitting with crossed legs.

Many people actually experience these feelings of numbness as threatening; this is reflected in the term "dead leg". So as therapists we can help by clearly announcing that these sensations will arise and by reassuring our help-seekers that the symptoms are in no way dangerous; it is simply the result of a few nerves being pinched. It is not a sign of blood circulation being cut off and there is no physical danger. The numbness should be accepted and our body will then become accustomed to this.

There are many other sensations people experience during meditation, such as itches, tingling and tickles. In some forms of meditation which help our mind to adopt a quiet trance-like mode whilst maintaining a very concentrated focus on some specific aspects, some people experience sensations going as far as the feeling that their body is dissolving. Normally we know where our arms and hands are even if our eyes are closed, but in a deep trance we may briefly lose this knowledge. Some of us may have no previous experience of these effects and become worried; carefully and mindfully touching the affected part of the body will restore contact and reassure us that our body has not dissolved.

Tiredness and drowsiness
Once again, we need to remind ourselves that meditation and relaxation are not one and the same. During relaxation our autonomous physical symptoms such as blood pressure, pulse, stress hormones and muscle tone all decrease. The opposite is the case during

meditation, hypnosis or trance. We can compare this difference with the difference between deep sleep (= relaxation) and the dreaming sleep phase (= meditation): During deep sleep both mind and body are resting but during the dream there is a high level of mental and physiological activity. Meditation is activity, not relaxation, but of course it is also not the same as dreaming.

If we regularly get tired during meditation we should reconsider the time of day for our practice and the activities which precede it. And we should again be clear that we are not using meditation primarily to relax but to train and clear our mind. The concept of the *Middle Way* can help us here. If we become tired, our tension is too weak; we have to build up more energy in order to move back into the middle. However, if we are too tense, we need to relax more in order to move back into the middle.

Restlessness

We have to distinguish between the normal restlessness of an untrained mind and the type or level of restlessness which will prevent us gaining any benefit from sitting meditation at all. We should talk this through and analyse it together with a Buddhist psychotherapist. If sitting meditation cannot be used at the beginning, there is a range of other methods which may be more appropriate, such as walking, cleaning, cooking, painting, dancing, drumming or gardening meditation, to name but a few.

Racing or compulsive thoughts (rumination)

The Buddha talked about this problem over 2500 years ago, using the analogy of a river: Initially our thoughts race like a rapidly flowing river. As we progress, the speed of flow reduces and the river becomes a gently flowing stream. Progressing further it slows ever more until eventually it is as if we as meditators are sitting in front of a beautiful, calm lake. Objects occasionally break through the surface and we see they are relevant to us. Nonetheless, the lake remains calm and the things which appear then disappear by themselves. The water in the lake is clear and we can see into the depths.

Daydreaming

Many beginners proudly report of visions, appearances and all sorts of daydreams which they had during meditation. However, Buddhists use meditation to come closer to (and eventually reach) their goal of liberation and the most continuous alertness and awareness possible. If we wanted to have "psychedelic" experiences, there are many drugs we could take, but actually we want to achieve the opposite of this: clarity, alertness, awareness and consciousness. If a Zen teacher has the impression that the meditation student is lost in thought or dreams, they will hit their students smartly on the back with a wooden stick. The message is more than clear: remain in the here and now.

Boredom

As civilised people we are accustomed to a high level of input and more or less continuous action, so we often actually experience quiet moments as boring. In this regard, too, we should respect the Middle Way. We should not demand too much from ourselves but we should also not persistently demand too little. For ourselves and for the help-seekers, we constantly have to check that we are remaining in the middle.

Doubt

As we progress in our meditation practice we will meet a wide variety of inner voices. We will hear our inner critic, our inner censor, and our eternal doubter etc. There are so many different voices within us: optimistic, pessimistic, arrogant, ambitious, jealous, aggressive, competitive, craving, covetous, addicted, timid, cautious, smart and clever, level-headed, adventurous and many more. When we try out something new and want to place a certain significance on this, a selection of these voices become active and want their comments to be heard. One of these is our inner doubting voice.

If we listen carefully to each voice we will understand that, for example, the doubting voice simply *has to* doubt—it cannot do anything else. So it becomes clear that our aim is not to weaken it (with the confident voice) or suppress it (with the strict voice of discipline). We aim to become more than just a mouthpiece of our inner voices. We remain the listener: "Oh yes, there's my old doubting voice again..."

Imagine coming back home after a long journey as a fully changed person; all of our relatives would have to get used to this new person. Some of them might like that but many would be surprised or even annoyed and unwilling to make changes. Changing the structure of our mind leads to similar reactions and processes. Regular, targeted meditation withdraws energy from a brooding intellect, which generally triggers a range of defensive reactions; these include even more brooding, a diversity of new ideas, restlessness, doubt, arguments, comparisons and judgements, and feelings of meaninglessness. When we first put our analytical intellect in its place, it will not necessarily thank us. So then we need to have patience with ourselves and to take advantage of the support on offer from Buddhist Psychotherapy.

Meditation and breath

Breathing has a particular significance during meditation. Why is training our breathing so important? What is the most important thing at all in our life? Family? Love? Money? Work? Food? We can do without these very important things for a while—food, drink, a roof over our head, money and even love. But if we try to do without breathing for even a few minutes, it will prove fatal. Breath, like our heartbeat, is necessary for our survival. We do not have any direct influence on our heartbeat, but we do have a certain scope for influencing our breath and changing it. So this gives us direct access to important control processes within our body, which is why breath plays a very important role right from the beginning of our meditation practice.

We did not choose this aspect by coincidence. Many centuries ago, before the Buddha's time, meditators had already recognised that particular breathing techniques can exercise significant influence on our body and mind. Today we know that our sympathetic nervous system can serve as a control centre for our stress symptoms and our parasympathetic nervous system can be used as a control centre to calm our mind and our body. But just how do we exercise our influence on these control centres, which act on elementary processes within us? As we presented in the 5th Fundamental, our autonomous nervous system controls most of our important survival processes such as blood pressure, blood values, digestion and muscle tone. And also our breathing.

Rapid flat breathing (each breath sharp as if we had just experienced a surprise) into the upper breast area just underneath the oesophagus activates our sympathetic nervous system and produces stress. Unfortunately, this is the normal type of breathing for many people not just in times of stress. A quick, shocked intake of breath will never reach beyond the *upper* breast area. However, abdominal breathing activates the parasympathetic nervous system, responsible for calming our body and mind. We can train ourselves to use abdominal breathing by placing our hand gently on our stomach. As we breathe in, our stomach should bulge *outwards*, pushing our hand *up*. As we breathe out, our hand will sink together with our stomach.

Controlling our breathing is therefore one of the few ways in which we can directly access one of our body's main control centres: the autonomous nervous system. It should now be clear that as well as being essential for survival, breathing also plays an essential role in our meditation practice.

The Buddha's Instructions on Meditation

Amongst the Buddha's many teachings, the most relevant for this topic are the *Satipatthana Sutta—Foundations of Mindfulness* and *Anapanasati Sutta—Mindfulness of Breathing*, which form the 10th and 118th Sutras in the Middle-Length Discourses respectively.

In the teachings, the Buddha asks his followers how a monk should meditate on his breathing and body, which both deserve their highest respect. He provides the answer himself:

Herein, monks, a monk, having gone to the forest, to the foot of a tree or to an empty place, sits down with his legs crossed, keeps his body erect and his mindfulness alert.

Ever mindful he breathes in, mindful he breathes out. Breathing in a long breath, he knows, 'I am breathing in a long breath'; breathing out a long breath, he knows, 'I am breathing out a long breath'; breathing in a short breath, he knows, 'I am breathing in a short breath'; breathing out a short breath, he knows, 'I am breathing out a short breath.'

'Experiencing the whole body, I shall breathe in,' thus he trains himself. 'Experiencing the whole body, I shall breathe out,' thus he trains himself. 'Calming the activity of the body, I shall breathe in,' thus he trains himself. 'Calming the activity of the body, I shall breathe out,' thus he trains himself.

The Buddha interrupts the instructions at this point to emphasise how we should direct our attention to our *body*, perceiving its desires and concerns and using our breathing to increase our awareness of our body. Then he continues:

He trains himself, 'I will breathe in sensitive to rapture and joy.' He trains himself, 'I will breathe out sensitive to rapture and joy.' He trains himself, 'I will breathe in sensitive to bliss.' He trains himself, 'I will breathe out sensitive to bliss.' He trains himself, 'I will breathe in sensitive to the associations of my thoughts.' He trains himself, 'I will breathe out sensitive to the associations of my thoughts.' He trains himself, 'I will breathe in calming the associations of my thoughts.' He trains himself, 'I will breathe out calming the associations of my thoughts.'

Again, the Buddha interrupts the instructions, this time emphasising how we should rest our attention on *feelings*, perceiving our desires and concerns and using our breathing to increase our awareness of our feelings. Then he continues:

He trains himself, 'I will breathe in sensitive to the thoughts and mind.' He trains himself, 'I will breathe out sensitive to the thoughts and mind.' He trains himself, 'I will breathe in satisfying the mind.' He trains himself, 'I will breathe out satisfying the mind.' He trains himself, 'I will breathe in steadying the mind.' He trains himself, 'I will breathe out steadying the mind.' He trains himself, 'I will breathe in releasing the mind.' He trains himself, 'I will breathe out releasing the mind.'

The Buddha interrupts again to emphasise constant mindfulness of our temperament or mind, perceiving our desires and concerns and using our breathing to increase our awareness of our mind. Then he continues:
He trains himself, 'I will breathe in focusing on impermanence.' He trains himself, 'I will breathe out focusing on impermanence.' He trains himself, 'I will breathe in focusing on dispassion.' He trains himself, 'I will breathe out focusing on dispassion.' He trains himself, 'I will breathe in focusing on cessation.' He trains himself, 'I will breathe out focusing on cessation.' He trains himself, 'I will breathe in focusing on relinquishment.' He trains himself, 'I will breathe out focusing on relinquishment.'

Finally, the Buddha emphasises the importance of constant mindfulness of *mental objects or appearances,* perceiving our desires and concerns and using our breathing to increase our awareness of these appearances.

So the Buddha describes how our body, feelings and mind, together with the appearances we are aware of (mental objects), can be observed with mindfulness. To do this, we use our most basic survival function—our breath—to direct our mindfulness to the important areas of body, feelings and mind.

Modern meditation teachers teach mindful breathing based on these original teachings from the Buddha. We can summarise the exercises as follows:

Summary of the Buddha's 16 Breathing Exercises
1) With a long, deep in-breath, I am aware that I am inhaling slowly and deeply.
    With a long, deep out-breath, I am aware that I am exhaling slowly and deeply.
2) With a short in-breath, I am aware that I am inhaling quickly.
    With a short out-breath, I am aware that I am exhaling quickly.
3) I breathe in, remaining very aware of my whole body.
    I breathe out, remaining very aware of my whole body.

4) I breathe in, letting my whole body become calm and peaceful.
I breathe out, letting my whole body become calm and peaceful.
5) I breathe in, experiencing a feeling of joy.
I breathe out, experiencing a feeling of joy.
6) I breathe in, experiencing a feeling of bliss.
I breathe out, experiencing a feeling of bliss.
7) I breathe in, remaining very aware of my mental activity.
I breathe out, remaining very aware of my mental activity.
8) I breathe in, letting my mental activity become calm and peaceful.
I breathe out, letting my mental activity become calm and peaceful.
9) I breathe in, being consciously aware of my mind.
I breathe out, being consciously aware of my mind.
10) I breathe in, letting my mind become calm and peaceful.
I breathe out, letting my mind become calm and peaceful.
11) I breathe in, composing and concentrating my mind.
I breathe out, composing and concentrating my mind.
12) I breathe in, releasing my mind.
I breathe out, releasing my mind.
13) I breathe in, contemplating the impermanent nature of all phenomena.
I breathe out, contemplating the impermanent nature of all phenomena.
14) I breathe in, contemplating the cessation of all phenomena.
I breathe out, contemplating the cessation of all phenomena.
15) I breathe in, contemplating perfect liberation.
I breathe out, contemplating perfect liberation.
16) I breathe in, contemplating relinquishment.
I breathe out, contemplating relinquishment.

As Buddhist psychotherapists, we can make wonderful use of these instructions to incorporate breathing meditation into our group meditation sessions. We can guide the group through the whole

16-stage process or alternatively, we can select one or more of the stages and repeat them to focus on specific aspects.

What is mind training actually?

We have already discovered that Buddhism is not only a religion but also a science of the mind and a system of practical mind training. The term "mind training" has now become very popular and appears very often in this book, but what does it actually mean? In fact, the term is potentially misleading because we do not have to directly train our mind and actually we cannot do this.

> In many respects, mind training is actually mind *discovery* and mind *awareness*.

Our meditation practice allows us to recognise and directly experience that we are not identical with our emotions, physical sensations and intellectual activities. Our mind (or consciousness) is another instance, including much more than just our emotions and our intellectual or rational mind. Unfortunately, we are not automatically or instantly aware of its existence and have to train ourselves to directly perceive it. The meditation we have described in this Fundamental is a very important technique within our mind training because it allows us to overcome the "cloudiness" which prevents us from seeing clearly (unhealthy consumerist habits and the unhealthy human factors of ignorance, attachment and aversion). We generally need much more mindfulness to truly discover our mind.

> When we say that meditation is a form of mind training, in practice this means that we use meditation to become *familiar* with our mind. *Meditate* can be translated as: *become acquainted with*.

Once we have rediscovered this way in and had our own experiences with our mind, we then proceed to expand and establish this access channel. This then enables us to become deeply aware of the true nature of our mind.

In addition, on a practical level we also rapidly develop inner clarity. Having become acquainted with both our emotional and rational sides, we can distinguish between the two and assume full command of how to deal with them both. We are resting calmly in our mind and no longer have to automatically follow the orders given by our restless intellect and emotions. We are free.

Letting Go

The concept of "letting go" or "relinquishing" has been proposed as a solution in several places in this book; this should not surprise us because Buddhism considers "holding on" or "attachment" to be one of the three main causes of suffering. Considering the issue practically, we need to pay careful attention to our motivation and find out precisely *what* we want to let go of and *why*.

The issue also presents some partially contradictory issues which need to be considered as part of the therapeutic alliance. For example, it is very important to assume responsibility for ourselves and for others, and so we as therapists will often need to work together with the help-seeker in order to check whether a particular case of letting go is perhaps actually an attempt to avoid something, flee or avoid responsibility. An old saying reminds us that even nomads do not move on if there is no reason to. Experience shows that people with a tendency to avoid responsibility find the concept of letting go very attractive and people who tend to be compulsive-obsessive grasp onto the teachings which emphasise self-responsibility. So, once again, the Wisdom of the Middle Way comes into play: Someone who walks too far to the right will be instructed to move to the left but someone walking too far to the left will receive instructions to move to the right.

We are all full of opinions, judgements and evaluations, and we all notice that at times we feel it would be nonsense to trust others but at other times helpful to hand over responsibility. At a general level many of us need to ask whether our decisions regarding trust and responsibility are really taken consciously, individually and flexibly, or whether a pattern has established itself.

Separation and letting go exercise

Here we present an exercise for *Separation and letting go* which has proved very particularly effective for people who have suffered the loss of a loved one or the end of a relationship.

Two chairs are placed opposite each other. The help-seeker sits on one of them, the other chair remains empty. In order to become calm, the help-seeker is led into a light trance. They are then instructed to imagine the person they wish to let go as sitting on the chair opposite them. The task is to visualise a tangible connection to the other person, permitting and using whatever images arise spontaneously and freely. Very often we see such things as ribbons, rubber bands, ropes or bands of light, but any form of connection and any material is allowed. It is important to notice which parts of the body are directly connected.

The next instruction is to cut this connection. Again, the first, freely imagined way of doing this should be allowed and accepted. After visualising this process of cutting, all of the materials and tools involved should then be put in an imaginary fire and burnt.

This short exercise should be enough to give a general impression of all possible methods of letting go and separation.

Trust and letting go exercise

This exercise is very suitable for group sessions, but if that is not possible, it can also be carried out individually. However, we do need a fairly large room or we can also go outside for this exercise.

The exercise is carried out by two people together. Firstly, one of the participants is "blind" (they close their eyes) and the other person guides the blind person as they walk around. This should last 3-10 minutes and then the participants swap roles. Beforehand, the participants are given the instruction to carefully observe how each role feels: giving up responsibility and letting go as the "blind" partner, or taking on responsibility and not being allowed to let go as the "guide".

Participants in this exercise often experience surprising results. For example, although many of us express a desire to let go, this direct experience reveals how it is often less frightening for us to be in control. In this section, we also refer the reader to the *letting* go exercise described in the 14th Fundamental on the topic of attachment as a cause of suffering. Recognising how complicated and sophisticated the issue of letting go is, we might find it useful to approach the issue from the other side as well. If we (unconsciously) associate letting go with significant fears or bad experiences, one possible approach, although it might seem paradoxical, is to practice complete acceptance of our problem as a form of inner relinquishment.

In order to take advantage of the opportunities which present themselves to us in our lives, we have to be active. We should truly accept the things as we find them today, fully aware that we will probably not be able to change them today. Both letting go and accepting our great challenges if they are to be performed authentically and not as an expression of our defence mechanisms. Our focus here is on a positive, *critical* appreciation of all the conditions around us in order to genuinely let go. The nature of the world is impermanence, sooner or later we will have to let go of everything anyway.

A drastic but very clear exercise in letting go

This exercise is suitable for both group and individual sessions. It starts with light relaxation and instructions to focus on our breathing. As the therapist, we set a breathing rhythm appropriate for harmonic, quiet breathing in a state of relaxation. Every now and again, we mix in instructions such as: "Hold your breath and hold on... and let go, breathe out." In a gentle voice, we remind the participants how difficult it is sometimes to let go. Then we change the instruction: "Hold your breath and hold on... and hold on... and hold on... and hold on... ." We try to keep this tension as long as reasonably possible before giving relief with the instruction: "And let go, breathe out... ." The message of the exercise is then emphasised with the comment: "Isn't it sometimes a great relief to let go?"

To summarise, meditation in all of its variations has long served as the "royal road" of mind training. The Buddha considered it to be very important, but also recognised that it has its limits. In the first years of his spiritual quest he benefited enormously from meditation, later recognising that it alone was not sufficient to achieve his goal. The further wisdom and insights which he understood, internalised and realised on his path to enlightenment form the source of the Fundamentals of Buddhist Psychotherapy presented in this book, offering all of us the opportunity to achieve lasting liberation.

Gerard K had very pronounced curvature of the back as he sat for his meditation sessions; it almost seemed as if he wanted to curl up into a ball. This body language was taken very seriously and his need for self-protection became one of the main issues in his individual therapy sessions. Parallel to this, Gerard was encouraged to choose a place in the room where he felt most secure during individual or group meditation sessions, in order to allow him to try out a more upright sitting position. This twofold approach, respecting and acknowledging his need for protection as well as the desirability of the proper posture, allowed him (and others) to clearly feel and see his own strengths and steadfastness. This in turn led to increasing progress in his therapy.

We now turn to another technique. Visualisation is very often used during meditation but it is an exercise in itself which we can also practice without meditative absorption.

Visualisation

Working with internal and external images can have a measurable influence on our body and mind. This is a fact which we need to have experienced ourselves in order to understand it and be able to convey it in a credible way. In several places in this book, we have already mentioned the *Torso Twist* exercise, which can be used as an opportunity for any doubters to gain their own tangible impression of the effects which can be achieved through visualisation techniques.

Jack Kornfield sums this up concisely when he says that whatever we visualise will change our body and our consciousness. Every image we regard triggers physiological reactions within us which can be measured. If we look at a gruesome picture of torture, or metabolic system will be affected in a way which we might feel as disgust, an urge to withdraw, fear, shivers, tension or queasiness. In the same way, regarding or visualising positive images leads to healthy psychosomatic processes in our body. Mandalas and yantras serve in this way to assist the development of a healthy basis within us. So it is very important for us to be careful about our input because it always has an effect.

The technique of visualisation, like all techniques we describe in this book, requires both theoretical knowledge and regular, independently carried out practical exercises. We need to be able to understand, internalise and convey the fact that we really do influence, change and shape our environment and our body through the power of our imagination. And we need to know and convey how this works. For many of us it initially appears unbelievable when we hear that images, ideas and visions have practical effects even if we do not act upon them. This is why exercises such as the *Torso Twist* are so useful.

If we take a closer look at the consequences of this and give ourselves time to think about its effects we may become slightly nervous because we realise that an influential mechanism has been working within us for a long time in a more or less uncontrolled way.

To put it very briefly: *Whatever we imagine in our mind changes both our body and our mind (since these cannot be separated).*

For example, if something happens to us and we spend a long time dreaming up ideas for revenge, our body will keep producing stress. This strengthens relevant neural networks, which form even more connections and therefore increase the effectiveness with which this aspect (revenge) takes place within us. So vengeful thoughts and vengeful images establish a vengeful mind in a vengeful body.

In the 6th Fundamental on the topic of our mind, we already discovered that we have an uncanny ability to spontaneously create *un-*

healthy mental states within us, such as anger, annoyance, rage and hate. However, we seem to lack the same level of skill when it comes to spontaneously developing *healthy* states such as loving-kindness, compassion or joy.

In Buddhist Psychotherapy we make use of the effects of healthy visualisations. We can take any positive objects for this which the help-seeker has a personal connection to, such as mandalas, Buddha statues and other symbols. We can regard this healthy connection between the practitioner and the object of visualisation as something akin to an "energy transfer".

Visualisation and triggering

At the beginning, it is helpful to restrict our exercises, meditations and visualisations to specific places, such as a quiet spot in nature, a healthy place we set up in our home, or community and group spaces established for these sorts of beneficial purposes. By practising regularly in one place, all of our sensory impressions "tune in" and are automatically triggered the next time we start. Perhaps the reader recognises this effect from an example such as trying out a new flavour of ice cream on holiday and then being flooded with memories of that holiday when eating the same flavour of ice cream at home. All sorts of sensations picked up by all of our senses can trigger these intense memories.

So the sensations created by the healthy places we choose to perform our exercises are automatically recorded within us. When we later find ourselves in difficult situations and want to use the exercises, by recreating some of the sensations (for example, the exact procedure of the exercise, or a particular incense smell) we can call up the other healthy sensations we had in the original place of practice. Many people report that when they practice elsewhere they suddenly see an image of the smiling Buddha from their usual location.

This effect or ability is called *Triggering*: One thing is used to set off, or trigger, a particular effect and in turn a particular connection. So when we find ourselves in a specific situation, the impulse to perform a certain exercise is like a key which opens a door within us leading to a room full of healthy sensations we can use.

The Safe Place exercise

The importance of the technique of visualisation should not be underestimated. Appropriate, inner, *healthy* images for each help-seeker need to be explored, trained, secured and established on an individual basis within Buddhist Psychotherapy. One example of this can be found as the *Safe Place* in which some psychotherapists will have already met within hypnosis and trauma therapy. In a light trance, the help-seeker is instructed to imagine a safe place where they are alone and completely secure. There are no other people there, not even people who are dead in real life. However, if we feel uncomfortable being alone in this place, we can imagine some other helpful beings. Once the help-seeker has a clear image of their safe place, this is anchored in their consciousness so they can return there in thought at any time. All of this takes place with our full awareness that our power of imagination can have very tangible effects on both body and mind. Especially in extreme crisis situations, this has been proven to be a very healthy method and resource, allowing the help-seeker to find temporary inner safety even if conditions around them are very difficult.

Furthermore, we will adopt other helpful symbols that we can use during visualisation exercises. Experience shows that Buddha and bodhisattva statues are very helpful in this regard; we can look at them for a long time, alternately opening and closing our eyes, internalising the image we see. Regular and frequent repetition is necessary for this.

When we integrate this element of visualisation into our daily practice, we have another method available to us which we can use in situations where we are distressed, angry, scared or discouraged. By applying this, we will experience a crucial situation where we become able to avoid our previously automatic responses, such as obeying our inner demon, going on the offensive or fleeing. Instead, we suddenly see the image of our beatific, smiling Buddha statue and literally feel the physiological processes within us calm down because of the visualisation.

The role of healthy visualisation objects

Buddha and bodhisattva statues are not primarily designed for worship in a conventional sense of this word. In other words, the Buddhist understanding of interconnection means that we actively create a link between the saintly figure before us and our own sacred qualities, instead of projecting or externalising positive characteristics onto the holy figure we are worshipping.

When, therefore, we turn our attention to symbols with a healthy meaning, whether we imagine and visualise them or look at them, our nervous system records these experiences and strengthens the appropriate neural pathways. And this in turn has a healthy, stabilising effect on metabolic processes in our whole body. Neuroscience has confirmed the extraordinarily high relevance of visualisation, proving that neural pathways can change permanently by means of our power of imagination. For our brain, it really does not seem to matter whether we actually move our fingers, for example, or simply imagine moving our fingers. In both cases, the structures in our brain responsible for finger movement are activated and trained. So visualisation can be recommended as an effective method of mental training.

By now it should have become clear that if we watch or imagine a brutal fight, our mind and our body could be said to "join in" the fight at a very deep level whereas participation in or observation of a more healthy event will result in healthy changes in our mind. The unhealthy or healthy changes will be reflected in a lasting and measurable effect on our neural networks after only a few repetitions.

The Western approach to visualisation

The power and significance of visualisation has also been recognised and taken up by Western therapists. For example, CG Jung worked with this approach in his analytical sessions, calling it *Active Imagination*. Clinical hypnosis therapists use this technique, as do those who work with Guided Affective Imagery (GAI). Trauma therapy also makes use of healthy visualisations, such as the *Safe Place* method mentioned above.

Effects of TV and video games

If we add up the hours we spend every day sitting in front of a screen (TV or computer) it amounts to quite a few years of our life. Of course, both of these media can be entertaining and informative but, with regard to the issue of "the power of visualisation", we need to understand that body and mind intensely orient themselves to what we are observing. Watching sport, our muscles and psycho-physiological coordination abilities are "joining in", but the exercise they receive here cannot be considered as a full replacement for our own physical exercise. Watching scenes of brutality will also form specific neural pathways; we will literally become more brutal or at least form a stronger tendency towards aggression. So it becomes crucial to consider what other intellectual, psychological and ethical input we are countering this with. There is not a 1:1-relationship between violent computer games and violent behaviour but the crucial factor is whether we balance the influence of the games with the mature competencies of an adult. Since children and teenagers do not yet have as many well-formed compensation structures, the effects on their behaviour can be significantly stronger.

We all carry within us the whole palette of possible healthy and unhealthy potentials. So it is our decision which of them we nourish.

The next Buddhist Psychotherapy technique we will present has a range of special features. Above all, it is expression of the peaceful and non-violent basic approach common to all Buddhists. It makes clear that this peacefulness is not only directed at other people but also at ourselves.

If we are suffering from *unhealthy* emotions such as anger, hate, annoyance and fear, we often might want to let them run wild; this is especially the case if our mental qualities are not yet completely conscious. As we improve our awareness, we may simply want to get rid of these emotions or even drive them out once and for all. In all of these cases, the language we are using is reminiscent of combat.

So now we will be introduced to an ancient Buddhist method which takes the opposite approach. It does not seek to combat our inner or outer enemies; instead it sets out to "feed" them.

Chöd—Feeding Our Demons

The American Buddhist Tsültrim Allione spent a long time living in Asia practising and researching. In her book *Feeding the Demons*, she presents us with a very powerful and important form of treatment.

When she refers to our inner demons, she is not referring to real creatures but rather to our inner impulses, drives and voices which influence us in an unhealthy way.

The *Chöd* method can give these inner forces a form and even turn them into something useful. So we do not need to fight them.

Originally, the *Chöd* technique was described by the Tibetan Buddhist teacher Machig Labdrön (1055-1145). This yogini was one of the few female practitioners who was able to establish their own lineage—a teaching tradition based on the handing down of wisdom from teacher to disciples and onto their disciples.

Machig Labdrön called her spiritual exercise *Chöd*, a Tibetan term which can be translated as "cutting through, cutting off". Although the term sounds quite violent, the method is actually much more about acceptance and reconciliation. However, in the end it does aim to cut through our false concept of self and bring about the realisation that all phenomena arise out of consciousness.

It is the inner voices expressing the various aspects of our personality (see 5th and 6th Fundamentals of BPT) which guide us (and very often misguide us). We have already seen how our mental balance is disturbed by these various aspects of our personality and their voices—our scared voice, angry voice, injured voice, greedy voice, comfortable voice, lazy voice, diligent voice or jealous voice etc. All of these voices deserve to be listened to—we will never be able to completely and definitively turn them off. Somehow we have to learn to live with them.

This is where the *Chöd* method comes in: It calls on us to enter into conscious communication with these voices and adopt an attitude of reconciliation and sharing. It addresses an utterly nourishing side within us all—an aspect of us which can be both giving *and* receiving at the same time.

A sufficiently stable and trusting alliance between the help-seeker and therapist is needed in order to carry out this exercise. Of course, this level of trust and the safe feeling it provides for the help-seeker are generally useful for all exercises and therapeutic measures, but they are especially important for measures where we come into contact with deep drives, such as our "demons".

It might sound a little unsettling when our therapist suggests we make contact with our "inner demon" but we can rest assured that these demons are actually creatures of our own imagination. In fact, we will discover that being ignored and left alone has made them bigger and scarier than they otherwise are. For more reassurance and background information, the reader is referred to Tsültrim Allione›s very useful book. Here we will present the basic structure of her technique.

The Five-Step Method
Feeding Your Demons

Preparations

Before beginning the work together, we talk through the whole procedure with the help-seeker, clearly describing the method and its background. Then we set up three chairs (or cushions): one for the therapist, one for the help-seeker and one empty seat for the 'demon'. Once the help-seeker is seated, they move this third chair or cushion so that it is facing them but close enough for them to easily shift onto it during the exercise (with their eyes still closed).

As therapist we help to guide them through the five stages of the exercise.

Step 1: Find the Demon
We instruct the help-seeker to sit comfortably, relax their shoulders and breathe into their stomach, calming and clearing their mind. When they are ready, they close their eyes and then keep them closed during the whole exercise.

As the help-seeker, to begin with we look for a very characteristic, frequent voice within us: our first demon. In subsequent sessions we can look for more demons. The first one is generally an impudent voice/demon that is constantly making itself heard anyway, so we do not need to look too far.

Examples include our "doubt-demon": "See, you won't manage to do this, either..." This "Doubting Thomas" within us probably has a whole host of doubts which it plants within us during the day, but for the purposes of the exercise we just take the first statement that we hear when we let the demon talk a little.

Now our attention is drawn by the therapist onto our body. Can we locate the demon in our body and its sensations? Is the doubting demon in our stomach? In our back? On our shoulders? When we find the bodily sensations we use our attention to focus on them and amplify them a little.

Step 2: Personify the Demon and Ask It What It Needs
The therapist now guides the help-seeker into the next stage, instructing us to imagine what the demon we have chosen actually looks like. We give it a shape and colour and imagine it sitting down on the seat opposite us, revealing itself as a tangible being instead of just an abstract concept. This might happen very quickly but we might need a little time to let our imagination find a clear image of the demon. As the help-seeker, we should then report to the therapist on what we see, clearly indicating the size, gender, shape and particular characteristics of the demon. We should also imagine what mood it is in and describe its charisma or presence.

We now move on to the next part of this stage, which was clearly described in the preparations for the exercise. It consists of the help-seeker asking the demon three questions, out loud and clear:

1. *What do you **want** from me?*
2. *What do you really **need** from me?*
3. *How will you feel if you get what you need?*

If as a help-seeker we forget the questions, our therapist can remind us. As soon as they have been asked, we change places (keeping our eyes closed) and sit on the demon's seat.

Step 3: Become the Demon

We now "become" the demon. Here, the therapist can help the help-seeker by asking specific questions about how it feels to be "in the demon's skin". What bodily sensations do we have in the demon's body we just described?

As the help-seeker, we now have the interesting opportunity to assume the role of the demon and also to take a look at ourselves "from outside", since we are now sitting opposite ourselves on the other seat.

The therapist asks us what the demon feels when it regards the person sitting opposite. How does this person come across? Keeping our eyes closed, we slip further into the role of the demon and regard this "me" and answer the question. The demon is then requested to answer the three questions which the help-seeker posed, speaking loudly and clearly:

1. *What I **want** from you is…*
2. *What I **need** from you is…*
3. *When my need is met, I will feel…*

These answers should be given fairly quickly, expressing the first ideas that come to mind without thinking too much. The therapist provides reminders or assistance as needed.

Experience shows that very interesting results can come out of this process. If we take our example of the 'doubting demon' above, we might hear it say:

1. *What I want from you is for you to doubt, hesitate and avoid acting.*
2. *What I need from you is more protection and security.*

3. When my need is met, I will feel safer and more relaxed.

The following table presents possible answers from other example demons.

The three steps	Four examples			
1. want →	alcohol	your effort	your vitality	cigarettes
2. need →	peace and quiet	security	power	emotional security
3. feel →	secure	relaxed	strong	peaceful

An alcohol demon might simply need some peace and quiet in order to feel secure. A discipline demon might need security in order to feel relaxed. A depression demon might just need some power to feel strong. And a cigarette demon might need emotional security. Then it would feel more peaceful.

In fact, whatever demon we are dealing with, it becomes obvious that behind the constant nagging or pestering there are always deeper, hidden needs. It can be a major insight to realise that there is a significant discrepancy between the demands the demon makes and the deeper needs it is really trying to satisfy.

Step 4: Feed the Demon and Meet the Ally

Once the demon has been allowed to express itself and has answered the three questions loudly and clearly, we (as the help-seeker) carefully swap seats again, returning to our original chair or cushion and *leaving the demon behind*. This is very important and the therapist needs to carefully question the help-seeker to ensure that the demon is clearly visible *opposite* them. Here it is usually helpful to enquire about bodily sensations and feelings.

So what happens with the demon now? Sometimes it has begun to change a little. And therapeutic support is now provided to drive this process on. We receive the instruction from the therapist: "Transform your entire body into the feeling that your demon needs." (This refers to the answer to the third question: *When my need is met, I will feel...*)

In our example the demon stated that it would feel *safe and relaxed* if it got what it needs. So the therapist prompts us to significantly increase and strengthen the feeling of *safety and relaxation* in our own body. It might be helpful here to visualise this power or quality streaming into us through the top of our head. Once this feeling has intensified sufficiently, we then imagine or visualise how this feeling then flows out of our body and across into the demon sitting opposite us.

The therapist's role here is to convey how we can develop inexhaustible supplies of this feeling. So in our example, we can feed our demon with as much *safety and relaxation* as it needs, while our own reserves are continuously replenished from these inexhaustible supplies flowing into us.

We feed our demon until it is completely satisfied. Some demons might claim to be insatiable, so after a while the therapist should instruct the help-seeker to imagine what the demon would look like if it was completely satisfied.

After feeding the demon, we regard the demon carefully: How has it changed? Experience shows that it always changes in a clearly positive way; in fact, in most cases it turns out to be a completely different being afterwards. The demon has been transformed. Or, in other words, there has been a transformation of our inner qualities, often resulting in tangible healthy inner changes.

This step of the exercise then has a second phase: meeting the ally. Here the therapist assists us as help-seekers to communicate with this transformed demon and ask three new questions:

1. *Are you an ally for me?*
2. *How will you help me?*
3. *How can I gain access to you?*

Again, as soon as we have asked the questions aloud, we swap cushions or seats and assume the role of the being opposite us. Taking a moment to slip into this role but without procrastinating or thinking too much, we then answer the questions.

If the answer to the first question is "*No*" then the exercise needs to be interrupted. We should then invite an ally to appear. When the answer is positive, we can move on to the other questions, answering clearly and aloud:

2. *I will help you by...*
3. *You can call me and gain access to me by...*

Then we change seats again, returning to ourselves and leaving the role of the demon/ally.

Assuming we have been able to find an ally (experience shows this is always the case), we imagine the ally merging with us, which leads naturally into the fifth step.

Step 5: Rest in Awareness

We know rest for a while in a relaxed state of peace and clarity. We should not try to force this but rather just let it happen by itself.

Sonya F appears to be under a lot of stress and always concerned about doing things correctly. At first she is very sceptical when she hears the detailed description of the exercise procedure for *Chöd* or *Feeding your Demon*. She is sure she will not be able to "see a demon". However, she agrees to attempt the exercise when her therapist assures her she will not have to "create anything". Together they will simply "take a look", as if they were curious spectators watching a film.

As the exercise progresses, Sonya is fascinated to see her demon appear as an extremely thin being, almost a skeleton. Previously she had always experienced her inner voice as being strict, merciless and sometimes even threatening.

When it comes to slipping into the role of her demon, Sonya feels somewhat sad and feels a great deal of tension. The therapist encourages her to continue. As the demon, she answers her three questions as follows:

1. *What I want from you is constant effort.*
2. *What I need from you is more safety and protection.*
3. *When my need is met, I will feel safer and more emotionally secure.*

Even though this is her first session of *Chöd*, Sonya is able to develop a great deal of the feeling of safety and emotional security within herself, helped by her own memories of when she felt secure. She then takes these healthy energies and begins to feed her skeletal demon, imagining how safety and security radiate over to the demon much like warmth from a heater. After a little while she can imagine how her demon slowly recovers and how its body begins to fill out. Then she sees how her demon is sitting in front of her as a small girl, which makes it even easier for Sonya to develop and feed safety and security.

With this little girl as an ally, Sonya now has support she can call on in situations where she feels under pressure. The girl helps Sonya to develop a feeling of safety and security and then they can reassure and calm each other down.

During further therapy sessions, Sonya then works on the goal of feeding the girl some more, finding an older and stronger woman to be an ally.

A variation:
When the demon appears to come from outside

So far we referred to *inner* voices and *inner* demons. However, we are frequently confronted with *external* situations and people who leave us with the feeling that they have an unhealthy effect on us. We tend to feel that another person triggers anger, sadness or fear within us—emotions we would not have felt if that person or situation had not been there.

Applying the *Feeding your Demon* exercise in these cases occurs in a very similar way. We need to identify the demon created within us by the external person or situation. Then we let this demon speak and answer the three questions. The only difference in procedure is then in the 4th step for a demon created by another person: Here we imagine both the demon and the other person front of us and visualise feeding them both.

Summary: The *Chöd* method described above provides us with both a very effective transformation tool and a very healthy set of instructions for dealing with our conflicts and fellow humans in general. The message is: Do not struggle or attempt to dominate and rule. Instead, take a peaceful path which allows the healthy aspects to develop in everyone, including demons. This is a message with beneficial consequences for us, our work as therapists and also for our societies, which are increasingly grappling to deal with issues related to integration.

Advanced Methods to Diagnose and Resolve Conflicts

When a help-seeker comes to us with a conflict situation which they want to work through deeply, it seems advisable to take a closer look at their personality structure. For this, we use the Buddhist categories of aversive, attaching and ignorant personality types and depth psychology's diagnostic system of personality accentuations. As therapists we need to determine whether the problems described by the help-seeker are ego-syntonic or ego-dystonic. In other words, can they signal a credible self-critical distance to what they are describing (= ego-dystonic: "Yes, I know I didn't behave completely appropriately") or are they self-protective without self-criticism (= ego-syntonic: "That is completely normal, everybody would do what I did"). An ego-syntonic attitude clearly makes it more difficult to process the situation.

The second question which we should ask ourselves as therapists is whether there are signs of a persistent (problematic) issue in the life of the help-seeker. What issues are they concerned about the most? Possible life issues include:
overload; overwhelming input
 · self-harming and self-injuring behaviour patterns
 · intimacy and distance
 · who is of value; who can be used for what
 · who has the power; who has control
 · urge to behave quietly or remain invisible

There are many other significant (problematic) issues which we can examine to better recognise any general tendencies towards particular patterns of behaviour and perception. Additionally, other aspects of the personality of the help-seeker are included in the analysis, such as the ego structures described in the 3rd Fundamental and social resources. Evaluating all of this should help the therapist to identify resources and obstacles for the resolution of the conflict. This whole process should be communicated transparently to the help-seeker.

According to the Buddhist understanding, all problems—including those at a structurally deep layer—are still located in the *outer* protective layers of a human being. These surround our core of Inner Nobility. They protect it and sometimes restrict it, but the problems in those layers will never be able to damage the core within.

Working with the resistant/aversive personality type

This temperament focuses quickly on deficits and problems so intensive exercises in *gratitude* and *humility* are indicated. The help-seeker could be given the following *Giving Inner Thanks* exercise as homework, for example. Here we silently say "Thank you" for both sunshine and rain; for the fact that a car is available to us; for the red traffic light, which helps to prevent traffic chaos and gridlock; for the fact that we have food to eat; for the fact that we feel thirsty; for the ability to move, see and talk (assuming the help-seeker has no disability which prevents this); and for much more as well.

The question we need to ask ourselves on a day when we practice this exercise is: What am I doing now, what am I experiencing, seeing, hearing, feelings, tasting, smelling and thinking? Whatever the answers may be, we immediately express gratitude for the present moment and what is happening in that moment even if it seems to be negative (for example, when we are being criticised, standing at a red light, or feeling hungry). We say thank you for what we have as often as possible. This constant repetition of our gratitude will help to turn the resistant or aversive person into a grateful one, but we need to remember that our basic temperament will always shine through a little. So this temperament will always have a propensity to offer criticism.

As always, when carrying out this exercise we should remember how constant repetition can influence and shape us at a deep psychological and physiological level. To paraphrase Mathieu Ricard: We can make 'Hate Street' narrower and narrower and set about widening 'Compassion Avenue'.

Gratitude exercises

We can frequently use a variety of gratitude exercises to change such aspects as the ways we deal with other people and also to change entirely inner aspects of our character.

We generally react with annoyance or other unhealthy impulses when we experience disturbances during a process which we want to run smoothly. We may have learnt that pressure, power, effort and possibly violence can all be applied in order to achieve what we need to achieve. However, if we want to have the choice of a less stressful alternative, we can practice gratitude exercises such as the *Giving Inner Thanks* exercise described above.

To prepare for these we should recall the frequently mentioned *Torso Twist* exercise, which demonstrates how mental imagery can have a tangible effect on physical processes. This should reduce any resistance we may have to purely mental exercises.

Another example of a gratitude exercise is the following *Basic Gratitude* exercise. We adopt a meditative composure, bringing our mind to rest, and then we say the following phrases to ourselves or out loud:

"Thank you feet for carrying me."
"Thank you knees for moving me."
"Thank you legs for letting me walk."
"Thank you hips for giving me the possibility of movement."
"Thank you back for allowing me to hold myself upright."
"Thank you shoulders for helping me to carry so much."
"Thank you arms."
"Thank you hands for allowing me to hold onto everything."
"Thank you head."
"Thank you heart for beating."

"Thank you eyes, ears, nose, mouth, skin for my experience of the world."
"Thank you stomach for digesting everything."
"Thank you organs for doing so much for me."
...and so on.

The statements as written here are just suggestions; everybody is encouraged to find their own words. And it is not essential to cover every single aspect; we may have our own particular problem zones which need special attention.

In this way we will gradually cease being so angry and judgemental with ourselves and start being much more grateful. If, for example, someone with severe pain carries out this exercise, they will initially find it very strange to express thanks for a body that hurts. After a while they will discover that the relevant sensations are changing. The exercise helps us to make contact and peace with ourselves.

Ideally, these gratitude exercises should be carried out several times a day.

Working with the attaching personality type

People with this temperament are easily excited, join in quickly and rapidly express desires. Working with them nonetheless needs just as much patience and time as the other two temperaments. We have to look out for the individual attachments of each help-seeker and come up with the most precise possible draft for the Middle Way as it could appear in their everyday life. And then this has to be trained, placing particular importance on various letting go exercises and a suitable way to find the balance between *letting go* and assuming responsibility.

The exercises will definitely need to be carried out often—perhaps every day. By applying our knowledge that constant repetition has a deep psychological and physiological effect on us, we can help an attaching temperament to develop into a relaxed and critical personality.

Working with the ignorant/confused personality type

As a therapist working with this temperament, we need a great deal of clarity, grounding and stability. Although we use the term ignorant here, the name for this personality type does not refer to intelligence; it describes people with characteristics which we regard as creative, quirky and volatile, floating and buzzing around. We may find ourselves also becoming confused—this is the much-discussed phenomenon referred to in psychoanalysis as counter-transference. Light braking manoeuvres are needed here, beginning with active forms of meditation such as walking, cleaning or cooking meditation and then moving on to more intensive exercises such as *Sacred Inner Moments*. And the Wisdom of the Middle Way also needs to be put into practice here.

Once again, secure in the knowledge that constant repetition will eventually produce a lasting psychological and physical change within us, we can help to produce behaviour patterns reflecting clarity instead of ignorance and confusion. However, this temperament will always retain its very lively and fun-loving energy.

Note on counter-transference: This term is used by psychoanalysts to describe the emotions arising within them which are triggered by the help-seeker. Theoretically, the training analyses undergone by a trainee psychoanalyst should lead to them being "fully analysed"; they should have overcome these unconscious tendencies. If this is true, their own role in this process should be very minor and therefore they can assume that any emotions which they do feel are actually indications of what their help-seeker is either experiencing themselves or not feeling and therefore suppressing, unconsciously delegating it to the person sitting opposite them (here, the therapist).

The Sacred Inner Moments exercise

This exercise (also described in the 17th Fundamental) is a very effective exercise suitable for almost everyone, but especially for people with tendencies to delusion or confusion. It is particularly difficult for them because it permanently demands that they put a brake on themselves: Whenever they are asked to do something or help someone, or whenever they feel the impulse to stand up and do or say something particular, then for the duration of two breaths they should hesitate a little, taking a moment to look inwards.

The Eye of the Hurricane

Sometimes we experience our life as a hurricane of tasks, duties, stress, appointments, work, effort and tests. However, we know that at the centre of every hurricane there is an "eye": an area of peace in the middle of the storm. Similarly to the exercise of taking a sacred inner moment, this exercise calls on us to take a step back and cast a mindful eye on the present moment. We do this by imagining stepping into the eye of the hurricane. It is a very effective measure which makes clear that we do not always have to change external circumstances and even that it is not a problem if we cannot change them: We can remain in the midst of tremendous chaos and just let it be the way it is. We simply change our position and enter the eye of the hurricane. We enter our inner zone of calmness. And we can rest assured that this zone is always there.

This is a further exercise which demonstrates very practically and tangibly that inner imagination can be very effective. Although exercises such as these often appear to be very unimpressive because they only present a small detail, a constant drip will wear down any stone in the end. And we will do well to remind ourselves how we can also change an apparently established character or even our destiny. We do this by starting at the beginning and paying attention to our *motivation*. This lays the foundation for our destiny, since motivation leads to *deeds*, which then become *habits* if repeated often enough. These habits then form the structure of our *character* which is responsible for shaping our *destiny*.

Now we move on to an aspect of Buddhist techniques which we have already seen and used in many places in this book in order to make particular issues clearer.

Myths and Short Instructional Tales

The Buddhist path offers a very rich pool of fables, myths, anecdotes and short tales which can be used to illustrate even the most complicated of topics. For example, there is a great selection of exemplary stories illustrating how mindfulness helps one to adopt a conciliatory approach towards disagreeable people or unwelcome aspects of one's own character. If we make use of these stories as a therapist, the help-seekers can listen and analyse them according to how open and motivated they are. Sticking to the level of pure discussion and logic can be a hopeless strategy when conveying insights relating to certain issues, such the common attitude that rage can somehow be justified in particular situations.

Of course, many people—particularly those in psychotherapy—need direct human contact. As Buddhist psychotherapists we will naturally be very present and active, but we do not adopt a "boxer stance"—allowing all affects to be thrown at us. Instead we stand shoulder to shoulder with the help-seeker and look at the situation together. This allows all the various energies coming from the help-seeker to find acceptance while the therapist also secures their own protective zone.

Metaphors and short instructional tales or anecdotes can be particularly helpful with very tense help-seekers. Perhaps the therapeutic situation allows us to compare a combative client to a bulldog. If they accept the metaphor for a moment, it can be used to consider the next steps: When is growling helpful and when not? Do we really want to be petted? What are the tasty bones we are fighting for? And a client who is a workaholic might be able to compare themselves to a donkey. In this way we can make use of creative resources whilst remaining aware of the possible danger of identification. Every one of us probably *has* a bulldog within us (large or small) but nobody *is* a bulldog.

The wise king

One example we can use to illustrate problematic ways of dealing with conflicts is the story of the wise king who one day had to leave his castle. Immediately, a demon came out of the castle dungeons, having waited for this opportunity, and sat on the empty throne. Loyal guards raced to the scene and cursed the demon, threatening it with an all-out attack. The stronger the threats, the stronger the demon became. The guards got scared and started to shoot, but the demon simply grew even more and became even stronger. The situation appeared hopeless.

When the King returned and saw the problem he hurried directly to the demon and apologised politely for the behaviour of his guards. He sympathised with the demon, agreeing that life in the dungeons could not be all that easy. The King ordered food and drink to be brought to the demon. As a consequence, it became ever smaller. Every nice gesture from the King and his servants led to the demon becoming less dangerous.

How to catch beavers

If we want to bring about healthy effects, we are repeatedly confronted with the difficult issue of how to put our knowledge into action. Therapists and help-seekers alike often complain about how the theory seems so plausible but the practice so difficult. The extraordinary power of old patterns and habits often seems to be almost overpowering.

In various Fundamentals we have explored how our neural pathways can be changed and how quickly new pathways can be established through regular training (neuroplasticity). Of course, this also means that old, well-worn pathways can also be very difficult to modify. This topic can be conveyed clearly by means of this story about catching beavers.

It is almost impossible to catch beavers in the water, since this is their element and the dams they build are very secure. However, on land they are more vulnerable because they have the tendency to always follow the same paths through the grass along the riverbank. Comparable to the well-trodden shepherding paths in the mountains, these tracks easily allow any hunter to find the beavers in the tall grass. They simply need to set a trap directly on a beaver path and they are almost guaranteed to go home successful that day. Although the beaver is a very intelligent animal in many regards, it does have its habits. As it searches for suitable trees to gnaw it regularly climbs out of the water and trots through the grass along the path which it knows. It does see the trap lying on the path but to the left and to the right of the trap is unknown grassland, so it continues along the path, knowingly heading directly towards the trap. We can imagine the beaver becoming more and more nervous and uneasy because it does not want to fall into the trap, but it also does not want to leave its familiar path. It becomes even more agitated as it gets nearer to the trap but it keeps on going... until the trap snaps shut.

Listening to this story, we may well consider the beaver to be a dumb animal, but we will surely also be able to identify with this friendly creature and his fixed habits. Considering the deeper meaning, we can then use the story to find the courage to try walking "straight through the tall grass" on an unknown path. As therapists, we should encourage our help-seekers to be creative and remain open for all possible experiences. Routine is undoubtedly very useful but we should also be careful not to let it lead us into a trap.

Dealing with interpersonal conflicts

This category of conflicts deserves special attention because it is a very common source of suffering. In fact, we seem to have an almost infinite number of conflicts with our relationship partners, children, relatives, neighbours, colleagues, superiors, authorities and other groups or nations etc. We can even go so far as to describe this whole field as a great adventure playground for our ignorance, attachments and resistances.

It is in interpersonal conflicts in particular that we experience the blurring of our respective limits and perceptions of responsibility. Each party to the conflict has a number of reasons to believe that they are right. Of course, every person always has good reasons for their behaviour. In the 15th Fundamental on the topic of our resistance, we discovered how we often exhibit the tendency to prefer "justice at any price" rather than react wisely (Michael Kohlhaas syndrome). And we learned about the issue of responsibility and forgiving in the 18th Fundamental. Unfortunately we still often remain very sure of ourselves when it comes to our emotions, in spite of their deceptive nature.

Interesting stories with a profound meaning can help to convey the wisdom we need in this regard, complementing the theory we convey by means of the Fundamentals of BPT and its practical exercises (meditation to cultivate healthy mental states such as love, kindness, compassion, joy and equanimity).

The story of
how to kill your mother-in-law

The reader may be surprised to hear that Buddhist literature includes a story advising us on the best way to kill our mother-in-law!

An old lady has spent her whole life working on the farm which she inherited from her parents; the farm has belonged to her family for many generations. She lives there with her adult son and they both have to work very hard to manage the farm. The old lady is worried about the future.

One day her son finally announces that he is going to marry. He met a woman in the nearby city and now they want to live together here on the farm. His mother is happy to hear this news but also a little worried about her son and the family farm. A woman from the city? The young woman is looking forward to life in the country with her husband, although she also knows that she will be moving into a well-established domestic situation and is not just gaining a husband but also a mother-in-law.

When the women meet each other for the first time, they greet each other in a friendly and polite way but also check each other out. They both initially remain sceptical and a few small issues lead them to remain somewhat aloof with each other. They both have considerable worries. The young woman would like to rearrange a few things, but the old woman wants to hear appreciation for what already exists. The tension between them slowly increases. The older woman expects respect and submission, the younger woman expects her to be open for her ideas as well. Now when the women meet, their faces are no longer so friendly and the atmosphere is grim. Mealtimes are characterised by a heavy mood, with each minute seeming to last an hour.

After months of mainly silent but occasionally vociferous struggle, the young woman begins to look for solutions. She does not want to lose her husband but can no longer live together with her mother-in-law under one roof. One day she finds herself talking to the old village pharmacist, who has a mixed reputation for the potions he creates. She hints that she needs a very strong powder and reassures him that she will be careful not to dose it too highly. The clever old pharmacist immediately sees through the situation and addresses the young woman directly. Everybody in the village already knows how difficult her life is. And her mother-in-law is actually very old. So she will be given a powder with a permanent and painless effect. But the young woman needs to be very patient and proceed strategically in order to avoid any suspicion that might arise if the old woman dies immediately after the young woman is seen visiting the pharmacist. When she returns home, she should begin to serve very tiny doses of the powder to her mother-in-law and remain extremely friendly for the time being.

Reassured, the young woman returns home and that very evening prepares her mother-in-law's favourite meal. She mixes in a little of the powder and serves the meal. She remains friendly and cannot help feeling more optimistic than she has felt for a long time. She smiles at the old woman and asks her about her day. Initially, the older woman is a little distrustful but after a while the good mood of her daughter-in-law becomes infectious and everybody has a very nice evening.

Life continues like this for a while. When the old woman returns from the fields, the younger woman has already prepared the evening meal and a pot of tea, carefully dosed with the powder from the pharmacist. The old woman slowly begins to have less ill will and begins to enquire about the young woman's life in the city and how well she is adapting to country life. As the days and weeks pass by they begin to talk more and more with each other. In fact, they slowly become friends.

At some point, the young woman's conscience starts to plague her and she stops dosing the meals with the powder. But her feelings of guilt are not completely eased, since she knows that she may well have already poisoned her mother-in-law significantly. So she soon returns to the pharmacist, confesses her feelings of guilt to him and asks him if there is an antidote to the powder he prepared. The wise old man smiles and shows the young woman a large jar of vitamin powder—this is the powder he gave her. At first she is very annoyed but then relief sets in and she is very happy.

Therapeutic tales like this one can be very useful during psychotherapy. Telling them in situations where the help-seeker is receptive to the details of their message can then be followed by short closing meditations. This prevents them from being over-analysed. The effect of the tale should be allowed to unfold on a deeper level; stories and images can have a very healthy effect in our storehouse consciousness. *Later*, individual aspects of the tales might be processed in more detail as part of therapy sessions; often it is the help-seeker themselves who initiates this.

Now we move on to another Buddhist technique: working with dreams.

Dream Yoga: Interpreting and Working with Dreams

Dreams were considered to be very valuable in ancient India. Sages were said to have interpreted a dream of the Buddha's mother as prophesying the birth of her son and his future importance for humanity.

However, the use of dreams within Buddhism has changed. The priority for Buddhists and Buddhist Psychotherapy lies in consciousness and alertness, which means that the actual contents of the dream are secondary, although they are still important.

We should never lose track of the overarching goal. In other words, we do not cling onto our dreams or identify with them. And our dreams do not bring with them freedom from attachments, resistance and ignorance. Our main focus should always remain the cultivation of an alert, clear mind, which will liberate us.

Correspondingly, *dream yoga* can be considered as a very advanced form of mind training. The higher goal consists of remaining clear and conscious while we are sleeping and dreaming. This is indeed an advanced goal which we will only be able to achieve with a great deal of patience and regular practice.

As the saying goes, it is not because things are difficult that we do not dare, it is because we do not dare that things are difficult. Anyone can easily start to become more conscious of their dreams by putting a dream diary next to their bed and, before they fall asleep, clearly affirming their intention to write down their dreams when they wake up. We will be astonished to discover how quickly we remember more dreams and more details. Our comprehensive and varied mind training will allow us to feel how we have many more fine types of consciousness than just sleeping, dreaming, being awake and being tired. Liberating our mind involves getting to know these better and learning how to influence them.

In this way we will be able to accompany our consciousness in a wakeful way when we send it to sleep. In fact, during the night there are hours of very lively mental activity during the dream phases and only a relatively short phase of deep sleep (generally less than two hours). Our training will allow us to experience a wakeful consciousness at night during dreams so we can actually learn how to shape our dreams.

Dream researchers and psychologists call this process "lucid dreaming". This has been researched scientifically, with its existence being established by researchers including scientists from Stanford University, who showed the possibility of consciously exercising control over our dreams and sleep.

Travelling

To conclude the 19th Fundamental, we will take a brief look at what is a relatively unorthodox topic for therapists, but one which Buddhism has nonetheless shown to be valuable for experiencing ourselves and bringing about therapeutic change: travelling. Stories, tales, fairytales and spiritual experiences constantly report about journeys undertaken by their participants. Although in many cases they may be a symbol for inner journeys, we should not underestimate the powerful magic we are exposed to when we set off for unfamiliar places, leaving our home and journeying into the unknown—especially if we do this alone.

In fact, if we travel mindfully, our experiences can be more intensive than in any course of psychotherapy. We will be confronted with our fears and longings, our anxieties and our strengths and weaknesses. Our established attitudes and opinions about ourselves and other people may be challenged. We will automatically be forced to think in new ways and to put our old experiences into perspective in order to develop a context for the new experiences we are subjected to. Suddenly our old concerns appear trivial and new worries may arise very quickly.

Travel broadens the mind: It opens up new mental horizons which can contribute to an improved self-critical approach, where we still take our own problems seriously but know how relative these can be.

Is healing possible?

The somewhat provocative answer is: We are already healed. Our suffering arises because we have lost access to our inner health. When we make use of Buddhist techniques to regain contact with this healthy core of Inner Nobility we will experience a tangible enrichment of our life energy and our health.

Slowly we are coming to the end of our short selection of Buddhist-psychotherapeutic techniques. There are still a lot of open questions, but within one book we can only present a limited yet important selection of Buddhist practices and the contents of Buddhist psychotherapy.

Is there an end to Buddhist Psychotherapy? When does a course of therapy end? Hopefully the reader now has a clear answer to this question: The end is our liberation! But now we also know that this is not a stable condition which we achieve once and then maintain forever. So in fact the end of our path turns out to be an open end. Or an open path.

We will go through life on the Middle Way, often veering off a little to the left or to the right but gradually increasing the speed with which we find our way back to the middle. Theoretical knowledge is not enough to achieve this; neither is a course of Buddhist therapy, no matter how long. However, the tangible, healthy changes which we will experience during our practice help us to develop increasing motivation and a firm commitment to continuing regular implementation of our Buddhist knowledge in our everyday life: for the benefit of ourselves and all other beings.

This Fundamental Should Convey the Following:

We have been introduced to the following techniques:
- The Four Principles of Change
- The Five Methods of Training Our Mind
- Torso Twist
- Meditation
- Breathing meditation
- Royal Posture
- Counting Thoughts
- Mindfulness exercises
- Switching
- Letting go exercises
- Visualisation
- *Chöd:* Feeding our Demons
- Sacred Inner Moments
- Eye of the Hurricane
- Gratitude exercises
- Giving Inner Thanks
- Therapeutic tales
- Dream yoga
- Travelling

Taking part in a course of Buddhist Psychotherapy can be very helpful to help us consolidate a stable psychological, psychosomatic and spiritual foundation. However, we can and should not live on foundations alone; a little comfort does not harm us. So we need to build a comfortable house, customised for our individual life, in which we can transfer the knowledge that we have acquired into our everyday life.

The general strategy of Buddhist Psychotherapy consists of securing, promoting and stabilising healthy actions (the latter by means of regular repetition). Unhealthy memories, experiences, actions and habits only form the focus of our attention for a short time where it is clearly appropriate for us to do so. Buddhist Psychotherapy should not be understood as a way of working through old problems. Instead, it concentrates on those elements of our behaviour which conduce to health.

Whatever we repeat becomes established.

The 20th Fundamental of BPT will now help us to find our own way of using our personal everyday life as practice.

The **20**th
Fundamental of Buddhist Psychotherapy

Our Whole Life is Practice

> When you're trained as a Buddhist, you don't think of Buddhism as a religion. You think of it as a type of science, a method of exploring your own experience through techniques that enable you to examine your actions and reactions in a non-judgmental way.
>
> YONGEY MINGYUR RINPOCHE

From Part-Time Buddha to Full-Time Buddha

The Buddhist teacher Thich Nhat Hanh coined the slogan "From part-time Buddha to full-time Buddha" to express the fact that we often begin slowly with our Buddhist exercises and move on to more regular and frequent practice once we begin to strongly feel their healthy effect and develop confidence and motivation. Perhaps most readers will consider the goal of becoming a Buddha to be well beyond their reach, but we need to remind ourselves of the Buddha's own clear words telling us all we already have our Buddha nature and have always had it. Our efforts to achieve liberation are nothing other than an attempt to find our way back to something we have always possessed. The Buddha was not and is not a distant god. Maybe his "awakening" does imply some form of divine power, but even if this is so, it is not reserved for a few saints. It is a power that we *all* have within us. Unfortunately it is often buried deep out of reach.

We study the Dharma; we work in Buddhist Psychotherapy; we experience the intense human efforts people are making there for the benefit of themselves and others. We attend the Buddhist teachings and meditation sessions. And we pay careful attention to putting our progress into practice every day; the emphasis on the latter aspect is one of the key reasons why Buddhist Psychotherapy offers such good chances of healing. In fact, as with Buddhist teachings in general, the supreme test of any progress is always its application and consolidation in everyday life. Our Buddhist focus on strengthening and stabilising ourselves as well as training, calming and clearing our mind may indeed be a sort of individual achievement, but it only really reveals its true quality when it proves helpful for all other sentient beings.

Applying this test very often puts a damper on our experiences: Perhaps we were sitting on our cushion and had an experience we consider to be ultimate peace. Now we want to secure and preserve this feeling; we discover this is just the beginning of the really exciting process. We go home after the meditation session and then we encounter the second, equally important aspect of our learning path; new teachers are always waiting around the corner, no matter what we believe we have achieved. They might be the neighbour's barking dog, our stressed-out partner, noisy children or the rip that appears in a newly purchased sofa. Opportunities to practice are found on a larger scale in the form of illness, aging, death and loss and on a smaller scale with examples such as minor conflicts, worries and fears.

Jack Kornfield writes: "Most masters agree that after the first illumination, there can still arise periods of fear, confusion, loss of spiritual bearings, and unskilful conduct."

As we discovered in the 1st Fundamental of BPT on liberation, we will never be able to "keep hold" of any progress we make—even when we achieve liberation. As the Buddhist teachings also tell us, the nature of our world is that we are part of a constantly changing flux. Our life is often a huge collection of challenges, drawing our attention in one direction after the other. We lose track of ourselves in thousands of everyday issues. The Wisdom of the Middle Way is perhaps easy to understand in theory as guidance for our path, but it is often very difficult to actually follow. Our everyday life rarely offers us clear indicators of the right measure and the right direction.

Rituals

We have an urgent need to revive *rituals* as a way of maintaining our inner and outer structures. We are using the term here for regular, meaningful actions and healthy habits. For example, little rituals to help us with our mindfulness practice. Initially it is very useful to set fixed times for our daily practice since it generally takes between six weeks and three months for a new regularly performed activity to really become a habit.

While we are still developing these healthy habits, a weekly plan can be very helpful. A course of Buddhist Psychotherapy is characterised by fairly fixed schedules with regular individual and group sessions as well as teaching sessions followed by meditation that take place several times a week. This rhythm should be continued even after a period of therapeutic work: fixed days for particular exercises, fixed times for our daily meditation, fixed days for one or two "practice days" each month.

This advice is based on years of accumulated experience which we can draw on to overcome the difficulties we encounter on the path. Conveying and becoming familiar with Buddhist practice and teachings takes place in cycles; it has its highs and lows but in general remains very accessible.

The Fourfold Challenge

In Buddhist Psychotherapy we definitely do not underestimate the eternal difficulties of putting theory into practice. Help-seekers are provided with instructions and homework in this regard, which make up their personal *Healing Quadrille* together with the daily exercises, weekly individual and group sessions, Dharma teachings and group meditations.

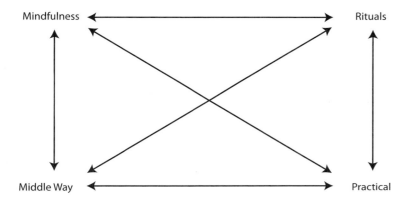

This Healing Quadrille has developed into one of the most effective aspects of Buddhist Psychotherapy. The four pillars are assigned individually to each help-seeker to bring it to life and make it as practical as possible, ensuring it is suitable for everyday implementation. Each of the factors interacts with each of the others; all of them are of equal value and importance for long-lasting effects.

Rituals

If carried out regularly, healthy actions help to establish our healthy mental states and cast light upon the intentions and motivations behind our deeds.

As we already described above, rituals initially need fixed times and clear procedures to ensure we carry them out and in turn ensure the development of healthy habits (since habits inevitably arise from any repeated actions). These habits then shape our temperament and character in a relatively short time, enabling us to play a role in determining our own destiny.

Mindfulness

Without mindfulness we are like a blind cross-country runner: We will end up running around in circles or running into obstacles and injuring ourselves. So we cannot do enough to train our mindfulness, including finding detailed answers to the questions: What does mindfulness really mean in our life? What does it feel like when we are mindful? How can we bring about mindfulness? How does it change our actions and behaviour? What do the changes caused by mindfulness look like exactly?

Middle Way

Every new path always fascinates us to begin with. So a new course of therapy or a new type of therapy, such as BPT, will naturally produce a few successes at first. But deciding to dedicate ourselves fully to this new path may well be a trap: We might be leaving the Middle Way. And the forks in the path do not stop there: There are an infinite number of ways to stray off the Middle Way. Like Little Red Riding Hood, we always have to beware of the Big Bad Wolf lurking in the forest, preventing us from reaching our destination.

The *Sacred Inner Moments* exercise is a very valuable support in this regard, allowing us to frequently check if we are still avoiding the extremes. Unfortunately there is no automatic navigation assistant for this. To stay on course, we have to develop our own inner GPS device.

Practical

The issue at hand is staying in the here and now. We are not aiming to reach some far-flung paradise or a promised afterlife; we are not concerned with "One day..." or "Once upon a time...". And the path is not about "blissful moments" on our meditation cushion. The Dharma teachings are vast but we should not get lost in their labyrinthine nature. We should make the most of our therapeutic support to ensure we are dealing with the *specific, practical* areas of our life and *exactly* the behaviour we need to deal with in order to *tangibly* put our progress into everyday practice.

So our challenge is as follows: To maintain an almost constant *mindfulness*, avoiding the extremes and remaining on the *Middle Way,* using *rituals* to support us every day and making sure we are aware of the opportunities we have to be of *practical* benefit to ourselves and others.

Buddhist Virtue is Active Virtue

Buddhism and Buddhist Psychotherapy place great value on *active* self-control; we assume responsibility for ourselves and for others, basing our thoughts and actions on virtue.

In some cultures, the term virtue has rather negative associations, appearing to emphasise renouncing or avoiding certain aspects of life. In contrast, as we have seen already in this book, the Buddhist concept of virtue is much more active: It is not enough to avoid unhealthy aspects—we have to actively cultivate healthy states and conditions. Virtue is both helpful and indispensable for our everyday life and our practice. Without orienting ourselves towards virtue, we will encounter great difficulties in our practice, for example during meditation. Non-virtuous behaviour confuses and unsettles our mind considerably. And since non-virtuous behaviour is inevitably a deviation from the Middle Way, we will definitely feel the consequences sooner or later—at the very latest during meditation sessions.

Here we present a three-stage process to develop an actively virtuous approach to life. Making the concept of virtue more tangible can be helpful, so we then present three realms, referred to as Three Gates, with practical guidance for each; this guidance allows us to have a significant influence on our karma.

The three stages of virtue

The high Buddhist goal of adopting a virtuous approach describes an integrity which is healthy for ourselves and all other beings. For Buddhists, virtue is much more interesting than just knowing what to avoid.

The first stage of virtue

The first stage is, however, initially focused on avoidance: we try to stop some of our unhealthy characteristics. For example, we avoid causing harm to ourselves and others, which corresponds to a Western approach to virtue. The *Five Lay Precepts* which the Buddha

taught for his non-monastic followers have already been presented in connection with the Noble Eightfold Path.
1. Refrain from deliberately killing or injuring living beings (including animals).
2. Refrain from taking anything that is not freely given.
4. Refrain from sexual misconduct.
5. Refrain from lying and harsh speech.
6. Refrain from blurring consciousness by taking drugs.

Once we have begun to implement this approach to virtue, we move on to the next stages, with a more active nature.

The second stage of virtue

Here we practice *active* care and providence. We can do this by building upon the precepts mentioned above:
1. Refrain from deliberately killing or injuring living beings *and also* actively contribute to the protection of life.
2. Refrain from taking anything that is not freely given *and also* actively serve others.
3. Avoid sexual misconduct *and also* actively cultivate mindfulness in sexual relationships.
4. Refrain from lying and harsh speech *and also* actively take steps to ensure truth and justice.
5. Refrain from blurring consciousness by taking drugs *and also* actively cultivate our own capacity to be alert and attentive.

The third stage of virtue

This stage focuses on establishing, internalising and practising our natural virtue and intuitive integrity—developing a secure feeling for the right path. No extra instructions are necessary to reach this third stage: It is a result of applying increased mindfulness to the regular practice of the first two stages.

Additional assistance for the practical implementation of the process mentioned above is provided in the form of the *Three Gates*.

The *Three Gates* of virtuous behaviour

Buddhist teachings make frequent reference to the trinity of *body*, *speech* and *mind* (the Three Gates) to help categorise the details of the topic being taught. Here, the three points take the form of appeals to *actively* practice particular virtuous behaviour.

Our body

Do not steal *and also* actively work for justice.

Do not commit sexual misconduct *and also* be very mindful in sexual relationships.

Do not kill *and also* actively work for the protection of life.

Our speech

Do not speak harshly *and also* actively cultivate positive communication.

Do not lie *and also* actively take steps to ensure truth is upheld.

Do not spread rumours *and also* actively pass on positive news.

Do not engage in meaningless speech *and also* cultivate the habit of thoughtful speech.

Our mind

Do not hate *and also* actively respect and appreciate others.

Tame desires *and also* actively cultivate liberation.

Avoid false views *and also* actively cultivate new knowledge and insights.

It has proven to be helpful to work through this list regularly in a slow and careful way in order to gradually internalise and realise this guidance and enable us to pass it on to our help-seekers.

Regular Practice Days

Even more structure can be provided for implementing our everyday practice by scheduling a retreat day once or twice a month, providing an opportunity to consolidate what we have learnt during our daily practice and meditation and in the teaching sessions. Initially it is advisable to have a fixed rhythm for this, for example, the first and third Sunday in every month. For some people it is also helpful to spend this practice day in their practice or therapeutic community and not alone.

The community of Buddhist practitioners—the *Sangha*—is considered to be one of the main pillars in our life. Joining together with others for exercises, meditation and discussions is a powerful tool to help us reach liberation more quickly. Practice in a particular group should not, however, be considered compulsory; we can spend our practice day alone, with our partner or with other like-minded people.

We should adopt a pre-determined schedule for the practice day and observe ten helpful precepts for the duration.

The schedule of our practice day

A few minor preparations are necessary for this day. We should tidy and clean the room we are going to use beforehand, although a few tasks can be left for the practice day itself, to be carried out in a mindful way. We should ensure that we are disturbed as little as possible on the day; for example, we should turn off our mobile and prepare a special message for the answering machine or mailbox.

The ten rules or precepts for a practice day are:
1. Do not kill (including animals).
2. Do not steal; do not demand anything; do not take what is not given.
3. No sexual conduct.
4. Do not lie; no loud, harsh speech; no verbal aggression.
5. No alcohol or drugs; no substances which cloud the mind.
6. Do not wear jewellery.
7. Do not use any media (TV, computer, newspapers, books, telephone, mobile phone).
8. Enjoy moderate meals, taken in silence.
9. Measured, mindful movement; do not play sport.
10. Conduct silent and walking meditation.

It is best to decide the schedule and details in advance, particularly regarding mealtimes. For point 10: Decide in advance how long and how often to meditate. Unless we have a lot of meditation experience, it is best to choose short meditation sessions of 15 to 20 minutes and then conduct these more often. Once we are used to the whole procedure, we can sit for longer.

In this way we can spend the day peacefully, with sitting and walking meditations, going for a walk, mindfully preparing our meals and engaged in mindful exchange with others (if we are spending our practice day in our community). On the day itself we will certainly have some interesting experiences; when we then bring these days into our life we will also notice tangible changes. The aim is always to enable our own practical experiences; the aim of the day is never to follow rules as precisely as possible or simply engage in something "we have to do". Every exercise we incorporate into the schedule should be carefully assessed.

Vows

Another helpful aid to carrying our progress over into our everyday life has proven to be the development and taking of our *own* clear rules in the form of vows. Tulku Lama Lobsang explained in his teachings and individual advice that we have to follow very many *external* rules, such as laws, ordinances and regulations but if we look closely we will see that we have comparably few *inner* rules.

He also points out that we generally take any opportunity to get around external rules and stipulations. And then when things go wrong we often call for more external rules and laws! For this reason, Tulku Lama Lobsang emphasises the necessity to create and specify our own inner rules in addition to the external ones.

If we take a moment and consider what inner rules we have created for ourselves to follow, can we name them?

Making positive use of inner rules, in Buddhist Psychotherapy we develop individual vows for every participant. Generally this is done considering important pillars of the Buddhist teachings designed to bring about positive and healthy change, such as the *Four Immeas-*

urables. The following text can be recited as a prayer or blessing for others and an aid to achieve inner composure, providing orientation for ourselves (a reminder of the qualities we wish to develop). It also serves well as a mantra to be recited in times of difficulties.

The Four Immeasurables
May all beings be happy and possess the causes of happiness.
May all beings be free of suffering and the causes of suffering.
May all beings experience joy and possess the causes of joy.
May all beings abide in equanimity, free of attachment and aversion.

In the Fundamentals relating to our body and mind, we discovered how effective mental imagination can be at influencing and changing both our moods and our body. Whatever we visualise changes our neural pathways. If we regularly develop healthy images, our nervous system will change measurably, creating a positive feedback effect which helps us to reach our goal more rapidly and effectively.

One form of vow the Buddha taught for lay people (not monks or nuns) is:

I vow not to kill any living beings.
I vow to refrain from taking what is not given.
I vow not to engage in sexual misconduct.
I vow to refrain from harsh speech.
I vow not to consume drugs which cloud my consciousness.

A form of these vows which could be considered to be even *more virtuous* according to the Buddhist concept of virtue would incorporate promises to engage actively for the opposite of what we refrain from. For example:

I vow to protect the life of all sentient beings.
I vow to commit myself actively for justice.
I vow to cultivate an appreciative attitude in all of my relationships.

I vow to communicate with all beings in a mindful and respectful way.

I vow to keep my consciousness as wakeful and mindful as possible.

For some people the Bodhisattva Vow may be appropriate, and others may want to make slight adjustments to the text. We already saw this vow in the 3rd Fundamental, where it was presented as being very helpful for therapists. Since it can never be harmful to repeat such a healthy text, we present it again here:

Beings are numberless; I vow to free them all.
Delusions are inexhaustible; I vow to end them fully.
Dharma gates are boundless; I vow to enter them all.
The ways to awakening are unsurpassable; I vow to embody them all.

Some others among us may choose to write our very own personal vows, referring to the weaknesses that we wish to change and the strengths we want to develop.

Whichever vow we choose, it is useful to recite it both at regular times each day and in situations where we feel a need for the support it can provide.

Walter G came to us exhibiting great esteem and respect; he would bow very deeply and could hardly conceal his reverence. It took quite a while before he began to notice how much remoteness he created with this. For Walter it seemed to be very helpful to recognise that our practice is not restricted to "sacred" ceremonies but is very much about the activities of everyday life.

This Fundamental Should Convey the Following:

No Buddhist teachings, no clever books, no intelligent lectures, and no course of intensive psychotherapy are by themselves sufficient to bring about our transformation and to liberate us. Our own effort is needed. We need patience for our regular practice and the support of like-minded people with healthy qualities.

Putting theory into practice is the path that only we can take; regular practice and patience will soon mean that we do not need special exercises—our whole life will become our practice.

The Buddha himself said: *Be your own master!*

The **21**st
Fundamental of Buddhist Psychotherapy

Recognise and Convey the Step from the Relative to the Absolute Truth

> If we succeed in arriving at the
> ultimate truth we recognise that
> happiness and suffering are one.
>
> THICH NHAT HANH

> All that is visible clings to the invisible,
> The audible to the inaudible,
> The tangible to the intangible,
> Perhaps the thinkable to the
> unthinkable.
>
> LAMA ANAGARIKA GOVINDA

We began the description of Buddhist Psychotherapy in the First Fundamental with a presentation of the essence of Buddhism—which also forms the essence of Buddhist Psychotherapy. We refer to this essence as liberation, freedom, enlightenment or Nirvana. By now the reader should hopefully have a clear idea of how this essence is actually a realistic goal and of how the path is the goal. The Fundamentals of BPT should also have served to demystify the term "liberation" or "enlightenment", revealing its realistic nature and the steps necessary to follow the path and reach the goal.

With this approach, we have tried to translate *absolute*, profound truths into our *relative* world.

Relative and Absolute

Many Buddhists differentiate between the *relative* or worldly truth and the *absolute* or *ultimate* truth. According to Thich Nhat Hanh, the whole of the Buddhist teachings belong to the *relative* truth. The teachings are not an end in themselves—they serve as a means to an end, simply pointing us to the *absolute* truth beyond them.

Perhaps we can compare the teachings with a sign showing us the way: Surely we should not focus on the sign so intensely that we forget to proceed in the direction we want to travel?! We could devote our life to the sign but it would be better simply to look at it carefully, understand it and then move on in the direction of our goal. Or perhaps a more modern comparison to a navigation system would be more appropriate, since Buddhist teachings accompany us for the whole journey. Even this very useful technology can never completely replace real life and the effort we need to put in ourselves to reach the goal.

The *relative* or worldly truth refers to the forms, words, terms, agreements and rules which are all expressions of or references to something beyond or behind them. They are all fundamentally important for our individual life and a functioning collective or society.

Absolute or *ultimate* truth refers to that which we cannot directly perceive. Nonetheless, with a high level of clarity and a very quiet mind we may indeed "catch a glimpse" of the absolute.

Both are equally important and of equal value. For example, the relative truth tells us that we want to avoid things that are unhealthy; this itself brings us closer to the absolute truth of Nirvana. Relative things can be described well using words. Absolute aspects are beyond words and so we always face the difficulty of how to refer to them.

We begin our path of practice with the relative truth. We learn to recognise what brings us satisfaction and what brings us dissatisfaction or suffering. We learn to maintain this ability to differentiate for ever longer periods of time and develop an ever surer feeling for positive and negative. To put this more accurately, we learn to differentiate between things that have healthy or unhealthy effects on ourselves or others.

Many spiritual seekers drift too quickly into apparently absolute worlds. This brings with it a significant risk of ignoring essential relative and real aspects of life, justified by the claim that everything is only sensory delusion, so the material world is unimportant—only the spiritual world has real meaning. However, the Buddha showed us how important it is to be *completely* in this world. So it is initially necessary to study real and relative references very carefully, internalising and implementing the knowledge and insights these bring. Without our relative aspects, the absolute truth has no value for us. To use a metaphor, we need very good roots in the earth in order to stretch up high into the absolute areas. In practical terms, this means that we initially secure and strengthen our ego; as we learn to progress further we learn to let go of our ego ever more frequently. Once we have a degree of security at this level, we can seek out support from helpful people in order to proceed even further.

When we manage to gain glimpses of and an understanding of the absolute truth, we will develop a wider perspective encompassing many different levels. For example, we will perceive how all opposites develop from one single source. We will recognise that happiness and suffering are one. Mind and body, nature and humans, us and them, emotions and rational mind, easy and difficult, funny and sad, birth and death: These are all useful categories for us but they are artificial separations of something at a deeper level. At that level it is one unity.

The recognition that there is no fixed self is a difficult and literally mind-blowing insight. It needs a great deal of courage to take a look at the absolute truth. We need firm stability in order to recognise and abide in our "airiness"—our non-substantial nature.

When the time comes and we are allowed a taste of the absolute truth, the degree of our liberation increases significantly. Even then we will remain firmly in this world and committed to important worldly affairs, as active, liberated human beings without attachments to grievances, hate, anger, frustration or disappointment etc.

We should not understand this to mean that liberation can only be found in distant, absolute realms: It is in the here and now.

Absolute or Relative Liberation?

The process of liberation is not a process of overcoming the relative world which happens in the absolute world. We cannot experience liberation *from* this world. Instead we experience freedom *in* this world. Perhaps this is different during the process of dying or afterwards, but we do not really know. As long as we are alive, boundaries will continue to exist—such as our physicality—which prevents us from experiencing the absolute truth as a permanent state. This is one of the reasons why we cannot "conserve" or hold onto liberation as a permanent condition.

It appears to be a very rewarding task to discover how we can develop our own access to the absolute levels and what they could mean for us. The path to this goal leads us through many obstacles, which we need to get to know, understand, internalise and realise. Many of our everyday experiences need to be examined very critically and a few paradoxes need to be deciphered.

Paradoxes help us to get closer to the truth

For example, we might describe very precisely (= relative truth) how the nature of the world beyond visible objects (= absolute truth) cannot be described. We use terms but come to the conclusion that our surroundings are devoid of terms. In other words, we need to recognise that every term or name is actually just a label that helps us to partially fathom the unfathomable. A symbol can never fully capture what it stands for. Terms have no inherent reality.

Everything is subject to constant change. There is no birth and no death; there is only an eternal process of "becoming and passing away" or perhaps "neither-coming-nor-going". We took a deeper look at this in the 13th Fundamental of BPT when we referred to the term "interbeing". However, we even try to compose a fundamental, written definition of this. We talk about human beings having an Inner Nobility at the same time as we refer to the illusion of our sense of self. We place great importance on practising in everyday life, there are so many teachers and masters, but at the same time we emphasise the extent of our ignorance about the true nature of all things. We learn to distinguish between healthy and unhealthy mental states, between good and bad, constructive and destructive, etc. We aspire for happiness and strive to reduce suffering. But as we progress we learn that at a deeper level there is neither happiness nor suffering, neither good nor bad, etc. Issues that are very important to us can be shown to have qualities that are surely very helpful and which we learn to recognise, but at another level these issues possess no qualities. And even Western sciences such as physics lead us to the paradoxical nature of matter. More than a century ago, scientists discovered that sub-atomic particles or atoms can be observed both as particles (= matter) and as waves (= energy = non-matter) although these two states of being should really be mutually exclusive. Einstein showed us that energy and matter are equivalent but scientists are still debating how specific particles can show themselves as material particles and energy waves *at the same time.*

Normally we experience our world and the objects within it to be either material or non-material, but not both at the same time. Physicists speak of the complementary nature of all things. At one level we perceive certain objects to be solid and hard but at another, more elementary, level these objects are no longer solid—they are void and space.

Our normal everyday consciousness has great problems in dealing with this type of paradox. A person is either alive or dead, so we can hardly imagine that at a deeper level, there are states of being where both are thought to be possible. Readers are probably familiar with the interesting thought experiment proposed by the physicist Erwin Schrödinger concerning his cat.

The Western understanding of relative and absolute truth

Physicists have been telling us for more than a century that our perception of solid bodies and objects is only true at a superficial (=

relative) level. Scientists proceeded analytically by taking apart our environment and things within it, reducing them to ever smaller components and building blocks. Many were searching for some form of solid core at the heart of all matter and they were disappointed because they found what appeared to be a very chaotic situation. At the atomic and sub-atomic levels, they found evidence which overturned all their previous assumptions. At deeper levels, everything appears to be mainly made up of space. There is no solid core. There are no causalities anymore; processes seem to take place backwards in time. Time and space merge. Atoms and their elementary particles are connected and interact in sometimes inexplicable ways (Einstein-Rosen Bridge). Sub-atomic particles appear to react to our observing them and even change their nature according to the experiment (wave or particle). So the foundations of our everyday experience appear to be disproven at this deeper level, which perhaps explains why we still have difficulty grasping this sort of information many decades after these ground-breaking discoveries.

Nonetheless, these insights are being applied practically, forming the basis of many everyday technological devices, so they are now considered as incontrovertible. For example, all modern communications technology is based on satellites, which only function because we incorporate calculations relating to the relativity of time. Without Einstein's special relativity theory from 1905, we would not have mobile phones today.

Natural sciences such as physics are often considered to produce "hard facts", in contrast to "soft" social sciences. Hard science appeals particularly to people who want to see proof or measure and analyse everything. This itself could perhaps be considered a paradox because it is these "hard sciences" which produce results leaving us in no doubt that:
- we can only perceive our surroundings on a *relative* level;
- our natural senses are unsuited to providing us with a deeper understanding;
- at a deeper level there is no such thing as a solid core or constancy;

- there appears to be an all-encompassing interconnection at deeper levels; and
- every answer we find simply reveals many more questions.

This understanding of the world was, however, present in the Western world much earlier. Among others, many Greek philosophers were looking to understand their environment more than 2000 years ago and left us with comprehensive literature full of their insights. Here we will merely mention Plato, whose *Theory of Forms* proposed that we humans are blinded and ignorant, incapable of recognising the "thing itself" and only ever seeing its reflection. We occupy ourselves with terms and objects but remain unable to see the deeper levels. We remain stuck in a relative layer. To recognise the absolute we need a rigorous act of liberation. In his *Allegory of the Cave*, Plato described humans as being trapped in a cave, seeing only the shadows cast by things on the wall of the cave. But the things themselves exist outside the cave, so we have to leave it in order to become free.

A useful distinction

For our goal of liberation and clearing our mind, it is helpful to maintain a clear distinction between the two levels of truth: *absolute* and *relative*. In the context of the *relative* level, we can form categories, deductions and precise descriptions, which all help us to understand particular situations. However, it will be an error to perform these mechanisms regarding the *absolute* aspects of our lives. It is almost impossible for us to perceive the deepest absolute truths, let alone measure or prove them in a reproducible way. For this we need spiritual insights.

To take a simple example: At the relative level we might be able to conclude that a help-seeker will develop physical tensions or pain because of their hunched posture during meditation sessions. However, we should exercise great caution before claiming that bad posture prevents us gaining access to our Buddha nature.

How Reliable Are Our Statements?

When we refer to the Dharma and at the same time try to carry over these Buddhist basics into our modern world, we notice that we have a certain room for manoeuvre which is actually given to us by the teachings. Even ancient Buddhist statements referring to inseparable interconnection, the illusion of self and constant change are compatible with modern scientific insights from the fields of physics or neuroscience, for example. Nonetheless, it is still very useful to pose the question as to whether Buddhist Psychotherapy really does convey the fundamental messages of Buddhism; in other words, whether our form of psychotherapy should really be allowed to call itself "Buddhist".

The Buddha gave us three "seals" which we can apply as a form of certification or control for any teaching. The quality of our Buddhist Psychotherapy should be measured according to the following three principles:

The Three Seals, or Quality Certification for Teachings

1) Nirvana: The essence of the whole Buddhist teachings is liberation or enlightenment: Nirvana. (See 1st Fundamental of BPT.)

2) Impermanence: If we try to keep hold of anything, suffering will arise. Change is the only constant. Nothing remains the way it is. (See 13th and 14th Fundamentals of BPT.)

3) No-Self: At a deeper level we are inseparably connected with everything else in a constant state of interaction. Nothing possesses properties which arose from themselves. Everything is composite—the result of a large number of prior conditions. There is no solid core; neither we nor any other things have a solid core (self). Everything is empty of an independent, separate existence. (See 13th Fundamental of BPT.)

If we study the Buddhist Psychotherapy Fundamentals and check them against these three criteria, we will see that they pass the test quite well. The basic principles of BPT include the Three Dharma Seals.

Understand the teachings and then go beyond them

The comprehensive Buddhist teachings (which we have presented only very briefly in this book) contain an enormous wealth of very significant insights. Nonetheless, they are only the means to an end and not an end in themselves. The Buddha compared them to a boat, which carries us across a river to the shore of awakening. The focus of our attention should not be how interesting the boat is. It is a means to cross the river (of recurrent suffering) and find freedom.

Here in the 21st Fundamental we want to remember this guidance. We have discovered a great deal about various aspects of Buddhist teachings and their theoretical and practical consequences for our Buddhist Psychotherapy. In fact, we have attempted nothing less than a presentation of something which by its very nature cannot truly be presented using words, metaphors, practical exercises or information.

Simone A questions every instruction. She relishes any chance to delve deeply into the details of the teachings. For a long time she finds it quite difficult to carry out a clear and peaceful meditation session on her own. Her therapist suggests that she initially try more active forms of meditation. Eventually she discovers an affinity for "singing bowl" meditation and she receives the instruction to ensure that she remains conscious and present, concentrating primarily not on the bowls themselves but on her own body and physical sensations. In this way, Simone slowly lessons her attachment to the theoretical teachings and increases her affinity with her own experiences.

Later, deep in meditative absorption, she has her first experiences of the dissolution of boundaries. Then Simone begins to understand what the difference between hearing a teaching and having one's own experience really feels like.

This Fundamental Should Convey the Following:

The comprehensive body of Buddhist teachings is very precious and very helpful. The teachings point us in the direction of liberation, showing us the path that the Buddha trod before us. He left us very clear, understandable descriptions of the path and we should study these descriptions very carefully. Nonetheless, our focus should remain on the direction we are heading in; the teachings are not an end in themselves.

Everything is important but at the same time insignificant. Everything possesses a noble spark but at the same time nothing exists independently. Even Buddhist teachings, as helpful and inspiring as they are, are insignificant at a deeper level. Even in the realm of Nirvana, everything is precious, valuable and unique but at the same time without appreciable significance.

Every contradiction is justified and at a deeper level resolves itself. All opposites are points along one spectrum.

These categories are expressions of an underlying unity which itself is beyond our direct perception. Opposites are not a problem; they are a sign that we are on the relative level. We should improve our knowledge of both absolute and relative levels and our ability to distinguish between them.

We achieve liberation when we discover for ourselves, recognise, internalise and realise what we are. When we leave the *relative* level...

The 22nd
Fundamental of Buddhist Psychotherapy

Study Buddhist Literature

> We need patience with ourselves and with everyone else. With patience we will be able to approach the truths at our own speed.
>
> BUDDHIST PSYCHOTHERAPY BPT

There is an almost inexhaustible supply of Buddhist literature to read, from the ancient classics to modern interpretations and from general practical advice for everyday life through to detailed treatment of very specialist individual aspects of the teachings. In addition, there are large numbers of CDs and DVDs and online media with talks, films, meditation instructions and music. So we have a wide variety of approaches on offer, allowing each of us to find the appropriate topic and level of detail for our current needs. Of course, we can make our choice entirely based on our own preferences, or we can seek recommendations and advice from Buddhist teachers and Buddhist psychotherapists.

BPT Recommendations

For an initial introduction to Buddha and Buddhist issues we recommend the book *Old Path, White Clouds: Walking in the Footsteps of the Buddha* from Thich Nhat Hanh, who successfully adopts the style of a novel to tell the life story of the Buddha. He conveys the depth of the Buddhist teachings in an entertaining yet profound and informative way.

For a deeper consideration of the psychological aspects of Buddhism, we recommend *The Wise Heart* from Jack Kornfield. His presentation is easy to read and very practical, with many examples.

Several English translations of the *Pali Canon* are available for readers seeking a flavour of how the Buddha himself gave his teachings—it may take a little patience to become accustomed to the ancient language and style. The *Access to Insight* project makes the canon available online (including alternative translations where available): http://www.accesstoinsight.org

The canon includes the *Middle-Length Discourses* referred to in this book. The translation by Bhikku Bodhi is highly acclaimed.

Recommended reading on Buddhist psychotherapy

Ajahn Brahm: *Opening the Door of Your Heart And Other Buddhist Tales of Happiness.*
Chödrön, P.: *When Things Fall Apart. Heart Advice for Difficult Times.*
Chodron, Thubten: *Working with Anger*
Dalai Lama: *Freedom in Exile: The Autobiography of the Dalai Lama*
Dalai Lama/V. Chan: *The Wisdom of Forgiveness*
Dalai Lama: *Ethics for the New Millennium*
Dalai Lama: *Mind in Comfort and Ease*
Dalai Lama: *The Four Noble Truths*
Dalai Lama/Cutler, H.C.: *The Art of Happiness*
Dalai Lama: *The World of Tibetan Buddhism*
Goleman, D.: *Destructive Emotions: How Can We Overcome Them? A Scientific Dialogue with the Dalai Lama*
Gunaratana, Ven. H.: *Mindfulness in Plain English*
Jung, C.G.: *Psychology and Religion: West and East*
Kornfield, J.: *After the Ecstasy, the Laundry*
Kuby, C. & Olvedi, U.: *Living Buddha*
Küng, H.: Tracing The Way: *Spiritual Dimensions of the World Religions*
Lama A. Govinda: *The Psychological Attitude of Early Buddhist Philosophy*
Lama Ole Nydahl: *The Great Seal: Limitless Space and Joy*
Mitchell, R.A.: *Buddha*
Oord, Thomas Jay: *The Love Racket: Defining Love and Agape for the Love-And-Science Research Program*
Osho: *The Way of the Buddha*
Shantideva: *Bodhicaryavatara—A Guide to the Bodhisattva's Way of Life*

Sogyal Rinpoche: *The Tibetan Book of Living and Dying*
Thich Nhat Hanh: *Buddha Mind, Buddha Body: Walking Toward Enlightenment*
Thich Nhat Hanh: *The Heart of the Buddha's Teaching*
Trungpa, Chögyam: *The Sanity We Are Born With: A Buddhist Approach to Psychology*
Tsültrim Allione: *Feeding your Demons*
Wetering, J. v.d.: *The Empty Mirror: Experiences in a Japanese Zen Monastery*
Wetering, J. v.d.: *Afterzen: Experiences of a Zen Student out on His Ear*
Wetering, J. v.d.: *A Glimpse of Nothingness*
Yongey Mingyur Rinpoche: *The Joy of Living: Unlocking the Secret and Science of Happiness*
Yongey Mingyur Rinpoche: *Joyful Wisdom*

Recommended reading on Western science, psychology and psychotherapy

Freud, Anna: *Ego and the Mechanisms of Defense*
Fromm, Erich: *To Have or to Be?*
Fromm, Erich, Daisetz T. Suzuki, Richard de Martino: *Zen Buddhism and Psychoanalysis*
Jung, C. G.: *Psychology and Religion: West and East*
Reich, Wilhelm: *Character Analysis*
Wilber, Ken: *No Boundary: Eastern and Western Approaches to Personal Growth*

Psychology and Neuroscience

Gleick, James: *Chaos: Making A New Science*
Grawe, Klaus: *Neuropsychotherapy: How the Neurosciences Inform Effective Psychotherapy*
Harris, Judith Rich: *No Two Alike: Human Nature and Human Individuality*
Libet, Benjamin: *Mind time: The temporal factor in consciousness*
Luria, Aleksandr R.: *The Working Brain*
Norretranders, Tor: *The User Illusion: Cutting Consciousness Down to Size*
Pert, Candace B.: *The Molecules of Emotion: Why You Feel the Way You Feel*
Ratey, John J.: *A User's Guide to the Brain*

Rüegg, Johann Caspar: *Psychosomatik, Psychotherapie und Gehirn [Psychosomatics, Psychotherapy and the Brain]*

Sacks, Oliver: *The Man Who Mistook His Wife for a Hat*

Sacks, Oliver: *A Leg to Stand On*

Schiepek, Günter (Ed.): *Neurobiologie der Psychotherapie [Neurobiology of Psychotherapy]*

About the Author

Dr. Matthias Ennenbach has 20 years' experience working in hospitals, psychiatric and psychosomatic clinics, rehab clinics and private therapy practices. He has an advanced degree in psychology and completed additional specialist training in psychotherapy to gain the statutory post-graduate accreditation as a practicing Psychological Psychotherapist. He completed his doctorate at the Faculty of Medicine at the University of Munich. Dr. Ennenbach has also been a Buddhist practitioner for many years. His Buddhist training included seminars, teachings, conferences, meditation retreats, talks, pilgrimages and ceremonies in Asia and Germany. Working as a therapist in hospitals and private practice he has been able to bring together Eastern-Buddhist and Western-psychotherapeutic forms of treatment, integrating them into a successful healing approach.

Buddhist Psychotherapy (BPT) is a new school of therapeutic treatment with deep-reaching ancient roots. It is designed to provide guidance, inspiration and support.

This book and Buddhist Psychotherapy as a whole are the results of the author's desire to initiate a "project of integration", enriching the realms of Western psychotherapy with well-tested theory and practice from the realms of Buddhism.

Further information on BPT (events, literature, concepts, contacts etc.) can be found online at
www.buddhistischepsychotherapie.de

Further publications from the author
(currently available only in German):

Ennenbach, Matthias: Befreit—Verbunden. Windpferd Verlag 2011 (*Liberated—Connected*)

Ennenbach, Matthias: Praxisbuch-Buddhistische Psychotherapie. Windpferd Verlag 2012 (*Handbook with Practical Guidance for Buddhist Psychotherapy*)

Ennenbach, Matthias: Einführung Buddhistische Psychotherapie. Windpferd Verlag 11/2012 (*Introduction to Buddhist Psychotherapy*)